INDIAN IMMIGRANTS IN USA
STRUGGLE FOR EQUALITY

To

My Parents

Ram Datta and Ram Piari/Kesar Kaur Varma

who set me in pursuit of learning,

learning and learning...

and my beloved Swarn

who has permitted it

INDIAN IMMIGRANTS IN USA

STRUGGLE FOR EQUALITY

PREMDATTA VARMA
M.A. Hons. Ph.D.

HERITAGE PUBLISHERS
NEW DELHI (India) 1995

Published in India 1995 by
B. R. Chawla
HERITAGE PUBLISHERS
5, Ansari Road, New Delhi (India) - 110002

ISBN 81-7026-196-1

Laser Typeset at Calligraphics, 13-D, Kamla Nagar, Delhi-110007 and Printed in India at Efficient Offset Press, 215, Shahzada Bagh, Industrial Complex, Phase II, Delhi - 110035

CONTENTS

PREFACE

The study being presented here is a research effort to reconstruct the struggle of the then tiny Indian community in the United States to gain the right to equal treatment. This struggle lasted almost fifty years. The succeeding decades witnessed a gradual widening of the gates and a smooth, an almost eventless upward swing in the immigrants' prosperity and numbers.

Even in those early decades of their settlement in America the unwelcome Indian residents had a high concentration of university educated leaders endowed with patents and contributing to science, literature, studies in economics, history and the law. There were preachers, scholars, students, farmers, railroad workers, all determined to make it good in America and whom the British failure to provide a sovereign's protection turned into rebels and seditionists. They made America an overseas headquarters of Vedanta, anti-British agitation, and financiers of education and social movements. Vivekananda, Swami Ram Tirth, Lajpat Rai, Har Dayal made themselves famous by their work in America and made America loved in India because of what they achieved here.

Inspired by the political upheaval which produced Tilak and Gandhi in India, Taraknath Das and Jagjit Singh in the United States, the peasants and Ph.D's of California and New York worked with farsighted Americans to win freedom for India and citizenship for the immigrants.

Victories on the battlefields of the global war emptied the ideological quivers of the American racists and the British chauvinists so that towards the end of the Roosevelt era both ideologies had to be abandoned as aids to the enemy on the threatened battlefields of the Cold War. The opponents of the immigrants' human rights lost their votes or special rights in all the three countries they once dominated. Moreover, after the tank-maker was demobilized India's consumers gained visibility in the eyes of the machine-makers of Chicago. In the mid-40's, therefore white racism retreated before the compelling persuasions of global opinion, global trade and the dreams of "the American century".

A NOTE OF THANKS

As a young participant in anti-government demonstrations, I saw two British police officers fatally wound Lajpat Rai hardly two yards away from me. The murder of one of these officers landed me and my friends in life-changing trouble with the law. While Haridas T. Muzumdar and Krishnalal Shridharani were marching to the sea with Gandhiji and Jagjit Singh our hero was advising the saint on American dress codes, the present writer was serving a five year sentence in West Punjab jails of British India.

In the late 1930s and early 1940s, the articles of Taraknath Das and Sudhindra Bose in the *Modern Review*, Calcutta, and Jagjit Singh's columns in *The Tribune*, Lahore, strengthened the patriotism and excited the hopes of the educated classes while making them mildly aware of an ongoing struggle between the white and the Asian skins.

This biographical background neither mellowed the writer nor could his ideological convictions be kept under wraps in the course of studying a topic like immigration, crowded as it was with racial conflicts and national claims, during the most racially oppressive and murderous period of human history, the first half of the twentieth century.

Reading the oratorical excesses of the so-called patriots of Canada and California and of their collusion with the alien rulers of India. I was reminded of the counter-eloquence of the oppressed, of a father on his son's arrest shouting, "I shall live to see the downfall of the British empire."

Writing this whole story has been a 5-year exercise in the restraint of emotions although, probably more often than intended, my phrases seem to radiate the heat of retaliation. For those phrases no apologies are being offered because the hurt from the British has been deep and timeless. In the end, however, the only emotions felt are admiration and joy because after a few dark decades both my countries emerged on the winning side—India became free and America became inviting.

The 1980s have been academically among the most rewarding and satisfying of my life's eight decades. The reward has come mostly from the encyclopedic knowledge and the satisfaction from the human touch of my teacher and guide Dr. Roger Daniels. The events concerning India's history discussed here have passed Dr. Barbara Ramusack's scholarly scrutiny without serious disagreement. This gave me a sense both of relief and gratification.

I am grateful to the Department of History of the University of Cincinnati for financing part of my research travel to New Delhi and recognize the decisive significance of the services of the Inter-University Loan Department of the University for scouring America's libraries for books, articles and newspapers needed for my work.

In New Delhi the custodians of the Sapru House Library granted me unobstructed access to their treasures which included the major part of the India League of America papers as well as the old magazines and journals. The Nehru Memorial Museum and Library materials make an impressive part of my Bibliography for which the officials and their assistants deserve deep appreciation.

The National Archives of India, a treasure-house of the records of British rule in Asia, also proved to be the mine of information on the life, struggles and seditions of the Indian emigrants to North America. It was a surprising discovery late in my stay in India but luckily not too late to discover the Commerce Treaty negotiations as well as eventful travels of the Indian citizenship bills through the United States Congress.

Mrs. Malti Singh lent me from her personal cabinet her husband's passports and the original copy of the India Bill signing ceremony photograph and several other documents which but for her kind favor would have escaped my knowledge and study. She has also offered to donate to the University gramophone records of the Indian League's public functions which are presently in the custody of the former office secretary of the League in New York, Mrs. Ruth (Beck) Greenbaum.

It is a pleasure to conclude this Preface with affectionate thanks to my wife Swarn who typed almost a thousand pages of the earlier drafts never complaining and never missing a deadline.

Premdatta Varma
Cincinnati

INTRODUCTION

This work is an attempt to do for the Asian Indian community in the United States what several scholars have done for immigrants from other Asian countries, namely, to research the history of their struggles in the United States from arrival to their reinstatement to the rights of immigration and naturalization. It is a contribution to those new American studies which represent the growing American sympathetic and understanding awareness of Asia abroad and Asians in the house. The emphasis of the study presented here is an examination of the forces and circumstances which deprived immigrants from British India of legal equality in America and their response to the national and racial insult by mounting a struggle to regain that equality.

Some primary and several secondary sources (not including Joan M. Jensen's *Passage from India* although our conclusions happen to be mostly identical) have been relied upon to reconstruct the story to 1924, the year which witnessed the completion of the imposition of inequality. The history of the recovery of those lost rights is however, based mostly on original sources.

The text presented here is the first research effort of its kind from two standpoints—the first to investigate the Asian Indian community's quest for civil rights in America, and secondly, the first effort by any scholar to study its political and legislative activities during the decades following the immigration legislation of 1924. Additionally the present writer is the first American scholar to study the papers of the India League of America and to bring to light the secret Indo-American treaty of commerce negotiations.

The basic argument of this whole essay is that proud, intelligent and industrious immigrants from India who had been awakened to national sensitivity by a wave of religious revival and political consciousness at home, were mistreated for their physical appearance and cultural possessions by the people of a country where they had come like millions of others to live, work and earn. Further in a spirit of racial exclusiveness, they were forbidden to enter and become citizens of a country where they should have had like white immigrants every right to live.

Asian Indians recovered those rights by a well-organised lobbying and legislative effort after the misdeeds of the German and Japanese aggressors had made racist ideologies indefensible and indifference towards the Asian people's self-respect harmful to America's national interest. This came at a time when America was seeking customers for her goods and allies for the Cold War.

From the vantage point adopted in this study, in contrast to the official and exclusionist advocacy current in the earlier decades of the century, the denial of legal equality to Asian Indians is seen as an insult, and Justice Sutherland's ruling against their eligibility to naturalization as a racially motivated injustice. The Gadar is hailed as an Indian nationalist uprising with a deep impact and the so-called "Hindu Conspiracy" trial as a British-American conspiracy to crush a threat to British rule. American friends of Asian Indians are seen here as fighting the battles of America at home to achieve the same objectives as American soldiers fighting on the battlefields of Europe and Asia.

The vocabulary of exclusionism has been examined from the Indian side of the argument. The alleged "low" standard of living of the immigrants in fact represented their habit of thrift, the obligation of support for families in India and donations to Indian causes. They were neither illiterate nor unskilled laborers. Most of them were literate in Urdu or Punjabi, and nearly all of them were either experienced cultivators or ex-soldiers, security guards and carpenters. Even university teachers can be reduced to the status of "unskilled laborers" by denial or lack of employment opportunities in their fields. It shall be repeatedly pointed out in the text that the leadership of the community was always in the hands of the university educated elite.

Most of the basic evidence for the work has come from the papers of the India League of America, the National Archives of India, Congressional Record and the House/Senate Hearings. There is heavy indebtedness to the periodicals of Indian organizations in America as well as the papers and writings of some of the prominent participants in the Asian Indian activities. Interviews over the telephone with some of the eyewitnesses yielded valuable insights.

Writings such as this one attempt to update American historiography particulary with regard to the country's racist past. American people looked upon immigration from Asian countries, including India, as a menace not only to the economic interests of the white workers but to the whole personality of the United States both as a nation in the Western Hemisphere and as the guardian of the western frontiers of European culture. The west coast exclusionists were very much conscious of the Persian wars with ancient Greece and of the white man's march towards the setting sun.

Around the years when Asian Indians started coming here, many Americans were busy becoming enmeshed in a philosophy of racism whose legislative agenda included restricting the immigration of Latin and Slav "races" and exclusion of all Asians. By 1924 the agenda had been achieved in the Congress, the courts, and the White House. Among the excluded nations, Japan blamed the insult on America, China blamed it on its helplessness, the Asian Indian immigrants blamed the British. All harbored a grudge. Indians urged America to rethink its priorities. Japan, losing equality in American law, started building equality in guns.

The expansion of American notions of equality and other developments following the Second World War made certain changes all but inevitable. The civil rights' movement, the emergence of new Asian and African nations on the ruins of western imperialism, the Cold War antagonists' use of the United Nations (U.N.) for purposes of propaganda and power politics dictated that the new members of the world community as well as their immigrant minorities in the United States be studied so as to understand the emotions and cultural preferences which guided their past and mold their opinions on social and political issues today.

These pages are an attempt to understand the mind, motives and methods of one of the newest constituents of the new American nation during the decades when about 5000 stranded immigrants with about two dozen vocal activitists carried the burden of symbolizing the struggles of a vast and ancient people trying to rise above the tide of British imperialism and American racism.

Starting with the origin and establishment of the community in America the investigation proceeds, in the first three chapters, to examine the hostile and finally successful efforts of the American exclusionists to persuade the executive, the Congress and the law courts to deprive Asian Indians of their eligibility to immigration and naturalization. The fourth chapter examines the life of the community at the bottom of the curve—a virtually outlawed and stateless people seeking and gradually discovering their inner vitality personified by a hardy peasantry and a brilliant elite leadership.

The last three chapters describe the emergence of this leadership and the organization for victory culminating in the legislative battles in Congress which were decided in the Indians' favor with the help of the world forces released by and the new racial philosophies generated by the Second World War. The investigation terminates with the signing of the Luce-Celler bill by President Harry S. Truman on July 2, 1946.

Sardar Jagjit Singh, successful hero of the struggle for equality holding the pen with which President Truman signed the Bill.

President Truman signing the Bill which granted legal equality to immigrants from India, July 2, 1946.

1

INDIA SENDS HER BEST SONS

America was discovered in the name of India. . . . The voyage of Columbus ended in a mistake. The next five hundred years will prove that his error was an accuracy of the gods.

— DHAN GOPAL MUKERJI

In This Chapter

A discussion as to the inevitability of the struggle for legal equality; significance of the epoch 1900-1946 in the history of India, U.S.A. and Britain; the beginning of the Asian Indian settlement in America, including the preachers, students and farmers; and the immigrants' successes in agriculture and business.

Struggle for Equality Became Inevitable

Indian emigrants came to the United States without the least apprehension of having ever to embark upon a battle for legal equality. They had come to realize their own individual purposes—spiritual, educational or economic—never expecting to meet a calculated official policy of denial of opportunities[1]. But they were victimized for decades by laws, formulas, and judicial rulings which withdrew from them opportunities and privileges generally available to alien residents and citizens of European origin.[2]

Spokesmen of the Indian community resented these instruments of inequality as un-American.[3] They appealed to what Senator Charles

Sumner (1811-1874) had called the "title-deeds of this Republic."[4] The concept of equality had been asserted at the very birth of the Republic among "powers of the earth" by the Jeffersonian invocation of "the laws of nature and of nature's God" and of the "self-evident truth" that "all men are created equal."

In two instances at least, Indian immigrants suffered the same "injuries" at the hands of the descendants of the colonists as the colonists themselves had suffered at the hands of the King and his British subjects. Jefferson alleged that the King had "endeavored to prevent the population of these states; for that purpose obstructing the laws for Naturalization of Foreigners; refusing to pass others to encourage their migration hither." As to "our British brethren" Jefferson wrote,

> We have reminded them of the circumstances of our emigration and settlement here. We have appealed to their native justice and magnanimity, and we have conjured them by the ties of our common kindred . . . . They too have been deaf to the voice of justice and consanguinity.

Here we see the parallels: the denial of citizenship to Asians, their exclusion, and the rejection of the Indian immigrants' plea of common Caucasian origin.

The colonists redressed their own grievances, including those concerning immigration and naturalization, by waging a successful war. Yet legal inequalities persisted even under the Republic. The Declaration had pronounced all men equal but the Constitution Article I, 2(3) recognized that there were slaves too in the American population.

During the era of Reconstruction Senator Sumner (R. Mass.) had proposed to remove the word "white" from the Naturalization Act of 1790. In February 1869 he had asked his colleagues in the Senate, "Can 'color' be a 'qualification'. . . (can) a race be disfranchised? . . . can any state undertake to establish a caste and organize an oligarchy of the skin? To put these questions is to answer, them'', he had concluded.[5]

Sumner repeated the proposal in 1870 "so that in naturalization there shall be no distinction of race and color;"[6]

> his intention being to bring our system into harmony with the Declaration of Independence, the Constitution of the United

> States. The word "white" cannot be found in either of these two great title-deeds of this Republic. How can you place it in your statutes ? he asked.

Some Senators were afraid that in case of relaxation of naturalization laws the Chinese might start pouring into the country. Sumner reminded them that if the Chinese come for citizenship, they would pledge loyalty to American institutions and "where is the peril in such vows ?" he asked.[7] On the contrary Congress adopted the Chinese Exclusion Act a few years later.

The history of the Republic shows several deviations from the ideals enunciated in the Declaration of Independence. A foreign scholar who studied the American Negro problem in the early 1940s called this lag, "an American dilemma." He defined it as the "ever-raging conflict" between an American's "moral valuations" with the "American Creed" on one side and several other valuations including "group prejudice against particular persons or types of people" on the other.[8]

This group prejudice brought about the Asian exclusion laws which, according to Clare Boothe Luce, signified the abandonment of "the great American principle perhaps the greatest of all: namely, that all men, regardless of color, race, or creed, are judged alike, not only in the eyes of God, but in the eyes of Uncle Sam."[9]

Scholars have found several reasons including "practical politics" and "social facts" for the growth of this contradiction between the American creed and the American conduct, even between the principles of the Declaration and the provisions of the Constitution.[10] For recognizing, though indirectly, the existence of slavery the Abolitionists had called the Constitution "a covenant with death and an agreement with hell." The first Congress had granted the privilege of citizenship to "free white persons" not to every person.

The makers of the Republic had developed and their descendants continued to abide by a national consensus rooted not always on the Declaration or the Constitution but on realpolitik or expediency.[11] The consensus demanded that American Indians be kept subdued and that slavery be maintained. Reconstruction witnessed a slight shift in the consensus. Slavery was abolished. Blacks were granted the right of citizenship. The same age, however, inaugurated the Jim Crow and the Asian exclusion laws. The political and ideological realities created by the Second World War gave the national consensus another push towards congruity with the American creed. In 1945 President Roosevelt seemed to be expressing the nations's view when he wrote that the exclusion laws "*now* serve no useful purpose."[12] Most of the Asian people were gradually granted equality in law but still not as "Men" of the Declaration but as Chinese, Filipinos, and Koreans. Asian Indians whose struggles we shall trace in detail were the beneficiaries with these three nationalities of the process of closing the gap between the ideal and the reality. Immigration quotas tied to national origins continued for another twenty years but the consensus was coming closer to the Declaration.

The Time Frame of the Epoch Under Study

The first period of Indian immigration to the United States lasted between forty-five and fifty years. It started when the United States was suppressing a rebellion in Asia, that of the Filippine General Emilio Aguinaldo (1899-1902) and ended one year after another American victory in Asia, that over Japan in August 1945.

In terms of Indian history the epoch extends from the viceroyalty of Lord Curzon (1899-1905) when some of the earliest Indian revolutionaries sought asylum in the United States, to Pandit Jawaharlal Nehru's assumption of office as Interim Prime Minister presaging the British surrender of power in India.

In Britain Queen Victoria had celebrated the Diamond Jubilee of her reign in 1899, a landmark in British history, before some of her Indian soldiers decided to emigrate to Canada. The fall of the Churchill War Cabinet came just three days after President Harry S. Truman signed the epoch-making Luce-Celler Bill on July 2, 1945.

Indian immigration became the concern of all these three countries. Persons and events mentioned above happened to play significant roles in the three ideologies that determined the fate of the immigrants—America's anti-Asianism, India's nationalism and Britain's imperialism. The immigrants by contributing their share of the nationalist effort—and their generation-long struggle (1923-1946) to achieve ethnic self-respect and equality contributed to the historic destiny of all these three ideologies. Indian nationalism achieved freedom for India which brought down the major pillar of British colonialism. The signing of the Luce-Celler Bill by President Truman a year after the end of the War proclaimed America's new pledge that the immigrants from friendly Asian countries would be legally equal both in war and peace.

The history of the Indian immigrant community was shaped by three major factors—the character of the immigrants, the type of reception which they met with and the struggle of this small minority to achieve for itself a status economically respectable and legally equal, as well as to remove from their country of origin and by association from themselves, the imposed stigma of inferiority. The part of the Indian community that had come from the rural areas of the Panjab, progressed on the road to readjustment by a process of trial and error, shifting its location mostly to California and its occupation to agriculture. At every uphill step it was sustained by a tenacious adherence to its cultural heritage and to Indian patriotism even to the extent of becoming almost an overseas extension of India's freedom movement. At the end of this period the whole community gained recognition of its equality from the American nation whose people had temporarily draped the Statue of Liberty with the black cloak of anti-Asianism. This recognition came just when the pioneers were aging in years and shrinking in numbers and the younger members—students and businessmen—were learning the American method of lobbying, propagandizing and salesmanship.

Such processes of learning and readjustment have been the fate of all ethnic groups that form the population of the United States today. Each one of them had to wage a continuous and multifaceted struggle until America changed the groups and the groups changed America.For instance, the English Puritans became American Yankees and the Southern aristocrats became anti- monarchists. Joining together they fought the war of immigrants' independence thereby creating a new America. This process of adjustment, assimilation and acceptance for over 350 years, has produced a national consensus in which race, color, and national origin no longer find ready endorsement in national policy. The road of progress has not been smooth. It had to pass through the bloody battlefields of the Civil War. It was often diverted by judicial and legislative battles, by the alarm bells of perverted intellectualism, or by the danger signs raised by the proponents of pseusdo-science.

When the Sikh immigrants started reaching the Pacific coast in noticeable numbers in the latter years of the first decade of the twentieth century, Canadian and American racism and anti- Asianism were there as guardians of the western frontiers of white civilization to ridicule their religion, dress, and customs and deny them economic mobility, indeed to give them the America-made Chinese treatment of total exclusion. The Canadians achieved this exclusion by the legislation of 1908 and the Americans by the Acts of 1917 and 1924 as well as by the Supreme Court ruling against Thind in 1923. Those who survived these blows were replenished in numbers by illegal arrivals and in spirit by a constant flow of religious preachers, students, businessmen, politicians, and visitors from India.

A discussion of forces that pushed the immigrants out of India and the story of their struggle for survival in a hostile environment in America will be sketched to illustrate the character of the Indo-American ethnic group as it existed in the 1940s. An effort will also be made to examine American racial prejudice at work against this group as part of a general attitude of color prejudice and anti-Asianism prevailing at this time. By denying to Indians the right of immigration and naturalization, this prejudice imposed inequality and thereby provoked a forty-year struggle to achieve those rights.

Emigration from India in modern times was a consequence of British conquest and the revolutions in transportation and communications. India had been made part of a world-wide empire under one sovereign and one flag and supposedly one common citizenship. There was a widening of geographical and cultural horizons; closer contacts were developed with both West and East. A fruitful age of learning, unlearning, reform, and defensive reaction in religion, politics, and culture opened within India. New social and economic classes emerged as the British sought to use India for their own benefit and Indians used the empire to get as much out of it as they could.

Like a shrewd businessman reinvesting his profits to increase his profits, Britain used India's martial manpower to conquer, occupy, and police more territories. India itself was subjected to famines made by official cooperation with nature and poverty made by law. Some of these impoverished masses were exported to meet the labor needs of new colonies and conquests. "The Equatorial life-line of the British Empire (became) effectively intersected with vast Indian concentrations."[13]

Indian bankers and entrepreneurs extended their operations abroad under the protection of British flag and British citizenship.

Ambitious families sent their sons abroad for higher studies in European sciences, law, and literature. Indian nationalist politicians travelled to Britain to plead for constitutional reform. Indian collaborators manned the British outposts in Southeast Asia.

Many of the Sikh peasant-proprietors of the Panjab victimized by colonial economy had sought to supplement the declining returns from their ancestral lands by serving the British in their overseas possessions in Malaya or China. Here they developed foreign contacts and wider horizons which eventually stretched to Canada and the United States.[14]

Bengali Bhadralok—the children of the Bengali renaissance and Hindu religious revival of the nineteenth century—sent to America preachers of Vedanta. Translated into politics the Hindu revival made Bengalis anti-British. Many came to America either as refugees from British justice or as students carrying heavy bags of patriotic dreams. Political radicalism spread in the Panjab with the teachings of the Arya Samaj (founded 1875) and in Maharashtra with the writings of Lokmanya Tilak (1856-1920).[15]

These groups, all of them products of British rule—the Hindu preacher, the ambitious and patriotic student, the businessman, the independent farmer from the Panjab, and the young revolutionary from Bengal, Maharashtra and the Panjab—were among the first Indian immigrants to come to the United States. They brought with them, consciously and unconsciously, cultural baggage which they had inherited as an ancestral bequest now sharpened by adverse contact with western culture and missionary propaganda. With regard to the spirit of adventure, political potential, intellectual acquirements, success in business and agriculture, they were those sons of India who would make events happen during the next forty years.

Hindu Preachers

India had no separate place in the community of nations. Its political identity was that of a conquered country, a subordinate part of the British empire. For its British rulers, India was a source of wealth, prestige, and labor supply. For the Christian missionaries, it was a vast field for evangelization.

Conditions, however, had started to change even before the first Indian immigrants reached the United States. European scholarship discovered India. The study, interpretation, and publication of Indian thought became a major achievement of European intellectuals. Gradually, however, the thirst for knowledge gave way to Victorian imperialism, when Hindu culture, history and religion started to be misrepresented and ridiculed. Lord Macaulay, the Law Member of the Government of India (1835), dismissed the accumulated knowledge of the Hindu as comprising of "medical doctrines which would disgrace an English farrier, astronomy which would move laughter in girls at an English boarding school, history abounding with kings thirty feet high and reigns 30,000 years long, and geography made up of seas of treacle and seas of butter."[16]

It seemed as if a joint effort had been unleashed by the Christian missions of the western world in alliance with the political interests of the British to wean Hindus away from loyalty to their ancient institutions. The Hindu reaction to this cultural aggression was widespread and of permanent significance. It gave birth to Hindu reform, resistance, and revivalism. It produced reform movements like the Brahmo Samaj and the Arya Samaj, the revivalist movements like the Ramakrishna Mission, the Sanatan Dharm Sabha, and the Theosophical Society. Resistance took the form of the Cow Protection movement, the Swadeshi movement in Bengal, and the rise of the revolutionary parties in Bengal, Maharashtra and the Panjab. Among the Sikhs there was the Kuka uprising, the Khalsa Dewan movement and a revived interest in Sikh history, rituals, and observances.

These developments within the body and spirit of Hinduism seemed like a message to the British and to the rest of the world that while India might be politically a conquered country, it was superior to the West in culture, in morality, and in philosophical thought. This new sense of superiority signified the Hindu's four-fold determination, namely to preserve his ancient heritage, to spread his spiritual message abroad, to modernize his social institutions, and to liberate the motherland.

The tradition of propagating the spiritual message of India in the United States started with Swami Vivekananda's address at the World Congress of Religions held in Chicago in September, 1893.[17] In 1830 Ram Mohan Roy (1774-1833) had expressed his hope of "ending his days in America." But for his death two years later he might have become not only the first preacher of Vedanta in America almost sixty years before Vivekananda but also probably the first Hindu immigrant to the United States.[18] Swami Dayananda (1824-1883), founder of the Arya Samaj, to whom also a foreign crusade had been suggested was more disposed to preach his Vedic faith to people at home than attempt to enlighten the foreigners abroad.[19]

Swami Vivekananda (1863-1902) revered by a Bengali Bhadralok, Dr. Taraknath Das as India's "most enlightened and sainted patriot"[20] was the disciple of Swami Ramakrishna Paramahansa (1836-1886), one of the most famous ascetics associated with the rise of the Hindu revivalist movement in the latter half of the nineteenth century.[21] Son of an attorney and a graduate of Calcutta University, young Narendra Nath Datta carried

> much further the teachings of his master, preached that Vedantism was the future religion of the world, and that, although India was now subject to a foreign power, she must still be careful to preserve the faith of mankind. She must seek freedom by the aid of the Mother of strength (Sakti).[22]

Vivekananda's significance in the history of the Indian immigrant community is that he opened a path, made America respected among Indian intellectuals, and established a Hindu religious presence in the United States that helped preserve the immigrants' religious and cultural identity.

He left little or no lasting impact on American minds. His emergence at Chicago was, like that of the Gadar Party in San Francisco, an event of Indian history taking place on foreign soil. Vivekananda was thirty when he addressed the Congress of Religions. Frederick Jackson Turner was not yet thirty-two when in July he had addressed the American Historical Association at the same Fair. Both young men had some new frontiers on their minds.[23]

With his first speech at the Congress, the Swami opened up a new frontier for the proper understanding of Hinduism. Forty-five years later a contemporary, the third in the famous nationalist trinity of Lal-Bal-Pal assessed what Vivekananda's mission to Chicago had meant to Indian history :

> It was all practically idolatry and polytheism and caste. This was in those days the universal judgment of Europe and America upon the religion of the Hindus. Vivekananda first offered a challenge to this universal British and American

> estimate of his national religion. It took his American audience by surprise. It offered a stupendous shock to their old convictions and prejudices. There was no hesitancy, no suspicion of apology, no attempt to explain away, not the least little trace of any 'inferiority complex' in this bold challenge to civilized conceit in Vivekananda's message of Hinduism to the crowded galleries of the Parliament of Religions.[24]

According to a recent American assessment,

> Swami Vivekananda revealed unusual talents. Demonstrating a fluent command of English, impressive stage manner, and gift for the memorable phrase, the Hindu spokesman was sensation from his first address. . . . His blunt rejection of the stereotypical view of Hinduism raised the hackles of mission-minded Christians, but attracted wide public attention.[25]

The *Boston Evening Transcript* testified that

> he is great favorite at the Parliament from the grandeur of his sentiments and his appearance as well. If he merely crossed the platform he is applauded. The Chairman used to keep Vivekananda until the end of the programme to make people stay till the end of the session.[26]

He founded the Vedanta Society in 1894 in New York as an extension of the mission and spirit of Ramakrishna Paramahansa. He paid his second and last visit to the United States in 1899 and died at his headquarters in Calcutta on July 4, 1902.[27]

Vivekananda was followed by several missionaries from the Ramakrishna Mission headquarters in Calcutta.[28] The most prominent were Saradanand, who succeeded Vivekananda; Abhedanand (1866-1939) who came to America in 1897, preached here and in Canada and England for twenty-five years; Paramananda (1883-1940) who arrived in 1906, published almost twenty-five works, and edited the Vedanta Society periodical, *Message of the East.*[29] They spread the message of Paramhansa by establishing Vedanta Centers, touring on lecture circuits, holding classes, publishing books and periodicals, and collecting donations. They were the first missionaries of modern orthodox Hinduism to preach abroad. They built the first Hindu temple in America and made the United States the strongest center of Vedanta after India.[30]

There were other preachers besides those connected with the Ramakrishna Mission. Swami Ram Tirth visited America 1902-1904.

A former professor of mathematics, he renounced the world after meeting Swami Vivekananda at Lahore. His American lectures were published as, "In the Backwoods of God Realization." In California he helped organize an association to assist Indian students.[31]

Swami Paramanand (Baba) Bharati was in the United States for almost five years (1904-1909). He was the first messenger of the Krishna cult in America. He published a work on Shri Krishna in New York (1904), built a Radha-Krishna temple in Los Angeles, and started a periodical, *The Light of India.*[32]

Swami Yoganand (1893-1952) came to the United States in 1920, established the headquarters of his Yogoda Sat-Sang at Mt. Washington, California in 1925. He was the Hindu preacher in America who served here the longest—over thirty years—and gained the widest following. He died in Los Angeles in March 1952.[33]

This religio-cultural effort of Indian immigrant and transient preachers does have an historical significance. It was one of the lasting outcomes of the World Congress of Religions. In the worldwide context of Christian/non-Christian confrontation, the Indian missionary effort was a counter-offensive into the adversary's home territories. It was the start of a tradition which helped to produce hippies on the one hand and the Hare-Krishna movement on the other. Many Americans who first heard of India and of Hindu immigrants from Yoga and Vedanta teachers later became sympathizers of the immigrants' demand for reform of naturalization and immigration laws.[34]

The literary products of these missionaries have become a precious asset of modern Hindu religious literature. The lectures of Swami Vivekananda and Swami Ram Tirtha and the works of Swami Parmananda are important as being modern interpretations of several ancient Hindu doctrines.[35]

The Swamis are important—not as missionaries among the Americans but like other Indian immigrants as representatives of a new India. They and their lay compatriots were men from the Hindu temples, Arya Samaj temples, and Sikh gurudwaras or from the temple of the Mother at Kalighat or participants in the Ganesh and Shivaji festivals in Maharashtra. They were proud patriots, proud of being Hindus, and imbued with a sense of cultural superiority. No assessment of the Hindu and Sikh immigrants is complete without taking into account this religious awakening that was molding the character of the Indian people and making them ready to fight the battles for freedom that were soon to be upon them.

In America the preachers and saints also played another significant role. They were the keepers of the religious conscience of the Sikh and Hindu immigrants. They maintained close contact with them—the Sikh priests with every *Jatha* (batch) of the Panjabi farmers, the Hindu priests with students, teachers, and businessmen. They arranged hostels for students, granted scholarships, helped to find employment, and organized associations to refute the hostile propaganda of the Christian missionaries. They also spoke out and wrote against racial discrimination and unjust immigration laws.[36] They built the first Hindu temples and Sikh gurudwaras in North America.[37]

It was not long before the Government of India recognized the political threat posed by the Vedanta leaders. According to a high British official, "A society which aims at restoring the supremacy of the Hindu religion naturally also glorifies the political status of the Hindu in the past and the teachings of the Vedanta society tend towards nationalism in politics."[38] A few years after Vivekananda's death, a revolt broke out in Bengal. One of its leaders was his younger brother who evaded a warrant for his arrest by escaping to the United States and taking refuge with the Swamis of the Vedanta Society at New York. According to the high official quoted above, this Society "was already a center of anti-British intrigue." One of its priests, Swami Abhedananda had published a book which "was in many parts objectionable, and in some places clearly seditious." The book was proscribed in India.[39] Religious awakening produced the Swadeshi agitation and the revolutionary movement in India. In America it produced the Gadar. All Gadar leaders were the products of religious revival—Sohan Singh Bhakhna was a devotee of the Kuka movement, Har Dayal and Ramchandra were Arya Samajists and Taraknath Das an ardent admirer of Swami Vivekananda.

These were the revolutionaries, the young men who favored violent overthrow of British rule. The men of peaceful means were no less intolerant of inequality or injustice. The two men most famous in the legal history of the Indian community's struggle for equality, Bhagat Singh Thind and S. G. Pandit, were men of the new age. Thind was a preacher and Pandit a Theosophist.

Students and Scholars

Vedanta preachers had come to teach spiritualism; young Indians followed a few years later to learn materialism. Indian students had been going to Britain for over thirty years before any of them came to the United states.[40] They sought British education generally though not in every case, with the ambition of joining the Indian bureaucracy in partnership with the British. It was the age of the Anglicized Indians. Soon, however, the hope for partnership received jolts. The British did not want partnership. "Anglicized Indians, disappointed in their aspirations, gave back her soul to India."[41] Although more and more students continued to go to Britain—their number multiplied "ten or twelve- fold" before the First World War[42]—the 1890's witnessed the birth of a new age of cultural loyalty and political dreams among the youth of India as a result of the revivalist upsurge. The new youth decried the idea of the permanence of British rule that they blamed for India's poverty, famines and industrial backwardness. In politics they believed in a free India, in economics, in an industrialized India—"the attainment of the kingdom of heaven once we could compete with the European in his own field," dreamed Dhan Gopal Mukerji, one of the leading products of the Indo- American cultural contact.[43]

The attainment of these political and economic goals involved defiance of British policy. Directing Indian students to Japan or the United States instead of to Britain became part of that defiance, both open and implied. Sending students abroad to learn modern science and technology became part of the nationalist urge and an item on the agenda of modernization beyond and above what the British rulers were willing to encourage.[44]

The nationalist plan germinated in Swami Vivekananda's mind. About October 1892, "he specifically declared to the Maharaja of Mysore his intention of going to the West" for finding means to ameliorate the material condition of India, "and to take it [sic] in exchange the Gospel of the Vedanta."[45] In one of his earliest speeches in the United States he told Americans that the "need of the people of India is not more religion—but—"practicality" and they, instead of sending out missionaries "would better send someone out to give them industrial education."[46]

Vivekananda planted the idea; Swami Ram Tirth seems to have been the first to give it practical shape in America in about 1902. He helped some Indian students who were in Japan to come to the United States and persuaded his American friends in Portland, Oregon, to organize a society to help Indian students.[47] Henceforth the plan gained endorsements from highly respectable quarters. For instance, in 1913, Rabindranath Tagore pointed out to the Indian students in the United States that their "first duty" was to "teach our countrymen to walk defiantly in the wide world in pursuit of modern scientific and industrial knowledge to modernize our ancient and glorious land."[48] A few years later Lajpat Rai told American professors that India's "young sons come to your shores to gain that knowledge which is a *sine qua non* of progress in this age—[to learn, what] America can teach them in science, in politics, in philosophy and the arts."[49]

"No one knows definitely when the first Indian student came to this country," wrote Dr. Sudhindra Bose, himself one of the early arrivals.[50] When Swami Ram Tirth visited America (1902-1904) he found Indian students already here. According to Girindra Mukerji, the "first pioneer students came to the Pacific Coast in 1900-1902."[51] If this is the firm date, students from India would then appear to have started getting American education in the first full school year of the new century.

Most of the students came "of their own accord and at their own expense" but in order to maintain themselves, there were several types of sponsorship arrangements.[52] Rich families could afford to send and maintain their children on their own. Such cases, however, were rare. Hardikar observed that the students were not from affluent class generally, they came rather from poor but hard-working families, like his own.[53]

Students who showed promise could expect to arouse the enthusiasm of public spirited patrons. Some Indian princes also sponsored talented students such as B.R. Ambedkar and Krishnalal Shridharani. Sometimes an Indian immigrant, such as Jawala Singh and Bhagat Singh Thind, would sponsor or support students. In a vast majority of cases, however, students worked their way through school with partial support from their families, patrons or the sponsoring organization.[54]

The Association for the Advancement of Scientific and Industrial Education of Indians located in Calcutta, was one of the "patriotic societies intent upon introducing Western science and Western methods into awakened India." It was founded in 1906 to send students to Britain, Europe, Japan, and the United States. It granted passage money and scholarships out of donations from the public. In the first eight years of its operations, it sent eighty-one students abroad. In a few years it seems to have deteriorated.[55]

The National Council of Education in Bengal (President : Rashbehari Ghosh) was another sponsoring organization in north India. The Madras National Fund and Industrial Association sponsored students from the southern Presidency. The Brahmo Samaj sponsored four scholars who received, in succession, the Meadville Theological School fellowships for Indian Students between 1906 and 1912. In 1929 Lajpat Rai informed N. S. Hardikar from Lahore that, "a large number of Panjabee boys are likely to reach New York before Septr./[sic]. I am referring them all to 1400 Broadway."[56]

The number of Indian students at one time in the United States never exceeded 400—the peak reached in 1926 and 1927—except in 1946 when almost 1000 came. In 1914 there had been less than 200 and by 1918 the War had halved even this number. Similarly the Second World War played havoc with numbers, there being only 100 when the War ended.[57] Students from China were far more numerous than those from India. India's educational connection with the United States was the child of private enthusiasm only. The Chinese students, in addition to private efforts, enjoyed the patronage of their national government as well as the financial resources made available as a result of the return of the Boxer indemnity by the host country. In 1913 more than half the Chinese students in America were government scholars. "We can never expect that the Government of India will send a twentieth of that number to foreign countries for education," lamented the *Hindusthanee Student*.[58]

Dhan Gopal Mukerji was a student in Japan where he happened to meet an Indian who had been in America. This man told him, "If you want to see civilized use of machinery, go to America," and he "drew an Arabian Nights' picture of the United States—his language sounded extremely romantic—and I felt irresistibly drawn to America." The moment the immigration authorities permitted him to land, "the reverence that I felt for this country was so great that nothing short of falling on my knees and kissing its soil would have sufficed to express my feelings."[59]

Sudhindra Bose came as "an assistant steward" on a Standard CGL tanker (1904); Taraknath Das left India in disguise (1905);

Sarangdhar Das came in defiance of his prince-patron in Orissa (1910); and Prafulla Mukerji came with letters of endorsement from an American visitor to India—William Jennings Bryan. Dalip Singh Saund's ship was delayed in the New York harbor by heavy fog for two days. "Then at last the fog lifted a little and I could see the faint outline of the Statue of Liberty. It was an exhilarating experience. I had finally arrived in the United States of America" (1920).[60] So had hundreds of others "finally arrived," each carrying his own story of adventure, hope and emotion. Several Indians who achieved prominence came as scholars and became teachers. Samuel Locus Joshi was a teacher of Oriental languages in New York before he left for Britain in 1909. Har Dayal came to Stanford as a teacher in June, 1911. Rajani Kant Das published his report on the Indian workers on the Pacific Coast in 1922 and became a lecturer in economics at New York University. Dr. Syed Hossain came in 1921.[61]

Individual students, their organization, the Hindusthan Association of America (H.A.A.), and its organ the *Hindusthanee Student* became advocates for America and the American universities. They started providing guidance for prospective students in India by publishing articles in magazines and issuing booklets of information.[62]

There were so many universities, colleges and institutions of technical education in the United States that the editor of the *Hindusthanee Student* asked rhetorically—"What nation on earth can vie with such a record ?". The 1920's brought a "tide" of foreign students to America because following the War "Uncle Sam (became) a pedagogue." Vast sums were invested in several specialized fields of education.[63]

Among other advantages that students enjoyed in America were the facility of earning one's way through college and the availability of paid practical training in factories. The former was praised by Lajpat Rai as providing to the ambitious student "a chance of building up his character and making a career for himself by his own efforts, unaided by patronage or charity, or even the help of parents and guardians." This chance the student "can get in America and perhaps nowhere else," he concluded. "Practicality" was what Vivekananda had asked America to provide. Indian students were not only getting it, but were being paid for it. In 1926 as many as seventy-eight percent of Indian students in America were studying "practical subjects" like engineering, chemistry, and agriculture whereas of those in Britain only thirty-three percent were enrolled for these subjects. America had become the "Mecca of practical education."[64]

Even these facilities could not persuade large numbers of Indian students to prefer American universities over the British. Krishnalal Shridharani offered several reasons but, "The main reason, however, has been the subtle British campaign in India against American education . . . ." In British eyes, Shridharani continues, American education

> is supposed to turn out university graduates 'spoiled beyond repair' for British rule in India. The Indian students who have a taste of the 'American Way' go back to India with 'dangerous ideas'. Upon their return, consequently they are treated as 'suspect' . . . . Only the adventurous and a few strays among Indian students ever think of coming to the United States. They are persons who either do not need or do not want a governmental appointment upon their return to India. Or they belong to that small species of self-reliant Indian students who are eager to learn new industries and new professions and who intend to embark upon private enterprises, instead of becoming cogs in a well-geared governmental set-up.[65]

This allegation of British hostility is corroborated from other sources including British official documents. For instance, twenty-two years before Shridharani wrote the foregoing paragraph, Sir W.H. Vincent, Home Member of the Viceroy's Executive Council, acknowledged "that many, if not most, of them return to India openly hostile to the British Government and indeed often full of seditious enterprises . . . . These remarks apply to students and emigrants generally. . . ."[66]

Looking back over the careers of most of those students who became prominent organizers and leaders of the Indian community hardly any one of them seems to have become a convert to nationalism after his arrival in the United States. They were nationalists already. British policy, not American education, had converted them. America only acted as a grinding stone sharpening their discontent and teaching them how "to carry the brown man's burden" and to claim their "royal kinship with men." Here they could shout nationalist slogans to their hearts' content with impunity. Some even had visions of doing for India what Sun Yat Sen had done for China.[67]

They, of course, could not escape British surveillance. The Empire was almost everywhere and friendly governments helped. Four governments—Indian, British, Canadian, and American—watched

Taraknath Das's activities in America, took away his job and obstructed his ambition to get military training although nothing he did or aspired to or wrote about violated American law. Pandurang Sadashiv Khankhoje, another student-immigrant, suffered a similar fate."[68] But not just governmental alliances were at work. There was a people's alliance as well. This latter included Indian immigrants, students, businessmen, and Americans interested in India. It took several names but under every name it worked as a pressure group for the advancement of Indo- American community's interests both with regard to British rule over India and their rights or welfare as residents of the United States.

The Vedanta Society, the Khalsa Dewan Society, the temples and the gurudwaras catered to the spiritual and very often also to the secular needs of the immigrants and students. The Hindu and Sikh religious preachers gained American adherents some of whom became helpful assets to the Indian community. The visiting politicians from India and the resident scholar-lecturers made some Americans skeptical of British propaganda. The admiration of university presidents and professors for their hard struggles to earn tuition fees as well as good grades was extended to their country and its culture. Finally their speeches and writings in favor of India's freedom won the "American opinion on its sentimental side (which) has a keen sympathy with 'peoples struggling to be free.' "[69] The appeal was to a broad spectrum of American opinion including anarchists, communists, anti-British isolationists, socialists, civil-libertarians, anti-imperialists, intellectuals, Irish Americans, German-Americans, Unitarians, and during the Gandhian age, pacifists.

When students started arriving, they needed help. The earliest organization concerned with students was the one established in Portland, Oregon, with Swami Ram Tirtha's efforts. In December, 1926 two former students, Taraknath Das and Profulla Mukerji, told a convention of the Hindusthan Association of America (H.A.A.) how after a few initial disappointments, they had finally succeeded in establishing this central organization of the students in 1911 by bringing local student societies under one umbrella.[70] Success came because there was by then a growing number of Indian students in American universities and the organizers had an almost missionary zeal to organize. As a former member of the secret revolutionary organization, Anushilan Samiti, Das had learned that organizing the youth was a key to effective nationalist indoctrination and united action.[71] The story of the foundation of the Hindusthan Association of America illustrates how for forty years sparks from India lighted flames in America. All major political associations of Indians in the United States were founded by those who had personally participated in the national movement in India or, as in the case of the India League of America, were reactivated by such participants.

In 1907 Profulla participated in the formation in New York of the short-lived Pan-Aryan Association, one of whose objectives was to assist students from India and Persia. Another effort in the following year also proved infructuous.

Meanwhile students associations had sprung up at several university centers including one organized by Taraknath Das in South Washington. In 1910 as the result of joint efforts of Profulla Mukerji and Taraknath Das, Sudhindra Bose and Y. M. Bose all "local societies were crystallized into the present Hindusthan Association of America." As K.D. Shastri told the students in August 1915, "the dream of years was translated into reality." The H.A.A. lived to become the "second such organization of the people of India in America," the oldest being the Vedanta Society. It had a longer life-span than that of the India League of America, which lasted less than quarter of century.[72] The first annual convention was held in December 1911 at Chicago where student-representatives from five universities attended. Though not "political" in the American sense, the H.A.A. became a patriotic organization with nationalist overtones. Its honorary members included Indian politicians prominently associated with the Indian National Congress, such as Congress Presidents, Dadabhai Naoroji and Sarojini Naidu.[73]

"The importance of foreign educated students in Asia's new life should never be minimized," wrote Shridharani, one of the presidents of the Association.[74] In America the Association built up this importance by training the future organizers, lobbyists, writers, cultural ambassadors and propagandists for India's freedom. For over thirty years the presence of Indian students at American universities was "the one continuous factor in bringing India and America nearer to one another."[75]

The Second World War virtually dried up the flow of new students, but by the end of the 1930s the "brain trust" was already in place to head new organizations, edit new journals, and to fight the seven years' war for India's freedom and immigration law reform. They came to learn; they stayed to lead.[76] Coming, learning, staying, and leading had not been and would not be easy affairs for most of them. The passage was long and inconvenient, sometimes neither money nor the ticket was available.[77] They had to struggle to maintain good grades at school, to work hard to supplement allowances from home or from patrons, and to suffer mental anguish at American race prejudice compounded by anti-Indian propaganda by the British and missionaries. The personal and the national insult of immigration laws was the final burden.[78]

Students who came during the early years of Indian immigration did not have to maintain a student status to remain in the United States. Nor did they have to produce written guarantees of financial help from India.[79] But within a few years the exclusion movement hit them, and restrictions began.[80] In 1914, Sarangdhar Das warned prospective students that "(1) They must have all the credentials they can obtain to prove that they are students; (2) they must have written guarantee from their relatives or some public body that they will be helped financially from India."

There was a special warning for Sikh students. Das advised them that the Immigration Department was "invariably returning all laborers (who) are mostly Sikhs." The Department had concluded that every Sikh was a laborer. "Therefore we warn the Sikh student against this danger," Das concluded.[81]

As a result of the Act of 1917, "the days when a student could earn his way through college are gone," wrote Sudhindra Bose in a rather gloomy mood, because, "under the new Immigration laws, no student from India will be allowed to land in America who has not a visible source of income from Hindusthan." The rules, however, were interpreted liberally, permitting the students to earn a part of their way through school.[82]

The part of the Immigration Act of 1924 that applied to students from countries like India, which did not have immigration quotas, was Section 4(e). A student had to be at least fifteen years of age and to enter an accredited educational institution, approved by the Secretary of Labor. He was permitted to stay so long as he maintained his status as a bona fide student but any student "who engages in any business occupation for profit, or who labors for hire, shall be deemed to have abandoned his status as an immigrant student and shall on the warrant of the Secretary of Labor be taken into custody and deported."[83]

It was the intent of the Congress to permit aliens belonging to countries excluded from the privilege of immigration to study in America, if they came solely for that purpose and not for remaining here permanently. The prohibition against working for hire or profit was relaxed by the Commissioner of Immigration in terms which made the students happy. The Commissioner said :

> It seems very probable before a (U.S.) Consul issues a non-quota student visa he will require an assurance that such financial provision has been made as to insure that the applicant will be able to maintain a student status here. However, it is not believed that if a student contributes to his own support by working, this would necessarily disqualify him for admission nor is it believed that he ought to be prohibited from working during vacation periods. The point is that he must be primarily a student and not a worker for wages with his studies as a secondary matter.[84]

The Commissioner ruled further in 1927 that an alien student may work full-time during vacation period or for a few hours each day during school year "provided he carries a full course and maintains passing grades in the same." Full course meant at least ten credits per week. The Immigration Rules and Regulations of January 1, 1930, incorporated the Commissioner's interpretations.

The Agricultural Farmers

Most of the immigrants from India who reached Canada or the United States in the early years of this century were agricultural farmers. A vast majority of them were Sikhs from the districts of Jullundur, Hoshiarpur, Gurdaspur, Amritsar, and Ludhiana in the Punjab.[85]

Leaving home to earn a living abroad had become a familiar phenomenon in almost every British Indian province. Hundreds of thousands had gone to overseas British Colonies as indentured or free laborers. Sikhs had gone overseas as soldiers or policemen to serve the British in Hong Kong, Singapore, and Shanghai. In 1896, thousands of them had been recruited to work on railroad construction in Uganda.[86]

The economic situation in the Punjab following the British conquest had made emigrants available. People had been displaced from their traditional economic systems. Land tenure schemes had been altered. The small holders having been forced off the land "had to become agricultural laborers in order to survive". Punjabis became victims of an undiversified economy where agriculture and money lending, not industry and commerce, were the "most profitable of all business ventures."[87]

The severity and high incidence of land revenue demand, rural indebtedness, increasing population, and the consequent land hunger contributed to "gross maldistribution of land." It is estimated that "sixty percent of the population did not own enough land to make ends meet," with the result that "if opportunities for emigration could be found; they would be readily seized."[88]

A combination of British strategic, political, and economic interests following the conquest of the Punjab in 1849 brought about "a veritable economic revolution" at this region of Sikh population.[89] In half a century, however, the benefits of economic opportunities were exhausted by the growth of population, famines that killed cattle, and the uneconomic subdivision of land.[90] The Sikh farmer had, therefore, started looking for economic opportunities abroad. The railroad network of about 2,000 miles in the province facilitated the exodus.[91]

In the matter of emigration to Canada or the United States across the Pacific, the Sikhs enjoyed a distinct advantage. Hundreds of them were already on or near the Pacific. Gurudwaras were important transit points, rest houses, and information banks. Shipping arrangements were often made through gurudwara contacts. Sikhs who were employed in East Asia could save enough money to pay for the journey without having to mortgage their lands in the villages back home.[92] Hundreds of Sikhs left for North America directly from Hong Kong. Those who came from the Punjab had to mortgage "an acre or two" of land to get to Vancouver or San Francisco.[93]

The Punjabis who left for the United States or for Canada were not hungry individuals driven out by the "howls of the hunger wolf."[94] They may have been poor and heavily in debt, but they had their lands and houses that they mortgaged to pay for the journey. They had on the average fifty dollars when they landed, twice the amount demanded by Canadian law before it was raised to the prohibitive figure of two hundred dollars in 1908. They "came from the class of peasant proprietors owning less than ten acres of land." Those who went from stations in Southeast Asia or China were wealthier.[95]

The voyage from Calcutta to the Pacific coast of the United States took almost two months if the steamer connections were made on time. Sohan Singh Bhakna left Calcutta on February 3 and reached Seattle, Washington on April 4. It took one month to reach Yokohama, from there twelve days for the cross-over to Angel Island detention camp in the San Francisco Bay and about four days to reach Seattle.[96]

The cost of the passage in the first decade of the century was about rupees 200 ($1 = 31/8 rupees). It reached almost 400 rupees later. The fare form Hong Kong to Vancouver or San Francisco was fifty dollars.[97]

There are several recorded instances of Indians coming to the United States even before Vivekananda, but immigration *per se* in noticeable numbers started, as already mentioned, from the first decade of the new century.[98] Three groups of Indians were the first to be economically attracted by North America, namely, Indians already living in Southeast Asia, Indian soldiers who attended Queen Victoria's Diamond Jubilee celebrations in London (1897) and were sent back home traveling through Canada, and the Indian soldiers who were sent to China to suppress the Boxer Uprising of 1900. "Traveling abroad and crossing the ocean fostered in them a spirit of wanderlust and either at the time of their retirement from service or while on leave of absence, some of them crossed the Pacific to Canada."[99] Those who settled here sent letters home thereby encouraging others to join them.[100] Over 5000 reached Canada between 1905 and 1908 when Canada shut its gates to them. Meanwhile, they had started coming to the United States, both directly from India and from stations in Southeast Asia. Between 1899 and 1914 about 6000 Indian immigrants had been admitted as alien residents, a vast majority of them from the Panjab and most of the Panjabis, Sikhs and farmers.[101]

Arriving in the midst of a violent anti-Asian movement in progress both in Canada and the United States, Bruce LaBrack determined that "the Sikh's timing was terribly unfortunate." The Canadians were in an "angry mood" towards Asian immigrants. In California, "opposition to Japanese immigrants had assumed a definitely organized form."[102]

Within a few years of their arrival the Sikh immigrants discovered a Panjab in California with the same sunshine and warmth of the plains and same rich farmlands. The farming opportunities in California offered irresistible temptation to them—Born agriculturists, "they might be profitable to the State if given an opportunity to cultivate land," suggestied a prominent journal while Rajani Kant Das applauded the Sikhs' decision to settle down in the "promised land" of the San Joaquin Valley where his compatriots started coming from 1907. At the same time they entered the Sacramento Valley and built the first Sikh Gurudwara in the United States at Stockton.[103]

Their potential as good workers was immediately recognized even by the reluctantly appreciative investigators of the Immigration Commission. An East Indian appeared to them a "slow but honest, steady and exceedingly tractable workman."[104]

In 1910, the earliest group of Sikhs reached the Imperial Valley where "the extreme heat of the summer does not attract many American settlers (but the Sikhs) found a great opportunity for carrying on their industrial activities." They worked in vineyards and fruit ranches in Fresno, in vegetable and fruit orchards in San Joaquin Valley, in rice fields in Sacramento, and in cotton and cantaloupe fields in the Imperial Valley.[105]

Being recent immigrants they "could not possibly have become farmers on arrival because they were almost completely without capital." Like other immigrants who dreamed of becoming farm owners as operatives, the immigrants from India had to spend a few years studying the country and earning capital. In India "only a few of them were wage-earners." According to H.A. Millis, who investigated the Hindu laborers for the Immigration Commission, 85 percent of them "belonged to the agricultural class" in India. Having been owners of farmland and homestead, the "spirit of freedom gained from the ownership of land is a dominant feature in their life."[106]

Even as wage labor, they behaved like capitalists. "Having been born on farms, the desire to become independent farm owners is very strong in them. Consequently they feel little interest in labor organization." In lumber mills, "some of the workers still hope that they may accumulate enough money to buy a share in the industry."[107]

A writer in 1908 had suggested that the workers pool their dollars "to buy seeds and apply to the land agents for grants of lands on rent, to be paid out of the produce." The writer had himself leased a forty-acre plot. The immigrants were learning fast because "being utterly at risk, moving into a new and dangerous land, makes the immigrant alert and quick to learn. It livens reflexes, pumps adrenalin."[108]

Farm labor was not the Sikh immigrant's concept of the American dream. Bruce LaBrack has pointed out that overseas Sikhs had generally gone into blue collar type wage labor or in small businesses. Canadian Sikhs did not go into agriculture. Their American compatriots were forced into it because "discriminatory legislation and social prejudice" left for them only the jobs that the Anglos considered too menial. This happened to the Chinese and the Japanese too who retreated "into areas of the economy where their conflicts with organized labor would be minimal."[109]

While working as farm labor, the pressure of upward mobility continued to work upon them. To some, success came early. Jawala Singh and Wasakha Singh became owners of potato ranches before 1913. By 1920 there were 2600 Indian immigrants in California, a majority of whom became farm operators who leased land alone or in partnership with fellow Indians, and even farmers who owned their own farms. Several farm operators also worked as agricultural laborers when they were free from work on their own leased farms. Some Indians settled in Chandler, Arizona, bought land and produced wheat and cotton. An official of the California Immigration and Housing Commission found that, "Hindus are rapidly leaving the employed list and are becoming employers . . . the change . . . is rapidly placing the Hindu in the position of 'little landlord'."[110]

The achievements of the Indian farmers are well-documented. Being few in numbers—only about 5 percent of the number of Japanese in California—the scale of their enterprise was necessarily limited. The quality of their work, however, has been widely acclaimed.

They overcame a heavy burden of disabilities. They had almost no capital to start with, little knowledge of the people or of the country; they were not welcome, and knew little or no English and had, unlike the Japanese, no national government to watch over their interests. They lost even the lower middle-class socioeconomic status they had enjoyed at home.

Starting at the lowest rung with "stoop labor" in the asparagus fields or on the railroads and the lumber mills, in less than a decade, several of them became rich operators. Their farms around Sacramento were soon considered models, and they planted cotton on the arid lands in Arizona in 1920. Good credit and honest dealings with American banks, attorneys, and absentee landlords helped them survive the Alien Land Laws without severe damage and to reach the same level as the best farmers in California and British Columbia. In 1920, they leased 30,000 acres in Joaquin Valley and elsewhere in California. At one time they controlled "a large percentage" of rice production in California.[111]

A high California official stated that

> The Hindu will not farm poor land. He wants the best and will pay for it. Consequently the American owner who can get a big rental for his land desires the Hindu. He will pay.

The Hindu not only demanded the best; he also worked the hardest. Soon the rewards came. He used to ride a cycle to work, then came horses and buggies, then Fords, and finally seven- passenger touring cars. Both by his hard work and by his rewards, he made some Americans jealous. One man complained that after the cotton season is over Hindus buy cars and "feel so far above everyone else that they drive right in the middle of the road." He also accused them of "hoarding money for cars or of sending it to India." "Industrial success" resulting in "conspicuous consumption" aroused ill- feeling against the Hindus because, "It takes more than ordinary patience for a native-born American or Canadian to see a Hindustanee ride a Hudson Super Six, when he cannot afford more than a Ford."[112]

His wealth was not always offensively "conspicuous". It was also donated for good causes here and in India, spent on the families back home or just saved. By about 1920 the Khalsa Diwan Societies of California and British Columbia had started several schools in the Panjab, the California Society alone spending about 193,000 dollars. Burjor found (his report is dated November 1914) that several Hindus returning to India carried with them 3000 to 5000 dollars. A Hindu returning from India "frankly admitted" that after living in California for a few years paying his living expenses, supporting his family in India, he had taken home from 2000 to 3000 dollars.[113]

If not the wealth, at least the munificence of the Canadian and American Hindus, Sikhs, and Muslims became a prominent item in the financial resources of Indian politicians, social workers, and religious organizations. Except during the Gadar times they never smuggled arms as the Irish-Americans were doing, but they made heavy donations of money and, in at least one instance, even of land. In the Hardikar Papers there is a legal deed signed by a Sikh immigrant donating his land in Hoshiarpur District to the Indian National Congress. Donations continued for over thirty years and for over thirty years complaints were voiced that the immigrants were getting little return from home in solving their own problems. The Sikhs blamed the "Loyalists." Lajpat Rai blamed "the religious and the political fanatic." Jagjit Singh blamed the visiting politicians and some activists in America for using the simple-minded peasant-patriots of California. The complaint was not universally valid. Any major effort on their behalf in India would have sooner or later coalesced with the mainstream of the freedom struggle. Solution to both problems ultimately lay in the weakening of British imperialism and of its ideological supporters in America. Nevertheless the blame did partly lay at the door of the Indian politicians who treated the immigrants not as Indians but as Indians abroad.[114]

By the early 1920s the "outstanding feature of the industrial life of the immigrant farmers on the Pacific Coast," according to Rajani Kant Das, was "their business success." They had "in the course of a few years, changed their status from that of common laborers to that of farm operators, farmers, independent businessmen and even employers."[115]

There were small traders on the west coast who sold "Hindu candies," dry goods, groceries, or did a brisk trade as street vendors of peanuts, enchiladas, and tamales. Dady Burjor was an importer of Manila cigars in San Francisco. Former Gadarite Godha Ram Channon was an importer and exporter in the same city and still a suspect in British eyes over twenty years later. Dalip Singh Saund was a lettuce farmer-businessman as was Pahkar Singh in Imperial Valley. Another Gadarite Ram Nath Puri was the Manager of India-America Trade Development Co. in Fair Oaks, California.[116]

In the Midwest Thakur Dev Sharma, a naturalized citizen, was a realtor in Detroit owing "lot of property." Mumtaz I. Kitchlew was the proprietor of the India Importing Company of Chicago, a former student, and in 1940s an activist of the India League.[117]

There were also Indian businessmen in the southern states. In Louisiana many were engaged in importing goods from India. Ali Ali, the head of the colony, is said to have amassed a fairly good-sized fortune. Sadeck Ali Mollah, the H.A.A. representative in the South, was a student and the owner of a dry goods store in Charleston. Abba Dolla, the hero of the naturalization case *U.S. v. Dolla*, had his business in Savannah, Georgia. He was a "regular importer of silks, linens and other goods from India—and a 'wholesaler in this line of business.'"[118]

The major concentration of Indian businessmen and professionals, however, was on the East coast particularly in the region of greater New York. A directory published in 1934 lists the names of seven businessmen in New York City. This is clearly a partial list. At the inaugural luncheon of the India Chamber of Commerce on June 16, 1938, even the twelve who attended did not exhaust the list. We know of one K.C. Choudhury, "organizer of the Ramola Perfumery," who gave a dinner in honor of Professor S. Radhakrishnan in 1926, a Mr. Verma of the India Commerce Company who was in close contact with Indian students in New York, and above all Moosa Rawjee, the "pepper king," one of the "prosperous merchants" and a prominent financier of the India League. There was also N.R. Checker, the rival of Jagjit Singh in organizing the India Chamber of Commerce, in revitalizing the India League of America, and in the campaign for the Luce-Celler bill.[119]

These were the Indian businessmen on the mainland. The wealthiest, the most famous and one with the widest commercial network was not on the continent, but in Hawaii. He was Gobindram Watumull of Honolulu. The family name is appropriate. It means, "Hero of Sales." An irrigation engineer, originally from Hyderabad, Sind (now in Pakistan), he came to Honolulu in 1917 to manage his brother Jamnadas's East India Store, which he did for forty years, dying in August 1958, at 68. By the end of 1943, the original store had expanded to five in addition to heavy real estate investment. In 1942, he and his wife, Ellen Jensen, whom he married in 1921, established the Watumull Foundation to provide grants and scholarships for Indian students studying in American universities. During the 1940s both Gobindram and Ellen Jensen became enthusiastic supporters of the India League efforts although often criticizing Jagjit Singh's methods and usually financing his rivals, Dr. Syud Hossain and Anup Singh.[120]

Contemporary Indian writers have mentioned with pride, and their American friends with appreciation, concrete instances of the Indian immigrant's contribution to the development of the states where they lived. Dr. Rajani Kant Das's investigative account is a classic instance of fraternal pride peeping out from behind phrases of scholarly restraint. Dady Burjor was another contemporary eyewitness who from his vantage point of interpreter for the Immigration Service and long residence in California, had occasion to appreciate the Hindu achievements. Large tracts of land in Sacramento and other counties were

> Considered by white people as barren and hard to cultivate and they could not be leased to the white men even on the most advantageous terms . . . . They looked like howling wildernesses before they were leased to the 'Hindu,' the Chinese and the Japanese who have transformed them into smiling gardens and prosperous farms. Where the white men could not even exist or at least imagined so, these so-called Asiatic hordes are thriving, and paying regular incomes to the owner of the lands in the shape of rents, or buying them out at prices which ten years ago their owners could not even dream of getting . It is the class of people who want more "Hindus" admitted to this country. I have met several of them at the Angel Island, where they come and actually offer bonds of $500 for each of these "Hindus" detained there on plea of being liable to become public charge."[121]

Other accounts came from Indian and American eyewitnesses who were attempting to persuade Congress that people who had done so much for America deserved to be rewarded with eligibility to citizenship. Mubarek Ali Khan, President of the Indian Welfare League, told a Senate hearing in 1944 what he knew of the Indian farmers' achievements. On lands, "where all was mud and sand and American farmers were not interested in taking this land for one nickel per acre, but these Indian farmers have taken it and cultivated it and have made good rice fields there." In Arizona the Indian farmers gave "tremendous profit" to that state where they were producing vegetables, wheat, rice, and barley.[122]

Joseph Tenner boasted that several Indian farmers were paying taxes ranging from 10,000 to 25,000 dollars. We have some "pretty rich Indian farmers," he told the Senate Committee. In Arizona some farmers had 2500 to 3000 acre farms. In the Imperial Valley three Muslim farmers held between them 5000 acres of fields, "where they raise wheat, barley and all kinds of vegetables which are shipped to the market every morning." In Casa Grande, one Divan Singh held 1600 acres in his wife's name. His farm machinery alone was worth about 100,000 dollars.[123]

In the course of a tour of the Asian Indian settlements in the west in 1943, Senator William Langer (D.--N.D.) met Governor Earl Warren of California who told him that some America-educated Indians first started to work on "these alkali lands and the swamplands (of the Imperial Valley) which were valueless." They kept trying "until today the rice crop is a tremendous item in California."[124]

Scholarly investigative essays on the social and economic life of the Indian community in the United States have described their good qualities as achievers and their alleged bad qualities as low-standard, un-assimilable men without morals. These are studies of the first generation Indians' reaction to their new environment like similar studies of the first generation immigrants of other nationalities including the vanguard of the Pilgrim sectarians who sailed in the *Mayflower*, the potato blight victims from Ireland, the railroad laborers from China, the refugees from Russian pogroms, and the Issei from Japan.

Some trials, hardships and experiences were the same for immigrants of all nationalities. For instance, they were almost never received with open arms. The immigration laws may have been liberal; the community itself was not overflowing with the spirit of those laws. They were received with suspicion directed towards the religion; the color, the language, the stereotype of the national character, in the numbers of the newcomers—in the case of the Asian immigrants, all the above; for Hindus, more than the above.

Secondly, national origin was never forgotten nor permitted to be forgotten. Right at the point of reception, a hyphen was awarded to each immigrant. Thereafter, it was a permanent possession. It was flaunted with pride, flung at you by traducers, and later foisted upon all nationalities by the Immigration Law of 1924. Color, religion, nationality persisted as potent factors in the lives of the immigrants for honor or for calumny. People were "Americans" only when at war or visiting abroad. At home America was a nation of hyphenates, a conglomeration, a mixture more than a chemical compound, the Turner thesis notwithstanding.

Both in the West and the East intolerance of the newcomers had become the American creed. As part of the national patriotism it was transmitted to other white nationalities through a process called "Americanization" so that the victims of today became the tormentors of tomorrow, sometime in less than one lifetime. It was in this intolerant society that the Hindus happened to have come.

Notes & References

1. Testifying before a House hearing in 1914, Dr. Sudhindra Bose said that Indians come here "because of the opportunities we have for social uplift, intellectual betterment, and economical advancement." *Hindu Immigration*, Committee on Immigration, House of Representatives, February 13, 1914, 4, henceforth referred to as *Sudhindra Hearings*; Dr. Haridas T. Muzumdar testifying at a hearing in 1939, said that some Indians were attracted "by the possibilities of making a new life in this country. Some of them came for idealistic reasons, some perhaps came in order to better material status in life." *India-Born Residents of the United States Request For Naturalization*; Hearing before House Committee on Immigration and Naturalization, 76th Cong., 1st sess., June 21, 1939, 11, henceforth referred to as, *June 1939 Hearing*.
2. A *Los Angeles Times* editorial quoted in an Indian journal seemed to hold out a hope and a promise : "The American missionaries and merchants have gone to India and carried to the natives the gladsome tidings that this is the land of the free and the home of the brave; that all men are created equal, ... They have merely represented what our Constitution and Declaration of Independence apparently guarantee," *Modern Review*, Calcutta, May 1919, 526.
3. Ramlal Bajpai called the denial of naturalization to Indians "incongruous," *June 1939 Hearing*, 1; Shridharani called it "a moral issue, an issue of human equality," "*To Permit the Naturalization of Approximately Three Thousand Natives of India*," Hearings Before a Subcommittee of the Committee on Immigration, United States Senate, 78th Cong., 2d sess., on S1595, September 13 and 14, 1944, Washington 1944, 49, henceforth referred to as *S1595 Hearings*. Dr. Anup Singh warned that "only by violating its own ideals can (the United States) discriminate against any people on the basis of race," *Asia and The Americas*, April 1944, 157.
4. *The Works of Charles Sumner*, Vol. XIII, Boston : Lee and Shepard, 1880, 475.
5. Ibid., 42.
6. Ibid., 474, 475.
7. Ibid., 483.
8. Gunnar Myrdal, *An American Dilemma : The Negro Problem and Modern Democracy*, New York, 1994, XLVII.

9. *Congressional Record*, 79th Cong., 1st sess., October 10, 1945, 9528.
10. This is Gunnar Myrdal's theme in his Chapter I, *An American Dilemma*, 1-25.
11. Indian Immigrants very early recognized the western nations' practice of "expediency," Nihal Singh complained in 1914, "No European nation has ever been able to justify the exclusion of Orientals from these regions (Australia, South Africa, North America) on moral grounds, but considerations of expediency are advanced." "Asiatic Immigration : A World Question," *Living Age*, August 15, 1914, 392.
12. Franklin, D. Roosevelt to Samuel Dickstein, March 5, 1945, *Cong. Rec.* 79th Cong., 1st sess., October 10, 1945, 9524. Emphasis added.
13. The quotation is from Rammanohar Lohia, *Indians in Foreign Lands.* All-India Congress Committee, Allahabad 1938, Introduction, 13 for heavy land revenue rates in the Panjab, Lucie Cheng and Edna Bonacich (eds.), *Labor Immigration Under Capitalism : Asian Workers in the United States before World War II*, Los Angeles, 1984, 324.
14. For a glimpse of how Indians basked under the protection of the British flag in Southeast Asia: Sant Nihal Singh, "Indians in the Far East," *Modern Review*, August 1908, 114-121. A Chinese view of the British use of India; to grow opium and sell it to the Chinese "because otherwise India might not prosper." and how Indians used the Empire: ". . . the rich Indians backed by the diplomatic force and physical strength of the British Empire, would not alone rob millions of degraded Chinese of their mental and bodily strength, but they would sop the last cash from the land of their victims. They would drain our beloved country in every way, and leave us helpless dupes of the poppy farmers of India," an extract from the memoirs of the Chinese statesman Li Hung Chang; *Cong. Rec.* 63rd Cong., 3rd sess., Extension of Remarks of Hon. Julius Kahn, Appendix, 490; Baba Gurdit Singh of the Komagata Maru fame prospered as a contractor in Singapore and Malaya where his father had started as a petty contractor, S.P. Sen (Ed), *Dictionary of National Biography*, Calcutta, 1972; in 1943 the investments of the Chettyar family of Indian bankers and landlords in Burma were "the most important foreign holding; estimated at Rs. 750 million in value, as well as at least one- quarter of the best cultivated land." Hugh Tinker, *Separate and Unequal : India and Indians in the British Commonwealth, 1920-1950*, Vancouver, 1976, 207.
15. For a general study of Bengal Renaissance and Hindu religious revival; R.C. Majumdar, *History and Culture of the Indian People: Struggle For Freedom*, Bombay 1969, Chapters XLII, XLIII; K.K. Datta, *Dawn of Renascent India*, Nagpur, 1969; A. C. Banerjee, *Brahmo Samaj and Freedom Movement*. 1960; S. N. Banerjee, *A Nation in the Making*, London, 1925; J. H. Broomfield, *Elite Conflict In a Plural Society:*

Twentieth Century Bengal, Berkeley, 1968. David Kopf, *British Orientalism and the Bengal Renaissance : The Dynamics of Indian Modernization*, Berkeley: University of California, 1969; Lajpat Rai, *The Arya Samaj*, New York, 1915; Ram Gopal, *Lokmanya Tilak, a Biography*, London, 1965; Biographies of Vishnu Bhicaji Gokhale, Brahma Bandhab Upadhyaya and Swami Satya Dev Parivrajak in Sen (ed.). *Dictionary*.

For Sikh religious revival, Fauja Singh Bajwa, *Kuka Movement*, Motilal Banarsidas, Delhi, 1965; Prem Raman Uprety, *Religion and Politics in the Punjab in the 1920s*, New Delhi; Sterling Publishers Private Ltd., 1980. Juergensmeyer and Barrier (Eds.). *Sikh Studies*, Berkeley, 1979, 173, 176, 177; Biographies of Baba Ram Singh, and Bhai Vir Singh, Sen (Ed.). *Dictionary*.

16. Quoted in Krishnalal Shridharani, *My India, My America*, New York: Duell, Sloan and Pearce, 1941, 440 with the following comment : "That a man of his intellectual stature failed to distinguish between figures of speech and imagery on one hand, and painstaking records on the other; that a man of his immense gusto failed to remember his own western and yet implausible *Ilaid* and his own English Chaucer and King Arthur, can be explained away only on the grounds of the selfrighteousness and complacency of his race and religion." Ibid.
17. "It was Swami Vivekananda who revived the old missionary spirit of Hinduism towards the close of the Nineteenth Century A.D." *India's Contribution to World Thought and Culture*; Vivekananda Rock Memorial Committee, Triplicane, Madras, 1970, Foreword by R.C. Majumdar, VII. Henceforth this work will be referred to as the Vivekananda Memorial Volume. Marie Louise Burke, *Swami Vivekananda in America: New Discoveries*; Advaita Ashram, Calcutta, 1958, describes his lecture tours over America and the contacts he established.
18. According to Lucy Aiken, Rammohan Roy had spoken to her on September 6, 1831, "of ending his days in America," David Kopf: *The Brahmo Samaj and the Shaping of Modern Indian Mind*, Princeton, N.C., 1979, 4.
19. Harbilas Sarda, *Life of Dayanand Saraswati : World Teacher*, Ajmer, 1968, 89.
20. His address, "The Struggle of Indians to Attain Equal Rights in the United States of America," delivered on August 4, 1946, 4.
21. A brief assessment of his life by a devotee, Swami Nikhilananda at the unveiling of the saint's bust in New York, *Modern Review*, April 1952, 307-309.
22. *Sedition Committee Report*, Calcutta, 1918, 17.
23. Richard Hofstadter, *The Progressive Historians: Turner, Beard. Parrington*, Chicago, 1968, 47.
24. Bepin Chandra Pal, "Five Months in the States'," *Modern Review*, January 1938, 12.

25. Carl T. Jackson, *The Oriental Religions and American Thought: Nineteenth Century Explorations,* Westport, Conn. 1981, 249.
26. *The Vivekananda Memorial Volume*, 668. Horatio W. Dresser, "An Interpretation of the Vedanta," *Arena*, Vol. XII, No. 4, October 1899; 489-508 mentions Vivekananda as "one of the most striking figures in that Parliament," 489.
27. Wendell Marshall Thomas, *Hinduism Invades America,* New York, 1930, 64, 78; *Open Court*, Vol. XVI, September 1902, 576.
28. Anna Josephine Ingersoll, "The Swamis in America" *Arena*, Vol. XXII. No. 4, October 1899, 484; Wendell Thomas, *Hinduism Invades*, says there were seventeen Swamis who succeeded Vivekananda till 1929, 82, 105.
29. *American Monthly Review of Reviews*, May 1908, 604; *Indian Review*, Madras, October 1939, 697; Wendell Thomas, *Hinduism Invades*, 86, 104; for Swami Parmananda: *Who's Who In America 1930-31*, Vol. 16, Vol. 17; *Modern Review*, 70, July-December 1941, 315; there is a list of his works in his *Secret of Right Activity*, Boston: Vedanta Center, 1923. For Swami Abhedananda: *Indian Review*, October 1939, 697; Haridas T. Muzumdar, *America's Contributions to India's Freedom*, Allahabad: Central Book Depot, 1962, 34; Moni Bagchi, *Swami Abhedananda: A Spiritual Biography*, Calcutta: Ramakrishna Vedanta Math, 1968, 276-78, 280, 282, 289. The Swami died September 8, 1939. Bagchi's claim that the Swami met President McKinley at the White House cannot be confirmed because the name of the Congressman who is supposed to have accompanied him seems to be wrong.
30. The work of the Swami-missionaries in the United States: Naeen Gul Rathore, *Indian Nationalist Agitation in the United States: Lajpat Rai and the India Home Rule League of America 1914-1920*, 4, says there were twelve centers in 1978, *Missionary Review of the World*, June 1934, 291; Wendell Thomas, *Hinduism Invades*, 7, 13, 14, 16, 86, 104, 106, 1119, 142; *Indian Review*. October 1939, 697; May 1940, 308; Swami Satprakashananda, *Swami Vivekananda's Contribution to the Present Age,* The Vedanta Society of St. Louis, Mo., 1978, 129; Rajani Kant Das, *Hindustani Workers on the Pacific Coast*, Berlin: Walter De Grunter & Co., 1923, 80; *Modern Review*, September 1926, 304-305; *San Francisco Chronicle*, 31 January 1926; K.C. Ker, *Political Trouble in India. 1907-1917*, Delhi, 1973, 216.

    On Hindu Temples in America: *Hindusthanee Student*, January 1916, 21; Wendell Thomas, *Hinduism Invades*, 112, 119, 120; *Modern Review*, June 1923, 693; July 1928, 90-91; *American Monthly Review of Reviews*. January 1907, 93; May 1908, 604.
31. Vitasta Prasad Fida, "Swami Rama and His Message," *The Tribune*, Ambala, October 22, 1957; S.S. Chawla, "Swami Ram Tirtha-Patriot and

Prophet," 27 ibid. October 1957; Hari Prasad Shastri, *Rama Tirtha: Scientist and Mahatma*, Shanti Sadan, London, 1955, 36-38, gives a disciples account of the Swami's visit to America; Wendell Thomas, *Hinduism Invades*, 205--206, Taraknath Das's appreciation of Ram Tirtha's work in America. *Hindustanee Student*, March 1926, 6.

32. Wendell Thomas, *Hinduism Invades*, 177; *American Monthly Review of Reviews*, January 1907, 92-93.
33. Wendell Thomas, *Hinduism Invades*, 134, 140- 142, 146-148, 151, 168, 171; *Modern Review*, November 1952, 398, 399. Ratification and confirmation of Naturalization of Certain Persons of the Hindu Race: Hearings before the Committee on Immigration, United States Senate, 69th Cong., 2d sess., on S.J. Res, 120, December 9, 1926, 37. Henceforth this Hearing shall be referred to as the Senate Hearings, December 1926. Swami Yoganand to Jagjit Singh, March 7, 1944; *Hinduism To-Day*, San Francisco, March 1, 1986, 9.
34. *Arena*, October, 1899, 483; Marie Louise Burke, *Swami Vivekananda*, 128-129; Baba Bharati's claim as to the recent "great upheaval of Hinduism in India," American Monthly, *Review of Reviews*, January 1907, 93.

Congressman James Manahan of Minnesota had studied Hath Yoga. As member of the House Immigration and Naturalization Committee 63rd Congress he attended all hearings held in 1913 and 1914 on Hindu exclusion bills. His attitude was uniformly helpful in explaining the Indian point of view; *Sudhindra Hearings* 9, 27, 28, 33; Ina Steele Hutchinson submitted testimony in support of the Celler Bill in the course of which she mentioned Vivekananda; Hearings Before the Committee of Immigration and Naturalization, House of Representatives, 79th Cong., 1st sess., on HR 173 (and five other) bills to grant a quota to Eastern Hemisphere Indians and to make them racially eligible for Naturalization, March 7, 8, 13, 14, 1945, Washington, D.C., 1945, 126, henceforth to be referred to as House Hearings, March 1945. Sometimes the Hindu preachers harmed their own cause, *vide*, Horace I. Paleman's remarks, "Some of your religious leaders have come to America and have had pronounced success. Wherein their interests are broadly and genuinely cultural and philosophical, their work is of value. When they indulge chiefly in the propagation of fads and isms—no matter how sincere they may be—their influence is not healthful." *India To-Day*, May 1941, Lala Lajpat Rai, devoted over four pages of his book on the United States to an assessment of the work of the Hindu preachers, as he found it in 1916. With the exception of Vivekananda and Ram Tirtha he thought that the "general run of Swamis that come to this country are not above criticism." *United States of America: A Hindu's Impression and a Study*, 2nd Ed., Calcutta, 1919, 470.

He also accused them of bringing into their organizations "a spirit of greed and commercialism." Ibid. Two decades later Shridharani was "shocked" to find that "some of his own countrymen in the United States (were) dragging spiritual qualities down to the market place." He found out that some of these priests were millionaires, *My India, My America*, 98- 99. Both these writers have, however, recognized the brighter side of the achievements of the Hindu priests in America. Lajpat Rai gave them credit for "disillusioning the people of America as to the civil and religious conditions of that 'heathen country' supposedly against the Christian missionary misrepresentations. Even in those first twenty years of Hindu religious preaching, Lajpat Rai found it 'marvelous to what a great extent Hinduism has influenced the religious thought of America. Reincarnation and the previous and future lives of the soul are accepted almost as an axiomatic truth. 'Karma' is a very common word in religious phraseology. The Bible is being very laboriously overhauled to bring it into conformity with modern religious thought, and many a Hindu idea is being given out to the world in Biblical language and Christian phraseology." Ibid., 469, 471-472.

Shridharani was well aware that, "There are probably half a dozen genuine Hindu Swamis in America . . . who have created a lasting place for themselves in various communities . . . They have also brought the wisdom of the Hindus to a distant shore, and unlike the Christian missionaries in the Orient, without any intention of proselytizing 'the heathens.' Shridharani, ibid. The author of *Hinduism Invades America* characterized this Hindu religious intrusion into America as an amazing adventure of an Eastern faith in a Western land," 7; "An expression of young India," 13 and "perhaps the first modern missionary movement of an Eastern religion to the west," 16.

35. Swami Ram Tirtha, *In the Woods of God Realization*, Ram Tirtha Publication League. Vitasta Prasad Fida, *The Tribune*, Ambala, October 22, 1957; Wendell Thomas, *Hinduism Invades*, 177, 180, 211; *Complete Works of Swami Vivekananda*, Calcutta, 1970-79

36. Preachers maintained contact with immigrants: Rajani Kant Das, *Hindustani Workers*, 81; Rathore, *Indian Nationalist Agitation*, 46, 47; Hardikar, *Lajpat Rai*. 40-41, *Hindusthanee Student*, September 1915, 6, 7; November 1915, 23; September-October, 1925, 24; January 1926, 7, 8; September-October 1926, 6; *Modern Review*, Vol. 70, July- December 1941, 572-573.

37. Rajani Kant Das, *Hindustani Workers*, 80, 81.

38. Ker, *Political Trouble*, 216; Wendell Thomas, *Hinduism Invades*, 64, the Chapter heading is "Vivekananda, A Champion of Mother India," and also mentioned "the son of Mother India," 72.

39. Ker, *Political Trouble*, 218.
40 ". . . about seventy-five years ago Indian students . . . began to go to England to study in British Universities." Taraknath Das and Gobindram J. Watumull's article in the *The Calcutta Review* reproduced in part in *Modern Review*, January 1944, 66; Surendranath Banerjee, the first Indian to pass the Indian Civil Service examination left for England in March 1868, S.N. Banerji, *A Nation in Making*, Calcutta, 1963, 4.
41. A. K. Mujamdar, *Advent of Independence* Bombay, 1963, IX.
42. J.M. Kumarappa and G.S. Krishnayya. *Indians Going to America: A Guide Book for Students,* Bombay; Byculla, 1947; henceforth mentioned as Kumarappa *Guide Book.*
43. *Caste and Outcast*, New York, 1923, 155.
44. The editor of the Indian students' journal in America complained that the Government of India was not doing "even a twentieth" of what is necessary to "shape the future destiny of India." He therefore appealed to "our readers, princes and merchants (to) come forward to take a lead in this matter." *The Hindusthanee Student*, November 1915, 20.
45. *Vivekananda Memorial Volume*, 657.
46. *Complete Works of Swami Vivekananda*, Vol. III, 365-356.
47. Vitasta Prasad Fida, "Swami Ram and His Message," *The Tribune* Ambala, 22 October 1957; S.S. Chawla, *Swami Ram Tirtha—Patriot and Prophet*, ibid. . October 27, 1957; Girindra Mukerji, "The Hindu in America," *Overland*, April 1908; 304; *Modern Review*, April 1925, 448: Taraknath Das, *Address, August 1946*, 5; Joan Jensen, *Passage from India.* 21.
48. *The Hindusthanee Student*, January 1914, 7.
49 Ibid., March 1916, 10.
50. Sudhindra Bose, *Fifteen Years In America*, New York 1974, 466; The Forum, Vol. LIII, 1915, 251; see Footnote 98 below.
51. *Modern Review*, May 1909, 471-472; Girindra, ibid.. 303-304; this seems to be confirmed by Lajpat Rai who writing in 1916 mentioned that Indian students had been getting education here within the last fifteen years," *The United States of America*, 458; *American Monthly Review of Reviews*, May 1908, 604.
52. Sudhindra, *Fifteen Years*, 466-467.
53. *Modern Review*, January 1909, 53; October 1912, 429; Rabindranath Tagore's son Rathindranath came as a student in 1906, Joseph Lister Dees, *Tagore and America*, 10. N.S. Hardikar, *Lala Lajpat Rai in America*, New Delhi. *Servants of the People Society*, 1966, 9; Lajpat Rai, *The United States of America*, describes the struggles and achievements of several children of middle class families who came here seeking higher education, 455-460.

54. Jawala Singh in S.P. Sen (ed.), *Dictionary*, Bhagat Singh Thind "helped to support nearly thirty-five students from India," including Dr. Anup, Singh and Pratap Singh Kairon, later Chief Minister of the Panjab. Mrs. Vivian Thind's interview with the present writer July 25, 1984: *Modern Review*, January 1911, 108; "Most of us live on regular remittance from home." *Hindusthanee Student*, January-February 1918. 20.
55. Sudhindra, *Fifteen Years*, 467; *Hindusthanee Student*, April-July, 1914, 49; May 1917, 9. *Modern Review*. January 1914, 32, October 1912, 428-129. In 1910 it demanded from each student a heavy cash security of 400 dollars and as a result no student came on its behalf in 1911 and 1912.
56. Lajpat Rai, *Young India*, Howard Fertig, New York, 1968, 171; *Modern Review*, January 1911, 109-110; December 1911, 625. The *Hindusthanee Student*, January 1916, 19; April; 1926, 5-6; Lajpat Rai to N.S. Hardikar, New York, March 10, 1920, Hardikar Papers, Jawaharlal Memorial Library, New Delhi. 1400 Broadway, New York was the main office of India Home Rule League of America.
57. *Hindusthanee Student*, April-July 1914, 49; January-February 1918, 20; September-October 1926, 3 and January-February 1927, 12; Jagjit Singh's broadcast speech on All-India Radio, Delhi in 1946. Jagjit Singh to Dinkar Sakrikar, October 17, 1946. As mentioned above the earliest Indian students had come to Berkeley, California in 1901-1902. In 1908 there were seventeen of them, Dalip Singh Saund found eighty in 1920. According to Sudhindra there were about two hundred in the whole country in 1915. Jacobi estimates that out of a thousand Indians coming to the United States in 1920-1926 most were students. According to another estimate there were five hundred students in 1934. Jacobi believes that there were almost no new arrivals till after 1946, Krishnalal Shridharani mentions the figure "over thirty" students in 1941. Among those who became prominent, Taraknath Das came in 1906, Sudhindra Bose the following year, Dhan Gopal Mukerji in 1910. Vaman Ramchandra Kokatnur, Profulla Mukerjee came about the same time as Dhan Gopal. Narayan Subarao Hardikar in 1914, Dalip Singh Saund and Haridas T. Muzumdar in 1920, Krishnalal Shridharani in 1934. *American Monthly Review of Reviews*, May 1908, 604; Dalip Singh Saund, *Congressman from India*, New York, 1960, 35, 37; Sudhindra Bose, "American Impressions of a Hindu Student." *The Forum*, Vol. LIII, 1915, 251; Harold S. Jacoby, *A Half-Century Appraisal of East Indians in the United States*, College of the Pacific, Stockton, 1957, 7; *Missionary Review*, June 1934, 291. Arun Coomer Bose, "Indian Nationalist Agitation in the U.S.A. and Canada till the arrival of Har Dayal in 1911." *Journal of Indian HIstory*, Vol. LIII, 1965, 234-235; for Das, Kokatnur and Dhan Gopal, *Who's Who in America 1932- 1933*, Vol. 17; Shridharani. *My India. My America*, 50, 72. For Profulla Mukerji, *New York Times*, 23 April 1982. N. S. Hardikar,

Lala Lajpat Rai in America, New Delhi, 1966, 1. Harold S. Jacoby, in Juergensmeyer and Barrier (eds.), *Sikh Studies*, 163. There also seems to be a similar though a shorter gap (1920-1930s) in the visits of Indian political leaders to the United States, Rathore, *Indian Nationalist Agitation*, 285.

58. November 1915, 10; It was believed that the British Government too was "making plans to use the Boxer Indemnity Fund to have Chinese students educated in England, " *Modern Review*. April 1924, 468.
59. *Caste and Outcast*, 162, 165.
60. Sudhindra Bose: In a short biographical note from Ersin Kalaycioglu to Prof. Samuel C. Patterson, dated May 26, 1976, in the present writer's possession; "I came to this country as a laborer." he told a Congressional Committee. Sudhindra Hearing, February 12, 1914, 4, *Modern Review*, November 1948, 365, Taraknath Das: Sen (Ed.) *Dictionary*; Sarangdhar Das: Frieda Mathilda Hauswirth, *A Marriage to India*, New York, 1930, 8. Profulla Mukerji, *Modern Review*, October 1932, 432; Maxine P. Fisher. *The Indians of New York City*, New Delhi, 1980, 13. Saund, *Congressman*, 35.
61. Arun Coomer Bose, *Indian Nationalist Agitation*, 229, 239; Rathore, *Indian Nationalist Agitation*, 8; Thomas, *Hinduism Invades*, 205, Rajani Kant Das: *Hindustani Workers*, IV. Dr. Syud Hossain came in 1921, *Bombay Chronicle*, Bombay, 7, April 1946, Haridas T. Muzumdar, *Oral History Transcripts*, 24, Nehru Memorial Library, New Delhi.
62. The Hindu student "never loses faith in the ultimate triumph of the vitalizing influence of American democracy." Sudhindra Bose, "American Impressions of a Hindu Student "*The Forum*, Vol. LIII, 1915, 257; his Presidential Address explaining the objectives of the H.A.A., *The Hindusthanee Student*, January 1914, 18, 19, 22; January 1916, 5. *Modern Review*, January 1909, 18-27, 30-34 September 1917, 262; April 1925, 448; Hardikar, *Lajpat Rai in America*, They also knew they were coming to better universities. Prof. M.M. Guptara, "American Universities and the 'Honor System', "*Indian Review*, October 1933.

Providing information and guidance became a permanent service of the Association. A representative in India was appointed in 1913 and information was circulated from several centres, *Hindusthanee Student*, January 1914, 18, and January 1926, 9-10; often the mail was heavy, *Young India*, New York, November 1919, 242; *Hindusthanee Student*, May 1925. Occasionally information was circulated in the form of a bulletin or pamphlet, Sudhindra Bose, Forum, Vol. VIII, 1915, 256; *Hindusthanee Student*, January 1914, 22; November 1916 December 1916, January 1917, 1; January 1926, 6. A large part of the information was concerning the courses offered in the universities but also about scholarships and immigration laws, *Hindusthanee Student*, April-July

1914, November 1916, 22; May 19[illegible], 7-8; March 1925, 5, 6 and January 1926, 6. Student-advocates of America were sometimes enthusiastically eloquent, for instance, "America today leads the world in engineering. America, so to speak, is a country made by engineers . . . . We must come to this country not by dozens but by hundreds.' *Modern Review*, May 1912, 481; Prof. Guptara wrote, "Not to patronise American Universities is national 'criminal ignorance'", *Indian Review*, Madras, October 1933, 647, *Young India*, August 1919, 189. The advantage of unrestricted admissions and an attitude of welcome to Indian students as well as comparative freedom from race prejudice on American campuses were recurrent themes in contemporary periodicals. See, *Mahratta*, Poona, Editorial, August 13, 1916, 9-10; *Hindusthanee Student*, November 1916, 6, 7; March 1925, Front Page.

63. January 1914, 19; a similar exhortation by Taraknath Das, *Modern Review*, November 1925, 607; New investment in education, ibid., August 1925, 225, 226; also see Taraknath Das, ibid., April 1924, 467-468.

64 *Hindusthanee Student*, March 1916, 10; "self-support" was explained in ibid., April-May 1930, 11. In 1941 Krishnalal Shridharani alleged that America "costs most to live in," *Asia And The Americas*, August 1941, 443, and in his *My India, My America*, 69, but on 73, he writes, "In fact the idea of studying and working for a living at the same time had been for me one of America's strongest attractions;" A 1918 estimate put a student's summer earnings at 175 dollars, *Young India*, October 1918, 3. *Modern Review*, October 1912, 429, 429. Laboratory fees in many west and midwestern state universities varied from 5 to 25 dollars per term of three or four months. "A student can live plainly in an university town" on 15 to 20 dollars with laboratory fees and books costing extra. Ibid., December 1911, 608; *Hindusthanee Student* figure was 30 dollars per month for board, room and sundry expenses, January 1914; Sudhindra Bose warned that "no one should think of coming here without a steady allowance from home of at least a hundred rupees a month," *Modern Review*, September 1917, 261. This would be almost 34 dollars a month; Mecca of practical education, *Hindustanee Student*, September-October 1926, 3; Kumarappa, *Guide Book*, iii; Dhan Gopal Mukherjee's experience with "self-support," *Caste and Outcast*, 272-275, 277; the Asiatic Exclusion League wanted this privilege withdrawn, *Proceedings*, February 1909, 11.

65. Shridharani, *My India, My America*, 69, 70; he also wrote "very few Indian students have ever come to the United States. It is farthest away, costs most to live and in the third place, there are those severe and even unfriendly immigration laws" *Asia and the Americas*, August 1941, 443.

66. Home/Political, March 1919. No. 21 Deposit, 11, National Archives of India, New Delhi. American professors also knew of the political suspicions their Indian students were laboring under : "I know that there are difficulties in the way of American-trained technologists when they return home . . . . British trained Hindu technologists will be preferred before them, and they will be under suspicion of having imbibed ideas too radical." Dr. Edwin Herbert Lewis, *The Hindusthanee Student*, May 1917, 14. Indian students continued to be suspected, watched, black-listed, *Modern Review*, February 1927, 170; Dr. Taraknath Das and Gobindram Watumull in *Modern Review*, January 1946, 66 and Anne Z. Bose's article on her husband Dr. Sudhindra, November 1948, 368; Rathore, *Indian Nationalist Agitation*, 5, 101; some steamship company officials who had refused passage to some Indian students told Rabindranath Tagore that "the British Government was exerting pressure upon them and California also and that they did not dare to transport them . . . . "*Modern Review*, June 1917, 663; "Of late the British Government has been refusing passports even to students." Lajpat Rai, *Young India*, March 1918, 8. It is interesting to note the assessment of the situation by the Director of Intelligence, Government of India in January 1919, "But when I see how the tendency to sedition has grown among Indians in England, I sometimes think that nothing can check that tendency among Indians abroad." Cleveland's Note dated January 14, 1919 Home/Political, National Archives of India, ibid., 8; "The educated Indians . . . are unfortunately all revolutionaries." British Consul-General in San Francisco to British Ambassador Sir C. Spring-Rice, February 13, 1914, Home/Political, November 1914, No. 77, Part B, Report by Mr. Burjor, 11, henceforth to be referred to as the *Burjor Report*. "All these Indian students I met were nationalists. They wanted to free India." Dhan Gopal Mukherji, *Caste and Outcast,* 253; "Every Hindu is a nationalist to some degree.", San Francisco Chronicle, January 31, 1926, 2, Col. 4; "I am told that the Indian student in America is engaged in making himself objectionable there to all but those cranks who find poison in the body politic nutritious to themselves, and is in process of acquiring ideas which will never help, but always hinder, the Government of India." F. Popham Young, Deposit, 13, National Archives of India. See also K. Inayatullah Khan's note dated February 22, 1919 in this document. Henceforth, to be referred to as the *Popham Young Proposal*.

67. St. Nihal Singh, "A Message America Gave me for India" *Modern Review*, October 1909, 376, 377; Sudhindra Bose, "The Challenge of ToDay", *Hindusthanee Student*, May 1917, 4. The Annual Intercollegiate Night at Schenectady, *Hindusthanee Student* April 1915, 9; September 1915, 9;

some students even made nationalist propoganda a source of pocket money, advertisements by Ramlal Bajpai and N. R. Chavre in *Young India*, April 1918, 5, May 1918, 9. Burjor Report, 11; Home/Political, December 1914, No. 96-98, National Archives of India, New Delhi, Part A, 3; *Christian Science Monitor* quoted in *Hindusthanee Student*, April-July 1914, 49, Saund, *Congressman*, 35.

68. N.S. Hardikar, *Lala Lajpat Rai*, 9; *Modern Review*, February 1927, 170; Ronald Spector, "The Vermont Education of Taraknath Das: An Episode in British-American-Indian Relations." *Vermont History*, Vol. 48 (1980), 89-95. Other instances of British surveillance activities : Hardikar, ibid., Rathore, *Indian Nationalist Agitation*, illustrates the swift action of the British-Indian authorities to suppress agitation of American sympathizers of India; 17-19; Lala Lajpat Rai's telephone was tapped, his correspondence opened, a detective lived in the adjoining part of his house, 101; Manoranjan Jha, "Britain and the pro-Indian Activities in the United States, 1917-1922," *Political Science Review*, India, 1973, 34, describes in detail the concern of the British authorities both in London and Delhi to counteract the propaganda which nationalist students were carrying on among other Indian students and the American public.

69. Congressman John R. Murdock (D-Ariz). had been an instructor at the University of California at Berkeley in 1929. Among his students were "several turbaned Hindus." "They were," the Congressman told the House of Representatives in 1945 during the most fateful debate in the history of the Indian community,—"very earnest men and I always had the feeling that I should learn from them . . ." Murdock voted for the passage of the Luce-Celler Bill, Congressional Record. 79 Cong., 1st sess., October 10, 1945, 9534, 9544. "One of the most characteristic and natural attitudes of public opinion in the United States has been that of sympathy with the national aspirations of subject peoples," Professor Morss Lovett in *Modern Review*, June 24, 14. The British Ambassador was aware of "the traditional (American) doctrine that this country is like the refuge for the oppressed of all nations" and of the American "dislike of any interference with the right of asylum or the aspiration of peoples 'rightly struggling to be free.' " Home/Political, December 1914, No. 96-98, Part A, 3; National Archives of India. Prevailing opinion among high British officials including the British Ambassador to Washington was that, "The ordinary American has a strong distaste for an Indian as a human being, but a sentimental regard for anyone . . . who claims to be champion of liberty." The "trend" of American opinion is against admitting Indians "but in favor of glorifying an individual *badmash* whatever his race, who stands for Liberty and Progress." M.C. Seton to Honourable Mr. H. Wheeler, July 31, 1914, ibid., 6, 7. "Badmash" means "scoundrel," literally a person who earns livelihood through evil ways. In British eyes all Indian patriots were

scoundrels. The use of this word in official correspondence says more about the character of the rulers than of the ruled.

70. See Footnote 47. For Taraknath Das's effort *Hindustanee Student*, March 1927, 6. In 1908 there were organized societies to assist the students from India in New York and Boston, St. Nihal Singh, "The Picturesque Immigrant from India's Coral Strand," *Out West*, January 1909, 54.

71. Ronald Spector, *Vermont Education*, 90; Sen (ed.) *Dictionary*; James Campbell Ker, *Political Trouble*, 119. Taraknath kept up this zeal for organization all his life. In August 1945 he "stressed upon the students the need of organizing among themselves, a strong and cooperative body . . . ." *Modern Review*, December 1945, 406.

72. *Hindustanee Student*, January-February 1927, 11; March, 6. Others whom Profulla consulted may have included Dr. S.L. Joshi and Khankhoje, ibid., May 1926, Front Page, and September-October, *Hindustanee Student*, September 1915, 3. Taraknath Das in *Hindustanee Student*, March 1927, 5.

73. *Hindusthanee Student*, September 1915, 2. The Commissioner of Immigration San Francisco believed that its "primary purposes are to foment and foster a revolutionary movement in India, to prepare and distribute circulars and pamphlets inciting their countrymen to such a revolution, to prepare and train leaders for the uprising and to collect funds for the promotion of their plans." The commissioner San Francisco to Commissioner-General Immigration, January 23, 1914. Home/Political, December 1914, No. 377- 378. Part B, National Archives of India.

Hindusthanee Student, January 1914, 2 and 17; the framework of H.A.A as explained by Sudhindra Bose in the *Modern Review*, September 1917, 261, 262; his *Fifteen Years*, 477, 478; Lajpat Rai, *The United States of America*, 458-459; Wendell Thomas, *Hinduism Invades*, 197; Brochure of H.A.A., Eleventh Summer Course, 1938. Reading the H.A.A. journal the *Hindusthanee Student* one would hardly guess that Har Dayal, the darling of several of these students, was ever here or the San Francisco trial ever took place. Nevertheless, Taraknath Das, Profulla Mukerji and S.N. Kar were for years closely associated with the journal as well as with the Association, J.C. Ker correctly pointed out that the Association "although nominally a non-political body, had a large numer of revolutionary Indians among its members," *Political Trouble*, 402, Taraknath Das was a "Councellor in the H.A.A. and S.N. Kar, Joint Secretary Western Section in 1914, *Hindusthanee Student*, January 1914, 3, 17; April 1916, 1; January 1926, 9; Mrs. Naidu's poem, "To India," published, April-July 1914, a banquet in her honor, November 1928, 9, 10. Sudhindra was not a Gadarite still the idea of patriotism he exhorted the students to adopt would have scared the British officials : "India," he told a gathering of students, "needs men of . . . liberalized national consciousness. Our country, right or wrong. It is our country ! . . . India needs just one hundred percent of 'Indianism,'—straight, unadulterated, unhyphenated . . . ." ibid., May 1917, 4-5.

74. *Warning To The West*, New York, 1942, 101-102.
75. H.K. Rakhit, the future secretary of the India League, *Hindustanee Student*, January 1926, 9.
76. The H.A.A. was "more or less inactive owing to very small number of Indian students at this time," *Modern Review*, July 1943, 49; The term "brain trust" is in Ramlal Bajpai's letter dated March 15, 1941 to Jagjit Singh. There were two brain trusts in competition with each other but, "My Washington brain trust is different than [sic] yours. They act quick." The other was in New York.
77. As in the case of Sudhindra Bose, *Modern Review*, November 1942; and Dhan Gopal, *Caste and Outcast*, 165; for money, Hardikar went "from door to door and begged for funds" to come to America. "Some Recollections," 5, Hardikar Papers, Nehru Memorial Museum and Library, New Delhi, hard to get tickets, S.N. Das finds, *Modern Review*, July 1924, 19.
78. S.N. Das Gupta's indictment of American prejudice and policies, "Indians In The United States," ibid. Shridharani mentions "unfriendly immigration laws," *My India*, 69, *Missionary Review*, June 1934, 267; St. Nihal Singh, "The Picturesque Immigrant from India's Coral Strand," *Out West*, Vol. XXX, January 1909, 52, Sudhindra Bose, "American Impressions," *The Forum*, Vol. LIII, 1915, 253-55, 257. Part of the reason why Lala Lajpat Rai chose to spend his exile on the east coast than in California was the climate of anti-Asian Prejudice, Rathore, *Indian Nationalist Agitation*, 79.
79. *Modern Review*, November, 1948, 465, so also Dhan Gopal, and Sarangdhar Das and others brought no written guarantee with them.
80. The Immigration Bureau's suspicion as to the revolutionery character of the H.A.A. and the fact that several Indians who entered claiming to be students were in fact "notorious agitators" seriously damaged the cause of persons coming as bona fide students. The Commissioner expressed his purpose hereafter "to scrutinize with the greatest care all Hindu applications for admission in order that we may bring the fullest strength of the immigration laws against those who may be coming to join in the movement referred to." He asked for the Commissioner-General's advice "to assist us in meeting the situation." He also warned the Bureau chief that "some of these Hindu students have already filed applications for naturalization with the local courts, and others are preparing to do so." Home-Political, December 1914, No. 377- 378, Part B, National Archives of India.

81. *Hindusthanee Student*, January 1914, 26-27.
82. *Hindusthanee Student*, April-July 1914, 42-44; Sudhindra called it "a most serious crisis" and explained the conditions to be imposed under the bill presently before the House. The article was written after his testimony at the House hearing in February 1913. It was the Raker bill and its proposed Section 47 that had alarmed him. *Modern Review*, September 1917, 261; Shridharani found that to enter the United States a student must show the authorities a "large enough bank account," *My India*, 73. *Modern Review*, May 1919, 522.
83. *Hindustanee Student*, January 1925, 4-5; January 1926, 10.
84. Ibid., January 1925, 5.
85. *Burjor Report*, 12; most of them were from the three well-known tracts of the Panjab—Manjha (or Majha), Malwa and Doaba Bist Jullundur, or Doaba, in brief. For the most part these tracts remained in India after Partition. For geographical demarcation in these tracts, *The Imperial Gazetteer of India : Provincial Series Panjab*, Calcutta : Superintendent of Government Printing, 1908. Vol I, 224.
86. Lucie Cheng and Edna Bonacich (eds.) *Labor Immigration Under Capitalism : Asian Workers in the United States before World War II*, Los Angeles, 1984,328; Hugh Tinker, *The Banyan Tree : Overseas Immigrants From India, Pakistan and Bangladesh*, Oxford, 1977, 175, 278; St. Nihal Singh, "Indians in America," *Modern Review*, India 1908, 204; Das, *Hindustani Workers*, 3; *Overland*, April 1908, 386.
87. Cheng and Bonchich (Eds.), *Labor Immigration*. The quotation is from page 323 of the first of the two chapters contributed by Sucheta Mazumdar to this work. Her conclusions as to the economic causes of immigration are professed to be based on "the central idea" that "capitalist development leads to imperialism, which in turn distorts the development of colonized territories. Consequently many people are displaced from their traditional economic systems, becoming available for emigration. They then provide the labor force necessary in the developed capitalist society for further development," 317- 318. This theory may well apply to emigration from India but not to that from self-governing Japan. The fate of small holders, 322,325.
88. Cheng and Bonacich (Eds.), *Labor Immigration*, 325. Heavy revenue demand, 324. Gurdev Singh Deol, *The Role of Ghadar Party in the National Movement*, Delhi, 1969, 38; Joan M. Jensen, "East Indians," Harvard Encyclopedia of American Ethnic Groups, Cambridge, Mass., 1980, 296-298; Bruce LaBrack and Karen Leonard, "Conflict and Compatibility in Pubjabi- Mexican Immigrant Families in Rural California, 1915-1965," *Journal of Marriage*, August 1984, 527. Poverty as the reason for emigration is also mentioned in *American Monthly Review of Reviews*, May 1908, 604; Das, *Hindustani Workers*, 6; but see ibid., 3, as

a corrective to Deol's observation above; Chandra Jayawardena, "Migration and Social Change : A Survey of Indian Communities Overseas," *Geographical Review*, Vol, 58, No. 3, July, 1968, 428.

89. Cheng and Bonacich (eds.) *Labor Immigration*, 323.
90. Ibid., 324, 325.
91. Ibid., 323.
92. Sant Nihal Singh, "Indians in the Far East." *Modern Review*, August 1908, 114-121. Wages they get in China "are high," 119. Those who receive ten or fifteen dollars a month can, according to Singh, manage to save considerable money.
93. Joan Jensen, "East Indians." Stephan Thernstrom (ed.), *Harvard Encyclopedia.* Cambridge, Mass., 1980s Cheng and Bonacich (eds.) *Labor Immigration*, 329, 330; S.P. Sen, *Dictionary* "Gurdit Singh (Baba)" who delivered speeches in gurudwaras exhorting the Sikhs to defy their exclusion from Canada, 123; land prices had been rising in the Punjab. Towards the end of the First World War price per acre was "between 250 and 400 rupees," Cheng and Bonacich (eds.), *Labor Immigration*, 323; some immigrants recalled having sold 1.5 acres for Rs. 400. Ibid., 331. Sikhs had started leaving for British service overseas since the 1880s, Mark Juergensmeyer and N. Gerald Barrier (eds.), *Sikh Studies : Comparative Perspectives on a Changing Tradition*, Berkeley, 1979, 143, Hong Kong had a mosque also, Burjor Report, 22; Indian immigrants coming directly from Hong Kong, Cheng and Bonacich (eds.), *Labor Immigration*, 327.
94. As alleged by St. Nihal Singh, *Out West*, January 1909, 45.
95. Taraknath Das, *Address*, 6; Sohan Singh Bhakna, a founder of the Gadar Party, for instance, had mortgaged five acres, was Rs. 3000 in debt and had with him Rs. 500 when he landed in Seattle, Josh, *Sohan Singh Bhakna*, 4. 7; Cheng and Bonacich, *Labor Immigration*, 331, the Sikh peasant's problem was not hunger but shortage of cash :

    At his heart is his daughter's wedding
    In his eye fore-knowledge of debt
    He toils and may not stop
    His life is a long drawn out question
    Between a crop and a crop.

    "The Masque of Plenty"

    The Panjab districts populated by the Sikhs were considered "prosperous" by contemporary standards—"The Sikh Districts of the Central Punjab and the submontane and Himalayan tracts are perhaps the most prosperous," *Punjab Gazetteer*, Vol. I, 72.
96. Josh, *Sohan Singh Bhakna*, 12; *Modern Review*, February 1911, 206, December 1911, 605.

97. This information gleaned from Sarangdhar Das "Information For Indian Students Intending to Come to the Pacific Coast of the United States," *Modern Review*, December 1911, 603-612; Extracts from G.D. Kumar's letter to the *Panjabee*, ibid., February 1911, 206-207; Cheng and Bonacich, *Labor Immigration*, 329-331; also see Joan Jensen, *Passage from India*, 26-27, fn. 5.

98. Scholars have discovered several pre-1900 references to the presence of Indians in the United States. Bruce LaBrack found some Indians in New England and in the California gold- fields, one as early as 1790. Jacoby, in Juergensmeyer and Barrier (eds.) *Sikh Studies*, 160. That Indian was from Madras, S. Chandrasekhar, *From India to America*, 12, "less than 200 Indians" had come to the United States between 1850-1870, ibid., 14; in 1851 half a dozen Indians participated in the July 4 parade of the East India Marine Society. Ibid., 12. A Hindu convert was sent to America on a goodwill mission by the Unitarians of Calcutta in 1858 and a certain "Mr. Joshee" lectured on Theosophy in 1886; Sujit Mukerjee, "Early American Images of India," *India Quarterly*, January-March 1954, 49-50; Ramanuj Pandita had come as a student in 1886, Sen (ed.), *Dictionary*.

Dr. Pramath Nath Roy was the Port Surgeon at Boston for several years, had lived in Massachusetts for about 25 years and died in Boston in 1917, *Hindusthanee Student*, October 1917, 23; January 1926, 8; September-October 1926, 9; Miss Anandabai Joshi came to Philadelphia for medical education in about 1885; ibid., January 1926, 8; Dinshah Ghádiali came to America in 1896, went back, returned in 1911 and was an "inventor and Patentee" in Malaya, New Jersey, in the late 1940s; his letter to Jagjit Singh, September 19, 1948; Bakshish Singh was the first immigrant to arrive in California in 1899; Das, *Hindustanee Workers*, 9-10, fn. 8.

99. Das, *Hindustani Workers*, 3, 4.

100. "... thousands of Hindoos, their fancy on fire with the tales they had heard of the rich and wonderful land across the Pacific (came here), and sent back golden tales of prosperity to their native villages." Herman Scheffauer, "The Tide of Turbans," *Forum*, June 1910, 617; Das, *Hindustani Workers*, 7, 9, 10, 11; Josh, *Bhakna*, 8; Taraknath Das *Address, August 1946*, 6.

101. Das, *Hindustani Workers*, 4, 5, 6; Bruce LaBrack, *The Sikhs of Northern California : A Socio- Historical Study*, 1981, 64.

102. Bruce LaBrack, ibid., "Indians in Canada," *Modern Review*, August 1913, 141; St. Nihal Singh in *Literary Digest*, July 18, 1914, 95; *Immigration Commission Report*, Vol. 23. Part I, 169-170.

103. Das, *Hindustani Workers*, 15, 18; *American Monthly Review of Reviews*, May 1908, 604; the Sikh farmer's decision to go into farming was dictated by his love for farm work and gradually "the choice became more common as other sources of day labor disappeared (particularly with the completion

of the Western Pacific railroad) or were available only to white workers." Joan M. Jenson, "*Passage from India*", 32-33; also see p. 55, the gurudwara at Stockton was started in 1912, foundation stone of the building was laid in spring of 1915. *Hindusthanee Student*, January 1916, 12-13. Funds for the gurudwara were collected through Jawala Singh's efforts, Sen. (ed.) *Dictionary*.

104. *Immigration Commission Report*, Vol. 24, 110.
105. Das, *Hindustani Workers*, 31, 32, 37, 41, 42, 52; Karen Leonard. "Punjabi Farmers and California's Alien Land Law," *Agricultural History*, No. IV, October 1985, 3, a skeptical view expressed by H.A. Millis, *American Economic Association Review*, March 1911, 75-76.
106. Maldwyn Allen Jones, *American Immigration*, Chicago, 1960, 214; Das, *Hindustani Workers*, 3, 15; H.A. Millis, "East Indian Immigration to British Columbia and the Pacific Coast States," *American Economic Association Review*, March 1911, 74.
107. Das, *Hindustani Workers*, 3, 15, 32, 34, 42-43; State Board of Control, *California and the Oriental*, New York, 1978, 109; Bruce LaBrack and Karen Leonard, "Conflict and Compatibility in Punjabi-Mexican Immigrant Families in Rural California, 1915-1965," *Journal of Marriage and Family*, August 1984, 530. Anonymous in *Modern Review*, January 1909, 57.
108. *Modern Review*, ibid., 56-57; *Time Weekly*, July 8, 1985, 25.
109. Bruce LaBrack, "Occupational Specialization Among Rural California Sikhs : The Interplay of Culture and Economics," *Amerasia Journal*, 9 : 2, 1982, 31. Roger Daniels, "Westerners from the East : Oriental Immigrants Reappraised," *Pacific Historical Review*, Vol. 35 (1966), 378.
110. Jawala Singh in Sen (Ed.), *Dictionary*, *Burjor Report*, 12. *California and the Oriental*, 47, 108, 109, figures supplied by M. P. Shaughnessy, Attorney to the Indians; Das, *Hindustani Workers*, 21, 23, 28, 31, 32, 44; La Brack, "Occupational Specialization", *Amerasia Journal*, 1982, 38.
111. Das, *Hindustani Workers*, 19, 44, 48, 93, 94; La Brack, "Occupational Specialization," *Amerasia*, 41. Karen Leonard, *Punjabi Farmers*, 3, 4, ,8 15; Karen Leonard, "The Pahkar Singh Murders : A Punjabi Response to California's Alien Land Law," *American Journal*, 11 : 1, 1984, 4, 5, 16; Francia J. Brown And Joseph S. Roucek (eds.) *One America*, New York, 1955, 456.
112. *California and the Oriental*, 109. Burjor Report, 13 : Karen Leonard, "Punjabi Farmers," 3, 15 : Das, *Hindustani Workers*, 37, 16, 113; "Riding cycle to work," *Missionary Review*, July 1916, 525, June 1934, 291. Emory S. Bogardus, *Immigration and Race Attitudes*, New York, 1928, 53; The quotation is from Das, *Hinduatani Workers*, 113; also see La Brack, *Sikhs of Northern California*, 137.
113. Das, *Hindustani Workers*, 105; $10,000 were sent by the Sikhs of Fresno locality "to further the cause of education in the Punjab," *Hindus-*

tanee Student, September-October 23, their donations to H.A.A. were numerous, ibid,—October 1915. 17 January 1916, 4; February 1916, 24; May 1916, 24; *San Francisco Chronicle*, January 31, 1926, 2 Col. 5; Burjor Report, 13.

114. Josh, *Bhakna*, 23; Lajpat Rai, *United States of America*, 467. It seems that the 1943 split within the India League was partly due to Jagjit Singh's intolerance of financial unaccountability over the Sikhs' donations for the Indian nationalist cause in America.

115. Das, *Hindustani Workers*, 93.

116. *Hindusthanee Student*, April-May 1916, Advertisements ; Salim Khan, "A Brief History of Pakistanis in the Western United States," M.A. Thesis, California State University, Sacramento, 1961, 23; *Burjor Report*, 10; Sant Nihal Singh, "Indians in America," *Modern Review*, Vol. III. 1908, 313. Godha Ram Channon to Jagjit Singh, August 8, 1949; British Consul-General. San Francisco to Lord Halifax, S-S Foreign Affairs, London, December 15, 1939, File 278-X (40). Secret 1940, External Affairs Department, National Archives of India. Saund, *Congressman*, 47, Biographical Directory of the American Congress; for Pahkar Singh, Karen Leonard. *Pahkar Singh Murders*, 76. S.A. Waiz (ed.), *Indians Abroad Directory. 1934*, Bombay, 57; *Hindusthanee Student*, March-April 1917, 15.

117. Thakur Dev's testimony at Senate Hearings, December 9, 1926, 33, 34; Mumtaz Kitchlew to Jagjit Singh, January 14, 1950, the letterhead.

118. For Ali Ali, *Modern Review*, Vol. III. 314; U.S. vs. Dolla, 1910, 177 F. 101, 102; for Sadeck Ali, *Hindusthanee Student*, January 1916, 18.

119. Waiz, *Indians Abroad Directory*, 569-571; For K.C. Choudhury, *Hindustanee Student*, September-October 1926, 10-11; Mr. Verma, ibid., November 1926, advertisement and September-October 1927, 12; Moosa Rawjee; information received from Mrs. Malti Singh and Mumtaz I. Kitchlew's letter to Jagjit Singh, January 14, 1950. India League papers, Sapru House.

120. Watu means one who can persuade customers to make the purchase; Mull means hero. *Honolulu Star Bulletin*, July 2, 1957; *New York Times*, August 14, 1958, 21, Col. I; *Honolulu Advertiser*, August 22, 1973; *Asia and the Americas*, October 1943, 490; *House Hearing*, March 1945, 72.

121. *Report*, 16.

122. *S 1595 Hearings*, 2, 37; Mubarek Ali in *New York Bulletin* 1946; La Brack, *Sikhs of Northern California*, 90, 99, 102, 103, 137; *Modern Review*, February 1927, 169; Lajpat Rai, *United States of America*, 461-463.

123. *S 1595 Hearings*, 51, 52.

124. *Senate Hearings December 1926*, 8-9; similar opinion expressed by Clare Boothe Luce, *S 1595 Hearings*, 24.

2A

TEMPTED BY THE LAND BUT CURSED BY THE LAW

It is not enough for Western people to know Asia through European and American eyes. Such knowledge cannot furnish a basis for a proper appreciation of the problems of Asia. We wish the Americans to know more of the Asia of the Asiatics as distinguished from the Asia of the Europeans.

LAJPAT RAI, 1918

The last chapter described the establishment of an Indian community in the United States. The present chapter shall examine why and how the American bureaucracy and the legislature imposed upon the community and its country of origin, certain inequalities that originally did not exist.[1]

It may, however, be stated at the outset that being Asians, Indians were already sentenced to inequality in the American mind. Their unequal political status at home and in South Africa confirmed further by exclusion from Canada with British consent, placed them even below the level of the Chinese and the Japanese. The green light to exclude them from America was given by the British Ambassador probably even before Canada had acted. To the regret of the U.S. officials, the enactment of the British advice was delayed by the procedures and politics of the American legislative process. The policies that the executive *could* enforce without breaking the law had been enforced—Indians were declared ineligible to naturalization in 1907 and from 1910 their immigration drastically cut by strict scrutiny under the law. A few hundred immigrants came through while the legislators debated and 69 Indians received citizenship while the judges debated.

The first half of this chapter describes how a racist society with a democratic constitution whose executive branch had already made its policy decisions, attempted to reach a consensus on the extent and the form of the exclusion. Thereafter one thing led to another—the harsh proposals, the Indian resentment, the rise of an Indian leadership, the Gadar, and the demise of that leadership for almost one generation.

The climate of the first decade of the twentieth century during which Indians started arriving was not conducive to their cordial welcome. The American WASPs were feeling threatened economically by the newly arriving immigrants' numbers and socially by their race and culture, irrespective of the color of their skin. A sort of American "Boxer movement" was said to be developing.[2] Legislators and the President were discovering more and more classes—anarchists, psychopaths, contract labor—that needed prohibition.[3] Several years earlier Senator Henry Cabot Lodge (R-Mass.) had urged the literacy test as a restrictive device to reduce the inflow from Europe. The President also urged Congress to stop the influx of "cheap labor."[4] There was rising interest in the tightening and continuation of the Chinese exclusion laws which did not abate even after their application had been extended in 1902. Roosevelt's exhortations to Congress to keep out undesirable immigrants became "more emphatic" and resulted in a "burst of legislative activity."[5] Both the Republican and Democratic party platforms called for Asian exclusion.[6]

A larger part of the Indian immigrants had poured into California whose constitution had warned the people of Asia that they were not wanted. It declared the presence of aliens ineligible to become citizens, "dangerous to the well-being of the State" and committed its legislature to "discourage their immigration by all means within its powers." "Asiatic coolieism" was "forever prohibited in the State" because it was "a form of human slavery."[7] Even as early as the 57th Congress, a few years before the Gentlemen's Agreement, the voice of the "Pacific Coast people" had been claimed as the "most experienced" and hence, "better fitted" to serve as America's guide on matters of Asian immigration.[8] The way Indians were being treated in Canada, Australia, Natal, and the Cape Colony, hardly enhanced the prospects of a warmer welcome on the Pacific Coast or for the people of these States saying some nice things about them in Congress. Indians had little time to know the country or let the country know them, before they were subjected to adverse scrutiny, hostile tests of character, biased official investigations, and even mob violence.[9]

There were four anti-Hindu riots in little over two years. With amazing speed almost the whole white population of entire cities like Bellingham, Washington had turned hostile to the newcomers. The Exclusion League included Hindus in the list of its targets for exclusion. H. A. Millis started his biased investigation of Hindu labor on behalf of the Immigration Commission. During these years the press continued to be hostile or condescending.

The Bellingham riot, a planned atrocity, started on the night of September 4, 1907, as the culmination of "friction between the community and the Hindu colony (which) had been growing for months."[10]

A month and a half later all Indians in Everett, Washington were "rounded up" by 500 white men. Indians "packed up and left." In January 1908 there was a riot at Live Oak, California and another at St. John, Oregon in March 1910.[11]

These riots, Bellingham particularly, are indicative of an American attitude toward the immigrants from India. The people of Bellingham were "almost entirely adverse to the Hindus"; no one would give testimony against the suspects. Organized labor was strongly anti-Asian. It was affiliated with the Exclusion League and "guarding" the western gates of Occidental civilization. The press was hostile though opposed to open violence. One paper called opposition to Hindus a "crusade" and viewed their departure from Bellingham with "intense satisfaction." *The Outlook* commented editorially: "Among the rights of every nation is the right to the character of its own civilization . . . the United States has the right to determine what sort of people it shall admit to the territory and what sort it shall bar out."[12]

The most surprising part of the story of riots, besides their violence, was the encouragement that it received from high quarters. Some lawmakers perhaps considered riots a more effective method of exclusion than legislation. Albert Johnson (R-Wash.) later Chairman of the House Committee on Immigration and Naturalization, boasted three times at a Committee hearing of his own involvement in anti-Indian riots. *(1)* "We can keep the Hindus from crowding into western Washington with the greatest difficulty, almost *riot* at times," *(2)* "I, myself, at home have taken part in the agitation which has grown out of this situation, (the prospect of his state being "filled up" with Hindus and other Asians), *(3)* "We have kept them out by local agitation . . ."[13]

The "Second American Revolution" with its expanded economic opportunities had created an almost insatiable demand for immigrants. Over ten million came during the thirty years from 1861 to 1890. The surfeit of colors, cultures and races they brought with them persuaded the Boston aristocrats, the conscience of the WASPs, to start thinking of restriction seriously. It was only restriction they were seeking, not exclusion. After all most of the newcomers were white; they were Christians, they were Europeans; and they were needed. Exclusion was for the Asian immigrants and the Chinese had already been made its first victims in 1882.[14]

During the forty years following Reconstruction American racism passed through several moods that together persuaded the nation to abandon its three-centuries old tradition of free immigration. One mood was that of aggravation and disgust at the "New" immigration in the East and Asian immigration in the West. The races of south—eastern Europe had taken Emma Lazarus's preferential invitation literally, and started sending their "wretched refuse" to America while the "huddled masses" of Asia began to arrive in California even though there was no Statue of Liberty lifting its "lamps beside the golden door" in the San Francisco Bay.

American victory in a three-month war over third-rate Spain in Cuba and the Philippines as well as the annexation of Hawaii (1898) gave a first-rate boost to Anglo-Saxon jingoism and imperialism. The first taste of becoming the rulers of an Asian people and the elevation to the rank of white nations with nonwhite overseas possessions, reinforced WASP pretensions to racial superiority.[15] Although the war had been fought against a white European country, the people who had been conquered were, according to Senator Albert T. Beveridge, among those "savages and senile peoples" to govern whom God "has been preparing English-speaking and Teutonic peoples for a thousand years."[16] To fulfill these "responsibilities," Theodore Roosevelt called upon Americans to maintain "masterful virtues" of "stern men with empires in their brains" and to avoid "slothful ease and ignoble peace" otherwise "stronger peoples will pass us by, and will win for themselves domination of the world."[17]

In this mood there could be no relaxation in the policy of Chinese exclusion. It was in fact made permanent in 1904. The Filipinos were not granted a status of equality even though their country had become a United States possession. Thirteen laws had been enacted and a Gentlemen's Agreement concluded between 1882 and 1923, all to exclude the Asian immigrants or to close the possible loopholes in exclusion. There was not a single law that imposed *racist* restrictions on European immigrants although some of them were coming from what the restrictionists considered inferior races.[18]

About nine million European immigrants came during the first decade of the twentieth century. They were absorbed, assimilated, and Americanized. Only Anarchists were excluded (1903). Less than 250,000 came from Asia during the same decade. Their fate was different. They were, like other colored Americans, "consistently refused admission into full membership in society."[19]

A large number of Indian immigrants arrived, while America was in its mood of imperialistic jubilation. They were immediately catalogued in the American mind as another Asian, nonwhite, non-Christian, unassimilable people. Although they were Caucasians, their turbans and beards and something more which had preceded their arrival, made them, in American opinion, the worst Asian immigrants to land on the western coast. That something more was the British, the missionary, the Kiplingese view of India, Indians, and Hinduism. The Indian immigrants as a consequence had to carry not only the burden of American racism and California anti-Asianism but also that of hostile and tendentious British and missionary writings on India which had spread over the English-speaking world including the United States.[20]

Politically the Indians were among the weakest Asian ethnic groups in America. The Chinese belonged to a free though a weak nation, the Japanese to a strong nation, the Filipinos to a United States territory. Indians were not only a subject people at home, but they were subject to the British whom the American Anglo-Saxons respected as their mentors in imperialistic adventures in Asia. They would do to Asians what the British were doing. The historian, James Hosmer, had in 1890 even proposed an Anglo-American alliance "powerful enough to withstand any challenge by the Slavs, Hindus or Chinese." They knew that Indians were being mistreated in South Africa, Australia and Canada. Exclusion was haunting Indians in one British colony after another. California too demanded their total exclusion. This is what Roger Daniels calls the "California position."[21]

American blacks were very much on the mind of the California exclusionists. To them the blacks were a problem. In course of time they collected several problems—Chinese, Japanese, Hindus, Koreans, Filipinos, and many others. They had fast and swift solutions for each of those problems—exclusion for the Asians, debarment and wrath for the "Okies" during the Depression, and concentration camps for the Japanese after Pearl Harbor. Towards the end of the Second World War a few enlightened Americans discovered that the Asians were not the problem, Californians were the problem.[22]

In the early years of the century the climate for Asian exclusion was being gradually built up. The Chinese exclusion as stated above was made permanent in 1904. The Japanese and Korean Exclusion League was established in 1905. The Pacific Coast exclusionists were representatives of those "muscular patriots" who were "vividly conscious of their position as the wardens of the Western mart [for whom] the possible crisis takes on the significance of a new "Thermopylae."[23] For them Asian exclusion was a "holy cause." In the later stages of the crusade V.S. McClatchy and Senator Hiram Johnson formed the "general staff of the exclusionist forces" that "directed the final exclusionist victory."[24]

"All manner of lies were invented, every conceivable means of questionable nature were employed to defame their character."[25] They urged the government to close the loopholes in the immigration laws that had enabled Indians to enter. Miss Anges Foster Buchanan proposed in 1908:

> The sacred writings of the Vedas say: "I gave the earth to Arya." This is a propitious moment for the State Department to adopt an amendment to the Vedas and to tell our brothers of the East that while the earth is large enough for us all, there is no one part of it that will comfortably accommodate both branches of the Aryan family."[26]

The Exclusion League's agenda for Asian immigrants was announced at its first annual convention in 1908. It proposed to the President and the Congress immediate passage of a law to exclude "absolutely and emphatically" all Asians from the United States. Segregated schools, a prohibition of interracial marriages, a ban on ownership of real estate, and withholding jobs from students were the other items to be lobbied for in the next election year, 1910. All political parties and both candidates for the Governor's office supported exclusion. To Sant Nihal Singh it appeared "almost a foregone conclusion that the Indian immigrant may be entirely shut out from North America" and that on "flimsy and fictitious reasons."[27]

Those reasons were eloquently expressed by Representative Denver S. Church (D-Calif), who maintained that the Hindus' "heathen and outlandish superstitions forbid even the thought of their living in this Christian land . . . Their darkness will spoil our light." Of more serious and urgent concern to him was the huge population of India, 350,000,000 out of which 50,000,000 "at least" may emigrate to California so that there will be "15 Hindus" to each white Californian. Three years before Congressman Church's speech, an editor had announced the California decision that no nation was large enough for two races. "This is the solution which the democratic instinct on the Pacific coast has hit upon. And the democratic instinct is right."[28]

The Exclusion League called immigration from India "an avalanche of death from the Himalayas." Indians had to be excluded before they developed roots in America because their children born here would be citizens and voters. It was also argued that when the Japanese workers were being excluded, Indians could not be treated more favorably without triggering a Japanese demand for the abrogation of the Gentlemen's Agreement.[29]

The Exclusion League suggested a strict interpretation of the existing law so as to achieve exclusion even in the absence of Indian exclusion legislation. Toward the end of 1909, the League protested to the Immigration Bureau against what it called "the wholesale landing" of Hindus at San Francisco and demanded that "the law be as strictly enforced against these people as it is against the Chinese and Japanese." The Bureau informed the League that "special legislation by Congress would be necessary before Hindu aliens could be excluded because of their race."[30]

Hart H. North, Commissioner of Immigration at San Francisco, who although believing "that the Hindus are not desirable as citizens" yet declared that

> he will take no steps to check their entry into California aside from those he would take to stop European immigration. . . . The Hindus are not governed by an exclusion law . . . they have the same legal standing that any European immigrant

> has . . . While the laws remain as they are these people must be allowed to enter.[31]

The League, on the contrary, insisted that "the present immigration law does proscribe Hindu coolies and laborers." This prescription, however was not possible, in the words of the Commissioner General of Immigration, "no matter how *efficiently* we may try to enforce the laws." As the first step of having the law enforced "efficiently" at San Francisco, the League submitted a 61 foot long petition to President Taft requesting North's removal from office. A few weeks later, the League reported that "As a result of this campaign the Hindu immigration has practically ceased and [North] had been suspended. . . ."[32]

An investigator for the Immigration Commission noticed the "change of policy" at San Francisco and remarked "That either a large percentage of those who apply for admission are unfit, or that the interpretation of the law had been severe. . . ." He also noticed that "the numerous rejections have worked much hardship."[33] There was, however, no relaxation in the severity of enforcement. Indian immigrants found it hard to land on the Pacific Coast, the students' newsletter reported, as it observed that "It is getting harder as days go by."[34]

Two more inlets had been closed in 1913. First, the privilege of entering the continental United States after securing admission to the Philippines was withdrawn. Second, the steamship companies agreed to suspend bringing Indians to the Pacific Coast "pending action on proposed (exclusion) laws in Congress" so that since the summer of 1913 there had been "practically a cessation of this immigration."[35]

The shipping companies might resume the traffic and the courts might rule favorably on the appeals of the rejected immigrants. The Commissioner General characterized the situation as an "urgency" even an "emergency" with appeals pending before the courts, shipping companies under only voluntary restraint, American labor organizations raising objections to Indian immigration, and "the apparent concert of action" among Indians in the Philippines and elsewhere to enter the United States. He felt helpless because unable to reject "under the present condition of the law, more than 50 per cent." He therefore appealed to Congress not to delay consideration of the pending bills.[36]

In this appeal to Congress the executive's policy decisions on Indian immigration mentioned at the opening of the chapter were starting to express itself in concrete terms. A letter from Labor Secretary William B. Wilson to the Speaker provides enough evidence of the official thinking on most aspects of the Indian question—their unacceptability for reason of culture; justification for exclusion provided by the actions of the British colonies; the use of "expedients and makeshifts" to prevent their "influx"; the Secretary's confession that the Indians were not physically defective; and now early in 1914 half measures having failed to restrict above 50 percent, the problem had become "urgent and imperative" hence the appeal to Congress. [See: Appendix I.]

These bills represented the revival of legislative activity concerning immigration that followed upon the submission of the Immigration Commission Report to the Congress in 1911. This activity kept three Congresses—62nd to 64th—busy hammering out new immigration legislation.[37]

The restrictionists aimed at reducing immigration from Europe by means of a literacy test of the intending immigrants. The exclusionists sought to strengthen Chinese exclusion by closing loopholes in the law, to convert the sanction of Japanese exclusion from the Gentlemen's Agreement to an American law, and to legislate a sweeping exclusion of all other Asians including Indians.

Indians were among their latest targets. Once marked for exclusion, they were subjected to the same treatment as the Chinese and the Japanese, such as unflattering descriptive phraseology, allegations of being a menace to American culture, alarmist estimates of their numbers allegedly sneaking in illegally across the borders, and characterizations as carriers of loathsome and contagious diseases.[38] These allegations and misrepresentations became virtually unanswerable in view of the treatment meted out to Indians in the British colonies.[39] The probable diplomatic implications of excluding British subjects would not be a deterrent in the face of Britain's acquiescence in what the white colonies were doing to its Indian subjects. Indeed an instance of British docility in Canada was the only good news which Commissioner Caminetti could present to the House Immigration Committee when he appealed to the Congress for help in the "emergency."[40]

The Exclusion League claimed to have been "requesting a rigid Exclusion Law" since 1905. In 1908 it gained support of the powerful Immigration Restriction League when the latter's Secretary agreed that "many are the reasons for excluding the coolie." The same year, two Congressmen from California "protested" in Congress against excluding the Japanese laborers by an arrangement with Japan rather than directly by an American law.[41]

The objective of Indian exclusion was pursued over the years by several individuals and organizations in the West. They received friendly hearing from Southern Democrats who were generally ready to applaud calls for "racial purity."[42] From 1911 came a further incentive in the recommendations of the Immigration Commission whose leading members proceeded to sponsor legislation to restrict immigration from Europe and bar that from Asia.

The Commission, consisting of three each of senators, representatives, and presidential appointees, was created by Section 39 of the Immigration Act of February 20, 1907 to make full inquiry into the subject of immigration.[43] The Commission worked for three years, produced an oversized report that gravely damaged the emotional unity of the nation by lending its prestigious sanction to the nativist bias pertaining to the so-called "new" immigration.[44] No Indian scholars were associated in investigating the "East Indians." Rajani Kant Das who researched for the Bureau of Labor Statistics had to write his own work to offer an "interpretation of their life to the American people."[45]

The Commission Report turned out to be like one of those writings about the Indians which Das had characterized as "generally prejudiced and erroneous." One instance was this summary judgement: "The caste system of the East Indians, as well as their training in their native land would seem to unfit them for rapid progress out of the ranks of common labor."[46] Here missionary and British writing had helped create a stereotype. Sikhs and Muslims who together formed the vast majority of "the ranks of common labor" did not believe in a "caste system." The Commission made no effort to explain the relationship between a "caste system" and unfitness for economic progress, rapid or not so rapid. The "training in their native land" did not "unfit them." It rather equipped them for life. Their training had been that of farmers, soldiers, security guards, and businessmen.

Attention was pointedly directed to the population of India particularly "in immigration questions where [it] is beginning to arouse some concern." The people of India "must emigrate or die by the millions in the famines that periodically reduce their numbers. The protection of the rest of the world against an Indian flood of migration is their poverty, their inability to provide the cost of transportation, and their lack of initiative."[47]

Two of the Commission's members, Senator William P. Dillingham (R-Vermont), and Rep. John L. Burnett (D-Ala.,) pushed Asian exclusion through Congress with the help of a third member, Senator Henry Cabot Lodge (R-Mass.), the chief advocate of the literacy test. Jeremiah W. Jenks, a Presidential appointee on the Commission and a university professor, published a work advocating the Commission recommendations. Another university professor, H.A. Millis investigated the Hindu immigrants on the Pacific Coast on behalf of the Commission. He publicized his views in magazine articles.[48]

The Commission had built its case for exclusion of Indian immigrants on several grounds. In its conclusions and recommendations the Commission summarised those arguments. The first one was that "the people of the coast states as a whole are opposed to such immigration and the facts and validity of their objections are recognized."[49] These "objections" were on racial grounds. The western states wanted European workers, not Asians. "There is a general demand" the report said, "for more Europeans, both as settlers on the land and as agricultural and other laborers" and the "West is in need of a larger population to settle the land."[50]

The reason for halting the further supply of Asian labor was not any glut in the labor market but upon other "considerations, in part social and political, in part economic." Asians were alleged to have "competed keenly and generally at a lower wage" thereby displacing European workers. In small businesses as well, they allegedly displaced small businessmen of "other races." By becoming farmers themselves, the Asians are "preventing the influx of other races and their settlement as farmers." In the end the Commission concluded that the policy of exclusion is endorsed by practically all classes represented in the West, save those who assert the moral necessity of according the same treatment to all races with little regard to consequences which result from so doing."[51]

The Commission's first recommendation was that "care should be taken that immigration be such both in quality and quantity as not to make too difficult the process of assimilation." This is a code phrase to exclude the Asians and to be selective regarding southeastern Europeans. Those aliens who "come to this country with no intention to become American citizens or even to maintain a permanent residence here, but merely to save enough, by the adoption, if necessary, of low standards of living, to return permanently to their home country," were recommended to be "excluded." As a mark of their identification, the Commission pointed out that "such persons are usually men unaccompanied by wives or children." These features described the Indian immigrants among others without mentioning the mitigating legal and administrative disabilities which made them so. "The exclusion of unskilled laborers unaccompanied by wives or families" was also suggested as one of the methods of restricting immigration.[52]

For Indians, the only direct recommendation was : "An understanding should be reached with the British Government whereby East Indian laborers would be effectively prevented from coming to the United States." The reason for preventing them from coming was that the Indian laborers are "from no point of view desirable members of the community." The route of diplomacy was selected following the earlier example of Canada by which the "British Government has consented to regulations which have effectively excluded the laborers of this race from Canada." The Commission probably had in mind a Gentlemen's Agreement with Britain of the type reached with Japan in 1907. At page 47 the word used is "understanding" perhaps of the Canadian type, on page 691 the word is "agreement."[53]

The Billingham Commission's views on Asian immigration are noteworthy because its views would become the nation's views and its recommendations become American law. The Commission had split on the issue of the literacy test—only a majority had favored it.[54] On Asian exclusion it was unanimous, and three of its most active members were in the Congress and determined to achieve it. The Commission's views and recommendations have to be studied carefully in order to be forewarned about the eventual futility of Hindu protests, pleadings, or petitions organized by Dr. Sudhindra Bose and followed up by Ramachandra to persuade this group of exclusionists to tone down the severity of their proposals.[55] As members of the Commission they had defined their objective as the "protection of the prosperity and economic well-being of *our* people."[56] Asian exclusion and the literacy test were the keystones of this "well-being." For their colleagues from the West, exclusion was part of national defense. Why would these legislators risk their political careers for the sake of a few thousand and unenfranchised Indian aliens? Lofty claims by Hindu immigrants to Aryan descent and ancient culture were not persuasive enough in the face of political realities. It was unfortunate for Indians that they had come at a time when American immigration laws, having lagged behind the latest advances in American racist untouchability, were being refurbished and modernized.[57]

This ongoing effort started to include Indians among the list of "excludables." From the 60th Congress (1907-1909) for a span of ten years 24 bills were introduced that named the Hindu directly or included them among those ineligible to citizenship and recommended their exclusion.[58] Many of these bills were introduced by Representative Everis Anson Hayes (R-Calif.) who served in six succeeding Congresses from 1905 to 1919. Although all of them died in committees, this fruit-grower and journalist from San Jose must be counted, for his tenacity, among the architects of Asian exclusion legislation.[59]

According to John E. Raker (D-Calif.), all Congressmen from California "for many years have given a written pledge to their people that they would work and vote for the exclusion of Asiatic labor."[60] Hayes and Raker were among the most active exclusionists on the House floor as well as at the Committee hearings though sometimes they were at cross purposes because of rival partisan loyalties.

Rep. Hayes attempted to strengthen and extend Asian exclusion in four ways, two of which would effect Indian immigrants, namely, to exclude all those who are ineligible to American citizenship by naturalization and second, to render liable to deportation all non-immigrants, such as preachers, scholars, merchants and students who failed to maintain the status or occupation under which they were admitted. He claimed to have been sponsoring bills to achieve the second objective in every Congress since the 59th.[61]

Raker seems to have kept the promise he made to his constituents to work for Asian exclusion. At the democratic party convention in 1908, he successfully lobbied the Platform Committee to include Asian exclusion as one of the planks. He worked "ardently, earnestly and industriously" for the intended legislation and was credited by his Republican rivals for having made the anti-Japanese agitation in the House "worse than it ever was before."[62] Denver S. Church (D-Calif.) who coined the most graphic phrases about the Hindus, sponsored two bills seeking their exclusion. Albert Johnson (R-Wash.) was their worthy colleague from the north. His adoption of street violence as a companion to legislation has already been mentioned. In the Senate the most persistent champions of Asian exclusion, all of them Democrats, were Senators James D. Phelan of California, Miles Poindexter of Washington, and a mid-western senator, James A. Reed of Missouri, with Ellison DuRant Smith of South Carolina bringing in the South.

Senator Phelan came to the Congress late (1915) and died in 1930, but he brought with him the well-earned reputation of being the "only anti-Japanese political leader in California before the First World War to subscribe to the yellow peril."[63] Senator Smith piloted two of the three exclusion bills (H.R. 6060 and H.R. 10384) in the Senate. For 36 years in the Senate, he was, according to a journalist, "one of the grimmest reactionaries on the Hill."[64] From 1905 to 1917 the Senate had a member, George Sutherland (D-Utah), whom we shall meet as Justice Sutherland in 1923. He voted both for Hindu exclusion and the literacy test. As a Senator he joined others in denying to the Hindus the right of immigration. As the spokesman of the Supreme Court in the *Thind* case, he denied to the Hindus the right to renounce their loyalty to Britain. As an Anglo- American, Sutherland belonged to that fortunate hyphenate community that could serve the cause of America and of its motherland at the same time, without being accused of "moral treason."[65]

The hero of Asian exclusion and the literacy test by the Act of 1917 was Representative John Lawson Burnett (D-Ala.) who, as Chairman of the Immigration and Naturalization Committee, a member of the Immigration Commission, and in charge of three House bills, one after the other, in three Congresses, prevailed against three vetoes. With single-minded determination to achieve the two objectives he had set his mind upon, he fought House members of both parties and defied Republican Taft and Democrat Wilson. He sincerely believed that by fighting for his bills he was serving America and the white race, but his loyalties appear to have been rather restricted both in time and space. He claimed there was

> no man in this House that more devotedly loves the white race than I do. I was 7 years old when the first gun was fired at Sumter and less than 12 when the flag went down at Appomattox . . . I come from a state where we had the horrors of reconstruction . . . Two brave Confederate soldiers from the South have told me that they would stand by me in my fight to pass this bill.[66]

The effort to legislate Hindu exclusion was only a small part of the large American effort in the course of the first two decades of the century, to reduce immigration from Europe as well as from Asia. On no occasion did the Congress debate a bill concerned exclusively with immigration from India as the 47th Congress had done about the Chinese immigration or the 79th would do about the Indian. Debates over the Chinese and the Japanese problems cover many more pages of the Congressional Record than those over the Hindu problem.

There was a conscious effort to exclude the Hindu without actually naming him in a bill. Recourse was sought in the formula of ineligibility—"persons who cannot become eligible, under existing law, to become citizens of the United States by naturalization"—being one of its several variations. Members from California and Washington however, generally insisted on naming their intended target in order to remove any probability of conflict of opinion in the courts.

Hindus had been classified among Caucasians by the Immigration Commission. Several members of Congress, exclusionists among them, agreed with the classification. A host of arguments, including diplomatic and treaty obligations, prevailed against naming of nationalities in the final version of the exclusion bill. It may be of interest to note that the United States Congress *never* declared Hindus ineligible to United States citizenship by naturalization. The Immigration Bureau declared them ineligible in 1908 by classifying them among the "Mongolic" grand division and Justice Sutherland by excluding them from the Caucasians in 1923.[67]

Several methods—legislative, executive, and diplomatic—were available to the host country for closing the door to Hindu immigration. The following chart shows the various options:

Methods of Hindu Exclusion

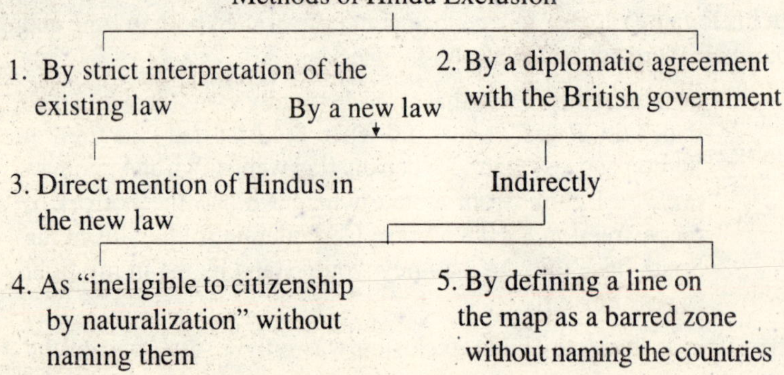

Of these options the Congress eventually invented the fifth.

Senator Dillingham embarked on his grand plan early in 1912 to overhaul the immigration system and to strengthen the Chinese exclusion law by his comprehensive bill S3175. It did not provide for exclusion of Indians probably because the Dillingham Commission had proposed to obtain this objective through negotiations with the British Government. An amendment was, however, adopted on the Senate floor which provided for the exclusion of "persons who are not eligible to become citizens of the United States by naturalization." Senator Lodge assured his colleagues that "the whole purpose of the amendment" was to keep the Chinese exclusion laws "in full force."[68] But this clause had a direct bearing on the Hindus. Dillingham recognized that by virtue of this clause it is "probable that at least the greater part of the people of India" are excluded from entering the United States as immigrants.[69]

Meanwhile the House had had before it the Burnett bill, H.R. 22527, which did not provide for Hindu exclusion. Congressman Raker insisted that the House adopt his H.R. 13500 which excluded all Asians. Burnett would rather "postpone that legislation for a year or two" because more Japanese were leaving than coming and the literacy test included in H.R. 22527 would keep out "a great many" of the 2,000 Chinese that are coming in. In his view conditions were not "acute" at the moment. Hindus were not mentioned at all in this Burnett-Raker argument.[70]

In December Rep. Hayes attempted to amend the Burnett bill by adding to it clauses regarding ineligibility to citizenship and making the failure to maintain one's status or profession a deportable offense. His amendment, however, was ruled out as not germane.[71]

Raker followed immediately with his interesting amendment proposing to exclude "all" Asians "who cannot read in some European language." He drew attention to the fact that "this amendment is in substance" the law in Australia, Cape Colony, Natal, and the province of British Columbia. His intention was to exclude "the coolie labor of India." But Rep. Augustus P. Gardner (R. Mass.) pointed out it did not exclude only coolies but every man in China, India, or in the East unless he can read some European language which he called "an unusual accomplishment" for Asians. Furthermore the amendment would embroil the United States with several Asian and European nations. The House rejected the amendment.[72]

During discussions on the conference report Raker again called the attention of the House "to Chinese, Hindu and Japanese immigration" and protested that the bill did not provide "real exclusion" of Asian labor. This bill, he agreed, "will exclude a few, but it does not cover the idea of those in the West . . . . While I shall vote for this conference report, it is not my idea as to what the law should be."[73]

The Senate adopted the bill S. 3175 that did not include a literacy test. The House adopted a bill that did not include exclusion of ineligibles. Therefore, it was claimed that "the whole subject of immigration came before the conference committee." Here major changes were agreed upon including the adoption of the ineligibility clause.[74]

In February both Houses agreed to S. 3175 as it emerged from Conference. President Taft vetoed it because, according to Burnett, a Democrat, "he fell overnight into the hands of evil influences." The Senate overrode the veto, but the House sustained it by a narrow margin "because four or five men who favored the measure and would have voted to pass it over the veto happened on that day to be absent."[75] Indians were saved from exclusion.

Almost a year passed before the next literacy test-Asian exclusion bill reached the House floor. Meanwhile developments had taken place both in the Indian consitutency and in exclusionists' determination. Har Dayal was here. The Gadar Party had been organized and the first issue of the *Gadar* published. The Immigration Bureau and several others had noticed the rising violence in the tone of anti-British sedition among students several of whom had allegedly drifted away from their regular status.[76]

The West Coast Congressmen—Hayes, Raker, Humphrey, Church—had introduced bills seeking Hindu exclusion. Commissioner General Caminetti had his official authority and nonofficial exclusionist convictions to give weight to his demand that Congress take immediate action.

The Taft veto had killed a bill, but not the issue. On the West Coast the Democratic-Bull Moose presidential contest of 1912 turned on the question of Asian exclusion. The Democrats were said to have a platform committing the party to "stringent immigration laws." They were also helped by their election propaganda that showed Wilson favoring Asian exclusion while Theodore Roosevelt was quoted as having once favored naturalization for the Japanese. The new Congress was, therefore, greeted with a spate of immigration bills.[77]

The House Immigration Committee reported Chairman Burnett's bill H.R. 6060 in December 1913—a 60 page text of proposed reforms including a literacy test and the exclusion of ineligibles by a formula carefully worded so as not to disturb the Gentlemen's Agreement with Japan.[78]

On February 2, 1914, the literacy test clause was adopted. Immediately what the *New York Times* reporter called "a flank movement" the opponents of the test joined to support an amendment proposed by Hayes to the clause excluding the ineligibles hoping thereby to ensure the bill's defeat in the Senate or a veto by the President. The amendment proposed to exclude "Hindoos, and all persons of the Mongolian or yellow race, the Malay or brown race, and the African or black race," thus, directly naming the targeted races and overriding the agreement with Japan.[79]

The exclusion of "black races" was proposed in order to win over the southern members. Hayes was applauded three times during his plea for "race purity." Burnett found it necessary to warn them not to "be swept off their feet" by that provision because "not a single one went to Louisiana; only two or three went to Mississippi; . . . scarcely any of them are coming to this country at all."[80]

Adoption of an amendment to the Hayes amendment kept the Japanese agreement intact and did not deprive the Administration of the power to negotiate similar understandings with other countries. The proposed exclusions remained. By the next day, however, the southern members had recovered their poise. Bryon P. Harrison (D-Miss.) rejecting the "sop" offered by Hayes asked him, "if you want to help us, why do not you assist us to repeal the fifteenth and modify the fourteenth amendments, and pass some Jim Crow car laws and segregation laws for the District of Columbia?"[81] Raker, who would not let a rival get the credit for inserting Asian exclusion in the Burnett bill, moved to exclude "all Asiatic laborers" without naming the races but defining the geographical boundaries of their native continent, Asia, and preserving the Gentlemen's Agreement. Hayes objected to it as liable to exclude all natives of Asia and of Australia as well. Burnett maintained it would hamper the Administration's efforts to settle matters with Japan by treaty negotiation. Raker's substitute was rejected by 6 to 182 and Hayes amendment as amended by Lenroot was lost by 54 to 203. Harrison of Mississippi had said earlier in the day that the crisis of the bill had been reached. Towards the end the crisis was over and Burnett back in control of his bill.[82]

What has just been described in exceptional detail illustrates the emotions involved in immigration reform. It shows how for almost a decade the problem of Hindu exclusion was caught up on America's treaty commitments to Japan, politicians' eagerness in Congress to gain partisan advantage, general reluctance to name the targets of exclusion legislation, West Coast attempts to win Southern votes for Asian exclusion, and the connection between this exclusion and the literacy test.

The House adopted H.R. 6060 on February 4 and sent it to the Senate where it was laid aside till the next session. When debate resumed in December, Senator James A Reed (D-Mo.) moved amendment after amendment to legislate the California plan. The one excluding "All aliens not of the Caucasian race," was rejected as was the one to exclude "All Turks and East Indians." The House members agreed to the amendment seeking the exclusion of "All members of the African or black race." The Senate rejected an amendment to grant exemption from the literacy test to those attempting to escape religious, political, or racial persecution.[83]

The Senate passed H.R. 6060 on January 2, 1915 by 50 to 7 with 39 not voting. President Wilson held a hearing in the White House at which the supporters and opponents of the literacy test and impartial scholars made their views known to him. He vetoed the bill on January 28, the House refused by 261 to 136 to pass it over the President's veto.[84]

The next and the final round in the Congress-White House struggle over the question of immigration control before America's entry in the World War was initiated by bills from Hayes, Humphrey, and Burnett. It was Burnett's H.R. 10384 that reached the House floor.

Except for their demand to exclude the Japanese by an American law than by a Japanese-American treaty this bill contained all the major features sought by the Californians. The ineligibility clause while preserving the Gentlemen's Agreement, made the exclusion of the Hindu, this time, doubly certain by adding the word "Hindus" at the end of the clauses. There was also a provision for deporting those non-immigrants who ceased to maintain their status. Hayes was glad to point out that the Hindu was after all added to the excluded races.[85]

Johnson (R-Wash.) advised the passage of the bill to meet an emergency. He told the House that the railroad magnate, James J. Hill, was planning "to fill both sides of our boundary line from St. Paul to Seattle with Hindu labourers, to work at 40 cents or 50 cents a day." That importation had been stopped, he maintained, by the "prodigious efforts" of Commissioner- General of Immigration Caminetti and the "leading citizens" of the Pacific Northwest who persuaded the steamship companies "to cease bringing Hindus until some legislation." The House adopted the bill on March 30.[86]

While the bill was with the Senate Immigration Committee, the Japanese Ambassador lodged a protest at the ineligibility clause and the threat of deportation for violation of status. The United States and Japanese governments were already engaged in negotiating a settlement over the California Land Laws. The new development forced the Senate Committee to take immediate action. It substituted the ineligibility clause by the Asian Barred Zone that named neither a country nor a race and did not include Japan.[87]

Senator John D. Works (R-Calif.) alleged that "this clause was inserted in the bill at the demand of Japan." Senator Ellison D. Smith (D-S.C.), in charge of the bill implied that Japan's intention in this affair was the same as in 1907, that is, it did not want the United States "putting them in the category of other nations with whom they did not care to be classed." On August 21 the Barred Zone was accepted by the Senate as one of the Committee amendments.[88] Senator Miles Poindexter (R-Wash.) moved to restore the original clause. His amendment was rejected but only after a long debate. Senator James A. Reed (D-Mo.) protested against the Barred Zone provision when the Senate was debating to override the veto. The Senators appeared to be so much concerned over the Japanese connection with the bill that at one time Senator Smith said, "I think, Mr. President, this is about the thirtieth time I have repeated the statement (as to why not name Japan directly in the bill)."[89]

The Senate adopted the bill on December 14. The House agreed to the Senate's Barred Zone provision. The President vetoed the bill on January 29, 1917. The House overrode the veto on February 1 by 287 to 106 and the Senate on February 5 by 62 to 19 thereby making the bill the Immigration Act of February 5, 1917 (39 Stat. 874).[90]

Twice the Presidential vetoes had saved the Hindus because the American whites differed over the acceptable qualities of the European whites and because of the American convention that a bill could not be vetoed in parts. In 1917, however, the preparedness hysteria, the dual loyalties of the German hyphenates, the alarming prospect of a resumption of flood of European immigrants after the War, and the fear of European anarchists, made enough converts in Congress to put the literacy test on the Statute Book and the Asiatic Barred Zone along with it.

Chinese exclusion held its own for over sixty years. Indian exclusion lasted almost thirty years. This longevity is impressive as is the near unanimity with which it was enacted. Presidents, Democrats, Republicans, organized labor, the press, were on the side of Hindu exclusion. None of the three Presidential veto messages argued against exclusion. On the contrary they implied approval.[91]

In his veto message President Taft had objected only to the literacy test. As for the rest of the bill he praised it for containing many "valuable amendments to the present immigration law which will ensure greater certainty in excluding undesirable immigrants."

His Secretary of Commerce and Labor, whose advice the President had accepted in vetoing the bill, had raised six objections to it. The second objection was: "The provision that persons shall be excluded who cannot become eligible under existing law to become citizens of the United States by naturalization is obscure because it leaves unsettled the question as to who are to be regarded as white persons. . . ." Clearly the Secretary was concerned that the formula may not exclude Indians.

This and four other objections, in the Secretary's view, furnished "no sufficient reason for disapproving this bill." But, he continued, "with respect to the literacy test I feel compelled to state a different conclusion" and he went on for almost 3000 words to argue for a veto. "As much as I regret it, " he concluded, "because the other provisions of the measure are in most respects excellent and in no respect really objectionable, I am forced to advise that you do not approve this bill."

Wilson's first veto was based on two grounds, namely the bill's attempt to "all but close entirely the gates of asylum and to exclude those whom the opportunities of elementary education have been denied, without regard to their character, their purposes, or their natural capacity." Clearly the President had no complaint about Asian exclusion, which also formed part of the bill. On the contrary he felt "great hesitation" in returning the bill without his signature because "this particular bill is in so many important respects admirable, well-conceived, and desirable." Without mentioning them directly, the President most probably included the Asians among those who were a "menace" to the "wholesome and essential relationships of life."

His second veto message came two years later almost to the day. This one also contained two grievances against the bill as enacted, one, the literacy test and the other a provision to grant asylum to victims of religious persecution. The latter, according to the President, would involve passing "judgement upon the laws and practices of a foreign Government" which "might lead to very delicate and hazardous diplomatic situation." As for other provisions of the bill, which included Asian exclusion, the President assured the House he "should be very glad to concur."

Enactment of Hindu exclusion by the Asiatic Barred Zone, i.e., by longitudinal and latitudinal lines on the map of Asia, rather than by written sentences as the Chinese had been excluded or by an executive agreement which excluded Japanese laborers, was induced by diplomatic considerations. The one that admittedly gave the Senate Immigration Committee "considerable trouble" was the Japanese objection to the way Asian exclusion had been proposed in H.R. 10384.[92] The Senate Committee therefore, drew lines on the map that excluded the people, including the Hindus, whom it wanted to exclude. The purpose of the change, as explained by the Secretary of Labor was not to give offense to Japan and at the same time not modify the effect of the excluding section of the bill. The bill was, therefore, amended to include the Barred Zone. Senator Poindexter's effort to retain the original formula was defeated.[93] Geographical lines served multiple purposes. They satisfied Japan, excluded the Indians, named no race and eliminated the need to seek an agreement with Britain for excluding the Indian subjects of the Empire.

The Immigration Commission and Sudhindra Bose had suggested this British route. It was, however, unacceptable to people of the west coast who were already expressing dissatisfaction with the procedure the United States followed with Japan. They wanted to stop immigration from India immediately whereas diplomatic processes, as Johnson of Washington felt "would delay us indefinitely." Commissioner-General Caminetti warned the House Committee that "the people of California waited patiently for diplomatic agreement on the Japanese question. I do not think they want to wait for diplomatic settlement of the Hindu question."[94] The Barred Zone provision excluded the Hindus by a unilateral action of the United States to which the British could not object even if they had wanted to do so.

Doubts had often been expressed about the potency of the ineligibility clause to exclude the Hindus. Even Dillingham had implied that some portion of the Indian population might be eligible to American citizenship by naturalization. In some bills, including H.R 10384 therefore, the Hindus were mentioned by name in addition to the ineligibility formula. The geographical lines excluded them effectively without naming them.[95]

Sudhindra Bose estimated that the Act of 1917 had excluded more than one-quarter of the population of Asia. The countries whose inhabitants were excluded were Indo-China, the Dutch East Indies, Malay, Burma, Afghanistan and India. China and Japan- Korea were already excluded.[96]

Huttington had called the Act of 1917 "an unmistakable declaration of a white immigration policy." Emanuel Celler called exclusion "an insufferable act of pompous racial ego." It completed the process of Asian exclusion—first the Chinese, then the Japanese, and now most of the rest. Sudhindra labored under an illusion in 1914 that "exclusion would never have been advocated by the American people as a whole. . . . The attitude of the labor unions and the politicians is, therefore to be regretted." But here it was now for the rest of his life.[97]

In November 1916 Rabindranath Tagore, the first Asian to win the Nobel Prize for Literature, had "strongly and ardently" enjoined on the United States not to exclude Indian students. The poet told the American people—"Perhaps your treatment of Asiatics is one of the darkest sides of your national life."

Lajpat Rai, a leading Indian nationalist and writer, in an open letter to Senator E.D. Smith protested against exclusion as " a gross injustice," "an outrageous reflection on the Hindus," "an undeserved and unjustifiable reflection on their national honour." He also pleaded with Senator Smith that students not be required to post a bond upon entering the country.[98]

As the years passed, this treatment worsened. The British Dominions enlisted the League of Nations on the side of discrimination. Tagore joined his voice to the shrill protests rising from China and Japan and accused the West of "every where raising thorny hedges of exclusion, offering human sacrifices to national self-seeking."[99]

For the Indian community in America, the passage of the Act virtually amounted to a sentence of death by attrition, which luckily did not happen. The part that the British were alleged to have played in the enactment of exclusion or by their refusal to prevent it, was added to the list of nationalist grievances against the alien rulers. Beyond that the new law did almost nothing new. Exclusion of laborers was already a fact except for a small trickle. The students' status was not rigidly shackled.[100] Merchants and preachers continued to come under the same restraints as before. In fact, by the Act of 1917 nothing was lost except honor. It was the implied insult that Lajpat and Tagore resented. It indeed was a national insult to be asked by a foreign country to keep out. But so were the Chinese and the Japanese being asked to stay out. Realistically speaking India had no case. The Indian immigrants too had no case. Very wisely, therefore, their leaders kept the question of immigration and quotas under wraps for almost a quarter of a century. Those merchants, students, and farmers who were to provide leadership and who wrought miracles in the 1940s had not been excluded.

Still the Act of 1917 is an important watershed. It was the first American law to impose inequality on India and Indians. Secondly, the riots, the agitation, and the official policies that shaped the Act's insulting provisions created a watershed in Indian history. It was called the Gadar.

2 B

After having described the Americans' riots, their exclusionist campaigns, and legislation, it is proper now to turn to the Indians to find out how *they* meditated upon their fate and came up with *their* solutions when forced to "watch for the turban."[101]

Indians had been reacting to the actions of the host countries in several ways. In Canada, they had appealed to the higher courts, sent deputations to India and England, and published periodicals to ventilate their grievances. The former soldiers among them had started to lodge public protests against Canadian immigration policies.[102]

In the United States the violent reaction of organized labor, the press, patriotic societies, and the West Coast politicians to the arrival of the Sikhs led to years of heart-searching debate within the community. For years the farmers, the students, and the intellectuals participated in this debate by open expression of opinion in periodicals, through organizations, and public meetings.[103]

It was almost unanimously conceded that the Indian community as an ethnic group of limited numbers and nonexistent political power, was too weak to fight the United States government, the Congress, and the California exclusionists. So far as America was concerned, therefore, the strategy was to appeal to the tolerant and democratic traditions of the nation, to ask for moderation in the exclusionist proposals, and to seek a settlement through a diplomatic understanding between the United States and Britain. The Indian spokesmen may probably have hoped that in this way they may save the students and gain the right of family reunion.[104]

Restricted immigration, in other words, the prohibition of "laborers," seems to have been accepted even by the Gadarites because they professed no quarrel with the United States.[105] The students, most of whom had come for studies and not for organizing an anti-British movement in America, pleaded for the continuation of their privileges. Lala Lajpat Rai, Rabindranath Tagore, and Sudhindra Bose insisted that students be permitted to come unburdened with severe restrictions. They looked upon students as the future hope of India.[106]

Ardent revolutionists among the students saw opportunities for creating a nationalist upsurge opening before them. American civil rights and the resentment of the immigrants provided them with the hammer and the anvil to shape the Sikhs into anti- British rebels. These were the Gadarites. The failure of the non-Gadarite Indian nationalists to persuade the British to protest against exclusonist bills in Congress deprived them of any *locus standi* with the radicals.[107]

The three years, from the arrival of Har Dayal in California in September 1911 to the late summer of 1914 when the Komagata Maru was forced to leave Vancouver, were also the years when the Indian community found its legal future in the United States threatened by bureaucratic decisions in California and hostile enactments in Washington, D.C. The stranded Indian community started organizing to protest against the British as well as to educate the American public here and Indian public opinion at home.

Sudhindra Bose emerged as the leader of the educational and the peaceful protest efforts. A university teacher at 30 and the first President of the H.A.A., he was one of those Indian revolutionaries who had no boats left to go back home. He received his naturalization certificate a fortnight before the Congress overrode the Wilson veto on February 5, 1917, enveloping his beloved India in a barbed wire zone. His most relevant efforts to ward off the threatened blow of exclusion took place in Washington, D.C., including his testimony at one Congressional hearing.

These hearings brought Indian witnesses and exclusionist legislators face to face in probing and often irritating question and answer sessions. Dr. Bose, a young intellectual, inexperienced in the tricks of his opponents' political game, was weakened still further by the open actions of the British colonies with the underhand encouragement of Great Britain. His arguments testifying to the high character of his country's laborers lost all validity in face of exclusion from the colonies. Commissioner-General Caminetti told him to his face that he was "possibly talking about a different class of people—a different race of people."[108]

Tishi Bhutia, a mystery man, a clever debater, a proud Hindu, an ardent nationalist, testified at another hearing. He often spoke as an embarrassing fanatic for caste and untouchability. Unlike Har Dayal he hated violence and anarchism but possessed a similar shiftiness in intellectual thought processes.[109]

Public hearings on bills proposing Hindu exclusion were held six times, twice each in December 1913, February 1914 and April 1914. Most bills that reached the hearing stage had come from the West Coast Representatives Raker, Hayes and Church of California, and William E. Humphrey of Washington.[110]

No Indian appeared at the December 1913 hearings. Chairman Burnett, after an initial refusal, permitted Dr. Sudhindra Bose and Bishen Singh to appear at the February hearings. In April the Committee heard Tishi Bhutia from New York.[111]

Dr. Bose came on behalf of the H.A.A., students' organization, and Bishen Singh represented the Pacific Coast Khalsa Diwan Society of Stockton, California. Tishi Bhutia also appeared as a representative of the H.A.A. These were the two most representative bodies of Indians in the United States next to the burgeoning Gadar party.[112]

At the hearings, Dr. Bose listened for long hours to what Canada was doing to his people and what the Californians intended to do to them here. Indian spokesmen hardly had any friend on the Committee except James Manahan (D-Minn.) who had studied yoga, and two members, Augustus P. Garner (D-Mass.) and J. Hampton Moore (R-Pa.) who were not yet convinced of the need to legislate Hindu exclusion. Adolph J. Sabath (D-Ill.), now as always, tried to soften the blow on immigrants, though just a few days before the start of the February hearings, he had told the House, "I am thoroughly in sympathy with [Representatives Hayes' and Raker's] views on [restricting Asiatic immigration]."[113]

The West Coast legislators openly expressed themselves opposed to assimilating Indians, justified the refusal of restaurants to serve them, resented the sale of city lots to Hindus, and did not consider them eligible to citizenship. They rejected Indians for their dress, their way of life, and their color. They sought to defame them as carriers of dangerous diseases, gave out exaggerated figures as to their numbers, and even threatened to use force to keep the figures down and the Hindus scattered.[114]

Sudhindra Bose and Bishen Singh proposed that the Indian problem be settled not by enacting an anti-Hindu law but through a "diplomatic arrangement" with the Government of India of the type of the Gentlemen's Agreement with Japan.

No concern had been openly expressed to Sudhindra Bose and Bishen Singh over the anti-British activities of the Indian community when they appeared for their testimony in February. When Tishi Bhutia appeared at the hearing at the end of April, these activities were one of the major topics for his questioning.

The proceedings show how closely and in detail the legislators had been watching the Indians' agitation. Representative Raker told Bhutia he had "a whole bundle of papers" to prove their anti-British purpose. Chairman Burnett introduced in the record about 400 words from one of Har Dayal's speeches. Raker and Johnson probingly examined Bhutia as to his contacts and associates in the several states.[115]

Bhutia agreed that "India is looking forward to the time when . . . she will overthrow the British yoke. That is what we all want." But he disavowed violence and anarchism. Freedom would be sought "by means of passive resistance . . . [and] utilitarianism" he told them. The principles of anarchism "are very far from India because Buddhism prevents the shedding of blood." Har Dayal's speech advocating overthrow of government including policemen and judges, Bhutia said, did not refer to the United States but to conditions in India. He informed the Committee that the shipload of Indians now on the high sea was going to Vancouver, Canada "to test the legality of their constitution" and to claim reciprocity. He assured the members that those Indians were headed towards Canada and not the United States.[116]

While in Washington, Dr. Bose had met Secretary of State Bryan to urge his proposal for a diplomatic settlement and unsuccessfully attempted to draw the British Ambassador on the side of the British Indians.[117] Advising the students to agitate against the Burnett bill, the scholar-patriot on his part broadcast in magazine articles his denunciation of the betrayal of his people by the British at this time. Concerned over the temper of the Sikhs of California in 1914 he was hardly bluffing when he told the Immigration Committee that "if the British Government sanctions any of this [Canadian restrictions] the whole Empire will have to be torn to pieces, and it will bring out one of the fiercest conflicts the world has ever seen."

It was probably at his initiative that the petition to Congress which was received in the Senate was organized. He also wrote to the Chinese and the Japanese Ambassadors, who told him they had protested

It was probably at his initiative that the petition to Congress which was received in the Senate was organized. He also wrote to the Chinese and the Japanese Ambassadors, who told him they had protested against the bills. The British never had. The editor of the *Hindustan Gadar*, Ramachandra, protested in letters to the *New York Times*: other people sent a collective telegram to the Secretary of State.[118]

The Gadar episode is relevant to this discussion not in its wider significance as a chapter in the national history of India but as part of the Indo-American community's struggle to preserve its status of equality, as an indication of the resentment at the apprehended loss of equality, and later as an inspiration to those who struggled for the restoration of equality. The abundance of documentation on the activities of the Indian community during those historic years reveals the high caliber of the immigrants that India sent. Among them were hundreds who when treated unjustly could stand up together in a common cause and manage to raise the largest body of men intent upon a violent overthrow of the British power second only to the one put together by Netaji Subhash Chandra Bose in the 1940s.[119]

The Sikh farmers and veterans who by 1912 had been disillusioned as to the real character of their British rulers, were looking for a strong leader. Har Dayal had come to California. Common friends brought about the meeting of minds. The Sikhs got a charismatic leader and Har Dayal got a following for his dream—a mass revolutionary movement in India.[120]

He told them the real cause for their hardships in America was not here but in India. He advised them to set up a party and a propaganda machine. The party headquarters were established in San Francisco, and the party paper *Gadar* made its first appearance on November 1, 1913. It was published in several Indian languages and was circulated in almost all countries where Indians lived. Efforts were made to smuggle it into India. Har Dayal fled from the United States in April 1914, before he could be deported for making speeches in support of anarchism.[121]

The ship Komagata Maru left Hong Kong on April 4, 1914. By the time it reached Vancouver it had 376 passengers eager to enter Canada. They were not permitted to land. Emotions ran high and there developed considerable tension among Indians in Canada and the United States. Taraknath Das said Indian workers on the Pacific Coast and in Canada spent more than $100,000 to meet the expenses of chartering the ship and feeding several hundred passengers for months. The ship was forced to leave on July 7. Ten days later World War I broke out. This was the opportunity the angry patriots had been told to look forward to.[122]

Hundreds returned to India to cause a rebellion. But where were the arms? "There would be lots of arms with the Indian soldiers of the British army so they should be won over to the cause," the Gadar leaders argued. There lay the tragedy.[123] Indian soldiers remained loyal to their British officers.

In the United States the new Gadar leader Ramachandra accepted German collaboration as did several young Indians in Europe. The American part in the Gadar-German effort included shipping of arms to India. Five Indians were sent with Gadar literature on S.S. *Maverick* which sailed from San Pedro near Los Angeles on 23 April 1915 for Socorro Islands off the west coast of Mexico. A schooner *Annie Larsen* was to be waiting for it there with a consignment of arms for the Indian rebels. The *Maverick* was to take the consignment to Batavia. The plan, however, miscarried. *Annie Larsen* was seized at Aberdeen, Washington; the *Maverick* sailed to Batavia without arms. The seditious literature had to be burnt. One of the five Indians on the *Maverick*, Harcharan Das became a prosecution witness at the Hindu-German conspiracy trial in 1917.[124]

This trial in San Francisco and the related trials in New York and Chicago are the only Gadar incidents in which America joined hands with Britain to suppress the revolutionaries. No Gadar activity injured any American interest. The allegations over *Annie Larsen* and *Maverick* and the German encouragement of any Gadar activity against the British did not violate American law whether of conspiracy or of neutrality. Even as late as February 28, 1917, President Wilson approved of the Secretary of State Lansing's memorandum that accused the British Ambassador of using "intemperate" language and insisting that neither of the ships had violated the neutrality laws.[125] Still Indians were brought to trial and punished because the British kept demanding that the Gadarites be suppressed, and the conviction of Franz Bopp, German consul general at San Francisco for conspiracy to violate the neutrality law convinced the Justice Department that the Germans might be involved in the Gadar too. Even after British spies with the help of New York Police arrested Chandra Chakravarti who immediately confessed and the German involvement was clearly documented, the violation of neutrality law was still not easy to prove in a court of law. Five Indian passengers on the S.S. *Maverick* hardly constituted a "military expedition." Moreover the Gadarites could not even be legally arrested for the kind of political activities they were pursuing in America.[126]

For some months before the United States became Britain's ally in war on April 6, 1917, their governments "were already collaborating on the case [against the Indians] below the diplomatic level." The British officials put "pressure" on the American government to arrest political activists to which the Justice Department officials "responded by using the conceptual framework of conspiracy" as part of the American "government attempt to discredit Indian revolutionaries."[127]

The conspiracy statute had previously been used to suppress nationalist agitations of the Irish, the Cubans, the Mexicans. In the present case it facilitated the prosecutor's job: only two people were needed to prove a "conspiracy", the government could arrest the Gadarites legally and justify that as an enforcement of neutrality laws. The prosecution did not even have to prove actual criminal acts. The government was also helped by the judges. Both in the San Francisco and in the earlier Chicago trial, the courts appeared to be cooperating with the prosecutors' version of the law against military expeditions by giving them their "broadest definition."[128]

In July 1917 the San Francisco grand jury returned indictments for conspiracy against 124 Indians, Germans, and Americans. The trial was planned to be "the showcase" of the "conspiracy". The evidence had been put together by British agents. Rules of evidence were relaxed in order to secure easy convictions. The British government got what it wanted. The Gadar had been crushed in India already. It was now discredited in America too, even dramatically so when Ramachandra was shot dead in open court by a colleague.[129]

Fifteen Indians received jail terms, far less than what they would have been awarded in India by the British. Among the convicted were Taraknath Das, Gobind Beharilal and Godha Ram Chanon all of whom lived to see a free India and a free Indian community in the United States.[130] One man who was neither convicted nor was destined to see India free was the leader who had fled. Har Dayal (1884-1939), a record-holder in university credentials, a talented speaker, possessor of a photographic memory, had attracted public attention by throwing away official British patronage, which thousands others would have sold their souls to own. He was 23 when he resigned the scholarship at Oxford, 29 when he offered himself as the community's savior, and hardly thirty when he wrote his own political obituary. For seven years a political arsonist rather than a statesman, he permitted his wayward intellectualism to forget India and the concrete political needs of his devoted followers in America to endorse anarchism and thereby remove himself from the protection of American law. Har Dayal needed a more stable intellect as badly as the Sikhs and their cause deserved a better leader.[131]

Although the British ruler's repressive and exploitative policies in India and their collaboration with the exclusionists of Canada and the United States called for a revolt, it was the Gadar leaders' political immaturity to declare war on Britain without providing for the sinews of war. It was even more fatal to believe that in case of war with Germany the Sikhs in the Punjab would want to go to war for the rebels.

Nobody knows exactly how many young men were hanged, shot or otherwise killed by the British. Scores of lives were lost, careers wasted, or cut short by imprisonment or exile. There was one gain, however. The list of martyrs grew.[132]

Collaboration with the enemy's enemy has never been a crime unless it fails. In the case of Gadar it failed badly. Next time around the strong nationalist forces, even those swearing by nonviolence, protected the "pro-Jap" Indian soldiers from attempted British vengeance."[133] It is all a question of balance of power. The Gadarites do not deserve to be condemned for collaborating with Germany. They are to be criticized for the way they did it and for making foreign aid a pillar of their ideology even before the nationalist forces at home had developed a cohesive strength of their own. The Germans could use them as "errand boys" because "the boys" had only a group and not the nation behind them.[134]

During the Second World War, Indian activists like Ramlal Bajpai in America looked back to their compatriots' activities during the First World War as a wasted first chance. He mentioned one, so far unreasearched, cause of political failure of the Gadar. He warned Jagjit Singh:

> My twenty-five years experience clearly shows that when young attractive women are taken in confidence to do independent political (serious) activities they prove mata-Haris [sic]. It was such a mistake that helped to land some of our patriots in American prison during last war. Pardon my timely word of caution."[135]

The British and the U.S. governments, the misdeeds of the German hyphenates, and the public hysteria aroused by the war had brought not only utter defeat but abject ridicule upon the Indians' attempt to use the war for their nationalist purposes. It is significant that when Taraknath Das recounted in 1946 a brief history of his community's struggles, he mentioned the Komagata Maru but forgot to say anything about the San Francisco trial. Another former Gadarite in America wished that the Indians' discontent had not resulted in "excess of enthusiasm" and wanted the ex-Kaiser to be tried for "attempting to corrupt Hindu nationalists." Lajpat Rai took the wise precaution to announce in his paper that Indian Home Rulers do not seek German collaboration.[136] The age of Gandhian pacifism aroused in some Indian intellectuals "excessive enthusiasm" for anti-Gadar hyperbole. Shridharani called the former Gadar leaders "anarchronisms—not only men without a country, but also men without a cause." He confused methods with the cause. Even Mahatma Gandhi could not but admire the revolutionary martyrs for their patriotism and sacrifices. Taraknath Das asserted "that Indians in America have contributed more than their share in the struggle for Indian Freedom." He was referring to their activities during the First World War.[137]

That share was contributed in several ways—the memory, the martyrs, the lessons learned—but most importantly by turning the Sikh farmers against the British. The former tempo of joining the armed forces would continue, but the old loyalty never returned.[138]

Notes & References

1. See fns. 29, 30, 35.
2. From a speech by Richard Bartholdt (R-Mo), *Cong. Record*, 63rd Cong., 2 sess., January 31, 1914, 2661.
3. President Roosevelt in his annual message to the 59th Congress suggested that "There should be an increase in the stringency of the laws to keep out epileptic and pauper immigrants . . . all violent and disorderly people, all people of bad character, the incompetent, the lazy and physically unfit,

defective, or degenerate should be kept out." Quoted in E.P. Hutchinson, *Legislative History*, 136.

4. Ibid., 121.
5. Ibid., 136, 155-56, 157, 158.
6. In 1900 the Demoratic Party "endorsed the Chinese exclusion law and recommended its application to the same classes of all Asiatic races." The Party's national platform of 1904 said : "We are opposed to the admission, of Asiatic Immigrants who cannot be amalgamated with our population." "*Cong. Record*, 62nd Cong., 3rd sess., 672; in 1908 two more reasons for exclusion were added; "whose presence among us would raise a race issue and involve us in diplomatic controversies with oriental powers," ibid., 63rd Cong., 2nd sess., 2782. The legislatures of Ohio, Pennsylvania and Virginia called for more stringent immigration laws, Hutchinson, "*Legislative History*, 145; K.J. Doyle, a Socialist, declared, "I do not see any difference between the two old parties and that is why I became a socialist. I am an Exclusionist, too (applause)." A.E.L. *Proceedings*, October 1908, 19; Jack London confessed to be 'first of all a white man and only then a Socialist," Daniels, *Prejudice*, 30.
7. *Cong. Record*, 63rd Cong., 2nd sess., January 31, 1914, 2679.
8. Hutchinson, *Legislative History*, 130, quoting from the report of the Industrial Commission presented to this Congress.
9. Hostile judgment had started while "the Hindoo invasion (was) yet in its infancy; only the head of the long procession (had) entered the Golden Gate." Herman Scheffauer, "The Tide of Turbans," *Forum*, vol. 43 (January- June 1910), 617. The Bellingham riot occurred the very first year of their arrival in more than small numbers; the Immigration Commission views on them were formed within less than two years of their arrival; the *Forum* article was published in less than three years; the Exclusion League started active opposition almost immediately with only "two or three years' acquaintance with Hindus" the authors of *Meat vs. Rice* were convinced that "they have no standard of morals by which a Caucasion may judge them." Samuel Gompers and Herman Gutscate, San Francisco, 1908 17; the year of Sant Nihal Singh's articles on Indian immigrants shows how early the unwelcome in Canada and the United States had started to become irksome. The titles of some of his articles published in the *Modern Review* in 1918 were : "The Spirit of the West," III, 46-49; "Indians in America," ibid., 204-209; "Indians in the 'Far East'," vol. IV, 114-121; "Indians in America," ibid., 311-314 : Indian immigrants found themselves subject to severe distress by riots soon after their arrival when they had "no organization and no leaders . . . no banks, no secure place in which to lodge their savings, no one to consult in sickness, no source of instruction, no lawyer, no medicine chest, no stores

of their own." *Modern Review*, vo. III, 56, C.F. Andrews visiting from India noticed the rising violence of anti-Asian feeling in America, "The racial outcry began to be raised four years ago and the mob of San Francisco could hardly be restrained from doing violence to the foreigners [the Japanese]." He also noticed that "At the present time the conditions of civilized life—law, order and personal security—are more immature in the Pacific than in the Atlantic States." *Modern Review*, March 1920, 212. The re- emergence of the spirit of anti-orientalism during these years has puzzled some scholars of the era which "historians continue to call "progressive," Joan M. Jensen, "Apartheid : Pacific Coast Style," *Pacific Historical Review*, 1969, 339; anti-orientalism was also used to embarrass the federal government, emphasize states' right and to attract publicity. Moreover, it was "typically in character, that the progressives' concern [for the plight of the European immigrant] was not coupled with an understanding of the aspirations of the nonwhite aliens." Spencer C. Olin Jr., "European Immigrant and the Oriental Alien," *Pacific Historical Review*, August 1966, 314-315; other instances of anti-orientalism are *California and the Oriental*, 101, 102; Mears, *Resident Orientals*, 193-195; Missionaries too supported Asian exclusion, ibid., 120, 121; "The Veto of Canada," *Living Age*, August 1, 1914, 310-312 is a plea for exclusion without "compromise."

10. Gerald N. Hallberg, "Bellingham, Washington's Anti-Hindu Riot," *Journal of the West*, vol. XII (1973) 163-175; Sant Nihal Singh called the riot an "unrighteous affair," "Message America Gave Me," *Modern Review*, October 1909, 373; "The Picturesque Immigrant from India's Coral Strand," *Out West*. vol. XXX (January 1909) 49; "The Riots at Bellingham and Vancouver," *The American Monthly Review of Reviews*, October 1907, 403- 404; Das, *Hindustani Workers*, 111, calls the riot an example of prejudice. An incident of retaliation by Indians is in *Asiatic Exclusion League Proceedings*, September 1908, 12, henceforth to be cited as A.E.L. *Proceedings*; an instance of the media ignorance and condescension is *The American Monthly Reviews of Reviews*, March 1907, editorial comment, 367-368; Founding and Expansion of the Exclusion League; Reports of the Immigration Commission, vol. 23, 169.
11. Das, *Hindustani Workers*, 111-112; for a later riot, that in Wheatland, California, Mark Juergensmeyer, "The Ghadar Syndrome : Immigrant Sikhs and Nationalist Pride." *Sikh Studies*, 181; Edith Abbott, *Immigration : Select Documents and Case Records*, Chicago, 1924, 489 gives August 3, 1913 as the date for the riot. According to Juergensmeyer the Gadar Party received its greatest expansion and widespread financial support following this riot. Ibid., 8.

12. Hallberg. *Bellingham riot*, 167. 168, 169, 173; *The Outlook*, September 21, 1907, 100.
13. Restriction of Immigration : House Committee on Immigration and Naturalization Hearing on December 6, 1913, 3, 4, 5, emphasis added; henceforth this document shall be cited as "*House Hearings, December 1913*"; Representative Johnson confessed to the same tactics, again, *Sudhindra Hearings*, 105; Exclusion League's threats to use violence against immigrants, A.E.L. *Proceedings*, September 1910, 47, 51, 52.
14. Speaking on the bill for restriction of Chinese immigration Senator James G. Blaine said on February 14, 1879; "I am opposed to the Chinese coming here. I am opposed to making them citizens. I am unalterably opposed to making them voters." One of the reasons for this opposition was that "you cannot work a man who must have beef and bread, alongside of a man who can live on rice," *Meat vs. Rice*, 22.
15. Brooks Adams welcomed the new present and visualized the expanding future "as the United States becomes an imperial market, she stretches out along the trade-routes which lead from foreign countries to her heart, as every empire has stretched out from the days of Sargon to our own. The West Indies drift toward us, the Republic of Mexico hardly longer has an independent life, and the city of Mexico is an American town. With the completion of the Panama Canal all Central America will become a part of our system. We have expanded into Asia, we have attracted the fragments of the Spanish dominions, and reaching out into China we have checked the advance of Russia and Germany in territory which, until yesterday, had been supposed to be beyond our sphere. We are penetrating into Europe, and Great Britain especially is gradually assuming the position of a dependency, which must rely on us as the base from which she draws her good in peace, and without which she could not stand in war," *The New Empire*, New York, 1903, 208-209. John Higham, *Strangers in the Land : Patterns of American Nativism 1860-1925*, New York, 1955, describes the "new confidence in America's position in the world" resulting from the acquisition of "far-flung dependencies on the pattern of the great European powers of the day," 107-108.
16. Richard Hofstadter, *Social Darwinism in American Thought*, Boston, 1944, 180.
17. Ibid.
18. These laws were enacted in the following years. Figures in brackets refer to their location in Carl B. Hyatt (Compiler), and Edwin Austin Avery (Ed.); *U.S. Department of Justice : Laws Applicable to Immigration and Nationality* (Washington, D.C., 1953), henceforth to be cited as *Laws*, 1882 (211), 1884 (218) 1888 (two laws enacted this year, 230, 236) 1892, (242), 1893 (247), 1894 (249), 1898 (251-253), 1900 (254), 1901 (255),

1902 (256-258), 1904 (276), and 1913 (316). Francis A. Walker, "one of the outstanding economists of his day"; Higham, *Strangers*, 142 characterized the "new" immigrants as "beaten men from beaten races." Quoted in Higham, ibid., 143. It has not been usually noticed by many writers that European laborers "cheap" or otherwise have never been called "coolies",

19. Roger Daniels and Harry Kitano, "The Ethnic Crisis of Our Time." in Roger Daniels and Spencer C. Olin, Jr. (Eds.), *Racism in California : A Reader in the History of Oppression*, New York, 1972, 332.
20. J.T. Sunderland, later a close associate of Lajpat Rai and a missionary himself agreed there were "two sources of this misunderstanding [about India in America, Europe and in England]. One is the Christian Missionaries . . . [and the other] is England." *Modern Review*, February 1911, 151. The Sikhs' turban "is becoming to the white population what a red rag is to an infuriated bull." *Burjor Report*, 17; Testifying before the House Committee on Immigration and Naturalization, Dr. Sudhindra Bose told of a "high Government official" in Washington, D.C. who had "never studied a page of Hindu philosophy, had never turned over the first page of Indian history, had not the remotest conception of the contribution of India to the world's progress and civilization, and yet this gentleman stated that the Hindus are the most undesirable people in the world," *Sudhindra Hearings*, 4.
21. Roger Daniels, *The Politics of Prejudice : The Anti-Japanese Movement in California and the Struggle for Japanese Exclusion*, Los Angeles, 1977, 46. This 'position' was claimed to have been sustained over the years by remaining "eternally on guard" in this matter. Rep. Burnett thought "the country owes the Pacific coast a debt of gratitude for keeping undesirable people out, because when they overrun California the whole country suffers." *Sudhindra Hearings*, 107; the Homer quotation is from Hofstandter, *Social Darwinism*, 182.
22. Blacks seen as a problem : A.E.L. *Proceedings*, April 1908, 15; C.O. Young quoted in Daniels, *Politics of Prejudice*, 16, Congressman Hayes' speech in Congress mentioned; ibid., 29, and *Cong., Record*, 64th Cong., 1st sess., 4784; Senator Poindexter's speech in Congress, ibid., 2nd sess., 263. "We ought to protect at this time even California against herself. [Applause and cries of "Vote!"] James R. Mann of Illinois, ibid., 63rd Cong., 2nd sess., February 3, 1914, 282; appealing to Californians in 1944 Pearl Buck insisted "that in our country all persons whatever their ancestry, be given their rights, in order that America be preserved" and reminded them that as their state faced the Pacific and Asia "You can, by what you decide, be a barrier—or you can be a gateway to a new and better world, for us and for all people." "An Appeal to California," *Asia and the Americas*, January 1944, 23.

23. Quoted in Mears, *Resident Orientals*, p. 1 from a statement in 1913 by Mr. Chester H. Rowell, Editor, Fresno *Republican*. Californians claimed to be the guardians of white civilization at the western point "like the Greeks who settled in Asia Minor 3000 years ago (who) stood at its eastern point," *California and the Oriental*, 10; the Chairman of the Board of Control under whose auspices this work had been published, asserted in a magazine article that it was "utterly unthinkable that America or an American State should be other than White."; Marshall DeMotte, "California White or Yellow?" *Annals of American Academy of Political and Social Sciences*, January 1921, 23; A.E.L. *Proceedings*, December 1910, 73 has this comment on Asian- European cultural exchange through the centuries : "Asia has been a menace to our civilization for many centuries past"; the phrase "muscular patriots" is in Higham, *Strangers*, 145.
24. Daniels, *Politics of Prejudice*, 91.
25. Sant Nihal Singh, "Indians in America, "*Modern Review*, March 1908, 206.
26. "The Hindu in America," *Overland Monthly*, April 1908 quoted in the *American Monthly Review of Reviews*, May 1908, 605.'
27. Sant Nihal Singh, *Modern Review*, March 1908, 207; A.E.L. *Proceedings*, April 1908, 14-15; also related to this same bias, ibid., January 5, 1908, 4, June 1909, 13; H.A. Millis, "East Indian Immigration," *American Economic Association Review*, 1911, Supplement I, 72, 73, 75, 249; Asians as carriers of diseases, A.E.L., ibid., October 1910, 62, 63, 67; December 1910, 70; Not all exclusionists came from the West coast states. Senator Charles S. Thomas (D-Co) wanted to deny Asians even the right to asylum for religious and political persecution. *Cong. Record*, 63rd Cong., 2nd sess., December 16, 1914, 263; the coming of the Indian immigrants had been characterized as a "crisis" even as early as 1908 and legislation in Washington had been suggested to bridge it, *American Monthly Review of Reviews*, May 1908, 605.
28. *Outlook*, New York, January 14, 1911, 64; Rep. Church's remarks are in his Extension of Remarks, *Cong. Record*, 63rd Cong., 2nd sess., August 20, 1914, Appendix, 844; fear of India's population among the exclusionists, *Sudhindra Hearings*, 82; Hearings on Hindu Immigration before Committee on Immigration, House of Representatives, 63rd Cong., 2nd sess., April 16, 1914 and April 30, 1914, 158, 161, henceforth to be referred to as the *Bhutia Hearings*; Caminetti's statement in *New York Times*, 14 February 1914; Senator Poindexter was concerned that 168 million Orientals were "ready to come in." *Cong. Record*, 64th Cong., 2nd sess., December 13, 1916, 263; exclusion because of religion; caption of an article arguing for Asian exclusion "Unless Future Peace and Protection

are Secured by Timely Legislative action, Christian Civilization and the White Race are Doomed," ending with "and [Orientals] having come here in sufficient numbers, it will soon be good-bye to liberty, Christian civilization and the Caucasian race," *Organized Labor*, February 20, 1909 quoted in A.E.L. *Proceedings*, February 1909, 10, 11.

29. A.E.L. *Proceedings*, February 1909, 11; "It must be remembered that the second generation of Asiatics would be voters," ibid., June 1910, 37; fear of the Japanese demand, ibid., October 1910, 61.

30. Ibid., January 1910, 11, the League mentions laws that had been used in "northern parts" and Seattle by the use of which "Hindus were debarred." Ibid., June 1910, 40, under caption "Good of the League," and September 1910, 46, 47, January 1910, 6, 7. This conflict between the exclusionists and the administration officials during these years of a legislative holiday over the execution of the law was not peculiar to the Pacific coast or to the case of the Hindus. Higham wrote that while the "Immigration Commission ground through its vast investigation, the nativists fumed impatiently. At first they used the legislative bill to try to secure *more drastic administration of existing statutes*." *Strangers*, 188, emphasis added.

31. A.E.L. *Proceedings*, September 1910, 46.

32. Ibid., 51, June 1910, 25; October 1910, 59-60; December 1910, 70; *Sudhindra Hearings*, emphasis added.

33. H.A. Millis, "East Indian Immigration to British Columbia and the Pacific Coast States," *American Economic Association Review*, 1911, 704; they were being turned back under the charge "liable to become public charges." Rep. Denver S. Church stated at a House hearing, "that is the only weapon we have, the only way by which we can prevent them from coming here (under) what little law we have on the subject." *Sudhindra Hearings*, 80; a student reported that "things wore an aspect of gloom and dismay specially for the Sikhs," *Modern Review*, August 1911, 210.

34. *The Hindusthanee Student*, January 1914, 20, 27.

35. *Sudhindra Hearings*, 49; Indian immigration had been practically blocked as Lajpat Rai wrote in 1916, "The immigration department admits no more Hindus into the United States. There is no law forbidding their entrance as such, but the laws and regulations are so administered as to shut out and effectively exclude the Hindu from entering America unless he comes on a short visit or for purposes of trade with plenty of money in his pockets, or as a student with sufficient evidence that he would be supported from home," *The United States of America*, 469; he expressed similar resentment at a students' gathering, *Hindusthanee Student*, March 1916,11.

36. "Urgency." "emergency," *Sudhindra Hearings*, 51; "not more than 50 percent," ibid., 50; alleged "concert of action," ibid., 51, 107; *Bhutia*

Hearings, 130, 131; the allegation of "concert of action" is also implied in Secretary of the Department of Labor, W.B. Wilson's words; the Indians' "immigration is now becoming systematized and financed," in his letter to the Speaker of the House, January 20, 1914 in *Bhutia Hearings*, 141. The document at page 107 of *Sudhindra Hearings* and Secretary Wilson's remark regarding Indian immigration are correct in the sense that hundreds of Sikhs were gathering at Hong Kong and that they were well financed. It was in fact the Komagata Maru affair that was starting to take shape. They were attempting to challenge Canada. They had no intention of coming to the United States. Chairman Burnett also thought that the Indian immigration was becoming an emergency—the Hindu question he agreed "was in danger of becoming an acute condition," *Bhutia Hearings*, April 16, 1914, 148. Another factor which was creating a sense of urgency was the approaching opening of the Panama Canal. Rep. Raker believed a law for the exclusion of undesirables was "going to be a vital one with the opening of the Panama Canal," House hearings December 1913, 13; a newspaper reported that Caminetti "will endeavor to strengthen the immigration laws generally before the Panama Canal opens in 1915." *The Seattle Times*, 12 December 1913, 212.

37. Some members of Congress have included in their speeches a brief history of the Asian exclusion-cum-literacy test legislation : *Cong. Record*, 63rd Cong., 3rd sess., February 14, 1915, 3014, 3056, Appendix. 325, Congressman Raker's summarization of the evolution of the ineligibility clause, ibid., 62nd Cong., 3rd sess., January 30, 1913, 2291-2292.

38. Louis Bromfield started his Introduction to Krishnalal Shridharani's *My India, My America* with this sentence : "I suspect that more rubbish has been thought, spoken and written about India than about any country in the world." The exclusionists produced much of this "rubbish." We find it in A.E.L. *Proceedings*, in Congressional hearings, House and Senate debates in newspapers and journals. The most eloquent contributions to this "literature" come from Congressman Denver S. Church—his statement at *Sudhindra Hearings*, 37-85; his three speeches preserved in the *Cong. Record*, 63rd Cong., 2nd sess., January 1, 1914, 2690-2691; 63rd Cong., 3rd sess., February 4, 1915, 3053-3056; and his masterpiece, 63rd Cong., 2nd sess., Appendix, August 20, 1914, 842-845. Abusive phrases, A.E.L. *Proceedings*, February 1909, 4; January 1910, 10; October 1910, 61; *San Francisco Chronicle*, 29 September 1910; carriers of diseases, A.E.L. *Proceedings*, January 1910, 22, 23; *Modern Review*, August 1911, 210; *San Francisco Chronicle*, ibid., flashed the allegation on the front page and confessed that it was used as "a device" to exclude the Hindus. An Indian's response was "Inasmuch as Americans enjoy the reputation of being the crime-centre of the world, they can ill afford to assume a self-

righteous air. Indeed it comes with ill grace for Americans to condemn other peoples as "vicious," "inferior," or degradingly "Asiatic," Sudhindra Bose, "World's Worst in Crime," *Modern Review*, February 1926, 154.

39. This fact proved embarrassing when Indian spokesmen were confronted with Canadian official documents confirming Indian exclusion. Dr. Bose did not object to restriction or exclusion on principle, only that "restrictive or exclusionary measures should not be taken by special legislative action," such as the ones directed specifically against Indians. He objected to such special legislation because "If you pass an exclusionary law it tends to lower us in the estimation of the civilized world. It renders it almost impossible for us to enter any country where there is no restriction against us. It may bring about international complications. It is very far reaching." In the course of his testimony, therefore, he refused to concede that British colonies were excluding or restricting Indians. For instance, he claimed that "The Canadian law has no specific exclusion provision against the Hindus .... In fact, the Government of India is contemplating retaliatory measures against Canada." Clearly he was leaning on a broken reed. The solution he suggested was, of course, moderate and reasonable but under the circumstance of the time unrealistic. Anthony Caminetti, Commissioner General of Immigration publicly rejected it the same evening. *Sudhindra Hearings*, 19, 20-21; *New York Times*, 14 February, 1914.

40. Caminetti had come before the Committee "to call attention" to what Canada had done about Indian immigration. A Canadian official document he introduced into the record showed that "as was to be expected, Canada has had not only the sympathy and understanding, but the hearty cooperation of the authorities in Great Britain and India as well." Canada had imposed two restrictions on an Indian immigrant—must have at least $200 when he arrives in Canada and "must have come by one direct line of communication from the country from which he starts until he arrives in Canada." "It is practical exclusion" he commented, correctly. Towards the end of his testimony he summarized the advantages that the United States gains from these happenings within the British Empire : "It is *fortunate* in this emergency that the action of the Dominion of Canada and other British Colonies affords abundant evidence that no objection can reasonably be made by the Government of Great Britain if Congress should by way of restrictive measures adopt substantially a course consented to by England and followed by Canada and other colonies of the Empire." *Sudhindra Hearings*, 36, 38, 51, emphasis added.

41. A.E.L. *Proceedings*, February 1910, 12, also see ibid., June 1908, 14, November 1908, 8; Congressman Raker proposed a resolution to ask the

President for copies of correspondence relating to Japanese immigration, Hutchinson, *Legislative History*, 149.

42. Speaking in the House, Congressman Hayes claimed. "I believe that I have no race prejudice whatever, but I do believe in racial purity [applause[." *Cong. Record*, 63rd Cong., 2nd sess., February 2, 1914, 2781.
43. Hutchinson, *Legislative History*, 142; *Reports of the Immigration Commission*, vol. 40, ii; some believed it was appointed to sidetrack the issue of the literacy test, "to afford a breathing spell, postponing another nativist assault until the opposition to restriction was better organized." Higham, *Strangers*, 130; Burnett complained that the matter of immigration restriction had been "sidetracked" in 1906 for an investigating immigration commission; *Cong. Record*, 62nd Cong., 3rd sess., December 14, 1912, 657; it was also alleged that a bill similar to the Burnett bill H.R. 22527 was before the House in February 1907, when those opposed to the literacy test moved a successful amendment providing for a commission of inquiry instead. Ibid., December 17, 1912, 796.
44. The Commission "cast its mountainous social and economic data in the form of an invidious contrast between the northwestern and the southeastern Europeans in the United States at that time." Higham, *Strangers*, 189.
45. *Hindustani Workers*, v.
46. Ibid.; *Reports of the Immigration Commission*, vol. 24, 104.
47. Ibid., vol. 5, *Dictionary of Races or Peoples*, 247, 234.
48. The Dillingham Commission "strongly influenced legislation for some years, perhaps less through the report itself than through the personal influence and prestige of its members, especially Dillingham and Lodge in the Senate and Burnett in the House, who played dominant roles in congressional work on immigration," Hutchinson, *Legislative History*, 156. Dillingham told the Senate that his bill S. 3175 embodied recommentions of the Commission offered in the first volume of their Report. Ibid., 151. Jenks wrote in collaboration with W. Jett Lauck, *The Immigration Problem : A Study of American Immigration Conditions and Needs*, New York, 1913. Of particular interest are pages 257-259; Jenks was Professor of Government, New York University; Lauck was Associate Professor of Economics and Politics, Washington and Lee University. Millis's articles pertaining to India were "East Indian Immigration to British and the Pacific Coast States," *American Economic Association Review*, 1911, 72-76; Supplement I, 248- 249; "East Indians Immigration to the Pacific Coast," *The Survey*, June 1, 1912, 379-386. Millis was Associate Professor of Economics, Stanford University during the years he investigated for the Immigration Commission.

49. *Reports of the Immigration Commission*, vol. 1, 41.
50. Ibid., 691; "State Labor Commissioner McKenzie says that the farmers need more Japanese labor. The labor unions say that the State needs a new Labor Commissioner," quoted from Berkeley Gazette in A.E.L. *Proceedings*, June 1910, 37; "According to the Labor Commission California cannot raise both fruit and American civilization," quoted from Niles Press, Ibid.
51. *Reports of the Immigration Commission*, vol. 1, 692.
52. Ibid., 45, 47.
53. Ibid., 47, 691.
54. Ibid., 48.
55. These efforts by Dr. Bose and Ramchandra are discussed elsewhere in this chapter.
56. *Report of the Immigration Commission*, vol. I, p. 45. Emphasis added.
57. Dr. Sudhindra Bose wrote in his diary in 1917, "I am sick and tired of this awful lonely life in America. I feel that my position in this country is precisely like that of the *ostracized man*. I have no social standing in this benighted, *caste-ridden* land." Anne Z. Bose. "Sudhindra Bose : Portrait," *Modern Review*, November 1948, 370; emphasis added.
58. Partial list of bills introduced in each Congress from the 58th to the 64th seeking to strengthen or expand Asian exclusion :

58th Congress :

James N. Robinson (D-Ind.) H.R. 5221, Hutchinson, *Legislative History*, 134.

59th Congress :

Duncan E. Mckinley (R-Calif.), ibid., 137, Hayes's legislative efforts also started in this Congress with his bill to strengthen Chinese exclusion by making violation of status a deportable offense; *Cong. Record*, 62nd Cong., 3rd sess., January 17, 1913, 1689. He claimed to have reintroduced this bill in every subsequent Congress.

He also introduced in this Congress his first bill to exclude aliens ineligible to naturalization, ibid.

60th Congress :

Hayes introduced H.R. 246, his first bill to exclude Indians as being ineligible to naturalization. Hutchinson, *Legislative History*, 143. He also had sponsored a bill H.R. 20379 proposing to exclude the ineligibles. The Exclusion League was dissatisfied with this formula and called the bill "an Exclusion Bill which does not exclude." A.E.L. *Proceedings*, February 1910, 11, 12; Button L. French (R- Idaho), introduced his H.R. 18790.

61st Congress :

According to Hutchinson, Rep. Hayes "reintroduced" his bill of the "preceding Congress" in the first session now called H.R. 2215, *Legislative History*, 146, In the third session we find another bill proposed by Hayes, H.R. 13404, *Cong. Record*, 61st Cong., 3rd sess., 64.

62nd Congress :

Hayes introduced several bills to deal with immigration and naturalization laws. They were H.R. 2870, H.R. 4668, H.R. 4669, H.R. 4672 and H.R. 4677. The last one was so comprehensive in its exclusion grasp that the Speaker referred it to the Committee on Foreign Affairs, *Cong. Record*, 62nd Cong., 1st sess., 244.

In the second session there was an exclusion bill H.R. 14126 proposed by Rep. Edwin E. Roberts (R-Nev.); ibid., 62nd Cong., 2nd sess., 13, Hutchinson, *Legislative History*, 123, 150; Rep. Raker's H.R. 102 was focus of attention at the Bhutia Hearings, 138-141.

63rd Congress :

First session Hayes offered H.R. 2870 besides which there were six more bills from other sponsors, Hutchinson, *Legislative History*, 159, Raker's H.R. 13500 was discussed at the House Hearing of December 1913, 6, text of this bill is at *Cong. Record*, 62nd Cong., 3rd sess., December 12, 1912, 691-692; William E. Humphrey's H.R. 6440, ibid., 3, 6, 8; in the second session there were Senator Ellison D. Smith's S. 5050, and Denver S. Church's H.R. 14627 and Albert Johnson's H.R. 9999 and H.R. 10249 from Hayes, Hutchinson, *Legislative History*, 160.

64th Congress :

H.R. 9926 proposed by Church, H.R. 363 by Raker, a total of ten bills "to regulate the immigration and residence of aliens," ibid., 164.

And finally the most famous of all were the bills pushed through Congress by Senators Dillingham and Smith and Rep. Burnett which in their final shape became the Act of 1917.

59. "I have since I have been a Member of this House, in season and out of season, at every session, practically since I have been here, for the last nine years, advocated the exclusion of all the Asiatic races; and I have had a bill for that purpose before this House ever since I have been here." *Cong. Record*, 63rd Cong., 2nd sess., April 15, 1912, 2784.
60. Ibid., 2782.
61. Ibid., 62nd Cong., 3rd sess., January 17, 1913, 1689.
62. Ibid., 63rd Cong., 2nd sess., February 2 and 3, 1914; 3819, 2782, 2821.
63. Daniels, *Politics*, 70-71. "The ex-Senator Phelan of California has been reported to have said that the Japanese must become day-labourers or get out of California." Taraknath Das, in *Modern Review*, March 1924, 264.
64. Allen Drury, A Senate *Journal 1943-1945*, 103.

65. President Theodore Roosevelt's phrase, Higham, *Strangers*, 198 : "The most subtle anti-Asian propagandists among us are the highly placed British visitors (and) . . . the Anglo-Americans." Elizabeth S. Kite, "An American Criticism of "The Other Side of the Medal" : India's Freedom and World Opinion," *Modern Review*, February 1927, 170.
66. *Cong. Record*, 63rd Cong., 3rd sess., January 7, 1915, 1138.
67. *Report of the Immigration Commission*, vol. 5. *Dictionary of Races or Peoples*, 53.
68. *Cong. Record*, 62nd Cong., 2nd sess., April 15, 1912; 4781.
69. Ibid., April 17, 1912, 4915.
70. Ibid., August 26, 1912, 11887.
71. Ibid., 3rd sess., December 17, 1912, 803, 804.
72. Ibid., 805, 806.
73. Ibid., January 30, 1913, 2292.
74. Ibid., January 17, 1913, 1682.
75. Ibid., 63rd Cong., 3rd sess., Appendix, Extension of Remarks, Rep. John L. Burnett, January 15, 1915, 171. The reason offered for failure in the House was Senator Dillingham's, ibid., 64th Cong., 1 sess., August 17, 1916, 12770.
76. The Immigration Bureau's concern over the "revolutionary propaganda of Indians" in California was conveyed to the British Ambassador. It was alleged that the "primary purposes" of the Indian students were "to forment and foster a revolutionary movement in India," that several students are "notorious agitators" and are actively engaged in rifle and revolver practice in the hills of Berkeley." The letter identified by name several Indians who came to the country claiming to be students but "who either have no intention whatever of pursuing courses of study or pursue such courses only incident to their other purposes." The British Ambassador in Washington, Cecil Spring Rice to Sir E. Grey, February 17, 1914; Commissioner (of Immigration), San Francisco to Commissioner-General of Immigration, January 23, 1914, in Home-Political, December 1914, No. 3773-78, Part B, Indian students in the U.S.A.; Pamphlet on the Subject of Naturalization Laws and Regulations in the USA, National Archives of India. Dady Burjor reported to the Government of India that "a feeling prevails amongst them [the non- student Indian immigrants] that . . . their interest is absolutely neglected, and allowed to be trampled under foot by their own Government." As to the students most of them were infected with "seditious ideas." Some of them have become "out and out anarchists and political fanatics of the most aggravated type." The *Burjor Report*, Home-Political, November 1914, No. 77, Part B, National Archives of India, 16, 21.
77.

Cong. Record, 62nd Cong., 3rd sess., December 14, 1912, 672; 63rd Cong., 2nd sess., Raker's statement, February 2, 1914, 2783, 2786, Rep. Church's statement, ibid., 2823; for bills introduced, 63rd Cong., 1st sess., 225, April 7, 1913, Hutchinson *Legislative History*, 160.

78. The text of the Burnett bill, *Cong. Record*, 63rd Cong., 2nd sess., December 16, 1913, 999.
79. The clause proposing to exclude ineligibles; ibid., 63rd Cong., 3rd sess., December 10, 1914, 92; *New York Times*, 3, February 1914.
80. *Cong. Record*, 63rd Cong., 2nd sess., February 3, 1914, 2820.
81. Ibid., 2820-2821.
82. Ibid., 2820, 2825.
83. Ibid., 3rd sess., December 31, 1914, 803, 807, 805, 787-788.
84. Ibid., 868; the text of Section 3 which provides for exclusion of ineligibles; ibid., January 31, 1914, White House hearing; ibid., Extension of Remarks of Oscar Callaway of Texas, February 4, 1915, 359-364.
85. Hayes said, "The Hindu, who claims to be a Caucasian, shall be excluded .... He is the only man whose status will be changed by this bill." Ibid., 64th Cong., 1st sess., March 24, 1916, 4784; the text of the clause providing for Hindu exclusion, ibid., July 14, 1916, 11023.
86. Ibid., March 24, 1916, 4785; March 30, 1916, 5194. The 'emergency' Johnson mentioned was the same that Caminetti had told the House Immigration Committee about at the *Sudhindra Hearings* in February 1914, see fn. 36; he had brought up the railroad magnet James Hill's alleged scheme to import Indian Labor twice at the *Bhutia Hearing* in April, 161, 175-176.
87. *Cong. Record*, 64th Cong. 1st sess., July 14, 1916, 11023.
88. Senator Works, ibid., 11023-11024; Senator Smith, August 21, 1916, 12928; the barred zone provision agreed to by the Senate, 12926.
89. Poindexter debate, ibid., 2nd sess., December 13, 1916, 261-265. His amendment rejected, 265; Senator Smith's protest, 262 : Senator Reed's protest, February 5, 1917, 2618- 2621.
90. Text of Wilson's veto message, ibid., February 2, 1917, 2465; House vote, February 1, 1917, 2456; Senate override, February 5, 1917, 2629.
91. The texts of the three veto messages and of Secretary Nagel's advice to President Taft, ibid., February 2, 1917, 2451- 2452. Taft vetoed the bill "because of the literacy test." Hutchinson. *Legislative History*, 157; President Wilson's reasons for vetoing H.R. 6060 according to Senator Dillingham were "almost wholly" because of the literacy test, *Cong. Record*, 64th Cong., 2nd sess., August 17, 1916, 12770.
92. Ibid., 1st sess., 21, 1916, 12928.
93. Having read in the morning paper about Asian exclusion by specification of lines on a map, Senator Phelan wrote to Labor Secretary William B.

Wilson in May 1917 to be advised on this subject adding, "I desire in every possible way, without giving needless offense to our neighbors, to protect the Pacific coast and the country against the blight of oriental immigration." The Secretary in his reply assured the Senator that "the only purpose [of the amendment] is so to change the form, without modifying the effect, as to eliminate even the least possibility of having the language employed in the measure giving any offense to Japan or to any other foreign nation. Incidentally, in perfecting these amendments, I believe that a general improvement has been brought about. The principle amendment is made in that provision of section 3 of the act having the object of excluding from this country orientals . . . *other than* Chinese and Japanese." Ibid., December, 13, 1916, 253, emphasis added.]

94. *Sudhindra Hearings*, 105, on the next page he called them "long diplomatic negotiations," Caminetti's statement, ibid., 44; *New York Times*, 14 February 1914; inasmuch as the Gentlemen's Agreement permitted the entry of parents, wives and children, the exclusionists insisted that "as a substitute for an exclusion law it was totally inadequate and utterly failed its purpose," *American Federationist*, March 1927, 304.
95. Doubts expressed for instance by Rep. Frank W. Mondell (R-Wy) who said that the ineligibility clause in the bill was "an accurate statement, *barring for some difference of opinion as to Hindus*." *Cong. Record*, 63rd Cong., 2nd sess., February 3, 1914, 2824.
96. Sudhindra's estimate, *Modern Review*, May 1919, 522; the Barred Zone map is included in *Senate Hearing on S. 236*, April 1945, the excluded countries are named on page 30 in the course of Jagjit Singh's testimony. A part of British Indian Baluchistan and eastern part of Afghanistan are shown outside the Zone.
97. *Legislative History*, 167; *You Never Leave Brooklyn : The Autobiography of Emanuel Celler*, New York, 1953, 212; Sudhindra in *Modern Review*, June 1914, 624. He died a few weeks before the Luce-Celler bill was adopted.
98. For Lajpat Rai, Rathore, *Indian Nationalist Agitation*, 78 and his, *United States*, 475; for Tagore, *Modern Review*, June 1917, 663-664; Professor Benoy Kumar Sarkar, Indian author and philosopher characterized America's treatment of Asian immigrants as "so drastic, inhuman, discriminative and unjust that it bids fair to be the most acute disturber of the world's peace in the coming decades. It is America's ultimatum to the Orient," quoted from the *Asian Review*, Tokyo in *Indian News Service*, June 5-12, 1920.
99. Tagore, "East and West," *Orient*, New York, April-May, 1923, 21; Walter Charles Maket, "Some Aspects of the Development of American Opinion

on India 1918—1947," Dissertation, University of California. Ph.D. History, June 1957, 124, 125.

100. Threat of death by attrition, Warren H. Atherton's letter to J. J. Singh, *March 1945 Hearings*, 93; students' status following the Act of 1917 has been explained in Chapter I; immigration was just a trickle, see fn. 33; this Act provided Justice Sutherland an additional argument to declare Indians ineligible to American citizenship—"it is not likely that Congress would be willing to accept as citizens a class of persons whom it rejects as immigrants," he wrote in his ruling against Thind.

101. During the political agitation of 1907 in the Panjab a Panjabi language song had become the slogan of the campaign. Its refrain was :

Pagari sambhal O; Jatta
Pagari Sambhaal Oey !
Enaahn farangiaan ne
Lut laya maal Oey!
Watch your turban, O Jat
Watch your turban,
These alien looters
Have wrought spoliation.

Within half a dozen years the Panjabi Jat had again to 'watch' for his self-respect.

102. Reaction to Canadian policies, J.C. Ker, *Political Trouble*, 227-242; Sant Nihal Singh's articles mentioned in Footnote 8 above; Nand Singh Sihra and others' "Indians in Canada," *Indian Review*, Madras, June 1913, 453-456; *Sedition Committee Report*, 146.

103. For heart-searching questions and the ways how the community should face the situation created by the opponents see Sant Nihal Singh's articles in Footnote 8 and other opinions expressed in the *Modern Review*, January 1911, 54, 55, 60, 61; February, 206; August, 210, 211; ibid., November 1912, 583, 584, and the *Open Court*, 1913, 623. Participants in the debate were intellectuals and students. These views are examined in Chapter IV.

104. Lajpat Rai suggested in 1916 that "it would be a good thing if some way could be found to let them send for womenfolk." *The United States of America*, 469; Taraknath had told the British people what rights and facilities Indians wanted in Canada, namely, same rights of immigration as European races; equal rights to what the Canadians enjoy in India; family unification and right of students, preachers and merchants to travel and reside on same terms as people of an independent nation: An Open Letter to the British Public by the Hindusthanees of North America, Home Political, October 1814 No. 60, Part-Deposit, National Archives of India, 2. Sudhindra Bose wrote his doctoral dissertation on British rule in India in the years when Indians were being excluded from Canada and the United States. His suggestions concerning Indian emigration to the British

colonies included right of free entry on the same terms as non-Indians, freedom to trade and to choose their residence, *Hindusthanee Student*, December 1916, 13.

105. The principle of restricted immigration had been conceded by Sudhindra Bose, *Sudhindra Hearings*, 52, by Bhutia, through a literacy test, *Bhutia Hearings*, 166 and by Ramchandra in his letters to the *New York Times* of 13 August and 9 September 1916; the Gadarites' regard for the United States : "Curiously, even though a major factor which contributed to the founding of the Ghadar movement in USA was the oppression and discrimination of Indian immigrants, yet there was hardly any reference made to that problem in *Ghadar* weekly. Har Dayal and Ramchandra did not avoid any criticism of American people or the U.S. authorities on that count, but also frequently acclaimed the support Americans gave to the cause of India's freedom." Harish K. Puri, *Ghadar Movement: Ideology, Organization and Strategy*. Amritsar, 1983, 110; ". . . these immigrants who came under the influence of the teachings of Ghadar, never thought of condemning America for their oppressions. If they were unprotected against white labor hooligans, the reason lay in the complete indifference of British consuls in the USA towards their requests and complaints. The Americans on the other hand, were regarded as the well wishers of Indians." Ibid., 118.

106. The community leaders recognized students as a national asset. Sudhindra Bose suggested three ways to attain the goal of a better understanding of the Orient by the Occident. The third way was: to arrive at an understanding with the Immigration Bureau of Washington to let students enter America unmolested, *Hindusthanee Student*, January 1916, 8. Students were considered a valuable revolutionary material, B.K.Roy, "Currents of Thought in the Orient," *Open Court*, 1913, 765-767; the coming of Indian students to America fosters "the revolutionary spirit" in India, Herman Scheffauer, "The Tide of Turbans," *Forum*, June 1910, 618; Tishi Bhutia's statement of Bhutia Hearings, 164, to use students to serve the nationalist purpose.

107. See fn. 131.

108. *Sudhindra Hearings*, 36-37; see fns. 39 and 40 above for Dr. Bose's weakness in argument; and instance of Britain's underhand encouragement—The "Calcutta Policeman," William C. Hopkinson. "worked with immigration officials and exclusionist politicians in support of legislation in the United States excluding East Indians." Joan M. Jensen, "The 'Hindu Conspiracy' : A Reassessment." *Pacific Historical Review*, vol. 48 (1979), 72.

109. His name and address as they appear in the printed hearings were : "Mr. Tishi Bhutia Kyagh Hla, of Darjeeling, India, and Brooklyn, N.Y." He told the Committee his article on Indians in South Africa would be

published in *Atlantic Monthly* for June. Bhutia Hearings, 154, A search in the *Atlantic Monthly* volumes failed to locate Bhutia's article.

110. Previous hearings on Asiastic exclusion legislation seem to have been held in executive sessions, *Cong. Records*, 63rd Cong., 2 sess., February 2, 1914, 2785, Congressman Nolan's statement.

111. Burnett's initial refusal mentioned by Dr. Bose, "The chairman of the committee in charge of the bill was at first reluctant to give us a hearing; but when due pressure was brought to bear upon him he yielded." His "Exclusion of the Indians from America," *Modern Review*, June 1914, 625. Har Dayal too may have desired to testify at a hearing, "In February, Spring-Rice reported that Dayal . . . was at the moment in Washington to plead the cause of Hindu immigrants and other Asiatics threatened with exclusion from the United States." Don K. Dignan, "The Hindu Conspiracy in Anglo-American Relations During World War I," *Pacific Historical Review*, February 1971, 60; and an unsolicited and favorable witness appeared at the February 1914 hearing—Mrs. R.F. Patterson, wife of a former American consul general at Calcutta, *Sudhindra Hearings*, 21-36.

112. *Sudhindra Hearings*, 3, 4, *Bhutia Hearings*, 159. Bose and Bishen Singh claimed to be a "delegation" sent by the H.A.A. and the Khalsa Diwan Society respectively to testify before the Committee. They also met the British Ambassador who denied their representative character. In a letter to the Foreign Secretary he said, "They did not form a deputation representative of the Indian colony in this country. The Sikh was dispatched at the expense of a Sikh employer of labour in California, who was anxious to increase the number of his labourers, and the Hindu came on his own account." Cecil Spring Rice to Sir Edward Grey, February 16, 1914, Home-Political, December 1914, No. 377- 378, Part B. Indian Students in USA, Pamphlets on the subject of Naturalization Laws and Regulations in the USA, National Archives of India.

113. Manahan had studied Hath Yoga, *Sudhindra Hearings*, 33; he helped the Indian side of the debate at all the hearings; Gardner believed few Indians were coming, *Cong. Record*, 63rd Cong., 2nd sess., February 2, 1914, 2784, February 3, 2822; both he and Moore made their views clear at the *Bhutia Hearings*, 145-147; Sabath's views on Indian exclusion, *Cong. Record*, ibid., 2822; 64th Cong., 2nd sess., February 1, 1917, 2455; at one Hindu hearing he argued for a stronger exclusion bill than had been proposed, *Sudhindra Hearings*, 87.

114. Unwilling to assimilate Indians, *Hearings of December 6, 1913*, 8, *Sudhindra Hearings*, 14, 15, 85; refusal of service in restaurants, ibid., 77; sale of city lots resented, ibid., 75; Rep. Sabath wanted to know whether

the person who sold city lots to a Hindu was "still alive ?"; ineligible to citizenship, ibid., 12-13; their dress not acceptable, Hearing of December 6, 1913, 8; *Sudhindra Hearings*, 77, 79; their way of life, ibid., 45, 51, 76, 79, 84; carriers of diseases, ibid., 48, 54, 65-73; exaggerated figures, ibid., 74, 90, 91, 98; *Bhutia Hearings*, 146, 177; threat of force :

Mr. Raker. I would like to ask Mr. Johnson a question. What is your estimate of the number of Hindus in Washington?

Mr. Johnson. I cannot say. They move around a great deal. In our state we have kept them on the move.

Mr. Raker. You keep them moving ?

Mr. Johnson. Yes, sir, I think if we had not had local agitation commencing four or five years ago that the very large number that worked their way down to California would have remained in our State." *Sudhindra Hearing*, 105.

115. Raker's claim, *Bhutia Hearing*, 164, other references to the Indians' anti-British activities, 170, 172, 182; Har Dayal's speech, 167-168. This is the speech which according to Harish Puri he delivered while "addressing the luncheon gathering on the eve of launching of *Ghadar* weekly." *Ghadar Movement*, 113. A view that a majority of Americans favored continuation of British rule over India, *Modern Review*, December 1924, 723.

116. What Bhutia told the Committee—that the ship was going to Canada "to test the legality of their constitution"—may have in fact been a free rendering of the Panjabi proverb which the organizers of the expedition must have had in their minds, namely: Jhuthe de ghar tak pujjo-literally, "follow the liar right to his house"; the Indian passengers were trying to put Canada's false professions to the test, to force the "liar" to reveal his real intentions. Disavowal to anarchism, *Bhutia Hearings*, 164, 167, in defence of Har Dayal, ibid., 171, 172; the ship not coming to USA, Ibid., 153, 181.

117. Sundhindra Bose, "Exclusion of Indians from America," *Modern Review*, June 1914, 627, 628. In refusing to be drawn to the Indians side, the British Ambassador had in fact told Sudhindra basically what he told London : "I do not think that foreign official interference in this matter would be favorably received as there is a strong feeling in Congress that this is a question which concerns the United States in the first instance and not the Governments whose subjects are anxious to come here." Cecil Spring Rice to Sir Edward Grey, February 15, 1914. Home-Political, December 1914, No. 377-378, Part B, Indian Students in the USA, Pamphlet on Naturalization Laws and Regulations, National Archives in India.

118. Students' agitation against the exclusion bills, *The Hindusthanee Student*, April-July 1914, 50, September 1915, 11, March 1916, 24, April 1916, 6

October 1916. 16. November 1916, 22. January 1917, 1, 3, 4, 5, 10, 11, 17, 22, March-April 1917, 13, January-February 1918, 21; Dr. Bose's articles, *Modern Review*, June 1914 May 1919, June 1923, *Hindusthanee Student*, April-July 1914, 42-44; his dire forecast as to the future of the British Empire, *Sudhindra Hearings*, 19, this could have been a threat delivered by the Gadarites through him. Bishen Singh who came for the hearing from California may have apprised the professor of the temper of the Sikhs. There is a coincidence which may seem to confirm the probability—the February 1914 issue of the *Gadar* was supplemented by a leaflet entitled "Declaration of War." One of the reasons for declaring war on Britain was its responsibility for the troubles Indians were facing in the British colonies and they , the British "now wish to ask the American Government to prohibit Indians from coming to America"—J.C. Ker, *Political Trouble*, 126. In this Declaration, Indians living in America had been invited to attend a meeting to be held at Stockton on February 15. The hearing took place on the 13th. The date for the meeting may have been fixed in consultation with Bishen Singh and Bose but we need more evidence to connect them with what was happening within the Gadar party or to make Dr. Bose one of the instigators of the Gadar. Sudhindra's threat may not have been inspired by the Gadarites of 1914 but it bears a striking resemblance to what Taraknath Das had written six years earlier in the first issue of his *Free Hindusthan* under the caption "Our National Life at Stake". It was a strong condemnation of British policy of excluding Indians from British colonies concluding with a threat of "an upheaval which will rend the Empire into pieces." quoted in Harish Puri, *Ghadar Movement*, 42; the Indians' petition was received in the Senate on August 2, 1916, *Cong. Record*, 64th Cong., 1st sess., 12945; Bose's letters to Ambassadors of China and Japan, his article in *Modern Review*, May 1919, 523-524. Ramchandra's letters to the press, San Francisco *Examiner*, 5 and 6 October 1916, *New York Times*, 8 July 1916, 13 August 1916, 14 September 1916; a collective telegram sent to the U.S. Secretary of State on May 1, 1916, *New York Sun*, a protest to San Francisco *Examiner* on 26 June 1916, and a telegram on August 12, 1916. In 1914 the Theosophist Mrs. Annie Besant had mentioned the possibility of Indian retaliation, *New York Times*, 21 June 1914, and an Indian writer had mentioned that Indians were bitter at the treatment they receive in the British colonies, ibid., October 30, 1915; Chamanlal, "Arsenal of Liberty' Is on Trial," *Modern Review*, June 1941, published much of the information preserved by Ramchandra's daughter.

119. Even in the judgment of a hostile writer, "the Ghadar movement in the Punjab possessed at the outset *some fine material* so far as men were concerned." Ker, *Political Trouble*, 372, emphasis added.

120. Common friends included Prof. Teja Singh, Kartar Singh Sarabha (the young man of 20 destined to become a part of the Gadar legend), and Gobind Behari Lal, *A Capsule of the Gadar Movement,* 3, 4; Emily C. Brown, *Har Dayal: Hindu Revolutionary and Rationalist,* Tucson,Arizona, 85, 138: the meeting of minds is explained by Harish Puri, "When Har Dayal came in their midst, his encounters with them aroused in him visions of organizing a mass revolutionary movement. It transformed him as much as it did his audience, giving a new sense of destiny to the hopeless Indian farmers and labourers in North America," *Ghadar Movement,* 53; Har Dayal became more to them than just a leader-"the cry was raised at Berkeley in 1914-Har Dayal is now our guru." Home-Political, 1919, No. 21, Deposit; Proposal to place Sir Frank Popham Young in charge of an Indian bureau on the West Coast of America. National Archives of India, 5; while the Sikhs may have hailed him as a guru, the students thought he was India's Sun Yet Sen, "The man was here now in the person of Har Dayal," some students told the U.S. Immigration authorities, *Burjor Report*, 11.
121. The *Gadar* bulletin seems to have been a large-scale affair—one million copies a week, according to Deol, *Role of the Ghadar Party*, 73 and its circulation was widespread, ibid., and Josh, *S.S.Bhakna*, 37.
122. Taraknath Das, Address August 1946, 8; the Gadar Party "turned the Komagata Maru affair into a Gadar affair." G.B. Lal, *Capsule*, 7; in 1914, Taraknath Das and six associates had in "An open letter to the British public by the Hindusthanees of North America" which had been posted to George V of England had complained that the ship's passengers "were unjustly deported from Canada; nay they were driven out of Canadian water by the naval forces of Great Britain as if they belonged to a hostile power." Home-Political, October 1914, No. 60, Part- Deposit open letter to the British public sent by Taraknath Das, National Archives of India. 2.
123. Harish Puri, *Ghadar Movement*, 82.
124. Ibid., 91-92.
125. Joan M. Jensen. "The Hindu Conspiracy'; A Reassessment," *Pacific Historical Review*, 1979, 68-87, 79.
126. Ibid., 80, 67.
127. Ibid., 70, 67; Gobind Behari Lal calls it "The Hindu-German Conspiracy against British rule in India, " *Capsule*, 10; in 1926 a high U.S. official referred to it as "The trial which had been designated the famous Hindu *revolution* case," *Senate Hearings, December 1926*, 5, emphasis added.
128. Joan M. Jensen, Ibid., 68, 69, 67, 82, 81.
129. Ibid., 82, *Young India*, May 1918, 24.
130.

L.P. Mathur, *Indian Revolutionary Movement in the USA*, Delhi, 1970, Appendix I, 166.

131. Even among the immigrants the Gadar ideology of violence was criticised and association with the Gadarites was often avoided. Rathore, *Indian Nationalist Agitation*, 67, Hardikar, *Lajpat Rai in America*, 45, *Young India*, New York January 1918, 22; March 1918, 8, 9; December 1918, 22- 23; September 1919, 214-215; for Har Dayal's views on Lajpat Rai's methods, L.P. Mathur, *Indian Revolutionary Movement*, 42 Lajpat Rai's comment on some Gadar leaders. Harish Puri, *Gadar Movement* 99 (on Ramchandra), 102 (on "Bengalees"), 108, (on Har Dayal), 109; Rabindranath Tagore's views on Gadar methods, Kalyan Kumar Banerjee, "Rabindranath Tagore and the San Francisco Trial," *Modern Review*, July 1964, 27-28; for a historian's view of the ideological controversy, R.C. Majumdar (ed.), *Struggle for Freedom*, 230-231; "challenge of terrorism to constitutional politics was formidable" Judith M. Brown, *Gandhi and Civil Disobedience : The Mahatma in Indian Politics 1928-34* (Cambridge, 1977), 71. For Gandhi's opposition to and embarrassment at the presence of the terrorists and their sympathisers within Congress and in Indian politics generally, Brown, ibid., 19, 35, and R.C. Majumdar, (ed.); ibid., 554. Dhan Gopal Murkerji was most probably drawing Har Dayal's portrait : "Take the typical Indian revolutionist. Many people remember him in San Francisco . . . . He devised ingenious plans to blow up garrisons of English soldiers as a disinfectant and a preventive of political hells, and once in a while he would grow lyrical about the joy of belonging to a free people. He imagined very suave massacres, and delicate assassinations." *Caste and Outcast*, 253; for a portrait by an unquestioning admirer; Dharmavira, *Lala Har Dayal and Revolutionary Movements of His Times*, New Delhi, 1970; for Har Dayal's wayward intellectualism, Emily C. Brown, *Har Dayal*, XI, 7, 103, 104 : "Dayal was impulsive and erratic," Joan M. Jensen, *Passage from India*, New Haven, 1988, 186.

132. Hardly any two estimates of the number of peoples sentenced to death or imprisonment or interned without trial agree. Below are a few figures : 189 interned in jail, 704 "restricted to their villages," *Sedition Committee Report*, 155; Interned in jail, 232, restricted to their villages, 1625, Ker, *Political Trouble*, 364. After trials, 42 sentenced to death, 200 to long terms of imprisonment, 18 belonging to 23 cavalry court martialed; 200 men of the 130th Baluchis were punished, 5th Infantry at Singapore killed their officers. Reinforcements wrecked their vengeance, Harish Puri, *Gadar Movement*, 88, 94; after trials 31 hanged, "large number" of the 7th Regiment in Delhi put to death, several others killed, Dharamavira, *Har Dayal*, 218, 219; 12 tribunals were set up to try the Gadarites, 135

convicted, 38 executed, 12 were executed in one Sikh Regiment, 8000 had returned to India from abroad during the war, Gobind Behari Lal, *Capsule*, 9; 400 hanged "by the British Government" during 1915 and 1916, and 5000 sent to various terms of imprisonment. *The Independent Hindustan*, San Francisco, November 1920; according to Dr. Deol the figures were : hanged 47, transportation for life 118, lesser jail sentences 46, executed after court martial 59, killed by police firing 2. "Lesser punishment" means up to 21 years; most often jait sentences included confiscation of property. Deol, "The Role of the Ghadar Party, Appendixes A to L, 203-222.

133. One of the contingents in the Azad Hind Fauj (Indian National Army) raised by Subhash Chandra Bose to collaborate with the Japanese forces was the Rani of Jhansi Regiment composed of women, under the command of Mrs. Lakshmi Swaminathan. She was also included in the provisional government of Free India as one of the colleagues of Subhash Chandra Bose. At the end of the war India received her as a heroine. Her mother Mrs. Ammu Swaminathan, member of the Madras Legislative Assembly, was after the war elected to the Central Legislative Assembly. On a visit to the United States she had met Jagjit Singh, President of the India League. In a letter to her in 1946 he asked her about Lakshmi. "Has your famous daughter returned to India as yet ? I would love to meet her. I think she should come to the United States to rest up after her harrowing experiences." Jagjit Singh to Mrs. Ammu Swaminathan, February 14, 1946, India League of America Papers, Sapru House, New Delhi. Collaboration with Britain's enemy had become an insignia of honor, a road to fame.

134. "In all these projects the Germans were in command and the Ghadar men were treated as enthusiastic *errand boys* to be financed, advised and ordered about." Harish Puri, ibid., emphasis added.

135. Ramlal B. Bajpai to "Dear Sardarji" October [sic] 27, 1942. Last year on March 13 in another letter to "Dear Sardarji" he had warned, "This is a second chance [sic] we have and failing that now we will have to wait till next bloody war which we may not live to see . . . . We will have to make big noise all over the country." I.L.A. Papers.

136. Y[G] obind Behari Lal, [Sic.] "Why the Hindus Detest the Huns ?" and unidentified newspaper clipping dated February 27, 1919 in Syud Hussain Papers in Nehru Memorial Museum and Library, New Delhi; Lajpat Rai's announcement, *Young India*, New York, January 1918, 4.

137. Shridharani, *My India, My America*, 507; R.C. Majumdar (ed.), *Struggle for Freedom*, 230, 541; Taraknath Das, Address, August 1946, 8.

138. The Director of Criminal Intelligence, Government of India at the time, C.R. Cleveland seems to have been a man of cool judgment and shrewd

insight. He agreed that the Sikhs had "real grievances" against American authorities. He estimated that the Sikhs in the Pacific coast areas had acquired "rabid and fanatical hostility to British rule" as the result of "the lies of the revolutionists and political agitators and by the harsh language and treatment of the anti- Indian white men." He suggested that the Indian government's endeavor should be "to prevent unnecessary complications and embitterments." In his judgement "hardships are inevitable for the Indian labourers, but there is really no necessity for the Sikh immigrant *to acquire fanatical hostility to the British Government as well as a small fortune*." Burjor Report, Notes, Political-B, November 1914, No. 77, 2, emphasis added. But it seems South Africa and Canada had greater clout in London and "consequently, the Sikh ex-soldiers and policemen swung violently away from the loyalty they had previously professed to the crown." Hugh Tinker, *Separate and Unequal*, 29. Taraknath Das asked the British public at the outbreak of the War—"What will be the internal situation in British India, if the loyal Sikhs who saved the British Empire in India in 1857 and who are now so much ill-treated in the British Colonies especially in Canada . . . refuse to shoot down their own countrymen for the interests of their overlords ?" Home-Political, October 1914, No. 60, Part-Deposit, An open letter to the British public by Taraknath Das, National Archives of India, 1. What Cleveland considered "the lies of the revolutionists" consisted of the Gadar propaganda items like this—"You go and fight for the sake of the whites. You always attack other countries. Why do you not take your own country into your charge? . . . Have you vowed to live as the slaves of the English ? Are your lives worth only nine rupees each ?" quoted from F.C. Isemonger and J. Slattery, An Account of the Ghadar Conspiracy 1913-1915, 93, in Deol, *Role of the Ghadar Party*, 133, fn. 39. "The conversion of many of the Sikhs—who had "traditionally" been so "loyal to the British"—into Nationalists (Gadarites) was Har Dayal's achievement." Gobind Behari Lal, *Capsule*, 1. Jagjit Singh, President of the India League of America in the course of a public speech indirectly recognized the significance of the First World War years in the politics of the Sikh community : "Yes. I would agree," he said, "that up to the year 1920 , the Sikhs were very backward politically . . . and did not take much of a part in the political life of India." Speech delivered at the New York City Town Hall meeting, September 29, 1942, I.L.A. Papers.

3

CITIZENSHIP DENIED

The racial discrimination in our naturalization law is entirely out of harmony with the general tenor of our law as a whole . . . . Legal equality of all permanent residents regardless of race is so throughgoingly accepted as sound policy in general that the exception made in naturalization is thrown on the defensive. It cannot be justified and can hardly be explained.

D. O. McGOVNEY, March 1923

Aspiration for American citizenship represented an attempt by Indian immigrants to carry their American dream a step further, to escape the discriminatory laws regarding landholding and the practice of certain professions and to receive a more humane treatment from the general public. It may also have been a rebuttal to the allegation of being birds of the passage. Revolutionaries like Taraknath Das, for whom the bridges back home had been burnt, could get a new country only by naturalization. Their concern is understandable. Becoming a citizen was like being reborn in America, another coming of age, a new adulthood. As Chief Justice Earl Warren once wrote, "citizenship is man's basic right for it is nothing less than the right to have rights." Eligibility to citizenship would remove from them an insult based on race and color and also break down the wall of isolation between them and the American people.[1]

The first Indians to obtain citizenship by naturalization were those living in the South. Abdul Hamid and Ballal Hussain received their certificates on the same day in March 1908, from a Federal District

Judge in New Orleans.[2] A year later Hamid's friend, Abba Dolla, was naturalized by the District Judge of Savannah, Georgia, over the objection of the United States Attorney. The judge held that the petitioner, though a native of India, was a white person within the meaning of the naturalization laws. The Circuit Court of Appeals sustained the ruling. The city of Savannah too considered him a white man to have sold him a lot in the white cemetery, "other cemeteries being provided for colored people."[3]

It appears that official opposition to the grant of naturalization to immigrants from India was neither spontaneous nor instant. The two New Orleans petitioners seem to have been naturalized without any official opposition. In the West also the Exclusion League complained that Indians "received sympathy" from a District Attorney in Washington State in their efforts to obtain naturalization.[4]

Instructions to oppose Indians' petition were probably issued sometime in 1908 after Abdul Hamid and Ballal Hussain had been naturalized, but before any Indian had received naturalization on the West coast. Charles J. Bonaparte, U.S. Attorney General, informed all U.S. Attorneys that Indians were not "white persons" according to the law. Richard K. Campbell, Chief of the Division of Naturalization, in a letter to the Asiatic Exclusion League explained that although the color of the Indian was in itself immaterial, it is the "mark, however, of a people who are . . . so diverse from white people or Occidentals as to make it no less a risk to admit them to citizenship" than it is to admit the Chinese and the Japanese. Official instructions with legal briefs seem to have reached the district attorneys in the course of the year 1908.[5]

The anti-Indian instructions were the result of a combination of bureaucratic ineptitude, failure of scholarly understanding and the victory of exclusionist philosophy within the Bureau of Immigration and Naturalization. The Bureau blundered into putting Indians and Mongoloids into one category called the 'Mongolic' grand division.

Several Indians became American citizens in spite of this opposition. Among them were many who were prominently active in the life of the community. The trinity of Taraknath Das, Sudhindra Bose and Profulla Mukherjee will appear in these pages as activists of decisive significance at almost every turn in the community history for forty years.. Rajani Kant Das gave us an authentic eyewitness account of the life and work of Indian immigrants on the West coast down to the early 1920s. Ram Nath Puri, Dhirendra Kumar Sarkar, and of course, Taraknath Das was convicted for their Gadar activities. Sant Ram Mandal was one of the devoted members of the India League of America. Sakharam Ganesh Pandit, Bhagat Singh Thind, Shankar Laxman Gokhale, and Taraknath Das fought in the courts the community's battle for legal eouality.

Of the immigrants who sought citizenship under the naturalization law, only fifty-nine had been fortunate enough to receive it.[6] The law officers of the Federal Government opposed their petitions, but the courts were not always hostile. In 1923, however, the executive and judiciary united in their opinion that by the language of the law Indians were ineligible to the high privilege. This historic meeting of minds, like the earlier rift, was made possible by the capriciousness of the two instruments of human legislation—language and the intended purpose of the law. Most of the judges whose rulings we shall examine complained of the absence of exactitude in the language and needed help in arriving at its meaning.[7]

A law is expected to be of consistent validity until amended but the world very often runs ahead of the law, changing the meaning of old words and the content of old situations. Worst happens when a philosophy of life and the plan for the future population of a new nation are sought to be included in one word—"white," and that word left in the law for over 175 years without defining what it precisely means.

During the last decades of the persistence of this word as the decisive part of the American naturalization law, scholars, judges, and demagogues attempted to get inside the mind of the original framers or learn of its original meaning. The hard task assumed by a great contemporary of these explorers was easier by comparison. Charles Beard had attempted to enter only the pocketbooks of the Founding Fathers. Trying to enter the mind is something else. Both efforts were investigating Federalist institutions. Both were motivated by a desire to understand the past in order to be able to face the present. But while Beard pulled down the elevated and worshipped Constitution to serve the more mundane needs of the slum-dweller and the sweated mother, the Justices in the Ozawa and the Thind cases and the demagogues who applauded their rulings, raised the word "white" to sanctified heights beyond the reach of Asian races.[8]

The first Congress under the Constitution adopted the first United States law of naturalization in 1790 by which "free white persons" were granted the statutory privilege to receive citizenship by naturalization. In 1870 this privilege was extended to "Aliens of African nativity and to persons of African descent."[9] Charles Sumner's unsuccessful attempt to secure the elimination of the phrase "free white person" from the naturalization law has already been mentioned. In 1882 the Chinese were by law expressly debarred from the privilege of naturalization. Supreme Court rulings debarred the Japanese in 1922 and Hindus in 1923. Other races or nationalities excluded by judicial rulings were the Koreans, Afghans, Filipinos, Burmese, Hawaiians, and American Indians.[10] There was a "conflict among cases" as to Parsees, Hindus, Arabs, and Mexicans.[11] On the other hand Amernians and Syrians were adjudged eligible to naturalization as "free white persons."[12] The Nationality Act of October 14, 1940 extended the privilege of naturalization to "descendants of races indigenous to the Western Hemisphere."[13] The Americans and the races of North and South America had thus been granted the privilege of naturalization not by amending the original phrase "free white persons" but by adding them to the original law in 1870 and 1940, respectively.

The debate over the eligibility of Hindus to be included among "free white persons" went on for about fifteen years before it was terminated in 1923 by the Supreme Court's verdict against them and in favour of the Bureau of Naturalization. The relevant arguments for and against first emerged prominently when four Armenian Christians petitioned the Massachusetts Circuit Court for naturalization. The judge admitted them to citizenship in December 1909, against the Assistant U.S. Attorney's arguments that he refuted in a scholarly opinion. This opinion, together with the refutation of the Thind ruling of 1923 co-authored by Chase and Pandit in 1926, present a strong case against the major arguments of those who opposed the naturalization of Hindus.

The government's contention was that the words "white persons" meant Europeans and persons of European descent and that they also expressed briefly the "ideals, standards and aspirations of the people of Europe," hence the petitioners must be "European by race." The Judge replied there is no such unmixed "European race."

The Government further contented that the petitioners belonged to "Asiatic or yellow race," but, according to the judge, "No authority to support this theory (that there is an Asiatic race) is cited by reference to history, to ethnological theory . . . or to physical appearance." The court also refused to accept the "average man in the street" test which Justice Sutherland would use as one of his basic arguments against Thind, thirteen years later. He went on:

> To its classification by European and Asiatic races the United States makes an extraordinary exception, viz., the Hebrews . . . Their origin is Asiatic. Yet the United States admits that they do not belong to the "Asiatic or yellow race" and that they should be admitted to citizenship . . . . Again, if Hindoos are to be excluded from naturalization as contended by the United States, because many Englishmen treat them with contempt and call them "niggers," a like argument applies to those who have suffered most cruelly among all men on the earth from European hatred and contempt.[14]

As for the "ideals, standards and aspirations" suggested by the Government attorney, the Judge insisted that the qualifications were there but one had to bend a little to see them. "A reasonable modesty may well remind Europeans," he wrote, "that the origin of their letters was in Phoenicia, the origin of much of their art in Egypt, . . . and that the Christian religion . . . was born in Palestine." On the authority of conclusions reached by fourteen scholars "taken at random" he decided that race "is not an easy working test of 'white' color as required by section 2169." He also found out that one of these scholars, Cuvier, "expressly included Armenians, as well as Hindoos, in the Caucasian race, as distinguished from the Mongolian."[15]

On the strength of over two dozen illustrations of the usage of the word "white" by the Colonies and the United States in their official documents such as statutes and census reports, he concluded that it was a "catch-all word" to designate persons not otherwise expressly classified. Among the latter were Africans, Indians, Chinese, and Japanese. In the census of 1790, the year when the first naturalization law was enacted "everybody but a negro [sic] or an American Indian was classed as a white person."

The Judge discovered that in the records of his own court "early instances have been found where not only western Asiatics, but even Chinese were admitted to naturalization" and further that Armenians, as well as Syrians and Turks, have been freely naturalized in this court until now, although the statutes in this respect have stood substantially unchanged since the First Congress."

Bhicaji Franyi Balsara, a Parsi from Bombay, was a merchant in New York City. In 1909 he petitioned for naturalization before the Circuit Judge. Although impressed by the "high character and exceptional intelligence" of the petitioner, the Judge could not arrive at a definite interpretation of the phrase "free white person." "It seems desirable," he ruled, "that some authoritative interpretation of this statute should be secured." By a kind of mutually agreed judgment, he admitted Balsara to citizenship, the Government attorney who had opposed the petition, expressed readiness to appeal so that a higher court may give the desired authoritative interpretation.[16]

The Circuit Court of Appeals ruled in Balsara's favor holding that "Parsees do belong to the white race," implying thereby that the Parsees were different from Hindus, whose eligibility was left in doubt.

Akhay Kumar Mozumdar was a Hindu from Bengal. His petition for naturalization filed in July 1912 came up for a final hearing on May 3, 1913 before the District Judge at Spokane, Washington. The Judge examined the petitioner, studied his testimony which had been "well summarized by counsel," Sakharam Ganesh Pandit, and himself studied historian Le Bon's views on the Hindu caste system. He was convinced that the applicant as a high-caste Hindu belonged to the Caucasian race. He further ruled that "it is now settled, by the great weight of authority, at least, that it was the intention of the Congress of 1790 to confer the privilege of naturalization upon members of the Caucasian race only." In support he cited nine cases including those of Halladjian and Balsara. Akhay Kumar was admitted to citizenship on June 30, 1913. Incidentally this was S.G. Pandit's first victory in a naturalization case. The verdict upset the West coast exclusionists.[17]

Faras Shahid, 50, was a Syrian Christian who had lived in the United States for about eleven years. In June 1913 his petition for naturalization was rejected by the District Judge, Eastern District, South Carolina on his "personal disqualifications." Still the Judge proceeded to discuss the varying interpretations of the Acts of 1790 and 1870. He considered the statute "most uncertain, ambiguous and difficult both of construction and application."[18] Most of his conclusions were against admitting non-Europeans to American citizenship. His interpretation would "exclude persons coming from the very cradle of the Jewish and Christian religions." The Judge, however, brushed aside such arguments as of the "*emotional ad captandum* order, that have no place in the judicial interpretation of a statute."

Rulings such as these gave substance to the taunt that even Christ would not be welcome in America."[19]

On December 11, 1917, Sadar Bhagwab Singh's application for rehearing of his petition for naturalization was refused and his petition denied by the District Judge of Philadelphia. This case is interesting as much for the judge's acute observations as for his lack of knowledge of the events around him and his erroneous understanding of the relevant cases he relied upon in his ruling.

The Judge believed that the term "white persons" "made no pretense to be a term of science, and was not chosen with a view to scientific definiteness or accuracy of expression. It was at all events the nearest approach to definiteness of expression among all the words which were at the command of the lawmaker."[20]

He admitted that in course of time other races were accommodated within the purview of the phrase by force of history. The French were included because of "gratitude" and "common heritage," the Spaniards, the Portuguese, the Italians "by the desire to be consistent." The meaning of the phrase expanded further by the "immigration of persons from Southern and Southeastern Europe." Clearly it was not the law but a willingness to expand the law that permitted the naturalization of these people. But he refused to expand the law for this Hindu petitioner.

The last paragraph of the ruling raised doubts about the extent of his knowledge of even those cases on which he claimed to have based his ruling. We quote in part : "The conclusion reached is we think in accord with the weight of authority as disclosed in the adjudged cases, among which are :

"----Halladjian ---Balsara---Mozumdar---."

The learned Judge was clearly ruling contrary to what he had recognized as "weight of authority". Two years later, another judge pointed out this contradiction saying that the ruling "does not seem to be supported in my judgement, by the controlling authorities, and its reasoning is to me inconclusive."[21]

Mohan Singh's petition for naturalization came up for a hearing on March 24, 1919 before the District Judge sitting in Los Angeles. He was represented by Sakharam Ganesh Pandit, of Los Angeles, himself a naturalized Hindu. The Bureau of Naturalization opposed the petition with the arguments it had presented against Balsara in the

Circuit Court of Appeals where it had lost, and against Bhagwab Singh in Philadelphia where it had won. The judge agreed with Pandit's arguments and granted Mohan Singh's petition. He ruled that "there is nothing that I can discover to indicate anywhere that either the Colonies originally or the United States Government later when the federal statute was first passed, had in mind the exclusion from citizenship of any other persons than those referred to, to wit negroes [sic], Indians and unfree whites." As to the argument that the Congress intended by the words "free white person" to confer the privilege of naturalization upon "members of the white or Caucasian race only," the Judge called it "reasonable and just."

His next step was to recognize the Hindus as belonging to the Aryan race and the Aryan race as the "branch or stock of the so-called Caucasian or white race." He referred the reader to the Immigration Commission Report in support of this contention. Indeed listening to the argument of the Counsel, he reached the conviction that *"Caucasians" are "white," whether they live under the tropic sun, and therefore have a very dark skin, or abide in northern climes and possess a light one. The possession of a "common racial stamp" is the basis of classifications."*

He saw justice in the petitioner's cause also from another angle. It seemed to him a "travesty on justice that a refined and enlightened high-caste Hindu should be denied admission on the ground that his skin is dark... (while) a Hottentot should be admitted merely because he is 'of African nativity.' "

By claiming to be an Aryan, a Caucasian, a high-caste person of pure ancient blood, the petitioner was in fact decorating himself with anthropological plumes to prove that he was the person the legislators of 1790 had meant to naturalize. He was attempting to use the caste system of the East to dazzle his way into the caste system of the West.

Mohan Singh's was the last case in which the decision turned on a lower court's interpretation of the word "white". The Supreme Court decision in the *Thind* case less than two years later shifted the judicial test from the legislation of 1790 to the Sutherland ruling of 1923.

Two months before the Supreme Court heard arguments in the Thind case, Justice Sutherland, this time also speaking on behalf of the whole Court, had held that a person of the Japanese race born in Japan was ineligible to citizenship under the naturalization laws.[22] There were certain similarities in the *Ozawa* and the *Thind* cases. Both petitioners were highly educated scholars; both cases reached the Supreme Court on questions certified by a Circuit Court of Appeals; and Sutherland was the Supreme Court's spokesman both times, and he rejected both petitions. The ruling in each case was decisive for several decades; each ruling turned on the meaning of the word "white"; each was considered an insult by the nation of origin and both had international repercussions.

When the Supreme Court declared its unanimous verdict against Ozawa, Hindus hoped that the principles enunciated therein by Justice Sutherland that thereby became the new law of the land instead of the ambiguity of the naturalization law would be adhered to. They seemed to favor the Hindu side of the argument. These principles were :

1. The word "white" imports race not color.
2. "White " is synonymous with "Caucasian" except in borderline cases.
3. The authority of previous judgments deserves proper weight.
4. Color test is impracticable because it does not provide a practical line of separation.

Bhagat Singh Thind (1893-1967) was an honors graduate of the Khalsa College, Amritsar, when he came to Seattle, Washington in September 1912 from Manila. During the war he served in the American army for six months, receiving, after the Armistice, an honorable discharge with his character designated as "excellent."

An Indian patriot like his father, he was on friendly terms with several Gadar leaders including Bhagwan Singh whom he visited in jail. Not receiving his expected naturalization as a veteran, he petitioned for it as a high-caste Hindu in which effort he received the organizational backing of the Indian community. Several years after leaving his imprint on the legal history of Indian immigration to the United States, he was naturalized as a veteran in March 1936. He earned respect and fame as a scholar, preacher, and publisher of the spiritual message of India.[23]

Charles Wolverton, Judge of the District Court of Portland, Oregon, granted a certificate of naturalization to Bhagat Singh Thind.[24] The Bureau of Naturalization brought a motion before him asking for cancellation of the certificate. Wolverton heard this motion on October 18, 1920 and rejected it saying that "I am content to rest my decision on the question upon a line of cases which (the Mohan

Singh, Halladjian and Balsara cases) are illustrative." Although aware of the cases with implications against the Hindus, he was "impressed that they are not in line with the greater weight of authority."

Judge Wolverton also ruled that Section 3 of the Act of February 5, 1917 that excluded Hindus from immigration did not deny the right of naturalization to Hindus like the petitioner who had already entered the country lawfully.

The Bureau of Naturalization took an appeal to the Circuit Court of Appeals. This Court heard arguments on behalf of Thind and decided to request the instruction of the Supreme Court in respect of two questions :

1. Is a high-caste Hindu a white person within the meaning of the naturalization law?
2. Does the Act of February 5,1917 disqualify from naturalization those Hindus who had lawfully entered the country prior to the passage of that Act ?

The case was argued before the Supreme Court on January 11 and 12, and Justice Sutherland delivered the opinion of the Court on February 19, 1923.[25]

Justice George Sutherland was sixty when he ruled against Thind's petition for naturalization. Born in England, his father, a recent convert to Mormonism, brought him to Utah when he was hardly a year old.

Although his father soon "deserted" the Mormons, George found a wife, some of his education, and most of his professional and political career in the Territory that became the Beehive State in 1896. He served successively as a state senator, a U.S. Congressman, and finally as Senator from 1905 to 1917. In 1920 he worked for the election of his former Senate colleague, Warren G. Harding. In September 1922 the grateful President at last appointed him to the Supreme Court after passing him over in favor of Taft in 1921. As an eminent jurist, Sutherland deserved the appointment. He had played a "major role in the revision and codification of federal criminal statues," had earned LL.D. degrees from three universities, Columbia (1913), Michigan (1917), and George Washington (1921), and had served as President of the American Bar Association in 1916-1917.[26]

As a conservative politician and Supreme Court Justice, Sutherland caused trouble not only to several weaker segments of society including, of course, the Indian immigrants, but also to President

Roosevelt and his New Deal legislation. As a Senator he voted against the Federal Reserve Act (1913), the Income Tax (xvi) Amendment (1913), Clayton Antitrust Act (1914), and the Federal Trade Commission Act (1914). In 1916 he sided with the organized bar against the nomination of Louis D. Brandeis to the Supreme Court.[27]

In the Supreme Court, Sutherland found two congenial souls in Willis Van Devanter and James C. McReynolds. Joined by Pierce Butler a couple of months later, these "Four Horsemen" with occasional help, first from Justice Edward Sanford and later from Justice Owen Roberts, defended with a majority of five to four a generally conservative interest for almost fourteen years till the "switch" and Van Devanter's retirement in 1937 scattered the "Horsemen" as well as President Roosevelt's "court packing" plan. Their earlier achievements were summarized thus by Professor Carl Swisher :

> During the early years of the nineteen-twenties the Supreme Court handed down decisions blocking liberal movement in a variety of directions. The subjects included child labor, minimum wages for women, the application of anti-trust legislation to labor, farm problems and utility-valuation problems. Some of the decisions angered large groups of people.[28]

In its issue of May 1, 1923, *Survey* carried a cartoon depicting Justice Sutherland handing a "Minimum Wage Decision" to a woman wage worker over the caption: "This decision affirms your constitutional right to starve."[29] Felix Frankfurter had appeared on behalf of the "girls and the law" but the court with a five to three majority and Brandeis abstaining, Sutherland, "almost always an opponent of legislation restricting the freedom of business enterprise," wrote the opinion of the Court.[30] This happened a few months after the Thind ruling in which, however, the whole Court was behind him. In 1927 Sutherland speaking on behalf of five to four majority declared unconstitutional a New York law "designed to protect the public against theater ticket scalpers"[31] and next year, on behalf of a six to three decision, struck down a New Jersey Statute regulating the rates charged by employment agencies.[32]

During the Depression when in the words of Justice Brandeis the country was "confronted with an emergency more serious than war," Sutherland insisted that the "present exigency is nothing new" and that recovery must be achieved not by emergency legislation but by "self-denial and painful effort."[33] These divergent views reflected a serious split among the nine Justices over economic and social policies. Over the naturalization of a Hindu, however, there was no divergence. The whole court was united against Thind and those whom he symbolized. This was the first time that the Supreme Court ruled on a Hindu's petition for naturalization, the first and the only occasion when it was called upon to rule on a petitioner claiming to be an Asian, a Caucasian, and white all in one.

The Court's judgment went against the Hindu, against the "weight of authority," and against its own conclusions in the *Ozawa* case. The Court spoke through a Justice who as a Senator had voted among the "Ayes" for the exclusion of Hindus and blacks from immigration.[34] Nor was Chief Justice Taft a neutral judge. As already mentioned, President Taft had vetoed the bill S3175 in 1913 not because it proposed to exclude Hindus from immigration but for other reasons.[35] An examination of the *Thind* case ruling reveals that the principles of the *Ozawa* case were not adhered to. By a clever manipulation of arguments the high court played the game of heads we win and tails you lose.

The Court reversed itself on the interpretation of the same law, the result both times being what the exclusionists wanted. Justice Sutherland proved that the law and the Supreme Court both were unreliable and capricious. Twenty-one years later a representative of a changing America, Mrs. Clare Booth Luce, characterized the *Thind* decision by an adjective that its Indian victims must have been eager to use all the time—that it was a "shameful page in the history of the Supreme Court of the United States."[36]

Of course, it is not just one page. It is over nine pages in print. Nor was it as "shameful" as the *Dred Scott* or the *Plessy* v. *Ferguson* decisions, though all three were products of the same ideology.

There is, however, one fact about the *Thind* decision which was lacking in the two nineteenth century rulings. Against Thind the Court was unanimous. Even Justice Brandeis, himself a member of a persecuted minority group, did not write a dissenting opinion. Eight of those "common men" of 1790 were Sutherland's own brethren on the bench.[37]

His most inexcusable sin, in Indian eyes, however, was his failure to uphold the principles he had enunciated in the *Ozawa* ruling. He paid no heed to the several recorded cases where federal and state courts had upheld the pro-Hindu arguments.[38] He practically refused to concede that the other side too had an arguable case. The totality of his one-sided judgment helped create the unfortunate impression among the victims of his ruling that even as an American citizen and as a member of the highest judicial court of the land, he carried in his mind the British prejudice against India and its people. In Indian eyes, Sutherland became an agent of British oppression.

We now examine the main arguments of Justice Sutherland's ruling against Thind and the way he turned his back on the judicial principles he had relied upon in his ruling against Ozawa.

In this ruling he had written that the decisions of the various state and federal courts are "to the effect that the words (white person) import *a racial and not an individual test,* and with this conclusion . . we entirely agree." In the *Thind* ruling he withdrew his agreement completely by the use of words "but" and "now":

> They (the words "white person") imply as we have said a racial test, *but* the term "race is one which, for the practical purposes of the statute, must be applied to a group of living persons *now* possessing in common the requisite characteristics, not to groups of persons who are supposed to be or really are descended from some remote, common ancestor,...

In the *Ozawa* case, Sutherland had agreed to apply the racial test to the petitioner, in other words to determine whether he belonged to the Caucasian race. The weight of authority being against the Japanese, he accepted the conclusions of those judgments and rejected Ozawa's petition on racial grounds.

Thind's petition could not be rejected on racial grounds because, both by weight of recorded judgments and the opinion of anthropologists, Indians were Caucasians. Sutherland, therefore, turned to color, thereby discarding one of his main arguments in the *Ozawa* case. Several judges who had naturalized Syrians, Armenians, Parsis, Hindus, and Sikhs had in fact ruled that color did not matter. Sutherland ruled that color was the only thing that mattered. Thind was disqualified because of "physical group characteristics." of the people from India.

Justice Sutherland's crucial argument against Indians being Caucasians was the "common man" argument. He did not invent it. The Judge in the *Bhagwab Singh* case did, but Sutherland defined it more sharply: He wrote, ". . . the words 'white persons' . . . are words of common speech and not of scientific origin. . . " "The words of the Statute are to be interpreted in accordance with the understanding of the common man from whose vacabulary they were taken." The Statute was "written in the words of common speech for common understanding, by unsicentific men. . . ." Immigrants from the British Isles and Northern Europe "whence they and their forbears had come . . . it was these immigrants . . . bone of their bone and flesh of their flesh . . . and their kind whom they must have had affirmatively in mind.[39]

Nobody need deny that the word "white" was of common usage at the time the law was enacted, nor can Justice Sutherland be denied credit for reading correctly the mind of the vast majority of his own *contemporaries* as to their prejudice against the Hindus. Congress had stopped their immigration. The Bureau of Naturalization had opposed their petitions. Several states denied them the right to own landed property. Only fifty- nine or sixty of them had succeeded in getting citizenship papers.

The ruling, though popular, was unjust. Sutherland's handling of the words "white" and "common man" was simplistic. The word "white" did come from current vocabulary but as the most important word in the statute of naturalization it took on a special, a manifold, a variegated meaning. Coming, no doubt, from "unscientific" men, it nevertheless became a scientific, a technical word in a statute. Sutherland denied that the word was complex or that it needed scientific analysis. He insisted that only the common man is competent to interpret it. But his "common man" was narrow in vision, restrictive in tolerance, and willfully ignorant of the widening frontiers of scientific knowledge, a wooden dummy in the hands of a ventriloquist who was determined to rule against Thind.

Common men are not the kind of dynamos who run on their own power all the time. They are very often educated, propagandized, or even brainwashed by teachers, politicians, churches, newspapers, and scientists. They are the makers but also the products of the socioeconomic and the intellectual climate of their age. Behind common men there are always uncommon men. There were uncommon men behind the "Indians" who dumped chests of tea in the Boston harbor, or marched in crowds as Sons of Liberty or forced the royal Governors to take refuge beyond the water front. During the age of the Revolution and the early Republic the common man was learning a few new concepts expressed in old familiar words. His vocabulary was changing. Instead of Whigs, Tories, and Burgesses,there were now Federalists, Anti-Federalists, Representatives, and Senators. Colonies were becoming states. He may have never heard of Montesquieu but he was starting to appreciate the new concept of balance of power. And then, of course, in place of thirteen colonies the common man had a country without a king, a Prestident without titles, states without sovereignty, and parties without taint of disloyalty. These words of common usage had become special words, technical words, part of the judicial vocabulary; they moved away from the meaning of the common man. When so many words were getting away from their "common man" meaning, why should Justice Sutherland insist that the word "white" did not have a special meaning containing more than what existed in the common man's understanding of it. Indeed his critics argue that for the common man and the legislature of 1790 and for that matter for those of 1870, the word "white" as part of the naturalization law meant more than the ordinary word "white" and was performing a well recognized, long-practiced function. The critics offer two arguments in this connection:

1. Judge Lowell's conclusion that the word "white" was a catch-all word to designate persons not otherwise expressly classified.
2. Chase and Pandit quoted from the third edition of the *Encylopedia Britannica* published in 1797 to show that the original framers knew that the "accepted" meaning of the term "white" in their day included the people of Europe and Asia up to the Ganges River.[40]

When the statute was re-enacted in 1870 and 1875, the geography textbooks taught in schools always included Hindus as part of the white race. They mention fourteen such textbooks and concluded that the "meaning given to words in the daily teachings of those schools which were maintained for the forming of thought habits of the children of the 'common man' were the meanings those words definitely had for him and them."[41]

Three years before the Chase-Pandit booklet was published, a law professor at the University of Iowa had suggested that the legal "profession, including judges, may consult the geograpahies in current use in 1875 and before in the little red school houses to see what the Congressmen and 'common people' were taught to regard as 'whites or Caucasians.'"[42]

In 1939 a Congressman reminded his colleagues what they all had been taught in their "little red school houses." Addressing the Chairman at a Committee hearing on the Indian immigrants' petition for naturalization, Rep. William R. Poage (D.-Tex.) said :

> Mr. Chairman, I would like to make an observation, maybe a question, in connection with this Supreme Court decision. It strikes me, without any desire to criticize the Court, that everybody who has gone to high school in the United States knows that the Indian people are Caucasian people. It is taught in every high school in the United States that I have ever heard of. It was taught when I went to school and while there is no law requiring Congressmen to have a high-school education, I take it that most every member of Congress now or at least in 1924, had approximately the equivalent of a high-school education anyhow and that the Congressmen who passed that law were perfectly familiar with the fact that the people of India were of the Caucasian race and were at least technically known as of the white race, and it seems to me that the Supreme Court certainly paid no compliment to the Members when they assumed that Congress had in mind that race depended upon the amount of pigmentation in the skin only, and I have been given to understand that that is the basis of the difference in appearnace between the Hindu and the men who went north from wherever their homeland was, that is, the men who went south and east stayed in a hotter climate and became of darker complexion, and those that moved up into the German forests and lived in the shade here for generations became fair- skinned.[43]

The critics' arguments may have scored a point over Sutherland's ruling but the common man of 1923 was pleased with his ruling. People do not always legislate their knowledge. Most often they legislate their fears. Their knowledge that Hindus were Caucasians and that a few judges had actually naturalized them, made them still more determined to oppose the Indians' claims. The results were the Barred Zone of 1917 and the Sutherland ruling of 1923. No critic has accused Justice Sutherland of ruling against the law. The ambiguity of the law gave him the chance to rule as he wished both against the Japanese and the Indians. He could not have ruled differently without ceasing to be Sutherland.

Indians and their spokesmen had attempted to prove for years the affinity of the Hindu with "white" or Caucasian. The more they spread the word, the more the exclusionists were convinced, and with deeper conviction came deeper fears. The pseudo-scientists' opinions had alarmed them about the immigrant flood from the West, the true scientists' opinions alarmed them about the immigrants from the East. The common man of the first quarter of the twentieth century was a nervous person imagining himself threatended from both oceans. He had lost faith in his digestive capabilities. He had become a nativist. In spite of Indians' efforts at pressuring Congress and organizing public support, no Indian was permitted to be naturalized on the basis of his Caucasian qualifications. When Congress at last agreed to grant naturalization privileges in 1946 it was by American favor, not by hereditary right. The "common man" would brook no rivals.

In the *Ozawa* case Sutherland had accepted the rulings of the Federal and State Courts that the words "white person" meant membership of the Caucasian race. In the *Thind* case ruling he denied that the two terms "were of identical meaning—idem per idem," and argued against the scholars and the scientists in an effort to exclude the Hindu from both the Caucasian and the Aryan categories and to assign him to an "intermediate classification."

On December 31, 1914 in the course of a Senate debate, Senator John Sharp Williams of Mississippi had said, "Caucasian" does not mean white. Senator Sutherland was present but apparently remained unconvinced for eight years because he ruled in the *Ozawa* case that Caucasian meant white. Then suddenly in three months be became a convert, light dawned upon him—or was it politics ? It was an amazing *volte-face.* "The Justice's mental dexterity was confusing to say the least," comments Dr. Chandrasekhar.[44]

Mrs. Mary K. Das was convinced that "in the *Thind* case, the Supreme Court rendered a '*political decision*' at the request of the Government of the United States and *for other considerations involving foreign governments*". She also believed that the ruling was given retroactive effect "for political reasons."[45] Twenty years later her husband alleged that during the Thind hearings the Solicitor General Beck "was aided by the experts of the British Embassy." Beck labelled the ruling itself "a significant political decision."[46] Pandit and Chase, although commenting on the Sutherland opinion as attorneys, found a way of expressing their suspicion that politics was involved. They wrote : "If the decision of the court in the *Thind* case is to be taken as a political decision, supposedly based on grounds of public policy, it should have no retroactive operation."[47] Whatever his motives, Sutherland had by his ruling denied to a few thousand immigrants the right to renounce their allegiance to the British Crown. A wide significance was seen by a representative of a missionary organization in 1945. Miss Sue Weddell protested at a Congressional hearing that

> keeping any country, any entire country, out because its people are of another color or race from ours is not in accordance with my religious concepts. Our laws now say that there is not one of the 390,000,000 people of India that is fit to be a citizen of this country. That is the thing I am speaking against.[48]

Notes & References

1. Hope of receiving humane treatment, Sant Nihal Singh, "Indians in America," *Modern Review*, III, March 1908, 207; Taraknath Das, *Address August 1946*, 2 I.L.A. Papers.
2. *Senate Hearings, December 1926*, 1.
3. U.S. vs. Dolla, 177 Fed. 101.
4. *Proceedings*, November 1909, 6.
5. Sant Nihal Singh's article cited in fn. 1 above mentions the official opposition to the Indians' petitions for naturalization and the Attorney-General's views. Obviously instructions to oppose had not reached New Orleans when those two Indians received naturalization certificates in March 1908. That the instructions had not reached the Fifth Judicial Circuit which included New Orleans may also be assumed from a document in the National Archives of India which is copy of a letter dated June 19, 1914 from the British Embassy in Washington sent by London to New Delhi. It says that "some six years ago five Hindus were admitted to U.S. citizenship in New Orleans, one at Galveston, Texas," and more recently "Abba Dolla in Georgia. The Attorney-General appealed against the decision *in this case* on behalf of the United States." The Dolla case was the first to be challenged in the South. Home-Political, November 1914, No. 239, Part B, National Archives of India, emphasis added.
6. *Senate Hearings, December 1926*, 1. The number fifty-nine is reached by excluding soldiers and including Balsara.
7. Judge Lowell, for instance, had to go through ". . . a casual examination of books on ethnology, standing together on the shelves of a large library, old and new, weighty and unimportant, . . . Figuier, Brace, Keane, Pickering, Brinton, Hutchinson, Jeffries, Prichett and Retzel, authors taken quite at random . . . Blumenbach, an influential author of the

eighteenth century, and ... Quatrefages and Huxley, about a century later. Cuvier ... modern travelers, such as Bryce and W.H. Ward ... Ripley .. Topinard ...." In re Halladjian et al. (174 F. 840.)

Judge Dickinson saw the difficulties of the lawmakers in their attempt to "approach definiteness of expression" but they in his opinion "'surmounted' those difficulties" by the expedient of transferring them to the interpreter. "Our difficulties are indeed increased."

Language has a bearing upon words used in the law. "Our language is a living thing," he wrote, "because it is alive, it is ever changing ... this fact has a bearing upon the meaning at different times given to the quoted phrase ('white person')." In re Sadar Bhagwab Singh (246 Fed. 496), 498.

8. The naturalization law (1 Stat. 103) had been adopted by the first Congress on March 26, 1790 and had come before the third Congress for amendment. Twenty-four members of the House and the Senate in these two Congresses had either signed the Declaration of Independence or had been members of the Constitutional Convention. Three of them had earned both honors; *White's Conspectus of American Biography*, New York, 1937, 33, 53; for debates on the bill, *Benton's Abridgement of the Debates of Congress*, New York, 1857, Vol. 1, 184-190, 555-566; Milton R. Konvitz, *The Alien and the Asiatic in American Law*, N.Y., 1946, 79.
9. (16 Stat., 254), signed by President Grant, July 14, 1870; Konvitz, *The Alien and the Asiatic*, 80; U.S. Department of Justice, *Laws Applicable to Immigration and Nationality*, Carl B. Hyatt (Compiler), and Edwina Austin Avery (ed.), Washington, D.C.; 1953; 755, this is the famous Section 2169 of the Revised Statutes. Henceforth this work will be referred to as Avery (ed.), *Laws*.
10. Konvitz, *The Alien and the Asiatic*, 96, 97; Sidney Kansas, *United States Immigration, Exclusion, Deportation and Citizenship*, New York, 1941, 327-28.
11. Eliot Grinnell Mears, *Resident Orientals on the American Pacific Coast: Their Legal and Economic Status*, Chicago, 1928, 101, Das, *Hindustani Workers*, 114.
12. Kansas, *United States Immigration*, 327; *Modern Review*, March 1926, comment by T(araknath) D(as), 349-50.
13. Avery (ed.) *Laws*, 912 fn. 40.
14. Ray E. Chase and S.G. Pandit, *An Examination of the Opinion of the Supreme Court of the United States Deciding Against the Eligibility of Hindus for Citizenship*, Los Angeles, 1926; the case was in re Halladjian et al., (174 Fed. 834).
15. Cuvier (1769-1832) was a French naturalist and the founder of the Science of Comparative anatomy.
16. In re Balsara (171 Fed., 294).
17. In re Akhay Kumar Mozumdar (207 Fed., 115), John E. Raker (D-Calif.) member of the Immigration and Naturalization Committee and a leading

exclusionist drew an alarming conclusion : "If one could be admitted, any other of the same race of 200,000,000 would be capable of being admitted because of their racial condition . . . ." *Sudhindra Hearings*, 12.

18. Ex parte Shahid (205 Fed., 812).
19. "When Christ comes again he will have to give up being an Asiatic and a carpenter if he wishes to be admitted into the Christian countries of America and Australia," M. Paul Richard quoted in *Orient*, New York, February, 1923, 31.
20. In re Sadar Bhagwab Singh (246 Fed., 496).
21. In re Mohan Singh (257 Fed., 209).
22. Ozawa vs. United States, No 1, Oct. term, 1922. (260 U.S. 178).
23. The writer is indebted to Mrs. Vivian Thind for several of her late husband's biographical details. He was born at his ancestral village Taragarh, near Amritsar. His father served in the Military Police but later, like thousands of others, served a term in jail as a nationalist. In America he worked in the lumber mills to earn his college tuition. He may have been the "Bhagat Singh" who contibuted three articles on Indian nationalistic topics in *Independent Hindustan* of October, November 1920 and January 1921. Sudhindra Bose alleged in 1927 that the United States "never kept its promise" to grant citizenship to Indian veterans including Thind, *Modern Review*, October 1927, 440. Thind was naturalized in 1936. See Chapter: Life Under Inequality, text p. 130 and footnote 5 on p. 159.

    According to Senator David A. Reed, Bhagat Singh was "a man of education," Senate Hearings December 1926, 10; he was "interpreting the spiritual heritage of India," Muzumdar, *Contributions*, 34, 35; in 1927 he is said to have given two courses of sixty lectures; Wendell Thomas. *Hinduism Invades*, 221; Mrs. Thind whom he married in 1941 has supplied the present writer with a printed list of her husband's writings "still in print." It has sixteen titles including *Jesus, The Christ, In the Light of Spiritual Science*, 3 Vols. Grewal remembered that "In fifty-two years of his teaching Truth, awakening the love of God in the hearts of his followers, five million Americans have heard Dr. Thind." He financially helped several Indian students including Dr. Anup Singh, Dr. Piara Singh Gill, Founder Gulmarg (Kashmir) Research Observatory, and Pratap Singh Kairon, Chief Minister, Panjab State.

    In a letter to the Editor, "*The Mahratta*," Poona, from Linnton, Oregon, dated January 22, 1922, Thind enclosed the brief of his case to draw the editor's attention to his fight for citizenship. He called it "a battle for recognition, we Indians are fighting in this country !" He hoped that the decision will be favorable and "will solve many irksome questions such as buying and leasing of land." The case was financed by the Hindustani Welfare and Reform Association of the Imperial Valley,

California, Hardikar Papers, Nehru Memorial Museum and Library, New Delhi.

24. In Re Bhagat Singh Thind (208 Fed., 683).
25. United States vs. Bhagat Singh Thind (216 U.S. 204).
26. George Sutherland was born in Bucking amshire, England, March 25, 1862. *Guide to United States Supreme Court*, 789, 845; *Who's Who In America*, Vol. 17, 1922- 23.
27. *Guide to the Supreme Court*, 845-46.
28. Carl Brent Swisher, *American Constitutional Development*, Cambridge, Mass. 1954; 771-72.
29. On 164.
30. Swisher, *Constitutional Development*, 805.
31. Alpheus Thomas Mason and William M. Beaney, *The Supreme Court in a Free Society*, New York, 1968, 246.
32. Swisher, *Constitutional Development*, 818.
33. Ibid.; Mason and Beaney, *The Supreme Court*, 208.
34. On the immigration of blacks from the West Indies; Sutherland promised, "... so far as I am concerned I do not want to see the negro population in this country added to; and for that reason I shall vote in favor of the amendment proposed by the Senator from Missouri" (James A. Reed, D.-Mo.). The amendment was adopted 29 : 25, with 42 not voting. *Cong. Rec.*, 63rd Cong., 3d sess., December 31, 1914, promise announced, 806, voting, 807; voted to override Wilson veto, *Ibid.*, 64th Cong., 2nd sess., February 5, 1917, 2629.
35. As explained in Chapter II.
36. One of the excerpts from her speech delivered at a public meeing held on May 4, 1944 in Washington, D.C. introduced into the record, *S1595 Hearings*, 24. On the other hand the Sutherland decision led the Californians "to a haven of overwhelming joy." *Modern Review*, July 1924, 16.
37. Jews are among "those who have suffered most cruelly among all men on the earth from European hatred and contempt," Circuit Judge Lowell in In re Halladjian et al. 174 F 839.
38. "We are unable to agree with the District Court, or with other lower Federal Courts, in the conclusion that a native Hindu is eligible for naturalization under article 2169," he wrote, thereby discarding all previous judgments that had favored the Hindus. Judge Wolverton had relied on what he had called "the greater weight of authority" and a scholar, one month after the Sutherland ruling called "the numerical preponderance of reported decisions." D.O. McGovney, "Race Discrimination in Naturalization," *Iowa Law Bulletin*, Vol. VIII, No. 3, (March 1923), 145; Jacoby believed that "the sizable number of successful petitioners seemingly would have indicated that the issue was fairly well settled."; "More Thind Against Than Sinning," *The Pacific Historian*, Vol. II, No. 4

(November 1958), 2; at one point long before the Sutherland ruling even the British Embassy in Washington had believed that the U.S. Government may Cease to Appeal against pro-Hindu verdicts. Its appeal against Abba Dolla had been rejected. "In view of that ruling it is unlikely that the Federal Government will take any action in the cases now reported." (These were the cases of the naturalization of Taraknath Das, Sakharam Ganesh Pandit, and Akhay Kumar Mozumdar.) The Embassy letter ended with two interesting observations : "It seems clear that theories of ethnological science carry more weight than the plain meaning of the Act." Secondly, "the fact that in the case of (Sakharam Ganesh) Pandit it was a Judge elected by the people of a State known for its antipathy to the influx of Asiatics who granted citizenship has caused considerable surprise." British Embassy, Washington, June 19, 1914 to Sir Edward Grey, Home-Political, November 1914, No. 239, Part B, National Archives of India; the Judges were so sure about the weight of authority being in favor of Hindus being "white persons" that a New York Court had granted naturalization to a Hindu (Dhirendra Kumar Sarkar) just ten days before the Sutherland ruling, *Senate Hearings, December 1926*, 1; a Circuit Court of Appeals ruling in 1928 recognized the fact that "in 1920 it was the understanding that Hindus were eligible to citizensip," United States vs. Gokhale, 26 Federal Report, 2d Series, 360.

39. These are Kipling's words—

    Flesh of the flesh that I bred, bone of the bone that I bare,
    Stark as your sons shall be, —stern as your
    Fathers were.

    "Racial Patriotism in Poetry," *Modern Review*, June 1917, 693.

40. *An Examination*, 3.
41. Ibid., 5, 6.
42. D. O. McGovney, "Race Discrimination In Naturalization," *Iowa Law Bulletin*, Vol. VIII (3 March 1923), 353-54.
43. *June 1939 Hearing*, 5.
44. Congressional Record, 63rd Cong., 3rd sess., 805; S. Chandrasekhar (ed.), *From India to America : A Brief History of Immigration; Problem of Discrimination: Admission and Assimilation,* La Jolla, California, 1982, 20.
45. *Modern Review*, April 1927, 462, 463, emphasis in original.
46. *Address August 1946*, 9.
47. *An Examination*, 16.
48. *House Hearings, March 1945*, 45.

4

LIFE UNDER INEQUALITY

Excluded from immigration, prosecuted for their political activities, threatened with deportation, excluded from citizenship, denaturalized, excluded from land ownership, and regulated even in the choice of a mate in the states where most of them lived, Indians now formed a small band of people set apart from Americans by what truly must have seemed a great white wall.

—JOAN M. JENSEN

By 1924 Indian immigrants had settled down to a life under inequality. A legal system of restriction and discrimination had closed around them. Family reunions, landownership, and citizenship had been declared outside their "racial" eligibilities. By voluntarily offering to agree to "restricted immigration," in other words, by dropping the claim to an annual immigration quota for persons of Indian origin and descent, the Indian leaders had themselves accepted a part of the code of inequality.

Indians were under a double exclusion—geographically by the Act of 1917 and racially by that of 1924. This latter legislation combining the exclusion from immigration with the exclusion from naturalization imposed by the *Thind* ruling of 1923, provided in its Section 13 (c) that "No alien ineligible to citizenship shall be admitted to the United States" as an immigrant.[1]

An Act of March 2, 1929 called the Registry Act, granted some relief to those Hindus who had entered the United States prior to July 1, 1924, but who could offer no record of their admission for permanent residence. If they could prove their arrival as prior to that date, they would be issued a certificate of arrival and the immigrant "shall be deemed to have been lawfully admitted to the United States for permanent residence as to the date of his entry." By an Act of June 8, 1934 this relief was extended to those who had entered prior to July 1, 1933.[2]

A wartime measure, the Alien Registration Act of June 28, 1940 obliged every alien to apply for registration and to be finger-printed within 30 days. This law applied to settlers, students, merchants, and visitors alike.[3]

Five categories of Indians continued to be admitted. They were :

1. Under Section 3 subdivision (1) of the Immigration Act of 1924: "A Government official, his family, attendants, servants and employees."

2. Section 3 subdivision (2) : An Indian "visiting the United States temporarily as a tourist or temporarily for business or pleasure."

These two categories were called "nonimmigrants." The other three were "nonquota immigrants."

3. Under Section 4(b): "An immigrant previously lawfully admitted to the United States who is returning from a temporary visit abroad."

4. Section 4(d): Religious preachers and University or college professors, their wives and unmarried children under 18.

5. Section 4(a): Bona fide students.

Indian immigrants suffered several legal disabilities because of ineligibility for citizenship. Their American wives could lose their own citizenship. They could not enter professions like medicine and law. For the same reason Indians "had great difficulty in obtaining employment. In many instances they were even unable to get emergency relief right here in New York City."[4]

People of Indian origin resident in the United States belonged to four categories according to their legal status—U.S. citizens, immigrants (permanent residents), nonimmigrants, and nonquota immigrants. Citizens could start any lawful business; noncitizen permanent residents too could become businessmen under certain restrictions as to professions and landholding without damaging their legal status. Nonquota immigrants like teachers and students had to change their legal status in order to become businessmen thereby becoming nonimmigrants under Section 3 subdivision 2 of the Immigration Act of 1924, i.e., Indians visiting the United States temporarily as tourists or temporarily for *business* or pleasure. Indians entering the United States after the exclusion legislation of 1917 and 1924 to start their own businesses fell under this legal status of Section 3 (2). They were all here "temporarily" for business.

Nine Indians had been granted naturalization before 1923 for service in World War I, a few more veterans, including Bhagat Singh Thind, were naturalized under a bill enacted by the 74th Congress in 1935.[5]

Section 303 of the Nationality Act of 1940 limited the right of naturalization to "white persons, persons of African nativity or descent and descendants of races indigenous to the Western Hemisphere . . ."[6] During World War II "less than 50" Indians serving in the American armed forces had been naturalized till 1945 under Title X of the Second War Powers Act of March 27, 1942.[7]

Attention was drawn in a previous chapter to the acceptance by the vocal elements in the community of the principle of restricted immigration, which involved sacrificing the laborers. This acquiescence in the demands of the exclusionists involved the loss of existing rights. The offer to accept the exclusion of laborers, however, was not considered by the students and businessmen as a defeat. Instead they themselves suggested it as a wholesome pruning operation so that they could continue to get education and gain wealth in America without attracting too much jealousy or prejudice.

The students were already in the United States when the farmers arrived. Exclusion from Canada, riots in American cities, hostile writings in the exclusionist press, forced the students to take note of the new situation. They had to structure a position which would take into account their interests as students and as Indians in the context of the American attitude towards the farmers.

They were the most vocal, though not the only participants in this intercommunity debate that ensued. Nonstudents and august visitors also helped in framing what in fact became the attitude of the English-educated intellectual segment of the community *vis-a-vis* the American immigration and naturalization policies for the next thirty years.

Sant Nihal Singh, who as journalist covered the Indians' early difficulties in Canada and the United States, considered the reasons for exclusion from Canada "flimsy and fictitious" and attributed it to the work of "yellow- press writers and selfish political agitators."[8]

Some of the west coast whites were in Nihal Singh's eyes "ignorant nincompoops," "hoodlums."[9] The rioters at Bellingham were chiefly composed of "the refuse of Europe."[10] He noticed what several others did later, the "significant fact" that "Indians at home and abroad resent the humiliating treatment accorded to their immigrants. This shows how an Indian nation is coming into being."[11] After having watched for years the treatment accorded to Indians in North America, he urged the immigrants to develop national pride, demand reciprocity and take up the brown man's burden.[12]

The revolutionists took up that burden by diverting the immigrants' wrath away from America and heaping almost the whole of it on Britain and its white colonies. They must have appreciated, for instance the question C. F. Andrews raised about Australia in one of these early years, "Can it be fair," he asked, "can it be just to make these lands. . . . the white man's preserve?"[13]

Most of the students were neither revolutionists nor Panjabis. They understood neither the language nor the religion of the Sikhs. There was little in common between them except India and the insult. For the latter each blamed a different source. The Sikh workers blamed the British; the students blamed the workers.

The students' Americanization had advanced to such a degree as to make them brown sahibs in language, dress, and eating habits.[14] Their advanced education and literacy in English tended to give them airs and developed in them an "unconscious contempt for the rustic Indian immigrants on the West Coast."[15] They started agreeing with the exclusionists' estimate of the Indian laborer.

Dady Burjor and Lajpat Rai had wished that the Sikhs would abandon the turban and the beard for the sake of peace with their white co-workers. They had patted them on the back for not abandoning them.[16] The students had no such wavering minds.

Even a Panjabi and a Gadarite, G. D. Kumar, did not want "any more laborers here" because they come with "bundles of superstitions and *eastern* habits."[17] Sarangdhar Das, a student from Orissa, thought Indians would be "desirable immigrants" if they "gave off their turbans, cut their long hair and shaved off their beard" and were not "blind religious fanatics by birth."[18]

An Indian correspondent referred to the farmers as "ignorant laborers" against whom Americans "seem determined to shut their doors . . . unless we ourselves create a favorable impression by sending *much better specimens of our race.*"[19] As already mentioned, Sudhindra Bose, Bishen Singh, Bhutia, and Ramachandra had all conceded "restricted immigration" a euphemism for excluding the Indian workers. They all thought of themselves as better specimens of their race.

S. V. Ketkar received his doctorate from Cornell in 1911. He thought India need not send laborers abroad. The government should instead create opportunities for employment within the country.[20] He recommended emigration, however, "even to countries like America" on the humanitarian grounds of relieving poverty at home. "It is a struggle for bread and for many other things. We should not shirk the struggle" he advised.[21] Students who were against laborers going to America were in his estimate "people without ambition and who do not know what is meant by struggle in life."[22] Besides relieving the pressure of population, he saw three significant advantages in emigration abroad. First, it helped "to advertise the existence of our country, a matter of no small importance."[23] Secondly, "some gross mis-statements, defaming the character of our 'heathen' country made by the American missionaries are being discounted in America." Thirdly, "the suffering [of Indians abroad] are an important factor in our nation making. All people . . . have felt the pinch, and in this matter we all unite."[24] As if responding to Sant Nihal Singh's call to shoulder the brown man's burden, Ketkar pledged, "We intend to demand treatment on terms of equality for our kinsmen abroad, a point which the Indian Government may not care to insist upon."[25]

Joan Jensen, Harold Jacoby, and Gary Hess have mentioned various figures for the total Indian population in the United States during this period. No figure reaches 4000; another figure—3896—is of Indians registered under the Alien Registration Act 1941." This figure would, therefore, include immigrants, students, businessmen, teachers, religious missionaries, and even white persons who may have come from India (and were eligible to naturalization).[26]

Meanwhile hundreds had returned to India. For those who stayed on, the paucity of privileges and the lack of numbers could have spelled a demographic disaster. For the British, the gradual withering away of a "seditious" community would have been a welcome finale[27] and for the American exclusionists a longed for end and, looking at the laws of vital statistics, not a vain hope. Both these opponents of a permanent Hindu presence in the United States were, however, to be disappointed because the disaster never took place. The small Indian community endured.[28]

By the early 1940s the Indo-American community was richer and better organized than twenty years previously. It was by then actively engaged in demanding redress of its grievances in America. Its commitment to the furtherance of India's nationalist cause had achieved organizational and popular strength that was beyond the dreams of Har Dayal and Lala Lajpat Rai.

Except in the matter of family reunification and Indian brides, the exclusion laws and the *Thind* decision did not exclude much from the social and economic life of the Indian residents. The two exceptions forced them to seek other families and other brides. The preachers and visiting scholars could come to fortify their faith and cultural morale. Tourists came bringing eyewitness news from the homeland. Students brought youth and organizing abilities. Professional lecturers and politicians supplied the latest rebuttals in the propaganda war with Britain.

Far from locking the Indian community out of society, the exclusion laws had left a large segment of its life free to find its own moorings. Legal residents could not be deported. Civil liberties protected them in their persons and property. They were free to pursue almost any profession, live anywhere in any state, and send any amount of money home. Moreover, the extension of legal disabilities to almost all Asians reduced the pain by distributing it.

The loss of the right to citizenship injured their national pride. It also restricted the farmers' freedom to own or lease landed property and denied him the right to bring over his wife and children. Otherwise it was mostly a racist discrimination rather than a fatal economic blow. It hardly persuaded any immigrant farmer to dub America as no longer a good provider. Infact, hundreds continued to sneak in even after the Thind ruling.[29]

The loss of political rights of franchise and elective office as a result of the Supreme Court decision was no loss at all because hardly any immigrant was likely to have enjoyed those rights in India. Not many of them could have qualified for the franchise under the Minto-Morley reforms. Dyarchy, which somewhat widened the franchise, was inaugurated only in 1921, almost four years after the enactment of the Asiatic Barred Zone.

Was there a U.S.-British treaty governing immigration from India the rights of Indians guaranteed under which were also lost at this time? The Commissioner-General of Immigration, Antony Caminetti, stated in 1913 that "India is British territory and we have a treaty with England governing immigration matters. (Therefore) the question of Hindu exclusion is one that we will have to take up with the British foreign office first."[30]

In a letter to the Speaker of the House, Labor Secretary William B. Wilson pointed out that the treaty in question was that of 1815.[31] According to Caminetti, that treaty "would be the only one that might be appealed to in connection with any possible diplomatic discussion of this (Hindu exclusion) question.[32]

This American official acceptance of the existence of a treaty was, however, always accompanied by an insistence that Hindu exclusion could be enacted in spite of it. For instance, Caminetti believed that "it is an established principle of international law, however, that any country has a right to designate who may or who may not enter its limits."[33] At one of the hearings he insisted that "not even the 'favored nation' clause" would prevent the United States from raising this question and from legislating upon it.[34] In this assertion he relied upon the judicial decisions mentioned in Secretary Wilson's letter upholding the "inherent and constitutional right of the Congress" to legislate the exclusion of the subjects of countries with which the United States had treaties containing the "most favored nation" clause.[35] The precaution to be taken was to exclude Hindu laborers only as part of the general exclusion of Asian laborers.[36] The State Department, which was accepted both by Caminetti and Secretary Wilson as the authoritative guide as to America's treaty commitments, declared that "no treaty would be violated if the recommendations [to exclude the Hindus] were carried out."[37]

Although official opinion in Washington emphasized America's freedom of action, American nonofficial opinion of a few years earlier had emphasized the Indian immigrants' freedom to come and settle. Sounding the alarm in 1910, an American who was scared of "the tide of turbans streaming westward out of the congested land of India" had warned that "no legal bar, under the present treaty, can be set up against the coming of the Hindoos. Being subjects of Great Britain, they possess an undisputed right of entry to the United States."[38]

The Indian nonofficial opinion took these suggested treaty rights to heart and made their denial one more cause of resentment against Britain. Dady Burjor sent his report to the British government the same month as Secretary Wilson publicly announced his decision to exclude the Hindus. He had heard "bitter complaints" made by the immigrants who were denied a landing and warned that there was "a strong undercurrent of disaffection and unrest among them." He was afraid that exclusion "will be considered as an infringement of the rights acquired by the people of India as British subjects" under the treaty of 1815.[39]

British officials denied that the Convention of 1815 applied to India. They had decided long ago in 1886 that the agreement of 1815 was "confined to the inhabitants of the territories of His Britannic Majesty in Europe."[40] This judgment was more hollow than an outright denial. As mentioned above, Caminetti and Secretary Wilson both accepted the applicability of the treaty of 1815 to Indian immigrants long after "1886" and were at pain to devise ways and means to sidetrack it.[41]

It appears, however, that in course of years the U.S. government also started to agree with the British view. In his testimony at the Congressional hearing in 1945 an official of the State Department repeated the British interpretation.[42] British subjects of non-European territories were, therefore, left unprotected in America. Indians lost the right to enter and live. Indian merchants lost the right to build permanent establishments. And all the while Americans were enjoying these rights in the land of the Indians, one of the non-European territories of His Britannic Majesty. Those Panjabis would have again consoled themselves saying, "Daade da Sattin Vin Sau," the stronger person's hundred is seven scores. His interpretation prevails.[43]

The law, the Supreme Court, and the one way flow of treaty rights having together deprived them of the best, the immigrants had resort to the next best. Immigration was banned; they increased their members by sheltering illegal immigrants. They could not bring wives from India; they married Anglo and Mexican women; several Indian Muslims married black women. They could not hold land in their own names, they held land in the names of their wives, their children, or their wives' relatives. They could not be citizens themselves; their children were born citizens.

The mercifully lax enforcement of law also helped. In most cases wives were not declared stateless persons and the state laws against interracial marriages were generally permitted to be violated with impunity.[44]

In race relations whites never treated the Hindus as they treated the blacks. They were better off in America than Gandhi's compatriots were in South Africa. The contemporary accounts of Rajani Kant Das and Burjor depict the Hindus as a distinct minority, but not as an oppressed minority. The law had done its mischief, but the mischief stopped in July 1924. The cancellation of naturalization certificates stopped before the 1920s were over. Racial ugliness persisted but never to the extent of becoming a paralyzing menace.[45]

There was one legal disability which Indians experienced, but the equally excluded Chinese and Japanese did not. In the absence of a treaty of trade between India and the United States, Indian businessmen could not enter the country as "treaty traders" but only on temporary visas which had to be periodically renewed. This and other disabilities, a price paid for being a subject people, had their compensations. They enabled Indians in the United States to share in the American people's sympathetic bias in favor of "peoples struggling to be free."[46] Both the disabilities and the compensation would help make history later.

Opponents of Indian immigration, who had hoped that in time the Indian community would gradually waste away, found instead that time had proved to be its savior. The story of its first forty years is not a tragic tale but an unfolding drama of a dawn tantalizingly slow but finally opening up to a bright day of hope.

The community was not dying. Of course, people do get old with years and the pioneers were getting old.[47] New blood, however, was pouring in from across the oceans. In return charities continued to flow for the national causes at home.[48] Gurudwaras, temples, and Vedanta preachers kept the cultural ideals alive. The Sikh-British alliance lay broken. Students were gaining knowledge; businessmen and the farmers in the West were gaining wealth. The freedom struggle in the old country was building up the racial consciousness which in turn made restrictive laws seem more insulting and, therefore, the demand for their repeal more insistent.

And then came the "Day of Infamy." Indian people's aspirations were welded together with American national interest under the seething heat of the burning ships at Pearl Harbor notwithstanding the Anglo-American cultural, political, and military alliances. The leaders of the Indian community, educated and enriched by more than a generation of American experience, were ready and organized to persuade the American people to understand that in order to liberate or save Asian countries from Japan abroad, they must also win Asian hearts at home.

The extent and character of the inequality that had been imposed upon Indians was determined by the tripartite concert of Britain, Canada, and the United States. The first party was motivated by reasons of empire, the other two by those of color. By the time of the First World War, the white British colonies had "imposed restrictions designed absolutely, to exclude Indian immigration." They wanted to remain white as well as members of the British imperial fraternity without having to accept Indians as their fellow countrymen.[49]

The reasons offered by the Secretary of State for India in 1909 for exclusion of Indians included his concern over "close familiarity" of Indians with whites which in his view did not "make for British prestige; and it is by prestige alone that India is held not by force."[50]

The reception of Indians in the United States need not necessarily have followed the Canadian precedent of harshness and exclusion. America had its tradition of harboring the Irish. Indian immigrants could possibly have become another such free, anti-British element under American protection. They may even have become American citizens—Sudhindra Bose and Taraknath Das multiplied a thousand times!

But there were factors besides the brotherhood of Anglo-Saxonism pulling Britain and America together. In the course of the first quarter of this century there was established a virtual Anglo-American alliance against Indians as destructive of their rights as the laws of the white dominions. It began as the alliance of the people—Americans applauding Canadian and Australian exclusions, eager to imitate them here, upholding the British line of argument against Indian aspirations, even suggesting denial of asylum to Hindus and

Muslims. A sort of "race religion" had grown upon the Pacific Coast. Indeed some observers saw these years as "an age of unprecedented white hegemony."[51]

The alliance of the two governments, informal but nonetheless vital, was sealed by several common interests — the need to keep their respective Asian subjects suppressed, the American desire to wean Britain away from its alliance with Japan, the American need for naval defense of the Panama Canal, and the Canadian and Australian need for American help against an Asian threat.[52] On the British side, "One of the consistent objectives of British policy was to prevent or retard the growth of a strong body of opinion in the United States that would be opposed to its continued rule over India."[53]

These mutual needs brought about mutual cooperation. William Jennings Bryan had violated the code of Anglo-Saxon conduct in 1906 by accusing Britain of having "impoverished the country (India) by legalized pillage." The damage was more than repaired by President Theodore Roosevelt who at John Morley's request pronounced British rule over India "one of the most notable and most admirable achievements of the white race during the past centuries."[54]

This cooperation had prevented Indian students from obtaining military training in American universities, secured the suppression of the Gadarites, and kept Lajpat Rai under surveillance. More damaging to Indian immigrants, however, was the silent Anglo-American concurrence over the issue of Indian immigration and naturalization.

All arguments and apprehensions counselling exclusion of Indians from Canada applied with equal validity to their exclusion from the United States. They were the same class of people—the Panjabi Sikhs and Hindus and Bengali revolutionaries. The Sikhs came from the same districts of recruitment to the Indian army and were exposed to a similar threat of nationalist and "anarchical" indoctrination.[55]

The policy, therefore, continued. It is said that after the Bellingham riot of 1907 Lord Bryce, the then British Ambassador to Washington, made a semi-official proposal to the U.S. authorities that "they should exclude Indians as they excluded the Chinese." The *Free Hindusthan* of Taraknath Das called it a "silly proposal." C. R. Cleveland, Director, Central Intelligence, Government of India, made a significant revelation about British policy in this respect—"I do not suppose," he wrote in an official note, "that it is the policy of our own

Government or of that of the United States of America to *encourage* the settling, permanent or temporary, of Indians in the United States of America."[56]

As in immigration so also in the matter of naturalization British policy was on the side of inequality. Their ambassador had protested against the grant of citizenship to Taraknath Das. Gokhale claimed he had been fired from his job in India because he had accepted American citizenship. The help rendered to Solicitor-General Beck by British experts in preparing his case against Thind has been mentioned in a previous chapter.[57]

Writing in about 1920 Dr. Rajani Kant Das had pointed out the "lack of a strong central organization" among Indians. The H.A.A. was primarily a student organization seeking to protect the interests of only one segment of the community. Other segments having been left unorganized "the whole burden of enlightening the merchants and the press," an H.A.A. leader complained, "falls upon our untrained shoulders."[58]

There were organizations to spread literacy in English among immigrants, to serve as local protective groups, and to foster the nationalist cause of India. There were religious organizations also such as the Pacific Coast Khalsa Diwan Society founded in 1907.[59] Rajani Kant Das's ideal of a central organization was not realistic because the community was spread all over the continent. The H.A.A., the Friends of Freedom for India, and the India League of America approached that ideal during the peak year of their popularity. Several Indians published newspapers here. Taraknath Das started *Free Hindustan* (1908-1911), the Gadarites published *Gadar* and *Hindustan Gadar* (1913-1917), the post-Gadarites, *Independent Hindustan* (1920-1928) and the *United States of India* (1920-1921). Other significant periodicals were Lajpat Rai's *Young India* (1918-1920), India League of America's *India To-Day* (1940-1959), and the National Committee for India's Freedom published the *Voice of India* (1944-1947). The H.A.A.'s *Hindusthanee Student* continued from 1914 to 1930 with some breaks. Hari Govil and Dr. Syud Hassain edited the *Oriental Magazine* and the *Orient* during the 1920s.

Harold Jacoby was impressed "by the extent to which the East Indians have organized themselves around a variety and multiplicity of interests." These organizations, besides satisfying "their demand for formalized group activity," built up their "comradeship" with other protest groups and provided them "institutional respectability" through which they "could exercise political persuasion greater than their voteless status would otherwise allow."[60]

The Indian community soon learned the advisability of abandoning violence and anarchism and of adopting instead the constitutional methods followed by Lajpat Rai. These would win them American friends and avoid giving the British a broad target to shoot at. The new strategists "quoted Wilson, not De Valera."[61]

Lala Lajpat Rai (1865-1928) was the only nationalist Indian leader of high stature ever to live in the United States. He had to work hard to divert the Indian community away from the path of political violence. Although Har Dayal had joined the anarchists, Lajpat Rai sought the support of the liberal intellectuals.[62] Jagjit Singh's India League inherited in the 1940s the friendships which almost a generation ago Lajpat Rai had built up with the liberals and Democratic Socialists, who though not in power themselves, were on speaking terms with the New Dealers on both ends of the Pennsylvania Avenue.[63]

Lalaji's methods were not new. He made them a permanent part of the armory of Indian political activism in America by dignifying moderation, constitutionalism, and restrained language with the endorsement of a respected and tested patriot.[64] He brought Americans into organizations of his founding rather than ask Americans to found one for him. He attempted to "influence the influencers" of American opinion by explaining the Indian viewpoint to the editors of the *Nation*, the *New Republic*, the *Masses*, to the brain trust of the Rand School and to the elite of the Civic Club.[65] With regard to these people, Lalaji "assumed the function of an Indian nationalist Ambassador to the United States."[66]

He trained young Indian students to handle organizational work, among whom N. S. Hardikar, Hemendra Rakhit, and Ramlal Bajpai were historically the most important.[67] Hardikar became his man Friday in America and founded the Congress Seva Dal in India. Rakhit and Bajpai became Jagjit Singh's close associates in the India League.

His American associates and friends included Rev. J. T. Sunderland, president of the Home Rule League after Lajpat Rai left for India, Rev. John Haynes Holmes, Norman Thomas, Roger Baldwin, Oswald

Garrison Villard, and the publisher B. G. Huebsch. All maintained a lifelong interest in India. Roger Baldwin, founder of the American Civil Liberties Union, was even among the policy makers of the India League of America as its treasurer for nineteen years.

Over three dozen associations are mentioned in contemporary documents as working for India or Indians during this period of about thirty years. Most of them originated in New York City, Detroit, Chicago, San Francisco and Seattle, the centers either of the Indian population or of their natural leaders, the Indian intellectuals and businessmen. New York City had the additional advantage of being the home of Americans who were most sympathetic to Indian causes. Washington D.C. attracted Indians' attention only after India had attracted Washington's attention after Pearl Harbor.

The objective of the most prominent organizations and periodicals was to fight India's and the community's most threatening enemies, namely, British hostility and American ignorance. Consequently, Indian nationalist agitation in America took the form of a war of arguments between the British and the spokesmen of Indian opinion. Lecturing for India and against British rule became an industry providing livelihood to several leading members of the Indian brain trust in America. Besides lecture tours and debates, the nationalist agitation progressed through celebration of Indian festivals and anniversaries, publishing books, taking visitors from India on grand tours, and seeking favourable publicity through the public media. Irish-Americans became their helpful allies while an occasional Congressman or Senator, generally an isolationist, brought up India's case in the Congress.

Hardly any American who believed in India's right to freedom did not believe in a Hindus' right to American citizenship. For Americans associated with Indians in one organization after another, support for India's freedom and for Hindu citizenship could have become a matter of habit and conviction. There must have been something decent, something deep and life-sustaining in these organizations that Indians and Americans who worked together for them, could retain their mutual loyalties and affections for one whole generation and finally pool their resources to win the Immigration Act of 1946.

Three Indian contemporaries—Dady Burjor (1914), Lajpat Rai (1916) and Dr. Rajani Kant Das (1920) have left us the results of their personal observations and investigations that are balanced and include sympathetic views of the life and habits of the Indian farmers in the United States. Burjor who acted as interpreter at the Immigration Office at San Francisco, came into daily contact with Indian immigrants. Lajpat Rai studied them sometimes without disclosing his identity and Dr. Das based his report on personal interviews and study of official documents and newspapers.[68]

Their observations show conclusively that although the Indian immigrants may not have been the best immigrants America was getting from Europe or Asia, neither were they the monsters depicted in the hostile and derogatory effusions of the North American press and the exclusonist politicians. "But for his race and color," Lajpat Rai was sure, "... there would be room enough for hundreds and thousands more." The "real objection" to the Hindu was his being "a formidable rival in the field of labor as well as trade," to which Rai's rebuttal was, "So is the Jew." But the Jew "has a white skin and has adopted the habits and manners of the European. He has been accepted."[69]

It may also be noticed that some of the allegedly ugly aspects of the Sikh conduct in America were forced upon him partly by the bias of the immigration law as well as its enforcement. For instance, according to the august exile from the Panjab, "Among the Sikhs and Hindus liquor creates havoc," but he adds,

> The reason is obvious; they have no other diversion. In the absence of female society [and other reasons] they see no harm in burying their fatigue . . . in a draught of beer or in a peg of whiskey.

Earlier on another page Lalaji had regretted that the Indian laborer drinks liquor and thereby "many a hard earned dollar goes into the cash register of the saloon keeper."[70]

In Burjor's estimate the former soliders and policemen among Indian immigrants "are very intelligent, pleasant and polite in manners and not at all timid or bashful. . . . They usually create a favorable impression as they have been properly trained by their English officers."[71]

But those who came directly from the Panjab "are densely ignorant and illiterate, with very uncouth manners and slovenly habits." He estimated that about half the immigrants were of this type. They "create a very unfavorable impression about India and its people." Later again about this 50 per cent, "Their manners are not at all pleasant, and they talk so loud on the sidewalk, ferries and in the street, that they annoy the public . . . they crowd on the sidewalks, and spit all around . . . and stare at [women] rudely."[72]

From interviews he had with American officials Rajani Kant Das ascertained that "a most common vice to which [the Indians] have fallen victim is drinking." Although they are "as a rule very clam and quiet people, when drunk they get extremely noisy and often disturb other people."[73]

With all his alleged filthy habits the Sikh immigrant was a mighty competitor to white labor. The cries of "cheap labor" with "low standard of living" were in fact the white workers' appeals to the politicians to save them from the Asian workers' competition.[74] "The Hindu is as tough as a whalebone, and instead of eating when hungry simply takes up another notch in his belt," Congressman Church complained, and confessed that it was "impossible" for the American laborer to compete with the Hindu laborer who "can work 20 hours a day if necessary."[75]

There were several reasons why Indian workers had to work hard, earn more, and spend less. They had to reclaim their mortgaged properties, to support their families in India, and to accumulate capital to become farmers themselves, the status that they had left behind in the Panjab.

They were not *Kammis* (agricultural laborers). They were peasant proprietors, capitalists, entrepreneurs, i.e., banias.[76] As farm owners they worked on their lands as hard as laborers, planned the crops as managers, sold them as merchants. In America they had had to start from the bottom. They were not professional laborers. They were only *working as* laborers. The distinction is important. When a Panjabi peasant declared before an immigration officer, as Sohan Singh Bhakna did, that he had come to work as a laborer, he in fact meant to work at any job"[77]

His decision to work as a laborer indicated several things—a condescension for wage labor, a temporary sacrifice as the price of his new adventure; his offer to America which America could not refuse; an implied "Situation Wanted" advertisement; a determination to work hard to regain or even improve upon his old status; an optimism that his time as laborer for others would not be a long one; an assurance that he was not here to disturb the status of others, that he will just lie low and not bother anyone. It was an appeal to be let in and be left alone. Finally his offer to work as a laborer was made in the hope born of the belief common in India that nobody is jealous of laborer, his status being too meek for envy. Mentally he still was a Kirsaan (a farmer), a Khud-Kashtkar (self-cultivator, not a tenant) and a Sardar Sahib, a former soldier of the British Empire who had won decorations for service or who had lorded it over the Chinese as a policeman in the British settlements.[78]

His official classification as a "laborer" has to be ignored in the interest of a correct understanding of the Sikh mind. It was his self-respect as an independent peasant or as a former soldier that was hurt by Canadian exclusion, by American prejudice, and by British collusion with his tormentors, not his dissatisfaction with the job he was holding that made him take that tragic but history-making lunge at the British lion which we call the Gadar. It was his sense of dignity born of his status *before* immigration, his determination as an ambitious entrepreneur to exploit all opportunities for upward mobility so plentifully available to him in America in spite of prejudice and the hostile law, that kept motivating him.

There are numerous other instances which illustrate the sense of dignity and self-respect of the Indian immigrants. Fears had been expressed by the Immigration Commission and by H. A. Millis, the Commission's investigator on the West Coast, that the low income of the East Indians and their practice of sending a substantial part of it to their families in India might render them liable to public charge during periods of seasonal unemployment.[79] No actual instance of an Indian immigrant becoming a public charge has been mentioned in the two volumes of the Commission Report dealing with "Charity-Seekers." Those who failed to succeed in America returned to India rather than become burdens on friends or on public revenues. No Sikh is ever a beggar and no beggar is a Sikh. According to Das, "they would rather lower their standard of living than borrow money."[80]

There were certain jobs which the whites avoided as being dirty or menial, leaving them for Asians. Sikhs too had this penchant for selection. They would certainly never have worked as garbage collectors.[81]

Discrimination, segregation, and hostile propaganda created a reaction among Sikhs and other Indian immigrants. The whites were racists. Indians became counterracists. They avoided social contact with whites except for business. This avoidance was not merely because of their lack of knowledge of English. They avoided marriages with white women. They did not patronize American restaurants, nor did they eat food cooked by others including Americans. Indeed, like most Indians at home or abroad who had not been westernized, Hindu and Sikh immigrants regarded all Americans, white, red, or black as inferior and impure people.[82]

For Hindus, the community of British citizenship with Canadians had not earned for them Canadian privileges. In the United States community of race, physical features, work ethics, and of economic and social ambitions did not earn them American privileges. Qualities claimed by the spokesmen of American pride as being the secret of their own success, were in the case of the Hindus, counted as disqualifications. Indian immigrants, therefore, resorted to several strategies to obtain relief. Scholars have noticed these strategies as indications of the Indians' attempts to seek assimilation. In fact they were seeking peace of mind. For a Sikh to abandon the external symbols of his faith was to avoid being, as Jagjit Singh complained "the cynosure of all eyes."[83] He was trying to overcome the prejudice around him. Others were trying to circumvent a bad law. Marriages with Mexican women were not attempts at assimilation, circuitous or direct. They were simply calculated measures to hold on to landed property in addition to satisfying the need for female companionship so inconsiderately denied to them by the exclusion law. Even when the marriage may have been for love and a desire to raise a family, the bride was a shield against escheat proceedings, a financial asset even if she was not working. When children came, the shield became stronger.

While the farmers were patching up their problems by solutions that looked like attempts at assimilation, the urbanites were trying to make their own peace with society. Indian students and businessmen in America absorbed several elements of Western life including dress and language just as millions of Indians were doing in India. Assimilation was not their aim. They were only trying to make their life easier. Saund had removed his beard and long hair for which he was roundly taunted by a prominent Sikh leader on his visit to India.[84] Sikhs like him were trying to achieve the purpose for which they came—to work, earn, and live in peace.

Did the Hindus ever attempt to assimilate? Before we can answer this we have to ask the question which Sudhindra Bose asked in 1914. "Now what does assimilation really mean?"[85] In fact he was asking—is it a reachable point or a mirage? There never has been a legal definition of assimilation. The terms under which Indians could be assimilated began to be discussed almost from the moment they arrived to the day their exclusion became law in 1917. This latter was the legislative judgment preceded by popular judgment. The judicial judgment came in 1923 in the *Thind* ruling. The popular, legislative, and judicial judgments received executive sanction in the Act of 1924. They all assumed that Hindus are unassimilable. Taken in combination with the utterances of the exclusionist leaders, the marriage laws, the Alien Land Laws, and the general atmosphere of prejudice and discrimination, these laws indicated that the American nation would not permit Indians to be assimilated. Until 1946, they would not become eligible for naturalization however high their standard of living, how deep their knowledge of the English language, how long their residence in America or how close they shave their heads and beards or even if they become Christians *en masse* or produce children who were American citizens.

What some writers have called trends towards assimilation were in fact trends towards modernization, and efforts to improve their quality of life. Hindus adopted the automobile, radio and farm implements from which Jacoby concluded that "in the area of material culture then, assimilation is virtually complete."[86] This was in fact "modernization." Even Jagjit Singh forgot the distinction. In a recorded interview a decade after his return to India, his unpleasant memories of several immigrants' way of life seemed very much alive:

> The accusation against the Indians (the working class people on the Pacific Coast and Detroit area) that they were not assimilating with the Americans was hundred percent correct. .. Their whole ambition seemed to collect money, live in dirty filthy surroundings, 20 people - 25 people in one room, a little *chulah* or something, any old thing, not to raise their standard of living, not to worry about the education, not to wear clean clothes . . . because their aim was not to settle down in the United States of America . . . no Indians are good assimilators . . . the same problem arose in Vancouver . . . some Kapoor Singh family . . . made millions but no mixing with the society

> . . . . At the time of the (Congressional) hearings . . . most of the questions were inimical and they were not for it . . . they tabled the motion.[87]

Just one year later "the motion" became the Act of 1946 although "the little *chulah*" was still there. The moral of the story is that the alleged "unassimilability" was an excuse for exclusion, again the Punjabi saying "Daade da Sattin Veen Sau"—"the stronger person's hundred is seven scores." By 1946 the American *nation* had changed not the Hindus here or in India. The definition of "assimilation" as offered by scholars remained the same as in the days when Sudhindra Bose had posed the question. It was the popular concept that had become wider and tolerant—a major feature of immigration history since the Second World War.

In 1914 Sudhindra found the definition in the words of Dr. David Starr Jordan that "assimilation is nothing more than appreciation of American ideals and institutions" and a similar one in 1919 offered by Prof. John R. Commons of Wisconsin—"To be great, a nation need not be of one blood, it must be of one mind. It is not physical amalgamation which unites mankind, it is mental community."[88]

Rep. John E. Raker of California said at a hearing in December 1913, "They (the Hindus) are not assimilating. You cannot assimilate with them, and they cannot intermarry." Rep. James L. Slayden of Texas asked, "Are you glad of that ?"

Raker replied, "Absolutely: and for that reason we ought to devise some method by law to exclude them."[89]

Under the scholars' definitions of the term, however, assimilation was attainable.[90] The Hindu immigrants loved the United States; they prospered under it and were decently protected by its laws. Several of them fought under its flag in the First World War. Even in their violent speeches or writings the Gadarites never criticized America. Emotionally they already were a part of the American nation. They were assimilable. They insisted that they were. Even Jagjit Singh confessed that in his verdict of Indian unassimilability, "I have disagreed with my own countrymen and Americans."[91]

The question most repeatedly asked them was about their religious affiliation with implications that conversion to Christianity could be part of the road to assimilation. Sudhindra Bose was asked this in 1914,[92] Gokhale, Taraknath Das, Profulla Mukerjee, and Kokatur in 1926.[93]

Burjor understood better than American exclusionists could, that

> devoutly religious and spiritual races like the Hindus . . . never will be assimilated with or absorbed by the vast white population . . . For it is only a race of superior moral calibre and tenacity that refuses to be engulfed in the vortex of superior force. To be assimilated or be absorbed is to go under and going under betrays physical, moral or spiritual inferiority and weakness.[94]

At the June 1939 hearing, Haridas T. Muzumdar told the committee, "I am not so sure that the conversion to Christianity in the Orient is a good test of whether or not the particular person from India would make a good citizen of the United States."[95] This argument was accepted by the American people just six years later but for almost forty years the Indian immigrants' religion was counted as another argument to exclude them from immigration, citizenship, and assimilation.

They were also excluded from the right to hold land. The *Thind* case ruling in 1923 brought them clearly within the scope of the California Alien Land Laws. These two laws, one enacted in 1913 and the other an initiative measure in 1920, were intended primarily to put an end to the Japanese occupation of agricultural land. The Hindus suffered because they were debarred from leasing or buying land for having been held "ineligible to citizenship" by the Supreme Court ruling and the Act of 1924.[96]

The Hindu immigrants employed four strategies to save their properties or even to add to them. The "front man" strategy involved a verbal understanding with a friendly citizen farmer, banker, or lawyer.[97] Nonprofit corporations were organized with American citizens as front men. Dalip Singh Saund organized one and the Gadar Party another, in the Imperial Valley. The "marriage strategy" was to marry an American citizen, usually of Mexican descent, who would then hold the property in her name.[98] Dalip Singh also took advantage of his marriage to an American citizen.[99] Marriages produced children who were citizens by birth. They were made the legal owners with their parents as legal guardians. The Alien Land Act of 1920 attempted to invalidate such as arrangement, but the courts ruled the attempt unconstitutional as violating the rights of the children-citizens to have parents as their guardians.[100] There were obvious dangers in all four strategies. Sometimes wives betrayed, the front men cheated. In one case a daughter tricked her father.[101]

A conference of District Attorneys from 49 counties took place in January 1924 in San Francisco. It gave notice that "Hindus must immediately negotiate for the disposal of their property." Several owners may have had to sell at 'nominal prices' or even "lost all the fruit of their labor."[102] Enforcement of the laws brought about several protracted prosecutions of Hindus including one in Imperial Valley in 1933 and another in Arizona (which had a similar anti-alien law) in 1934.[103] Wanton betrayals by front men or wives sometimes resulted in murder.[104] The alien land laws were an upsetting element in the economic life of the Sikhs which made the "haves" nervous and the "have-nots" disappointed.

Taraknath Das called them "the logical development of the policy of the people of the United States regarding Asiatic Immigration."[105] Ramlal Bajpai alleged that about 2000 "successful agriculturists" had lost their farms as a result of these laws, which, according to him, were a violation of India's rights under the Jay Treaty of 1794.[106] He was probably not wrong about the treaty rights but the British Government did not protest. Indian immigrants lost another right.

These laws may have driven several Indian immigrants to seek other sources of livelihood or to equip themselves with other qualifications.[107] The Hindu land holdings did increase during the next thirty years from 2097 acres in 1920 to 13000 in 1955[108]—but without the legal wall, more Sikhs could have purchased more acres.[109]

The strategies of concealment, the prosecutions, the widely publicized trials, the murders, highlighted the root of all trouble—ineligibility to citizenship. Most Sikhs wanted to be farmers. They could not be, unless they were citizens. To become citizens, therefore, became for the Californian Sikhs not just the removal of a personal or national insult, which was the main emphasis of the urbanites, but the key to economic emancipation.

During the decades of inequality the immigrants had survived on the strength of the cultural traits they brought from home. Their struggle for survival here was often made harder by a few negative qualities, which they also had brought from home. At the same time they enjoyed an advantage. A foreign domicile generally brings out one's utmost effort. "He bends all his talents and strength to succeed in the teeth of opposition."[110] When that domicile happens to be a rewarding country like America, the stretch of hand to grasp at the reward was pushed forward by precedents of success and the prevalence of hope.

Indian students worked harder in America than in India. Farmers were backed by their bankers, lawyers, and friends even after crop failures and bankruptcies because they were considered shrewd businessmen and good borrowers.[111] "To be square in all their dealing with others is a part of their religion" was Rajani Kant Das's assessment.[112] In the asparagus fields "it was walk and bend, bend and walk, from half past four or thereabouts until seven in the evening" till Dhan Gopal Mukerji, their student co-worker, became both angry and proud. "What used to disgust me so with these men was their love of work . . . it was no wonder the American union laborer wanted to exclude them. They were underselling the Americans in their own fields."[113] "The white man feels that the day is not far distant when the brown man is going to run him a pretty hard race . . . the sign "keep out" that is posted before our immigrants . . . is about the sincerest and most gratifying compliment that the (white men) could pay us."[114]

Individuals as well as the community at large helped fight for causes of common interest. Organizations financed Bhagat Singh Thind's fight for naturalization and Pahkar Singh's legal defence. Loans on low or no interest were advanced to help a fellow villager or a cousin from India to get a start in life. Evidence was withheld in order to save a friend from conviction for crime. Indian employers paid higher wages to Indian workers.[115]

Loyalty to families they had left behind generally continued to be a well-discharged obligation. Those who came first sent money home "to buy transportation to this country for their cousins. They always talk about their cousins." Several had left their wives in India. Money continued to be sent for their support and for recovery of the property mortgaged to pay for their own voyage to the United States.[116] This sense of familial faith, a quality deserving of applause like their quality of hard work, gave the exclusionists another argument to use against them because the faith was expressed in bullion exported out of the country.[117]

"I have never seen a Hindu woman in my life" and "I certainly do not want them, but in time they will come" confessed Rep. Church in

1914. For Dhan Gopal Mukerji probably one day in the same year "was the first time in my life that I had come across a real divorced person and I did not know what to make of her." Around the early years of this century, very few Americans had seen a Greek woman in America, "but as soon as the first comers had established themselves, they [the Greek males] were usually joined by their wives and families."[118]

This happy consummation was denied to the Hindus. The divorced lady in Mukerji's story confessed to have "abolished" marriage. The Hindu males could not "abolish" marriage because several of them were already married and others were naturally eager to abolish their bachelorhoods. Like Rep. Church, they too probably never saw a Hindu woman in America because there were almost none.[119]

Interracial marriages were at first avoided by both sides for reasons of legal consequences and mutual racial repulsion. Rep. Church pointed out rightly that the Hindus "would not want to marry with our people and I am sure our people would not want to marry with them." Sudhindra Bose believed assimilation could be achieved by the Hindus as had been achieved by the Jews without extensive marriages into families of other races and religions. Although Hindus always preferred to have Hindu wives, interfaith and interracial marriages started taking place. Sikhs married Mexican women, and several students, scholars and businessmen married white American women. According to Ramlal Bajpai, 35 percent of Hindus had married American women by 1944.[120]

This left almost two-thirds of all Hindus in America without marriage companions. In California the sex ratio among Indians as late as 1940 was about 4.6 to 1 (1211 males, 263 females). In Rajani Kant Das's days only about 50 to 55 Hindus on the Pacific Coast (this included Canada) had any home life. "The evil effects of such a condition on the social and moral life of these people cannot be exaggerated," he concluded.[121]

In the absence of women of their own culture to bring tenderness and discipline into their lives, the Indian immigrants' existence became lonely, lackluster, and dull. The soft music which a Panjabi finds in the image of a Jat girl singing while picking mustard leaves in the village fields was taken out of his life by innocuous-looking words like "law" or "policy."[122] As a result the uncouth side of the Jat character started to express itself in harsher tones among fellow workers and longer hours in the saloons.

These immigrants were condemned to have no children of their own race and culture to leave behind a Sikh impact on America. Biologically they were forced to seek or purchase love elsewhere and to lose their identity in a hybrid progeny which would scarcely understand or be proud of India or of its Gurus. Later generations may attempt to search for their roots, but they would be just inquisitive alien explorers not long-separated children looking for their mother.

"It is not always a profound interest in man that carries travellers nowadays to distant lands. More often it is the facility for rapid movement," wrote Rabindranath Tagore who himself used this "facility for rapid movement" to visit the United States five times in eighteen years.[123] He was the fourth prominent Indian to visit this country since Vivekananda started the tradition in 1893. Swami Ram Tirth (1902-1904) and Baba Bharti (1904-1909) followed the young disciple of Ramakrishna to bring the message of Hinduism to America, in those years the rising star of the West. They were followed by hundreds of others, some who came for pleasure, others to see and be seen, to lecture for or against British rule in India, to attend scholarly or political conferences. The most prominent Indian who came soon after Tagore's first visit, Lajpat Rai, was an exile. Ragini Devi came to sing and dance, Uday Shankar to dance, A. B. Hakim was applauded as one of the three Indian cyclists to cross Asia and Europe.[124] Visiting scholars included philosopher Surendranath Das Gupta, Radhakrishnan destined to become a President of the Republic of India and Jagdish Chandra Bose, the world-famous botanist who made the plants respond to music. The Honorable Sir Srinivas Shastri came but was not honored. Sarojini Naidu, Kamaladevi Chattopadhyaya, Mrs. Vijayalakshmi told their appreciative Indian audiences what they wanted to hear.[125]

The welcome offered to the visiting showpieces of the nation expressed the Indian community's patriotism. Their visit helped to bring them together around a common cause or a common pride. Besides, the occasional presence of a Lajpat Rai, Tagore, or Jagdish Chandra Bose "had done much to unfold to the enquiring mind of the American public the composite culture of India."[126]

Every time the great Tagore visited the United States the Indian community welcomed him with pride except once at the height of the Gadar movement. Most of the praise and honor showered upon him by Americans in the banquet halls and the press columns was genuine. On his part Rabindranath too had genuine faith that "This America is a wonder worker. . . ."[127] These mutual showers of praise and friendship had, however, to pass through the pollutants of national, racial, and cultural diversities so that showers turned into acid rain. As a poet Tagore looked into the future, as a thinker he preached a message, as an Indian he openly resented the sad plight of his community here and of his nation at home, and as an aristocrat he felt himself the equal of the tallest ones in America. Neither the Nobel Prize nor the Knighthood—both the gifts of the West—could draw from him homage to what he considered the false gods of the Anglo-Saxon race.

As for the "message of the East," America had its own message *for* the East—"Keep Out." Rejection of political, cultural, or racial participation with Asia on terms of equality was an almost unanimous American decision expressed from time to time under different names—Open Door, Exclusion Acts, Boxer Rebellion, Spanish-American War, Christian missions, Treaty of Versailles, Washington Conferences, the Stimson Doctrine. Repulsion for the "yellow" coolies from the East was tempered only under the menace of "Mongoloid" fascists of Japan and the white Communists of Russia. In the age of Rabindranath's visits America was not in a mood to listen to any Asian, particularly if he struck a high pose as Tagore did.

The young Gadarites too disowned him. An admirer alleged that the poet's knighthood "sticks in [Ramchandra's] throat.[128] Gobind Behari Lal accused Tagore of standing aloof from the nationalist movement. There was even a furor in the press that the "Indian anarchists" had plotted to slay the poet.[129] His renunciation of knighthood following the Amritsar massacre of 1919 must, however, have rehabilitated him with the extremists. But sympathy for him may have developed even earlier.

At the Gadar trial in San Francisco, "My name was dragged into this case . . . I sent an explanatory telegram to President Wilson asking for his protection, which remained unacknowledged." The Prosecuting Attorney had made a remark that Rabindranath was not one of the defendants because "We overlooked him in our haste." He later confessed that the remarks were intended to be facetious and should not have been recorded by the reporter.[130]

But the mischief had been done. The *New York Times* published prominently that Tagore's name had been linked with German plots and that he "had enlisted the interest" of prominent Japanese and Chinese politicians "to establish an independent Government in India." His innocence was later officially established in the Departments of State and Justice, but the exoneration was never communicated to Tagore. Only research efforts in the 1960s retrieved the official correspondence from the Department of State.[131]

The Indian revolutionaries and Tagore may have differed on India's political issues, but they were of one mind as to the plight of the Indian immigrants. Both resented it and pleaded for liberalization of the immigration laws. In 1929 Tagore's own brief but painful contact with an administrator of those laws proved to him how inhuman and insensitive those laws could be to an Asian's feelings.

In 1916 Dr. N. S. Hardikar acquainted him with the Burnett Immigration Bill and "requested his attention to the objectionable provisions therein." In the course of this visit someone asked him if he would visit Canada. The poet said "most emphatically 'No!'" In 1929, however, he did go to Canada.[132]

In a press interview in November 1916 he pleaded against excluding Indian students as was proposed in a bill. "I think that to pass the bill will be a crime," he said.[133] In the spring of 1929 he was in Vancouver, Canada as India's representative at the conference of the Canadian National Council of Education. While there he received invitations from some American universities. He decided to pay another visit to the United States. "Unfortunately he lost his passport in Vancouver and the U.S. Consul whom he applied for a visa treated him disrespectfully."[134] This is what the Consul did to him: kept "him waiting for more than half an hour; "curtly" beckoned to him in his office; asked him "if he was able to pay his passage home"; asked him "did he realize the penalty for overstaying the time allowed by his visa"; "the winner of the Nobel Prize for Literature was asked if he could read and write."

He was fingerprinted on his arrival in California, a "privilege" which he felt"was confined by the Americans to criminals and people of colour from Asia and Africa." After this experience with the working of the Act of 1924 both in its spirit and practice, he cancelled his engagements in the United States and left.[135]

Contemporaries and recent scholars have pointed out the reasons why the "status of the small East Indian community remained low in comparison with other groups." Several causes were held responsible—small numbers, patterns of isolated living, by 1940 only 4 percent held professional positions, high percentage of illiteracy among them.[136] Yet the community had survived. In the next few years, it would win a decisive struggle. We must, therefore, look elsewhere for the elements of strength which must have been there, but have escaped adequate notice of scholars. As for Jagjit Singh, his urban, elitist, and secular bias prevented him at times from appreciating the cementing forces acting within the community that carried him on its shoulders to victory in 1946.[137] When we discuss this problem in another chapter we will find how big a help these "95% uneducated" were to the struggle for legal immigration. Indeed sometimes he had more trouble with the white collar professionals than with the farmers in California.

Common Indian patriotism was the strongest cementing force even for Muslims until at least the end of 1941 when most of them drifted away to the Indian Muslim League. Even after this separation they continued to support the demand for the right to citizenship. Identical demands were, therefore, the force that held them together with Sikh and the Hindus. For the latter two, community of religion and culture, combined with a common pride in the Congress leadership in India maintained high morale.

The farmers, though illiterate and scattered, were making money enough to contribute to famine relief and to the support of the Indian organizations working in America. During the last twenty years these organizations had won friends among the Irish-Americans, the American blacks, and most profitable of all, organized labor. Having no votes of their own, Indian leaders had been attempting to nurse the constituencies that had votes. The blacks were attracted by the community of suffering and the labor leaders were gradually abandoning old economics and starting to widen their international horizons.

At the top of the Indian community stood a tiny minority—to estimate its number as being even 100 might be a slight exaggeration—which was intensely partiotic, highly motivated, and extremely sensitive to national self-respect. This minority took the lead and used the opportunity presented by the Second World War to widen and to exploit to the noblest extent the capital of goodwill that previous Indian organizers had accumulated among the healthy, forward-looking, enlightened segments of American opinion.

The real strength of the community, of course, lay in its majority, the farmers, the troublemakers for the British, the image-spoilers of the Indian elitists, and for the American exclusionists, the epitome of the Hindu stereotype. The Sikhs had to draw heavily upon their spiritual resources to be able to withstand the wrath of the British, the hostility of the American laws, and the indifference of the compatriots at home. They survived "*Guruan de Aasarey*," with the grace of the Gurus. Let us try to understand a part of that grace in order to appreciate the Sikhs' survivability.

The Sikh faith prescribes three guiding principles of personal conduct : *kirt karna*, to perform active work; "*vand chakna*, to share what you consume; and *Naam japna*, to recite God's name. Added to these three—work, share, worship—and arising out of them is the principle of Seva, i.e., service, a very distinctive feature of the Sikh brotherhood, almost unique in its pervasive intensity in practice. The way to earn respect is through self-sacrifice and service—"Ap gavaye, seva kare, ta kich paye man" says the sacred song, *Asa di Var* which a Sikh recites every morning. This spirit of service and brotherhood was solidified among the Sikhs by their experience of the Ghallu Ghara, the holocaust attempted by the Muslim invaders from Afghanistan during the latter half of the eighteenth century. In practice the ideal of service is expressed in various ways, glamorous or routine. It may range from martyrdom in the cause of the faith to menial service in a gurudwara such as cleaning the place of worship, fanning the congregation, and helping in the langar, the free community kitchen. Free kitchen, a well-known feature of the Hindu faith, is a prominent, well-organized and an inevitable part of Sikh religious performances.[138]

Every gurudwara must have a free langar—the Sikhs pray together, eat together and in America they also lived together in groups for many years. The first gurudwara in North America was founded at Vancouver in 1908 and the first in America was built in 1912 at Stockton through the efforts of Santokh Singh, Jwala Singh Thathian, and Wasakha Singh Dadehar.[139]

A gurudwara is more than a place of worship. It is a community center, a hub of community life, a free rest house, a bank of information, an employment agency, a Sikh information center and emotionally a symbol of community pride. Das counted nine gurudwaras on the Pacific coast. Sikhism was the second immigrant church from India.[140]

The religion the Sikhs brought with them to North America was the old religion of the Gurus with its observances (rahats) more scrupulously obeyed and consciousness as a distinct community sharpened and revitalized by the impact of Namdhari, Singh Sabha and Khalsa Diwan movements.[141] Their attachment to the Sikh rahats was very visible to the unaccustomed eyes of Canadians and Americans from their turbans and beards. If the immigration officers had subjected them to a body search, which they did not, they would have found four more symbols of the Sikh faith—an iron bracelet on a wrist, an underwear reaching above the knees, long hair under the turban, a comb stuck into the kesh (long hair) and a small dagger slung over the shoulder between the shirt and the coat. The spiritual part of the Sikh religion, however, lay not on his body but in his heart from where it was expressed every morning in his prayers, every day in his tenacious adherence to it despite ridicule in America, and over the years in his struggles and achievements.

Most of the Sikhs continued to wear the physical symbols of their faith. Even those who, like Dalip Singh Saund, became clean-shaven, preserved their loyalty to the Sikh Panth that so very often they openly proclaimed in word and deed.[142] Several Sikhs went from Canada and America to India to participate in the gurudwara reform movement of the midtwenties. The Sikh organizations donated respectable amounts to Sikh and several other patriotic causes in India.[143] In all their four capacities—as Indians, Sikhs, Jat warriors, and immigrants—they provided the mass support, the money, and the manpower to the Gadar movement.

Under British classification they were one of the "martial races" of India whom they were eager to use, but also eager to screen from political education.[144] But with the Canal Colony agitation of 1907 under the leadership of Lajpat Rai and Ajit Singh the dam began to show fissures. The Sikhs' price for further collaboration began to rise in terms of political reform, civil services, and legislative representation. The Sikh Jat's emigration to Canada and the United States was an unwelcome development for the British because America particularly was the witch's brew of dangerous ideas. The rise of the Gadar Party was soon to prove that their apprehensions were not unfounded.[145]

The Sikhs' hardships and struggles in North America gave them a clear vision of the white man's world, of India and of Britain. In about half a dozen years the Sikhs received a political education of tremendous intensity and historical significance. The sixty years old Anglo-Sikh alliance started to wither away.[146] They would not always wholeheartedly side with Mahatma Gandhi's agitations and programs but they would never again side with the British against India's march towards freedom. They formed a significant part of the Indian National Army of Netaji Subhash Chandra Bose. This political awareness of the Sikhs in the twentieth century on a large scale originated in North America. It is Canada's and America's gift to India's freedom movement through both aspects of their national character—racist deeds and democratic societies.

The so-called "Hindu Conspiracy" trial was the product of Anglo-American alliance, the English doing all the spying and the Americans supplying all the law, the site, the cost of the trial and of jailing. In India, America was forgiven, the British never. There is something mysterious, almost mystic about the Indians' affection for the United States. There has been inequality, racial violence and exploded myths about American help in Indian causes but the love affair persists.[147] The reasons may lie in economic opportunities, an American national endowment for justice and fairplay or in a few immortal documents written by a few immortal men which from time to time have recovered control of the steering wheel to set the ship of American state back to its course.

Notes and References

1. Sidney Kansas, *U.S. Immigration, Exclusion and Deportation and Citizenship of the United States of America*, New York, 1941, 56. This Act granted an annual quota of 100 to India for the use of those who were born in India and were eligible to naturalization such as Europeans. Between 1925 and 1944 about 1020 Englishmen, Dutch and Frenchmen took advantage of it. *Cong. Record*, 79th Cong., Ist sess., October 10, 1945, 9531.
2. Ibid., the Act of March 2, 1929 (45 Stat. 1512), 168; that of June 8, 1934 (Public Law No. 299, 73rd Congress, S. 2692), 169.
3. Ibid., Alien registration, 141, fingerprinting, 144.
4. Wives losing their own citizenship, discussed in Chapter VI; barred from several professions, Hearings before a Subcommittee of the Committee

on Immigration United States Senate Seventy-Eighth Congress, Second Session on S.1595 a bill to Permit the Naturalization of Approximately Three Thousand Natives of India, 78 Congress. Second Session, on S. 1593, September 13 and 14, 1944, 42, hereafter to be cited as *S. 1595 Hearings*: Indians denied emergency relief, Mubarek Ali Khan's testimony. Ibid., 36, his Address in *The New India Bulletin*, July 31, 1945, I.L.A. Papers.

5. Senate Hearings on Ratification and Confirmation of Naturalization of Certain Persons of the Hindu Race, 69th Congress, Second Session, on S.J. Res. 128, December 9, 1926, 7; henceforth to be cited as *Senate Hearings, December 1926*. Thind's naturalization was granted under S. 2508 adopted by the 74th Congress and signed by the President on June 25, 1935, *Cong. Record*, 74th Cong., 1st sess., June 25, 1935, 10031, text of the bill. Ibid., June 10, 1935, 8977.
6. Kansas, ibid., 326.
7. For Second War Powers Act of March 22, 1942, *S. 1595 Hearings*, 6, Indians naturalized under it, Hearings Before a Subcommittee of the Committee on Immigration, United States Senate, 79th Congress, First Session on S. 236, a bill to permit all people from India in the United States to be naturalized, April 26, 1945, 5, henceforth to be cited as *Senate Hearings on S.236.*
8. "Indians in America," *Modern Review*, March 1908, 207, 208. B.K. Roy's articles in *Open Court* 1913 like those of Saint Nihal Singh in *Modern Review* in earlier years were creating a conscious ethnic identity based on resentment against immigration laws and policies both of Canada and the U.S.A. For instance, to visualize the possibility that one day these resentments may carry the Asian people "across the Pacific to teach the colorphobe and 'democratic' Americans a lesson in return for the American laws of exclusion and discrimination" Vol. 27 (1913), 623.
9. "The Spirit of the 'West'," *Modern Review*, January 1908, 47.
10. "A Message America Gave Me for India," ibid., October 1909, 373.
11. "The Triumph of Indians in Canada," ibid., August, 100.
12. "A Message America Gave Me for India," ibid., October 1909, national pride 374, reciprocity, 375, Brown Man's Burden, 377.
13. "The Situation in Australia," ibid. (February 1910), 117. A similar question was asked by K. M. Panikkar in 1917: whether any race had a right to consider any part of the world as its special preserve, ibid., March 1917, 337.
14. Their eating habits—"The uneducated Hindu and Sikh laborer does not eat beef. . . . On the other hand it is hard to come across a Hindu student who does not take beef." Lajpat Rai, *United States of America,* 465.

15. Arun Coomer Bose, "Indian Nationalist Agitations in the U.S.A. and Canada till the Arrival of Har Dayal in 1911," *Journal of Indian History* (1965): 227-239, 231; this elitist attitude continued over the decades. Sucheta Muzumdar in Lucie Chang and Edna Bonacich, ed., *Labor Immigration Under Capitalism,* 558.
16. "The Sikh has intensified the prejudice against him by his pagri (turban) and by long hair. Personally I have nothing but praise for this trait of his character. Go wherever he may, he maintains his Indian character; he keeps his distinctive dress and cooks his own food." Lajpat Rai, *United States of America*, 464-465; "They positively refuse to discard their turban on the plea of its being against their religion or "dharam." This turban "stands as an emblem of their power of resistance against being assimilated with their new environment." "The 'Hindus' . . . will never be assimilated with or absorbed by" the white population of America. "It is a peculiar trait in the Oriental character and instead of running it down or deprecating it it deserved [sic] to be commended and appreciated at its true value." Home-Political, November 1914, No. 77, Part B. *Report by Dady Burjor,* National Archives of India, 17, 18. Henceforth cited as the *Burjor Report*.
17. *Modern Review*, October 1911, 398, 399, emphasis added.
18. *Modern Review*, August 1911, 210, July 1911, 70.
19. Ibid., (August), 210, emphasis added; Dr. K. D. Shastri addressing an H.A.A. Convention regretted that "Not only the Americans have not duly realized our conditions but they have been largely led to misunderstand us as most of our adventurous fellow countrymen who arrived in this country happened to be illiterate and unassimilable." *Hindusthanee Student*, September 1915, 3.
20. S.P. Sen, *Dictionary of National Biography*, Calcutta, 1972, S.V. Ketkar, "Indian Emigration, Ancient and Modern," *Modern Review*, December 1912, 585; similar views expressed by Sarangdhar Das, ibid., November 1910, 533.
21. Ibid., December 1912, 583.
22. Ibid., 584.
23. Ibid., 583.
24. Ibid., 584; similar views by Sarangdhar, Das, ibid., November 1911, 532-533.
25. Ibid., December 1912, 584.
26. Joan M. Jensen : "fewer than 1500" were legal immigrants in 1946 while 3000 had "entered surreptitiously" in 1920s, Stephen Thernstrom, ed., *Harvard Encyclopedia of American Ethnic Groups*, Cambridge, Mass., 1980, 296; according to Jacoby the number of "officially admitted" Indians residing in the United States in 1950 should be 1625. The Census of 1950 however gives the figure 2649 which may include those who had

come illegally but had survived death or deportation, Mark Juergensmeyer and N. Gerald Barrier, Eds., *Sikh Studies : Comparative Perspectives on a Changing Tradition*, Berkeley, 1979, 164; according to Gary Hess the population was 2405 in 1940 but to this figure should be added the "several hundred" of the 3000 who had entered illegally and had "managed to remain," S. Chandrasekhar, ed., *From India to America*, La Jolla, California, 1982, 31.

27. For instance, "About five hundred of them have left for India the last year." M.P. Shaughnessy, the Indians' attorney, told the California State Board of Control on February 16, 1920. *California and the Oriental*, 108; Deportations and voluntary departures, 1906-1920 amounted to 1900, LaBrack, *Sikhs of Northern California*, 64; in twenty years 1911-1930 almost 4500 left, Joan M. Jensen in Thernstrom, ed., *Harvard Encyclopedia of American Ethnic Groups*, 296; also see *Modern Review*, June 1914, 627; May 1919, 524. There was wishful hope among high officials of the Government of India that under the Act of 1917 "the number of Indian labourers in the United States *must steadity diminish.*" Home Member, W.H. Vincent's Note dated January 27, 1919, Notes, Political Deposit, June 1919, No. 9, Further Papers Regarding Sir F. Popham-Young's Proposal, Home-Political, June 1919, No. 9, Deposit, 11, emphasis added.

"The period of 1917-1947 was one of cultural and numerical decline . . . ." LaBrack, "Sikhs Real and Ideal," Juergensmeyer and Barrier, eds., *Sikh Studies*, 134; Marriages with Mexican Women were "not so much an assimilation as a cultural genocide brought about by restrictive immigration laws." Ibid., fn. 20. Also see his *Sikhs of Northern California*, 145, 146; Harold S. Jacoby, *A Half- Century Appraisal of the East Indians in the United States*, Stockton, 1956, 9, 28; Rajani Kant Das, *Hindustani Workers On the Pacific Coast*, Berlin, 1923, 116; Dr. Anup Singh's statement, *S.1595 Hearings*, 20; "if the presence of Indians in America creates a "race problem" . . . nature would soon remove it. The average age of Indians in the United States is well above 50. Less than 1 percent of them are married. In a few short years the number of Indians in the United States must of necessity be negligible. Warren H. Atherton to Jagjit Singh, March 13, 1945, *House Hearings March 1945*, 93. "Had not immigration and naturalization laws changed in 1946, the East India community would almost certainly have eroded significantly perhaps to the point of extinction," S. Chandrasekhar, ed., *From India to America*, 32.

28. Gary R. Hess in Chandrasekhar, *From India to America*, 29.
29. See fn. 26, for Indians coming in illegally.
30. House, *Hearings on Restriction of Immigration*, 63rd Congress, 2nd Session, December 11, 1913, 212; Caminetti's press interview at Seattle,

Washington introduced into the record by Congressman Johnson. Date of the interview not given but not many weeks old.

31. Secretary Wilson mentions the Treaty, House Hearings on Hindu Immigration, 63rd Congress, second session, February 13, 1914, 47, hereafter to be cited as *Sudhindra Hearings*; full text of his letter, House Hearings on Hindu Immigration, 63rd Congress, Second Session, April 16 and 30, 1914, 141-144, hereafter to be cited as the *Bhutia Hearings*. See Appendix I.
32. *Sudhindra Hearings*, 47.
33. *House Hearings, December 11, 1913*, 212.
34. *Sudhindra Hearings*, 46.
35. Ibid., 47.
36. Ibid.
37. *San Francisco Examiner*, 24 January 1914. But Secretary Wilson was determined to exclude Hindus anyway—"regardless of physical test." Ibid.
38. Herman Scheffauer, "The Tide of Turbans," *Forum* (June 1910) : 618.
39. *Burjor Report*, 14, 16, 17.
40. *Burjor Report*, Notes, Political-B, November 1914, No. 77, 1.
41. Fns. 33-36; Rep. Burnett agreed, "There is danger in putting through the bill excluding the Orientals, of diplomatic relations between England and the United States." *Cong. Record*, 63rd Cong., 2nd sess., February 3, 1914, 2820.
42. House, *Hearings to Grant a Quota to Eastern Hemisphere Indians and to Make Them Racially Eligible for Naturalization*, 79th Congress, 1st sess., March 7, 8, 13, 14, 1945, Testimony of Richard W. Flournoy Jr., 137; henceforth cited as *House Hearings, March 1945*.
43. One Member of the Viceroy's Executive Council, an Additional Secretary in the Government of India, External Affairs Department and one in Commerce Department agreed that Americans were enjoying rights in India under the Treaty of 1815 which they were denying to Indians in the United States. Sir Feroz Khan Noon's Note dated May 14, 1942, 95, H. Prior's Note dated August 5, 1940, 12, and Pillai's Note dated January 29, 1942, 77, File 300-X/40, External Affairs, Notes, National Archives of India. Three nonofficial Indians resented that while Americans were enjoying rights in India under the treaty of 1815, Indians were denied those rights in America—Hemendra Rakhit, *Modern Review*, November 1938, 585; Kodand Rao, *The Annals of the American Academy of Political and Social Science*, May 1944, 205; Krishnalal Shridharani, *Asia and the Americas*, March 1945, 151.
44. "Some counties permit marriages, in others they don't let you marry." Dr. D.S. Saund, *Indian National Congress Association Newsletter*, I, 9. Some

counties which presumably permitted interracial marriages are mentioned in Bruce LaBrack and Karen Leonard, "Conflict and Compatibility," *Journal of Marriage and the Family*, August 1984, 528.

45. "Even men of labouring classes never molest or maltreat him. . . . He can live wherever he likes . . . without having any of those degrading checks and restraints [imposed upon him in South Africa]. Two Sikhs were arrested for alleged rowdy conduct, fined $50 and sent to jail for refusal to pay "such a heavy fine." "Next day the San Francisco *Examiner* came out with a strong editorial, denouncing the Magistrate and characterising the proceedings in the court as a mockery." *Burjor Report*, 20.
46. This phrase is quoted in Demi-official letter from M.C. Seton, Esq., to the Honourable Mr. H. Wheeler, dated India Office, Whitehall, July 31, 1914, its origin not indicated, National Archives of India. An instance of such American sympathy was that "the Chinese Republican movement was hailed with delight."

    "The ordinary American has . . . a sentimental regard for anyone . . who claims to be a champion of Liberty." Home-Political, December 1914, No. 96-98, Part A : Question of placing 'Ghadr' on list of prohibited publications. Suggestions made by British Ambassador in Washington in connection with seditious propaganda of Indian students at San Francisco, 6, National Archives of India.
47. The Indian community was "rapidly becoming geriatric as sixty-six percent were over forty years of age, thirty-two percent over fifty, and nine percent over sixty," Bruce LaBrack in S. Chandrasekhar, ed., *From India to America*, 61.
48. Sikhs of Fresno locality sent "more than" $10,000 to further the cause of education in the Panjab; *Hindustanee Student*, September-October 1925, 23; Sikh donations for schools and colleges in India, San Francisco *Chronicle*, 31 January 1926, p. 2, col. 5.
49. The quotation is from Hugh Tinker, *Separate and Unequal : India and Indians in the British Commonwealth 1920- 1950*, Vancouver, 1976, 37; a young I.C.S. officer, Girja Shankar Bajpai noted in 1931 that "The tradition of white supremacy (in the Dominions) had hardened into a dogma," ibid., 46; "Everybody loves the Hindus so long as they stay at home," Editorial comment, *New York Times*, 14 November 1923,16, quoted in Walter Charles Mackett, "Some Aspects of the Development of American Opinion on India 1918-1947" (Ph. D. diss., University of Southern California, June 1957), 119.
50. Harish K. Puri, *Ghadar Movement : Ideology, Organisation & Strategy* (Amritsar, 1983) 32, emphasis removed.
51. Senator William J. Stone (D-Mo) speculated on the implications of "excepting from the operation of" the literacy test people who have been

persecuted for racial, religious or political reasons. But he added, "provided the immigrant was not otherwise subject to exclusion" for other reasons. As an instance the Chinese would not be included in the exception. "In the manner the people of any other particular race could be excluded from our citizenship." *Cong. Record*, 63rd Cong., 3 sess., December 16, 1914, 264, 265; the phrase "race religion" is from Andre Siegfried, *America Comes of Age : A French Analysis*, New York, 1927, 325; "white harmony," *Modern Review*, January 1924, Editorial Note, 213.

52. "An entirely new American viewpoint on India was inaugurated when in 1898 'America's irresponsibility'—namely, traditional sympathy for such British irritants as the Irish, the Egyptians, the Boers, the Indians—"came to an end" because the Philippine Islands came under American administration," quoted from Ignatius Thayer, "America's Own India" by Sujit Mukherjee, "Early American Images of India." *India Quarterly* (January-March 1964) : 48-49, fn. 33.

In October 1923 the municipality of Allahabad, India attempted to impose punitive taxes on its British and American residents "in retaliation for [anti-Indian] actions in Kenya and the United States." Mackett concludes that "here was an indication that the Indian problem involved more than a mere parting with power by Britain, and that it might bring pressure even upon America," "Some Aspects," 118 and fn. 112; the oppressive character of British rule over India prevented the Government of India from protesting too much against American treatment of Indian immigrants. "We should remember," S.V. Ketkar wrote in 1912 "that when our public officers begin to speak about the subject [of Indians' disabilities] with the officers who represent the colonies as well as the United States, the former are easily silenced by the latter by asking whether the Indian Government itself treats us with equality in our own land. This question silences our officers and makes them feel shy to insist upon the matter further. Our Government becomes seriously handicapped in pressing our cause abroad." "Indian Immigration, Ancient and Modern," *Modern Review*, November 1912, 584. Identical policies toward Indians helped create another incentive for a united Anglo-American front against Asian aspirations. Some Americans "protested that Hindu revolutionists were sheltered in Washington," a policy which they claimed "would drive England to retain her ties with Japan," quoted from a letter published in the *New York Times*, 8 January 1922, in Mackett, ibid., 102, fn. 69.

"When the Anglo-Japanese Alliance terminated in 1921, the [British] Foreign Office wished to renew it" but owing to the insistence of Canada and Australia "London was persuaded to abandon this alliance, which the American public considered most unsuitable for a white nation. The

Washington Agreement is, in reality, an *entente* of all the white nations of the Pacific to keep Japan in *status quo*." Siegfried. ibid., 339.

"The more this small colony of 6,000,000 whites [Australia] . . . realize their terrifying situation, confronted by the "Yellow Peril," the more they respect the might of America . . . . Mr. Hughes premier of Australia once said "that he saluted with joy the launching of every new American battleship," Siegfried, ibid., 338. In 1924 Mr. Hughes visited the United States. Sudhindra Bose found out that the ex- Premier was "reaching hundreds and thousands of Americans with his "great message" . . . that America should go to war with Japan." Hughes told Dr. Bose "in blunt, homely words" that "One of the greatest problems which concern the world at the present time is the increase in Asiatic population. It is a disease," "So This Is An Australian Statesman," *Modern Review*, September 1924, 287, 286.

As in Australia but "To a lesser extent a similar psychological reaction is taking place in British Columbia and possibly throughout the whole of Canada . . . [which] "knows that she can depend on America, who will never tolerate the slightest attack on either her territorial integrity or her racial status. In actual practice, therefore, Canada has a complete guarantee without counting on England at all . . . Canada's security does repose on force, but on the force of her neighbor," Siegfried, ibid., 338-339.

53. M.S. Venkataramani and B.K. Shrivastava, *Quit India : The American Response to the 1942 Struggle*, New Delhi, 1979, 10.
54. Ibid., 10-11, nf. 14; according to Har Dayal major topics of conversation among Indians in America included "the greatness of the American people, the blessings of democracy, the honourableness of manual labour, *the meanness of Theodore Roosevelt* and the necessity of education," *Modern Review*, July 1911, 3, emphasis added.
55. The Director Central Intelligence, Government of India had reported in December 1914 that "The doings of the returned and returning "Ghadr" people in India itself are now our primary objection [objects ?] of watch and action." To this the Home Member added a crucial objective of British imperial policy and the purpose behind it : ". . . undoubtedly the Far East and the Pacific Coast will require our closer vigilance in the near future, since the campaign there can get into touch with the masses and the fighting races of India in a way that is impossible for continental anarchists in Europe." R.H. Cradock's Note dated December 10, 1914, Home Political, December 1914, No. 96-98, Part A. Suggestion made by British Ambassador in Washington in connection with seditious propaganda of Indian students at San Francisco, 11, National Archives of India. Clearly the objective was to prevent the Indian revolutionaries in East Asia and North America from indoctrinating the Sikhs. They must, therefore, be excluded from the United States also.

56. *Modern Review*, February 1927, 169; Puri, *Ghadar Movement*, 32-33; C.R. Cleveland's Note dated January 14, 1919, Home-Political, March 1919, No. 21, Deposit, Proposal to place Sir Frank Popham Young in charge of an Indian Bureau on the West Coast of America, 8, National Archives of India.
57. Chapter III.
58. Dr. K.D. Shastri's Address, *Hindusthanee Student*, September 1915, 3.
59. Das, *Hindusthani Workers*, 89.
60. Jacoby, *A Half-Century Appraisal*, 24; "To a considerable degree, the history of the East Indians in the United States has been the history of the organizations they built and through which they carried on much of their life activity," Jacoby in Juergenemeyer and Barrier, eds., *Sikh Studies*, 168.

    Several of these newspapers, magazines and organizations had been established in retaliation to British policy. For instance Ram Nath Puri's *Circular-i-Azadi* and Taraknath Das's *Free Hindusthan*. This latter stopped publication in November 1910, Arun Coomer Bose, *Indian Nationalist Agitations*, 235.
61. Krishnalal Shridharani, *My India, My America*, New York, 1941, 507.
62. Lajpat Rai's hard work, a summary, "My Farewell," *Young India*, December 1919; 276-278.
63. Before Roosevelt came into power," these liberal-radical intellectuals [were] ineffective and alienated from power but not hope in their own society . . . ." Alan Raucher, "American Anti-Imperialists and the Pro-India Movement, 1900-1932," *Pacific Historical Review*, 1974, 103.
64. Naeen Gul Rathore, "Indian Nationalist Agitation in the United States : Lajpat Rai and the Indian Home Rule League of America 1914-1920" (Ph. D. diss., Columbia University, 1965), 288.
65. Rathore, ibid., 84, 145, 286; Raucher, "American Anti-Imperialist," 91, 92.
66. Rathore, ibid., 73.
67. Lalaji's contacts with students, *Hindusthanee Student*, March, May, October 1916, January 1917; Hardikar Biography, 10, Hardikar Papers; hard training under him, Hardikar Biography, 12-13; N.S. Hardikar, *Lala Lajpat Rai in America*, New Delhi, 1966, 77; Rathore, ibid., 99.
68. Lajpat Rai, *United States of America*, 468; Das, *Hindustani Workers*, v, 118-124.
69. Lajpat Rai, ibid., 461, 463-464.
70. Ibid., 466, 461; some got drunk and "were expelled in consequence of their riotous conduct in public," Har Dayal in *Modern Review*, July 1911, 3.
71. *Burjor Report*, 12-13.
72. Ibid., 13; 18.

73. Das, *Hindustani Workers*, 84. Hardly anyone has accused the Sikhs of emigrating to America to drink. For the Europeans inexpensive liquor was alleged to be one of America's major attractions. They came to the United States "because the financial opportunities are greater, because more pumpkins can be grown on an acre of land; and because red wine costs but 19 cents a gallon." Congressman Denver S. Church, *Cong. Record*, 63rd Cong., 3rd sess., February 4, 1915, 3055.
74. Allegations made, Herman Scheffauer, "The Tide of Turbans," *Forum*, June 1910, 617, *Burjor Report*, 16, 17, 18-19. Asia was not the only supplier of "cheap labor" with "low standard of living." "They [the American workers of north European extraction] could not compete with those laborers from southeastern Europe who lived on 30 cents a day and who were willing to work 12 hours for a wage of $1.80 a day," Senator Henry F. Ashurst of Arizona speaking, *Cong. Record*, 64th Cong., 2nd sess., August 17, 1916, 12768.
75. *Cong. Record*, 63rd Cong., 3rd sess., February 4, 1915, 3055.
76. The Sikh is "half agriculturist, half soldier, and wholly bania," *Punjab Gazetteer*, Vol. I, 63. He believed in capitalism, never thought of himself as a proletarian. The Stockton, California Chief of Police told Das that the Hindu "has no socialistic, I.W.W., or Bolshevik tendencies," *Hindustani Workers", 86.*
77. S.S. Josh, *Sohan Singh Bhakna : Founder of the Ghadar Party*, New Delhi, 1970, 12.
78. "In some of the China towns, tall, plump forms of swarthy Sikhs tower over the Chinamen. In his hand the Indian policeman holds the queues of perhaps a dozen celestial criminals. Triumphant the Sikh marches in the streets, covering many blocks, piloting the ten or twelve captives to the police station." Sant Nihal Singh, "Indians in the 'Far East'," *Modern Review*, August 1908, 120; *Overland* of April 1908 has a photograph showing "one of king Edward's Sikh policemen in Hong Kong" with this comment printed under it : "The magnificent Sikhs are a race from the north of India; they make excellent soldiers and police, and as they bear Aryan blood in their veins, they are naturally ready to fall in line with the ideas of the Westerner."
79. H.A. Millis, "East Indian Immigration to British Columbia and the Pacific Coast States," *American Economic Association Review*, 1911, 75.
80. *Hindustani Workers*, 76. Impartial contemporary American witnesses as to the Indian immigrant's spirit of self-respect and "aversion to seeking charity" are plentiful, several of them quoted in the pages of this work. Four such witnesses are on page 102. There is one instance when "In the winter of 1907-8 the East Indians in northern California were desperate and in great distress. They were assisted by money sent to them by the British consul-general." The reasons for lack of money were "general

aversion to employing them." Soon they started earning so that by July 1908 they sent to India $34,000 from Marysville post office alone. Reports of the Immigration Commission, Vol. 23, 347. However there is another view as to the economic fate of Indian immigrants during the 1930s when "a few . . . received aid from relief agencies since the depression began." Frances J. Brown and Joseph S. Roucek (eds.), *One America*, New York, 1945, 456.

81. *Reviews in American History*, Vol. 12, No. 1, March 1984, 111.
82. "They dislike us as a people as much even as we dislike them," Denver S. Church said. *Cong. Record*, 63rd Cong., 2nd sess., August 20, 1914, Appendix 843; "As long as there is any ill-feeling, the possibility of social intercourse is remote." Das, Hindustani Workers, 115, avoiding food cooked by others : Denver S. Church, ibid.; Brown and Roucek, eds., *One America*, 457-458, "I was cruelly discriminated against many a time because of the place of my birth," Dilip Singh Saund, *Congressman From India*, New York, 1960, 36, also see 40-41, 61-62.
83. Robert Shaplen, "One-Man Lobby," *The New Yorker* (March 24, 1951), 50.
84. Master Tara Singh's speech at Saund's reception in Amritsar, *Akali Patrika*, December 11, 1957.
85. *Modern Review*, June 1914, 616.
86. *A Half-Century Appraisal*, 16. The Sikh Temple at Stockton was modernizing not "assimilating" when it "installed Short Wave Receiver" to hear news from Delhi, Bhola Singh to Jagjit Singh, August 3 (year illegible), I.L.A. Papers.

    To do justice to Dr. Jacoby's wider interpretation of "assimilation" here is what he wrote on ibid., 32 : "In a very real sense, there are no people wholly 'unassimilible' [sic]; and even if we were to establish a scale of 'assimilability', the East Indians would undoubtedly stand high on any list of the peoples of the world."
87. Transcript of interview given to Dr. R. Narayanan, 16, 17. Parentheses in the original.
88. See fn. 85. For Prof. Commons' definition, *Modern Review*, May 1919, 524.
89. *House Hearing, December 6, 1913*, 8.
90. Every essay in Sudhindra Bose's *Fifteen Years in America* shows it. Also see *San Francisco Chronicle*, 31 January 1926, p. 2F, col. 5.
91. Transcript of interview given to Dr. R. Narayanan, 17. The "Americans" of course would be his friends and colleagues of the 1940s and 1950s not the general public.
92. *Sudhindra Hearings*, 9.
93. Senate Hearings, December 1926, 16, 24, 28, 30 for Gohkale, Das, Mukerjee and Kokatnur respectively. Sudhindra Bose rejected the notion

of conversion, *Modern Review*, March 1933, 279; he was turned out of school because he declined to convert, ibid., November 1948, 365. Dr. Kokatnur is shown as a "Unitarian" in *Who's Who In America*, Vol. XVII, 1932-1933 but see the story how he helped save a Hindu lady from conversion, Hardikar, *Lala Lajpat Rai*, 47-51. Jacoby, on the other hand calls converts to Christianity "emancipated," *A Half-Century Appraisal*, 23. In this connection it may be interesting to note the position of some officials of the Indian National Congress : "To the extent that the religious quality of Indian culture has saved our overseas communities from the strangle-grip of Christianity and, consequently, from the nameless merging into a dull hybrid and cultureless existence, it has been useful." Rammanohar Lohia, *Indians in Foreign Lands*, A.I.C.C. Allahabad, 1938, 3, General Secretary.

94. *Report*, 18.
95. India-born Residents of the United States Request for Naturalization : Hearing Before House Committee on Immigration and Naturalization, 76th Cong., 1st sess., June 21, 1939, 17, henceforth this Hearing would be cited as *June 1939 Hearing*.
96. There are indications that the law of 1913 did not operate harshly against Indians who, according to one modern authority, were "able to move into the ranks of owner/tenants within *about ten years of arrival*." Sucheta Mazumdar, "Punjabi Agricultural Workers in California 1905-1945," in Lucie Cheng and Edna Bonacich, eds., *Labor Immigration Under Capitalism*, 571; several Indians had become big landlords, and farmers, before the Sutherland ruling of 1923 in spite of the Land Laws. Burjor Report, 12, Das, *Hindustani Workers*, 23-25, 28. Kanshi Ram donated a large piece of land to the Gadar Party; Josh, *Bhakna*, 27. These land laws were aimed primarily at the Japanese, California Board of Control, *California and the Oriental*, 11, 12, 13; the Supreme Court had upheld their validity, Carl Brent Swisher, *American Constitutional Development*, Boston, 1954, 800-801, Taraknath Das, "What is at the Back of Anti-Asianism of the Anglo-Saxon World ?" *Modern Review*, March 1924, 262-264.
97. Dr. Karen Leonard, "Punjabi Farmers and California's Alien Land Law," *Agricultural History*, No. 4 (October 1985) : 7, 8. Roger Deniels, *Politics of Prejudice*, 63.
98. Leonard, "Punjabi Farmers," 7; Lawrence A. Wenzel, "The Rural Punjabis of California : A Religio-Ethnic Group," *Phylon* (February 29, 1968) : 251.
99. Ibid., 9; D.S. Saund, *Congressman From India*, 59, 65.
100. Leonard, "Punjabi Farmers," 9, 10; Deniels, *Politics of Prejudice*, 88.
101. Leonard, "Punjabi Farmers," 10; *Christian Century*, March 13, 1940, 357; LaBrack, *The Sikhs of Northern California*, 167. For a modest estimate

of cheatings and persecutions relating to the Alien Land Laws, see his, "Occupational Specialization among Rural California Sikhs : The interplay of Culture and Economics," *AMERASIA*, 1982, 37, more serious consequences, Karen Leonard, "The Pahkar Singh Murders : A Punjabi Response to California's Alien Land Law," *AMERASIA*, 1984, 80, 85.

102. *Modern Review*, July 1924, 17; February 1927, 169; *Christian Century*, March 13, 1940, 357.
103. Leonard, "Punjabi Farmers," 11, 13.
104. Transcript of Jagjit Singh's interview with Dr. Narayanan, 1, 2 : Leonard, "The Pahkar Singh Murders," *AMERASIA*, 11 ; 1 (1984), 75-87, deals with one of the most remembered cases.
105. *Modern Review*, March 1924, 264.
106. Ibid., December 1927, 677-678.
107. Leonard, "Punjabi Farmers," 6.
108. Ibid., 17; *California and the Oriental*, 48.
109. Leonard, "Punjabi Farmers," 17.
110. Sant Nihal Singh, "The Triumph of Indians in Canada," *Modern Review*, August 1909, 100.
111. Leonard, "Punjabi Farmers," 15.
112. *Hindustanee Workers*, 94-95, 97-102.
113. *Caste and Outcast*, 270.
114. Sant Nihal Singh in *Modern Review*, August 1909, 99. Also see *Burjor Report*, 13, 17; Leonard, "Punjabi Farmers," 3. There is a story in the Panjab illustrative of this work mania. A Sikh Jat's mother died just during the busy harvest season. "Keep her wrapped till we are done with harvesting," he told his family.
115. Help for Bhagat Singh Thind, Thind's letter to the Editor, *The Mahratta*, Poona, January 22, 1922, Hardikar papers, subject File No. 1, 1922; help in Pahkar's defence, Leonard, "Pahkar Singh Murders," *AMERASIA*, 9. Lawrence A. Wenzel, "The Rural Punjabis of California : A testimony, *Sudhindra Hearings*, 78-79. Das, *Hindustani Workers*, 45, 46, 58-59. The tradition of employing fellow-Indians still continues but with a slight change, "Cementing Ties that Pay Off," *New York Times*, 30 September 1984.
116. LaBrack, *Sikhs of Northern California*, 81, 82. Rep. Denver S. Church testimony, *Sudhindra Hearings*, 82. *Burjor Report*, 13.
117. Allegation made, *Sudhindra Hearings*, 79-81; the rejoinder *Burjor Report*, 19, *Cong. Record*, 62nd Cong., 2nd sess., April 19, 1912, 5017.
118. *Sudhindra Hearings*, 75. *Caste and Outcast*, 205. Maldwyn Allen Jones, *American Immigration*, 181.
119. "Only six Sikh women were in the country from 1904 to 1947," LaBrack, *Sikh Studies*, 134, fn. 20; "A singular fact is that the whole (Indian) population is male with the exception of about a score of girl students in

various universities," *Indian Review*, August 1933, 535; there were no women students in America at least till July 1911, *Modern Review*, July 1911, 70 and footnote; there was a suspicion among exclusionists that there were Hindu women in America disguised as men, *Sudhindra Hearings*, 75; during the Indian Students' convention at the Panama Pacific Exposition "a couple of young ladies dressed like Hindu women" served tea and sweets to guests, *Hindusthanee Student*, September 1915, 10.

120. *Sudhindra Hearings*, 14-16, 30, 82, 85; Sudhindra Bose, *Fifteen Years in America*, 426-430; *Modern Review*, June 1914, 626, July 1924, 18, 19. Bajpai testimony, *House Hearings, March 1945*, 70. The marriage aspect of Hindu social life in America has been studied in Yusuf Dadabhoy, "Circuitous Assimilation Among Rural Hindustanis in California," *Social Forces*, December 1954; Bruce LaBrack and Karen Leonard, "Conflict and Compatibility," *Journal of Marriage and the Family* (August 1984); LaBrack, *Sikhs of Northern California*; Jacoby, *A Half-Century Appraisal*, 28-31.
121. Dadabhoy, "Circuitous Assimilation," 40; Das, *Hindustani Workers*, 77.
122. "The West, in its relation to us, is all plan and purpose incarnate, without any superfluous humanity." Rabindranath Tagore, *Orient*, New York, Vol. 1, No. 2, April-May 1923,18.
123. Ibid., 17.
124. *Hindustanee Student*, May 1925, 3; for Uday Shankar, Press Release by Basant Kumar Ray, I.L.A. Papers.
125. *Hindustanee Student*, December 1926, December 1928, 10; *Modern Review*, March 1927, 323-329. Taraknath Das's Open Letter to Shastri and Jawala Singh's letter from Vancouver, September 1, 1922 to N.S. Hardikar in India. The part of the letter pertaining to him reads : "S.N. Shashtri came here in Aug. 1922 & was not treated, he himself came to the temple but told him that you are not reliable man & we are non co operated if you want to talk us, be follower of the Congress." Both these documents are in Hardikar Papers, Nehru Museum and Library, New Delhi. I.L.A. Papers.
126. Hemendra Rakhit, *Hindustanee Student*, January 1926, 9.
127. *Los Angeles Times*, 19 September 1916, quoted in Stephen N. Hay, "Rabindranath Tagore in America," *American Quarterly*, Vol. 14, No. 3 (Fall 1962), 458.
128. *Modern Review*, May 1917, 553.
129. *Atlantic Monthly*, June 1927, 730. His assertion was not exactly correct. The protest was published in the Los Angeles *Examiner* of 7 October 1916.
130. *Atlantic Monthly*, June 1927, 730; Kalyan Kumar Banerjee, "Rabindranath Tagore and the San Francisco Trial," *Modern Review*, July 1964, 27. For this whole incident see Banerjee's article and Stephen N. Hay, "Rabindranath Tagore in America," 450-452.

131. *Hindusthanee Student*. January 1917, 20, 5; N.S. Hardikar, *Biography*, 12-13 in Hardikar Papers, Nehru Memorial Museum and Library; *Modern Review*, August 1926, 219.
132. *Modern Review*, June 1917, 663-644.
133. Stephen N. Hay, "Rabindranath Tagore in America," 457.
134. Ibid., Joseph Lister Dees, *Tagore in America*, Calcutta, 1961, 25.
135. Krishna Kriplani, *Rabindranath Tagore : A Biography*, New York, 1962, 343.
136. Gary Hess in S. Chandrasekhar, Ed., *From India to America*, 31.
137. His article, "Why Do Americans know So Little About India ?" September 30, 1946, 11, I.L.A. Papers.
138. The following are good introductions to the study of Sikh history and religion; Hari Ram Gupta, *A History of the Sikhs*, 3 vols., Lahore, 1944; Indubhushan Banerjee, *The Evolution of the Khalsa*, 2 vols., Calcutta, 1962; N.K. Sinha, *The Rise of Sikh Power*, Calcutta, 1960; W.H. McLeod, *The Evolution of the Sikh Community*, Oxford, 1976.
139. Gurdial Singh, "East Indians," *Sociology and Social Research*, January-February 1946, 214; Pritam Singh Panchi, *Gadar Ki Goonj aur Kamagata Maru Ka Romanch* (Hindi), Rajdhani Granthagar, New Delhi, 1977, 22; Juergensmeyer and Barrier, eds., *Sikh Studies*, 180.
140. Das, *Hindustani Workers*, 73, 80, 81; S.S. Josh, *Sohan Singh Bhakna*, 16; Gary R. Hess, "The Asian Immigrants in the United States : The Early Phase, 1900-65," *From India to America*, 32.
141. Sant Singh Sekhon, "The Minorities of India - 1. The Militant Sikhs," *Asia and The Americas*, May 1942, 301; Josh, *Sohan Singh Bhakna*, 9, 11.
142. An instance is Congressman D.S. Saund's declaration of loyalty on behalf of American Sikhs. *Akali Patrika* Jullundur, December 11, 1957.
143. Das, *Hindustani Workers*, 104-106.
144. S.C. Mittal, *Freedom Movement in Punjab, 1905- 1929*, Delhi, 1977, 49, cites the Panjab Government concern at the politicians' attempts to educate the Sikh military pensioners by persuading them to attend public meetings. Josh, *Sohan Singh Bhakna*, 11.
145. With the Sikhs in America the British were nervous but Har Dayal was proud of the change his Sikh compatriots were undergoing here : "He becomes a changed man . . . He learnes to respect himself. He no longer thinks that a risaldarship in the Indian army is the summit of earthly ambition for him. He sees that there are other powers in the world besides Great Britain. Silently but surely, a great internal revolution occurs within him . . . This process of moral and material improvement is watched with keen anxiety and many misgivings by interested parties. But it cannot be checked so long as the Sikhs emigrate to this country." "India in America," *Modern Review*, July 1911, 4. "The British Government itself does not

wish the Hindus to come here. They might become imbued with pestiferous ideas of political freedom." Ramchandra. Editor *Hindustan Gadar* to Editor of the New York Times. August 7. 1916. *New York Times*. 13 August 1916.

146. Josh, *Sohan Singh Bhakna*, 20-23; Deol, *Role of the Ghadar Party*, 81, 82. The Sikh deputation mentioned here failed to secure British official support in getting their grievances remedied. This failure caused widespread disillusionment among the Sikh immigrants with the British as well as with the Sikh communal organizations in the Panjab. "To hell with this loyalty to British rule, to hell with these decorations and the citizenship of British empire," the Indian settlers started saying. Josh, ibid., 34. *Sedition Committee Report*, 146. Deol, ibid., 133, fn. 59 where collaboration is now seen in a different light. "With their awakening, the entire edifice of the British Empire in India would be endangered." Surendra Karr wrote about the Sikhs in 1919, *Open Court*, vol. 33 (1919), 474.

147. Rathore, *Indian Nationalist Movement*, 285 on the "myth of American support for India" and Jawaharlal Nehru's tribute to American efforts on behalf of India's freedom; also *Modern Review*, April 1917, 422. Love and admiration for America, Das, *Hindustani Workers*, 103-104. In the Gadar Party songs the blame and curses are hurled only against the British, Josh, *Sohan Singh Bhakna*, 29, 30, 31. The whites were, in popular Indian parlance, ridiculed as "monkeys" but here on p. 31 it is "British" monkeys. Bankim Chandra Chatterji, the author of India's national song 'Vande Mataram' and the famous Urdu poet, Akbar Allahabadi have also indulged in the same stereotype but always against the British. British sovereignty over India was sometimes called Bundershahi—the rule of the monkeys, S.C. Mittal, *Freedom Movement in The Punjab*, 48, fn. 92. Har Dayal put his admiration for the United States in eloquent pharases : "No one can breath [sic] beneath the stars and stripes without being lifted to a higher level of thought and action. The great flag of the greatest democratic state in the world's history burns up all cowardice, servility, pessimism and indifference," *Modern Review*, July 1911, 4.

5

THE COMMUNITY FINDS A LEADER

Your work here on behalf of India's liberty has been truly remarkable. You have functioned in various capacities as scholar, teacher, propagandist, orator, and advocate of a nation's cause, and all of these upon the highest level of integrity, honor, and resourceful leadership. You have been like the watchman on the towers, always alert, always fearless, militant and courageous.

—REV. JOHN HAYNES HOLMES

There is no duplicate of J.J.

—PEARL BUCK

Of all the Indian residents of the United States during the first half of the present century, Jagjit Singh possessed a combination of advantages that few others possessed. These were advantages of birth, comparative youth, financial independence, business success, intellect, personal charm, length of involvement in the struggle for freedom at home, and a capacity to win American friends. Together they formed a combination that enabled him to become an all but unrivaled leader. In his effort to improve the legal status of his community, he exploited his talents as an organizer and the circumstances created by World War II, to become a successful leader—the only successful leader that the Indian community produced in its first half century in America.

He worked for the enactment of the immigration law of 1946 with the unanimous support of seven opinions that had formerly gone their separate ways on this subject. The Luce-Celler bill was supported by public opinion in India, by the British government, the American administration, the U.S. Congress, organized labor, the churches, and the Indian immigrants in America. Such unanimity had never before been achieved. The times and the man had united to justify Jagjit Singh's claim to have been "the right man in the right place at the right time."[1]

His advantages started with his parentage. Both his parents came from wealthy families—"filthy rich" as he would call them later—and he was their only son, "spoiled" by his father's status as a high Government official in the North-West Frontier Province of India.[2]

Jagjit Singh Ahluwalia[3] was born on October 5, 1897 in Rawalpindi in the Panjab where his mother had come, in the Hindu tradition as old as the Buddha and Guru Nanak to her own mother's home for her first confinement. His parents' household dialect made him a Panjabi, their faith made him a Sikh, and the location of his ancestral residence in the N.W.F.P. enabled him to boast of being a Pathan.[4]

His father, Rup Singh Ahluwalia, retired as an Extra Assistant Commissioner, the highest executive-judicial office an Indian could reach in the Provincial Service in the days when the richest plums were reserved for British men. Only the most talented Indians could reach even that subordinate status. According to the son's testimony, the father indeed was a talented man, a scholar of Sanskrit and Persian, a writer, and an orator. He did not send Jagjit to school but the intellectual qualities his son displayed show that by his home schooling he had achieved excellence in the mastery over a foreign language, a bold handwriting, logical organization of thought and a diligence to understand a problem before starting to work on it whether it be famine in India or immigration in the United States. The seeds of several other qualities that flowered in the work of the "One-Man Lobby" made their first appearance before he was twenty-four. Recognizing the importance of "influencing the influencers" as well as of the significance of the press, he wrote a letter to an editor in 1920 complaining of official high-handedness in his hometown and sold shares of a friend's newspaper. When his property was confiscated or a passport refused for participation in the noncooperation movement, he lobbied some of the major Indian politicians including Motilal Nehru, Tej Bahadur Sapru and Madan Mohan Malaviya to have the official orders reversed.[5]

Jagjit Singh's political education started, as did that of countless other Indians in that "Annus Mirabilis," the year 1919, when the British government terrorized the Panjab, a British general massacred Indians in Amritsar, the British governor of the Panjab supported his military man on-the-spot, the British House of Lords rewarded the butcher, Mahatma Gandhi declared the dissolution of his loyalty to the British Empire, Tagore returned his knighthood, and the "bug of nationalism got" our young hero.[6]

He was a student in Lahore when he felt "repulsed" by the stories of the cruelties and bestiality of the British action in Jallianwala Baag in Amritsar, 32 mile, away. He later wrote, "It just struck me that I had no business to do anything else but follow the nationalist movement."[7]

While leading demonstrations in Lahore, he escaped being hit by British bullets twice. He organized a Congress Committee in his hometown, Abbotabad, in 1921 and a shutdown of shops and buses on the arrival of the Prince of Wales in India in November for which he had to stay overnight in jail, his only incarceration. A month later, he attended the Congress session at Ahmedabad defying the Deputy Commissioner's orders by obeying Gandhi's advice to attend. For this defiance he was exiled from the Province and his property confiscated.[8]

Meanwhile he had been elected to the Panjab Provincial Congress Committee (P.P.C.C.) and in 1921 to his prized achievement—membership of the All-India Congress Committee (A.I.C.C). Along with his activities in the Congress movement, he participated in the Sikh Gurdwara Reform agitation of the early 1920s. Had he stayed on in India he might have emerged a leading Congress figure in the N.W.F.P. that was virgin soil for the nationalists. But he was neither a charkha-spinning, khaddar-wearing orthodox Congressman nor a votary of the Gandhian brand of nonviolence. The sudden withdrawal of the Congress agitation by Gandhi in February 1922 because some people had indulged in violence at a village, Chauri-Chaura, made him feel "like a pricked balloon" and forced him, like many other young participants, to reshape his life and seek another career.[9]

The credentials he won during the three years of his active participation in the Congress movement were of lasting inspiration and pride to him personally and proved of immense value to his later career: They were his passport to the affection and confidence of Americans and Indians in the United States. They were an insignia of his superiority over all other Indian activists, few of whom had risked so much, participated for so long, or reached such high offices.[10]

In 1923, he decided to study law in England. This decision to become barrister may have been suggested by his friend Dewan Chaman Lal, a barrister himself and by the example of his cousin, H.K.S Malik, another barrister. He may have hoped to build up a lucrative practice in an independent profession on the goodwill his family had earned in the N.W.F. Province. The road to government employment had been blocked by his participation in the national movement.[11]

To travel to England he needed a passport. Motilal Nehru, Dewan Chaman Lal and T.C. Goswami pulled some wires for him and got the passport directly from the head of the Province on February 23, 1924. Handing him the passport the official warned "Don't get involved in Gadar activities," to which Jagjit Singh, who had more accurate knowledge, replied, "I am going to England not America."[12]

Within six weeks he was in London. He was twenty-six and this was his first voyage overseas. He returned to India about seven times and entered America perhaps 14 times during the next 35 years. The British officer's instinct was not completely wrong. He was letting loose a patriot who proved to be more enduring than Har Dayal and who instead of getting involved in "Gadar," created a new Gadar of his own.

If in April 1919 "the bug of nationalism" got him, five years later, the bug of money-making possessed him. Instead of studying law he joined the British Empire Exhibition at Wembley as a concessionaire for Indian textiles in 1924 and 1925. The importing of Indian textiles became his life's occupation. Profits earned at Wembley made the business attractive. Losses suffered at Philadelphia in 1926 and again during the stock market crash of 1929 made recovery a moral obligation, a psychological necessity for a man who proudly called himself a "fighter."[13]

The year 1925 was "the turning point": he decided to abandon the Eastern Hemisphere in order to make more money. Much of what we know of his first twelve years in the United States comes from what he told journalists in 1943, 1945, and 1951, and what is recorded in his oral history in 1970. In addition, several autobiographical references are scattered in the documents of the India League.

The 150th anniversary of the signing of the Declaration of Independence was an opportunity for the city of Philadelphia to make a profit out of it in the "American way." A Sesquicentennial International Exposition was proposed to run from June to November 1926. It was billed as "the greatest international exposition ever arranged."[14] One million delegates were expected to attend the nearly 200 conventions to be held during the Exposition where discussions on every subject under the sun and "some beyond that luminary" would take place. The official estimate of fifty million visitors was labelled as "a very conservative figure." Jagjit Singh was told by the Americans that sixty million would come. The Exposition received so much coverage in the press that the entries in the New York *Times* Index for three months run to almost two columns.[15]

Jagjit Singh learned that the Exposition was an American "racket" to raise the value of the swamp south of the city of brotherly love. Only about one-tenth of the advertised number of visitors came and the whole thing turned out to be the "biggest flop." But in 1925 enthusiasm was the rule.[16]

Indian students in America urged commercial and industrial associations of India "to represent India in a fitting manner" at the coming Exposition. A delegation of the Sesquicentennial organizers tried to persuade A.C. Chatterjee, India's High Commissioner in London, to set up an India Pavilion at the Exposition. He directed them to Jagjit Singh to persuade him to win over Indian merchants to make an India Pavilion. Jagjit turned out to be more enthusiastic than the Americans or the High Commissioner could have expected.[17]

He traveled to India and persuaded 29 merchants to participate. The total Indian delegation at Philadelphia was 35 including a few Englishmen. He left Bombay in February 1926, got the British Foreign Office endorsement for travel to the U.S.A. on April 15, an American visa the same month, and in June entered the United States for the first time at Niagara Falls, New York in June.[18]

Most of the Indian merchants lost money. Jagjit said he "lost his shirt" so much so that a journalist alleged he was "too broke for passage home." On April 16, 1927 the Indian students in New York gave a farewell dinner to the "returning" Indian merchants of the Sesquicentennial including "Mr. Singh of Kashmere." This is probably the first mention of Jagjit Singh in press in the United States. His family had moved from the Frontier Province to Srinagar, Kashmir. It was here that the son would send during the 1940s an occasional American friend including Congressman James G. Fulton (R-PA) to enjoy its "good hospitality" of the Valley.[19]

Jagjit Singh exaggerated the extent of his losses at the Exposition. He did not "lose his shirt" nor is it correct that all the money he made at Wembley "was just drowned there."

He did lose $50,000 at the Exposition but still had $30,000 left with him as well as the unsold merchandise : "semi- precious stones and bolts of cloth mostly." To get rid of this merchandise he opened a retail store in Philadelphia at Walnut Street not very far from where Sudhindra Bose had rented his first room in America 22 years before. There "to his surprise, the stuff sold readily and profitably." In April 1927 when the New York students honored the Indian merchants, Jagjit was there to stay. He "opened a wholesale importing house on lower Fifth Avenue where in three years he recouped his Exposition losses."[20]

He did not stay in America because he was "broke" but because "I have a streak of a fighter," he said in 1970, "I am a born fighter, I do not take defeat easily." He said to himself, "No, I am not going back defeated." He had to repeat the same slogan to himself when the Crash of 1929 treated him probably worse than the Exposition.[21]

When the Depression sent him again "down to hell" he became "his own travelling salesman" carrying a 40 1b. sample case through New England, Midwest and the South.[22] By 1934 when he entered the Chicago World Fair as Director of the India Exhibit he had probably succeeded in driving away the wolf. In a Directory published in 1934 he is listed among prominent Indian merchants in America. By 1939 he was a well-established New York importer specializing "in the marketing of Indian textiles for women's fashions and has been fairly successful in that line . . . . Mr. Singh's firm has both wholesale and retail establishments located in two of the best locations in this City." The wholesale establishment was Singh, Singh & Co. Inc. and the retail store was India Arts and Crafts Inc.[23]

In Miss Suzanne Goutal he found an aide capable of taking over full charge of his business when he got involved in the India League. He claimed to have made money through two venturesome ideas that paid off—introduction of raw silk textiles into the American market and ladies' coats made out of Indian bedspreads into the American fashion world.[24]

Jagjit never ceased to be proud of being a Sikh, but the pressure of living in America started to bear heavily on the outward symbols of his faith. They had "attracted customers" at the Philadelphia Exposition, and made him "the cynosure of all eyes" who "stop [ped] traffic at every corner" but caused him "an awful mental strain." The strain brought about a decision to surrender which he later rationalized as if it was a spiritual revelation. "After travelling around and learning a lot more than I used to know," he told Shaplen in 1951, "I came to the conclusion that religion was a good thing but that it had nothing to do with having a beard and turban." So he decided to shave off his hair and beard.

The decision was made in Toronto, Canada and the cutting took place in New York. This Toronto visit seems to be the one shown on his Passport No. 1 as that of September 1929, thereby placing the removal of his hair in the fall of 1929. His next Passport issued on July 15, 1932 shows him without beard and turban. In the third Passport even the mustache is gone. No passport shows him with a Vandyke which he says he kept for some time.[25]

In 1932 he scored a *coup de maitre* which brought about a radical uplift in his legal status as an Indian merchant. He made his firm technically a British concern by the simple process of showing in his papers a friend's office in London as his firm's office in England. This paper trick could get him a Treaty of Commerce visa, if the American Consul in London agreed to look at things the way Jagjit wanted him to. A complaint to him by an American customer of Jagjit Singh's Wembley concession seven years before which turned out to have been made in haste, had convinced James E. Callahan, the Consul, that Jagjit was not one of those "dishonest orientals." He and Callahan, a Bostonian with an English wife born in India, became good friends. In 1932 Jagjit talked to him. "I am also operating from England," he told Callahan, who was neither the first nor the last person to come under Jagjit's charm. "I think he actually stretched the point—technically I do not think that was right—and gave me Treaty of Commerce visa," commented the beneficiary 38 years later. In any case, an "oriental's" headaches if not his reputation for "honesty" had been saved.[26]

He had understood the American people because he gained entry into some American social circles. He "used to go to parties," he recalled in 1946, all sorts of parties. He was invited to high class clubs and social parties where, incidentally, he saw the Prohibition Amendment violated openly. He was young and handsome, was making good money and was a bachelor. He loved to dance, enjoyed night life, horseback riding, hiking and tennis. He did not drink till 1942 and then only moderately. No scandal tarnished his public image. Jagjit's acceptance of the American value system may have disturbed some of his compatriots but never to the extent of open hostility. His social contacts helped his business, satisfied his youthful urges of self-expression, and fortified his inherited elitism. Above all they helped him become a dual ambassador, speaking the language of India's self-respect to Americans and demonstrating the advantage of acculturation to his own compatriots.[27]

Among the Americans on his social circuit was James Roosevelt. Jagjit tried to reach inside the White House through the President's son. He did not succeed, but his request was not rejected. Whereas several Indians who had sought to meet President Roosevelt were asked to come through the British Embassy which in effect implied rejection, Jagjit's visit was only sought to be postponed till "he will return again in 1938 (from India), at which time he may be able to see him (the President)."[28]

Although he did not have a formal high school diploma, a State Department official reported in 1937 that he "talks and looks like a man who had been to Oxford or Cambridge." Anup Singh who knew him more closely congratulated him on his "very concise, eloquent and the outstanding talk" on Gandhi Day and concluded that "you have missed your vocation. You should be on the plateform [sic]."[29]

During the so-called "period of his development," the post-Philadelphia 1920s and the early 1930s the "ups and downs of my fortune kept me busy, to keep the wolf from the door." In fact, "To be absolutely frank, I think not till 1938 did I take any active part in the Indian national movement."[30]

Between 1926 and the middle of 1937 his political activity consisted mostly of self-education. He not only watched the unfolding drama of the New Deal, he wrote well-organized articles about it. He also sent a letter bearing political overtones to James Roosevelt commending both the President and his son "very highly" before leaving on his trip to India in 1937.[31]

On June 5, 1931 Jagjit Singh wrote a letter to Mahatma Gandhi from New York suggesting that he should not visit the United States and offered reasons for his recommendation based on his estimate of the American people. The Mahatma not only acknowledged the letter, but he also published it in *Young India* with his comments. Thereafter the letter appeared in the *New York Times* identifying the writer only as "an Indian resident" and a "six-foot Sikh".[32] This incident which gave him no name–recognition in America, however, shows his genuine concern for Gandhi's and India's self- respect abroad and reconfirmed him as "no lover of Englishmen in India inasmuch as they represent the cursed system of government existing in our country." Two other persons, both of them Americans, had also advised Gandhi against visiting the United States for almost the same reasons as Jagjit's. The latter had not yet met Roger Baldwin but may already have known Rev. John Haynes Holmes. The identity of arguments in 1931 foreshadows that deeper community of views which pervaded their relationship when they became colleagues several years later.

During these years of his stay in America he had become familiar but "mixed rather rarely with" those who were "interested in doing something about Indian nationalism." He expressed his dissatisfaction with what they were doing and how they were doing it.[33]

Jagjit Singh has pleaded two major reasons for his prolonged noninvolvement in the public affairs of the Indian community. The first is his own struggle to establish his business, "to keep the wolf from the door" as he characterized it. The second needs close attention because in the final analysis it proves to be hollow, leaving us guessing as to the real reasons for his noninvolvement. He concedes that "some good was being done . . . certain amount of contact was being established by these people" including Dr. Taraknath Das all of whom were "patriots of the first order"; "true Indians and true patriots." But he complains that "they were not at all effective." Miss Mayo's *Mother India* was published soon after he came to America but "there was no one to answer, no one to write a book there, none of our people were in a position to do that," he complained. There were "some small associations," he agreed but "I do not even remember their names" because "If there were any really good associations you would know them."

Some organizations, he complained, talked to the American people "more on the spiritual side of India than the birth right of India to be free." People like Das Gupta would hold "gatherings in small little places and invite a few Americans . . . and would pass the hat," because they "were always short of money."

Every worker, he reveals, was short of money. That "always remained the major problem because they never earned enough." No cohesive movement could develop because "They were all apart. Before my advent on the scene they were busy lecturing."[34]

The intellectuals among the Indian community in New York who gathered at the Ceylon India Inn "ran these rather sombre gatherings" or "sleepy, sporadic meetings" and regarded "Singh as a shallow fellow who had never known his Bhagavad-Gita," and "looked down on whatever merchants there were in their midst with the traditional consciousness of caste and they were especially leery of Singh, who they felt had 'become an American' with a vengeance."

"Clash of personalities" and the appeal of great Indian visitors like Swami Vivekananda, Lala Lajpat Rai and Rabindranath Tagore only to "a restricted number of people" may also have been contributory causes why the Indian community had "no vocal, strong, dependable organization."[35]

This is Jagjit Singh's analysis of the status of Indian public activities before his own advent. Coming from the man who radically changed the tempo of these activities, and who had watched them for twelve years before participating in them, this status report may seem to be accurate, unbiased, impartial. It is none of these. In fact, it is unjust to those who had spent whole lifetimes working for India. In the background of his adverse remarks stand the images of the India League and of his own achievements which he is trying to glorify by contrast. For instance, take this comment : "If there were any really good associations, you would know them too because why did you hear about India League of America? Because it did something."

The drawbacks he complains of did not vanish after his advent. Even in its best days, those in the mid-1940s, the League treasury was never full. Anup Singh had to go on the lecture circuit to survive financially, even at the cost of his duties as Director of the League's Research Bureau; Jagjit himself kept the performance of his patriotic duties in abeyance for several years even after his business had been fully reestablished. The "clash of personalities" split the League as seriously as it did the Gadar Party. Although there was no murder in a courtroom, the bitter after-tastes lingered. For instance, he never forgave Syud Hossian.

One of his statements reveals a lapse of memory. There were at least two books published by Indian residents in reply to *Mother India*, Katharine Mayo's wholesale and sleazy condemnation of the Hindu social system that was published in 1927. Dhan Gopal Mukerji wrote *A Son of Mother India Answers* and Dalip Singh Saund wrote *My Mother India* which he dedicated to Bhagat Singh Thind. The December 1927 issue of the *Hindustanee Student* was almost entirely devoted to a discussion of that book. This fact was also noticed back in India.[36]

His whole argument about the alleged ineffectiveness of the earlier associations falls to the ground when he tells us how America and Americans being isolationists, were indifferent to, ignorant of and unconcerned with India, India's freedom and Indian national interests before Pearl Harbor. According to his own showing even during the War American legislators felt puzzled as if saying : "We don't know were India is." He also emphasized the scattered geography of the Indian community as a hindrance in the way of building up a "cohesive" organization. As for his own city of New York where there where only "thirty or forty people," he asked "how could one create an impact on the Americans ?" In those circumstances it is doubtful how even he with his charisma and "push" could have built an organization which would meet his standards and arouse the interest of the American people.[37]

He was forgetting that, although he inherited the allegedly week associations with few members and the intellectuals' caste discrimination *vis-a-vis* the merchants, the Indians had been running those associations for years and they helped him rise to his glory. Not a single member of "the Brain Trust" except S. Chandrasekhar came to America *after* he joined the League. Associating Americans with Indian organizations as full members which, according to Shaplen caused "one of those violent internal battles" was not Jagjit Singh's innovation. Lajpat Rai's India Home Rule League had American office-holders and the Friends of Freedom For India maintained the practice. Lajpat Rai's advocacy of India's cause which Jagjit Singh thought appealed "only to a restricted number of people" gave to the India League at least three staunch supporters of India's freedom—

Rev. John Holmes, Roger Baldwin and Norman Thomas—and several Indians including Bajpai, Rakhit and S.S. Sarna.[38]

The Hindusthan Association of America made the larger University centers like New York, Chicago, and Detroit hubs of Indian activities later taken over by the League. For instance the very page of the *Hindustanee Student* where Jagjit's name appears among other merchants, shows six activities planned for April and May in New York and names five Indian associations working there.[39]

Any estimate of the status of Indian political activities before 1938 that belittles the work of organizations like the H.A.A., the India Society, the India Welfare League and of individuals like Taraknath Das, Sudhindra Bose, and Ramlal would be historically inaccurate. Jagjit's report is no exception.

Every political lecturer, he tells us, had to earn his living. This is correct but they hardly took a day off from their patriotic activities. The writings and lectures that financed their living always carried patriotic themes like India's culture, India's freedom, Mahatma Gandhi, and the evils of British imperialism. Syud Hossian lectured, wrote and debated for over twenty years; Haridas T. Muzumdar wrote and lectured in the 1930s. Sudhindra Bose and Taraknath Das were two of India's most prolific writers during the first half of the twentieth century.

Although Jagjit Singh took twelve years off, some of these scholars and organizers never gave themselves a vacation. Taraknath Das became a political eyesore to the British soon after his arrival in 1906. Gobind Biharilal, another patriot whom Jagjit seeks to belittle, reached here in 1911 and became a Gadarite almost immediately, Ramlal Bajpai, Rakhit and Surendra Kar who also came as students became political activists in H.A.A. and other organizations. Of the most prominent intellectuals—Taraknath Das, Sudhindra Bose, V.R. Kokatnur, Syud Hossian, Anup Singh, Haridas T. Muzumdar, and Krishnalal Shridharani were Ph.D.'s. and four of them were university professors. Some of them wrote works of lasting value such as Taraknath Das's *India in World Politics* and Shridharani's *War Without Violence*. They mounted propaganda campaigns that caused the British serious concern both before and after the outbreak of the World War II. One may concede brilliance and success to Jagjit Singh because the facts are incontrovertible, even without swallowing wholesale his assessment of his predecessors, colleagues and competitors.[40]

His lobbying and publicity probably hastened India's freedom by not a single day, whereas the Gadar people in the First World War succeeded in starting a chain-reaction that Gandhi used to shake the British Empire in India. In the matter of immigration reform, relief for Asians came to a large extent as a consequence of Americans fighting in Asia. Jagjit ignored this matter for almost three years after Pearl Harbor whereas Bajpai, Muzumdar, and Mubarek Ali had lobbied the Congress for a hearing in June 1939, 30 months before Pearl Harbor.

It was not the community that was inactive or ineffective; it was Jagjit Singh who was inactive as his patriotic urge was quiescent for over a decade. No unpatriotic motives were involved. It all happened, both the sleep and the awakening, because the son of the rugged frontier, emotionally a Pathan and in determination, once aroused, a Sikh, Jagjit was the man he was.

He never invented a new idea. He was never unique except in the combination of his qualities and advantages. He was the first to organize a Congress Committee in Hazara, but in those days Congress Committees were established like mushrooms. Lobbying the Congress was a tradition established by Sudhindra Bose, Lajpat Rai, and Ramlal Bajpai. The Gadarites were the first Indians to use a war situation against Britain and several earlier sufferers had sought to change the immigration laws.

Although never original in his thinking, Jagjit would adopt a program as his own once it caught his imagination. The nationalist movement, the Wembley exhibition, and the Sesquicentennial had enthused him, the first by the lure of slogans and the other two by the lure of gold. True to character, for twelve years he was probably waiting for the return of days similar to the 1922 pre-Chauri Chaura days, which had sparked his enthusiasm. They arrived slowly, but when they came in 1937, he was ready to join the mainstream.

Jagjit may have been inactive himself, but he was not out of touch with activists. On his frequent visits to London, he had, in 1935 or 1936, struck up a friendship with Krishna Menon, secretary of the India League. He may have already read Nehru's autobiography. During 1937, 1938, and 1939 he returned to India where he met people and saw things for himself that changed the tenor of his life. He started participating in public events prominently. Before he left for India in 1937, he addressed an early celebration of Gandhi's birthday—probably his first public speech in America. Even his friends were taken by surprise at the high quality of his maiden speech. Dr. Anup Singh may have been flattering him because the letter asks for a loan but he adds, "I heard so many fine comments."[41]

The events that swept Jagjit Singh into public life followed the British Government's decision to implement the provisions for provincial autonomy of the Government of India Act 1935. An unprecedented 35 million people had been enfranchised by the Act. The elections to the Provincial legislatures held early in 1937 returned the Congress candidates in numbers which surprised the people as well as the Government. Congress emerged as the most cherished organization of the Hindus and Jawaharlal Nehru, its president and the master-campaigner, as their idol next to Mahatma Gandhi. In July 1937 Congress ministries took office in six out of eleven provinces of British India. Prisoners and "non-cooperators" of former days had become Government ministers, the Congress flag "the same flag that I used to carry at Anarkali and the Mall Road, Lahore and get beaten up" was now flying over the ministers' houses.[42]

After his return from India early in 1938, he spoke at a meeting of businessmen in New York "on the new temper of our people and suggested that we in America were lagging behind our countrymen in India in the matter of national work." A few weeks later he was billed as having recently returned from India after "a conference with" Nehru and who "will reveal some startling facts for the first time in America bearing on the present crisis in India and prospects for world peace" at a dinner in "joyous celebration of the inauguration of" Subhash Chandra Bose as the new Congress president.[43]

On June 16, 1938, Jagjit Singh delivered his address as the president of the India Chamber of Commerce of America at the formal launching of the Chamber, "India is a-stir today" he told his audience. "England has now decided to accept the inevitable" and "reluctantly but definitely, is preparing to yield and give to India her long sought-for freedom . . . seven out of eleven provinces in India are governed by the Congress Party."[44]

He had shown taste for office and responsibility as early as 1920 when he had organized the Congress Committee at Abbotabad. None of the offices he held were showpieces or sinecures. He had suffered heavily, as we have seen, for performing his duty as a member of the A.I.C.C., and had travelled to India to canvass for the Philadelphia Exposition as a member of the India Chamber at Wembley. This willingness to assume or the effort to achieve responsible office and having once achieved it, to give his heart and soul to the duties involved, remained a Jagjitian trademark in America as it had been in India and London. The precondition always was that Jagjit had to be emotionally convinced about the purpose of the organization. The Indian National Congress had aroused his nationalist emotions, Wembley and the Exposition held prospects of wealth, the India Chamber of Commerce established in 1938 involved questions of national self-respect and legal status and the India League stood for every dream of his public life except the pursuit of wealth.[45]

He was a bachelor whose youthful love for nightlife was restrained not by religious inhibitions or by any regard for an elder relative around but by an inner discipline and a consciousness of responsibility. These qualities helped him in bringing Indian merchants to Philadelphia, in campaigning for the Treaty of Trade, in rehabilitating his business twice in half a dozen years and finally in revitalizing the League. He was a Karmyogi, a man of action, according to the Geeta and a human "sparkplug" according to Roger Baldwin.[46]

None of the other prominent Indian workers in the 1940s had served the cause of India at home for three continuous years in a period of crisis. None had become a member of the A.I.C.C. Syud Hossain had never led demonstrations or risked facing British bullets or loss of property. Haridas T. Muzumdar and Krishnalal Shridharani had joined Gandhi's Salt March in 1930. Muzumdar returned to America in 1931 to pursue his career while Shridharani went first to Tagore's University, Shantiniketan, and then came to Columbia on a Maharaja's scholarship in 1934. Anup Singh never had to go through a baptism by fire.[47]

There were several talented Indians in America at the time—successful immigrants, graduates of American universities, scholars and scientists of high repute, scholar- patriots like Taraknath and Sudhindra. But most of them were now getting too old for an active public life. Sudhindra was senior in age to Jagjit Singh by 14 years, Taraknath by 13, Gobind Behari Lal probably by 10 and Profulla Mukerji by 9,

Dr. Kokatnur, the industrial chemist and a member of the India League before Jagjit took over, by 11.[48]

Bhagat Singh Thind who lived till 1967 continued to serve his community. His interests lay rather in the spirit of man than in the spirit of the law. He could have, by his close association, given Jagjit's successful fight for the naturalization law a romantic flavor of past memories. But Thind seems never to have been asked nor would he have agreed to play such a role because, as Mr. Vivian Thind said, "Thind was not a man who lived in the past."[49]

Dalip Singh Saund who came in 1920 remained in a class by himself. He was neither Jagjit's active associate nor a damaging rival. Though fellow Sikhs and occasional correspondents, their mutual relations do not seem to have advanced beyond formal social exchanges. Saund was building his own agricultural empire and personal popularity in the West that yielded political dividends in the early 1950s. His substantial participation in the immigration reform campaign is discussed in the following chapters.[50]

Ramlal Bajpai and Hemendra K. Rakshit deserve special mention. The former had a clearer perception than Jagjit Singh had as to the strategies Indians should adopt in America to make their nationalist viewpoint heard. For instance, the phrase "influencing the influencers" is Bajpai's not Jagjit's as the latter claimed. But in 1940 Bajpai was already 57 years old. "I regret very much I am physically, mentally and economically unable to help you," he told Jagjit Singh.[51] Rakshit (or Rakhit) with his several years of training in the Hindusthan Association of America and as one of the young associates of Lala Lajpat Rai was like Bajpai and Dalip Singh Saund another student-turned-businessman. He was Jagjit's closest Indian associate and secretary of the India League for 17 of the 18 years that Jagjit Singh was its president. He, like his president, became an almost full-time worker of the League.[52]

In India, hundreds of young men who, like Jagjit Singh, had participated in the Gandhian movement of 1919-1922 took up the "service of the country as a whole time job." This involvement was, according to the great historian of India's freedom movement, one of the "most significant and far-reaching consequences" of that movement. Jagjit Singh reached that ideal as best as an Indian merchant in America could under the limitations of his legal status.[53]

It seems that he never had to sacrifice League affairs because of his business commitments. His priorities were firmly fixed especially from August 1942 onward until around the time he started to have a family.[54] Jagjit enjoyed this advantage that except for Rakhit no other prominent Indian public worker did. Syud Hossain had to supplement his income as a teacher by travelling all over the country delivering lectures. In his first four years in America he covered almost 60,000 miles. In early 1941 he sent an application for a teaching job in India. Part of the reason for returning home may have been his exhaustion from the "nomadic existence," he had led for almost twenty years.[55] Haridas T. Muzumdar earned enough from his books and lectures to support an organization in New York during his earlier years in America. These lecture tours, however, took him out of town so often that he could not serve as an effective secretary of the India League after it was founded in 1937. He resigned. Even when, as a university teacher, he became less dependent on lecturing for living, he was removed from a day to day contact with the centers of activity both in New York and Washington, D.C. too often to make more than a minimal contribution toward actual achievements.[56]

The dictum of "publish or perish" dictated the American careers of both Anup Singh and Shridharani to a substantial extent. It seems Shridharani was more successful as an author than Anup in terms of financial returns. The latter, however, was more active, first in the India League and later in the Washington, D.C. based National Committee for India's Freedom. Even in his case lecturing schedules seriously interfered with the performance of his functions as the director of the India League Research Bureau. More significantly, in this instance, lecturing took precedence over directorship.[57]

There were some watchful eyes in the United States which noticed Jagjit's long-delayed reentry into the mainstream just at the moment of 'India's first taste of power." Three years later Shridharani wrote that

> The long line of candidates waiting for a turn to swing themselves up on the swaying back of India's playful elephant included several new mahouts from the United States. *Some* of the few Indian businessmen in America had always kept aloof from nationalist "propagandists" and had fought shy of joining groups which tried to help the struggle at home. These

> people now became the *most ardent* members of such circles. The whole spirit was changed.[58]

How much intellectual "castism" was packed in the word "businessmen" we have no way of knowing.

Although Jagjit Singh had suffered for several years the indignities implied in an Indian merchant's legal status, they do not seem to have provoked him to seek a general remedy. In later life he called such an attempt "selfish." The personal escape-hatch that he had devised for himself in 1932 kept him unconcerned with the lot of other merchants for several more years.

It seems that Magan S. Dave, the New York jeweller, was, according to Jagjit, the "main thinker" on this subject. Since the early 1930s Dave had been busy trying to save his wife from deportation. She was still in the United States in 1946 and her case still pending, because her influential relatives in India, including Sir Chimanlal Setalvad, had kept making representation for over thirteen years through the Government of India and the British Ambassador in Washington, D.C. This conflict between love and the law gave Dave strong reasons to seek changes in the law and made him "a pioneer' in bringing this question to the notice of the authorities in India."[59]

Dave's concern over immigration laws seems to have convinced Jagjit Singh of the need to demand a trade treaty between India and the United States so that Indian merchants too may become entitled to "treaty of commerce" privileges, as, for example, Chinese merchants had enjoyed since 1882. On his visit to India in the winter of 1937-1938, he campaigned for it through the press, by correspondence, and by personal meetings. He published an article on the subject and sent copies of it to several industrialists including G. D. Birla and Sir Purshotamdas Thakurdas and to the American Trade Commissioner in Calcutta. He also urged several Indian legislators to ask questions on the subject in the Legislative Assembly.

He may also have discussed it with Jawaharlal Nehru, whom he found in an excellent mood at their lunch meeting. He was grateful to Vijayalakshmi Pandit, Nehru's sister, who had donated to him her own time for meeting the Congress President. Having caught the contagious mood of optimism that prevailed in the Congress-ruled provinces, Jagjit returned to America determined to establish an organization of Indian merchants.[60]

His rise to power in the community, first among businessmen and a year later among political workers, was, however, obstructed by one man—Nibahu Ram Checker whose first name ironically means "a man with a cooperative bent of mind." Only a few months earlier while Jagjit was still in India, Checker had established the India League of America as one comprehensive organization which would cover other needs of the Indian community under its separate divisions. The businessmen's division was the Indo- American Association of Commerce with Checker as Chairman and Dr. V. R. Kokatnur as Vice-Chairman. Checker's opponents' first target was this Association.

If Jagjit Singh is correct in his guess that Nibahu came from Mianwali, the struggle was then between two Panjabis each adopting one of the two Panjabi style strategies of grabbing power. His oral history testimony that Checker was ambitious, unscrupulous, undemocratic, and domineering is supported by the words and actions of the Indian merchants of New York transmitted to us by Jagjit as well as by the minutes of businessmen's meetings held preparatory to the establishment of the Chamber of Commerce.

Jagjit's low assessment of Checker's educational equipment is not supported by available documentary evidence. The man who founded the organizations, the need for which others including Jagjit Singh realized years later, who established contacts with intellectuals and merchants in the East and the West, who won the support of even some eminent Indian immigrants like V.R. Kokatnur, and was later accepted as a member of the League's Research Bureau, could not have built his public life on "ginger ale and cookie" parties as alleged by Jagjit. But Nibahu Ram did indeed frighten a few Indians including some of the richest and the most intelligent members of the community. That was his tactical blunder.

In his profession, and in its ups and downs, in his vision of an organized community, in his aggressive pursuit of power, he was Jagjit Singh's double. Both wanted power—Nibahu, in what Jagjit Singh alleged to be the "gangster style" to which the latter used the support of the anti-Checker businessmen. Ramlal Bajpai asked him, "Are you strong enough to fight Checker?" to which Jagjit replied, "Ramlal don't worry of my being strong enough to fight. Are you also strong enough to join me?" And he said, "I will join you. But I know this man and he will adopt all kind of crookedness." "I said never mind. This is America and we are doing nothing wrong."[61]

The first meeting of businessmen invited by the anti-Checker coalition was held on March 4, 1938. "About 25 Indians" attended. Some "differences of opinion" were expressed at this meeting, but they came out forcefully at the next meeting held on March 21. "A heated discussion followed." Haridas T. Muzumdar mentioned Checker's organizations as the "so- called" Commerce Department of the "so-called" India League of America. This drew "instantaneous response" from Checker. Muzumdar insisted that elections to the India League "were not in his judgment properly held [and that its] constitution is vested in one person's hat."[62]

Forced by Checker's behavior at this and subsequent meetings at one of which he walked in with his men "in gangster style" Jagjit decided to bypass Checker, his supporters and his Commerce Department. At his suggestion it was decided to get a charter for an India Chamber of Commerce, something "higher than anything we had thought of."

> The decision was made, they needed a fighter now. They said—then you become the President instead of Magan Dave. I agreed. Called my lawyer to make corporation papers and started India Chamber of commerce of America Inc. Held a meeting at a very nice little club where people like Checker and his gang could not even be allowed to enter. Checker was completely taken aback.

The Chamber became a fact on June 4, 1938 the day its By- Laws were adopted, Board of Directors elected, and a bank designed as the depository of its funds. Two days later the charter of incorporation was registered at Albany, New York and the inaugural meeting at which Jagjit Singh presided, was held on June 16.[63]

During the whole span of his public life, Jagjit probably never had to confront an adversary of the type of Checker. Dr. Syud Hossain, Dr. Anup Singh, and Mrs. Vijaylakshmi Pandit would oppose him in the mid-1940s. But there was a difference in the character of confrontation. Checker challenged Jagjit's manly courage and spirit of determination, the other three provoked his anger and contempt. Their behaviour did not appear to him to be of the gangster type, just plain immoral, unethical, dishonest. Jagjit would neither be cowed by gangsterism nor forgive dishonesty in public life.Even his once adored Jawaharlal Nehru, who ruled an empire as the result of India's partition, was not forgiven. On his visit to India in 1946 Jagjit Singh learned from Mahatma Gandhi himself that "he had been kept in the dark" about the "the negotiations for partition that had been afoot for at least two or three months." "All I can say is," he regretfully confessed several years later, "that I never again had the same warm regard for Jawaharlal Nehru and Sardar Patel."[64]

Jagjit's colleagues elected him their President. His business success may have appealed to these businessmen, his services to the nation may also have carried weight with these patriots—"they are all nationalists"—the Indian Trade Commissioner in New York testified to this in a secret report to his Government—but the quality that mattered immediately was his determination to face up to a bully. In short, they needed him in 1938 for what Motilal Nehru needed him in 1919—protection. The merchants needed protection from a gang, the Congress President, from the crush of an admiring crowd. Both times it was this six-foot Sikh who happened to be around at the right time. Other qualities aside—and they were all impressive already—in the matter of election to the Chamber's highest office, the fact of Jagjit being a Sikh and at that a tall Sikh must have counted with them. His Indian colleagues felt safe under his leadership.[65]

The following winter Jagjit decided to take a business trip to India. Taking advantage of the opportunity "he was deputized (by the Champer) to explore all means and methods of creating enough interest in India so that the Government of India may feel the pressure of public opinion and also realize the absolute necessity of bringing about such a trade treaty at as early a date as possible."[66]

He met the key officials of the Government of India Department of Commerce and External Affairs who would be directly involved in negotiating the treaty and the presidents of the various Indian Chambers of Commerce whose support was crucial in pressuring the Government to negotiate in good faith. Above all he had a "long talk" with Jawaharlal Nehru through whom he secured the support of Bhulabhai Desai and S. Satyamurti, leader and deputy leader respectively of the Congress Party in the Central Legislative Assembly. He urged these legislators to ask questions in the Assembly about the trade treaty and the treatment of Indians in the United States. He also interviewed the U.S. Consul-General and the U.S. Trade Commissioner in Calcutta.[67]

He so effectively charmed Sir Aubrey Metcalfe, secretary of the External Affairs Department, that the British official became a staunch friend at court. The talks between the Governments of India and the United States over the desirability of concluding a treaty had started even before the India Chamber had been established. The Government of India favored the elimination of American restrictions on Indian merchants. Neither of these events had been revealed to Jagjit Singh but the talks he held with officials and nonofficials in India made him "feel certain that the conclusion of a trade treaty between the United States and India is not far distant." He proved to be too optimistic.

Within a fortnight of his arrival back in New York, he was sent off by the Chamber to Washington, D.C. on a lobbying mission. He met the British Ambassador and Mr. Wallace Murray Chief of the Far Eastern Division of the U.S. Department of State to try to expedite the completion of the draft of the proposed treaty.[68]

Unknown to Jagjit Singh the Indian Government's Commerce Department had decided to ignore both the Chamber and its president thereby rendering both of them ineffective. The Indian Trade Commissioner had written quite truly that the Chamber "is not in any sense representative of the more important lines of trade between India and the United States, e.g., burlap, hides and skins, shellac, cashew nuts, etc. . . . Commercially speaking, therefore, the Chamber is of little importance, and indeed, what little importance it has is due to the fact that it is representative of the very small number . . . of the Indian businessmen settled in this country. . . " The other side of the story was told by Jagjit Singh himself. "But it is regrettable," he told a newspaper in India, "not 1 percent of the trade passes through Indian hands in the United States" because Indian businessmen could not open offices in the United States.

The Government of India Commerce Department nevertheless reached a damaging conclusion. "It appears that it (the India Chamber of Commerce) could not be considered a genuine business association as its members were mostly small curio dealers of no substance" ignoring altogether that part of Malik's letter stating that the Chamber indeed represented the Indian merchants settled in the United States.

Sir Aubrey Metcalfe washed his hands off Jagjit and the Chamber. "I hold no brief," he wrote, "for Mr. Singh and as the Commerce Dept.

appear to hold a poor opinion of him I agree that he should get no encouragement from us."[69]

The torrent of events in the sphere of politics, including Indian politics, in the world of 1939, on the one hand and the official conspiracy of boycott that condemned him to inactivity on the other, offered Jagjit two options. He chose politics over inactivity.

The promise of Indian politics as visualized by the faithful of the Indian National Congress from their seats of provincial power in the late 1930s served as music celebrating Jagjit's political rebirth. Baldwin bears witness that "J.J. Singh, a New York merchant who had not previously been active [was now] enthused by the struggle." Jagjit announced the optimism in terms almost approaching the compulsions of historical determinism. "The tide of Nationalism can no longer be stemmed. . . England, reluctantly but definitely is preparing to yield."

Krishna Menon had suggested that Jagjit Singh start an India League. There already *was* an India League in New York. Then the War started which reduced the already inactive India Chamber into a "paper organization." Jagjit Singh now had even greater reason to look for an organization which would enable him to serve India politically. "I am thinking of doing something. I may start a new organization" he confided to Dr. Anup Singh.

In July 1938 Anup got a taste of the U.S. immigration laws in action. Having gone to Canada on a lecture tour probably without equipping himself with a reentry permit, he was detained by the Immigration authorities at Seattle, Washington. Dr. Taraknath Das as friend and Jagjit as president of the India Chamber had to send assurances that Anup was a Ph. D. from Harvard and not a laborer which helped him with the Board of Special Inquiry. This help may have gained a political ally for Jagjit.[70]

His young confident wanted Jagjit to come into the League to rescue it from Checker. An understanding was reached. Anup would try to have Checker ("dead wood") replaced as president by Hemendra Rakhit. After Checker was out, Jagjit would join the League and later replace Rakhit as President. This understanding, as Jagjit remembered it, was reached in 1939 and seems to have been acted upon before the year was out.

Jagjit Singh was a member of both the League's Executive Committee and its Research Bureau in 1940, added the post of treasurer in

1941 and president from 1942 onward. Hemendra Rakhit was president in 1940 and 1941, treasurer in 1942 and secretary from 1943 onward. Anup Singh was director of the Research Bureau till he resigned in July 1944 and secretary of the League in 1942.[71]

Robert Shaplen described in 1951, obviously as related to him by its hero, the story of "one night in 1939" when the India League is supposed to have been converted at one sitting and at one man's command, from a medieval monastic institution into a modern one-issue pressure group :

Jagjit Singh

> appeared one night in 1939 at one of the sleepy, sporadic meetings in New York of the India League, then an organization of the Ceylon India Inn intellectuals whose active membership had dwindled to twelve. Singh listened to the expression of lofty thoughts for a while and then proposed that the League pay less attention to culture and philosophy and more to politics and propaganda. He also proposed that the League abandon its policy of restricting its membership to Indians and that it set about corralling some prominent American members. . . . There ensued one of those violent internal battles that frequently shake such organizations. The upshot was that Singh became the dominant figure in a revamped League, with no racial restrictions on its membership, and the intellectuals established a rival, all-Indian group called the National Committee for India's Independence [sic], with headquarters in Washington.[72]

Actually the events were less dramatic and spread over several years. Derogatory reference to "culture and philosophy" and "the intellectuals" correctly reflect Jagjit's anti-intellectualism. They also show a realist's exasperation at the compatriots' supposed persistence with subjects that better be shelved during the political emergency that was developing in India as a result of the War. They also remind us of Jagjit Singh's bitter experience with those intellectuals particularly Syud Hossain and Anup Singh, so frankly explained by him in letters to friends and later in his interviews.

Regarding the organizational efforts of the Indian community in New York City in 1939, Shaplen's paragraph ignores more than it describes. The India League had purposely been established in 1937 for "politics and propaganda" the absence of which Jagjit complained of on that "night in 1939." Dr. Haridas T. Muzumdar, its first secretary says that the League was established as "a sort of analogue of the India League in England spreaheaded by Mr. V.K. Krishna Menon" and as "an organized effort to promote India's cause." The League's intended methods were apparent in its plans "to issue a monthly bulletin and to send out appropriate releases to the press at frequent intervals," a plan dear to Anup's heart for which he had sought the advice of Roger Baldwin before Jagjit joined the League. Indeed the press reports of League's activities during the Checker years even including Tagore's birthday celebrations were laced with political and patriotic interpretations.

In fact there were at least three organizations in New York City which were responding to political events as soon as they happened in India, in the way the India League would do later. Two of them were certainly known to Jagjit Singh. They were also cultivating friendship with American sympathizers of India and at least one of them had even "abandoned" the policy of restricting its membership to Indians as Jagjit Singh is supposed to have demanded of the League on that mythical night in 1939.

The Indo-American Association held a dinner in April 1938 to celebrate Subhash Bose's election as the President of the Indian National Congress. Jagjit Singh was billed as the main speaker. The India Political Council sponsored a dinner on June 29, 1938 at which the topic for speeches was "The Dawn of the New Day in India—How Does America propose to Respond to it?" Jagjit Singh was one of the sponsors of the dinner. The American League for India's Freedom was an organization of American liberals with Indians associated only as "Advisors" not as full members. The League sent a fraternal message to the annual session of the Indian National Congress held in February 1938. It also published a quarterly bulletin.[73]

An interesting thing happened in the last four months of 1937. Not one but two organizations were established. One was the India League of N.R. Checker, the other the India Political Council. The ostensible purpose of the League was " to interpret India and America to each other," the India Council was established for "coordinating pro-Nationalist activities." Its chairman was Ramlal Bajpal and its executive council had both Indian and American members including Roger Baldwin.

Contrary to the impressions that Shaplen's eloquent paragraph might convey, Jagjit Singh clearly was not the first to feel the need for "publicity and propaganda" and the elimination of "racial restrictions" in the composition of Indian organizations in New York City. Ramlal Bajpai was ahead of him in these two respects as in others mentioned already. It was the Lajpat Rai tradition as represented by Bajpai, Baldwin and Rev. J.H. Holmes which was spearheading the new Indian nationalist offensive at the outbreak of the Second World War. Jagjit Singh was only its latest, most efficient and the most successful adherent. He chose the India League rather than the India Political Council as the medium for his exploits probably because of the advantages of the more famous name. He took the name from the League and the practice of interracial membership from the India Council.[74]

The League was not a dying organization when Jagjit Singh joined it. It was rather "quite an active society doing a great deal of good." It was most probably the League's celebration of Gandhi Day that Jagjit had addressed in September 1937. Even after its rival, the India Chamber had been inaugurated, the League's Commerce Department held a dinner-conference on July 21, 1938. The *Modern Review* devoted eleven pages to its proceedings in which 39 American and Indian business concerns and their representatives participated. Eight papers on Indo-American trade and its problems were presented including one each by Hemendra Rakhit and Dr. V. Kokatnur.[74]

Anup and Jagjit attributed the decline in the League's membership to 12 or 13 to Checker's weak leadership. Jagjit, however, also knew the more basic reason which he told Bromfield: "The story is this. As you know, there are only thirty to forty so-called educated Indians in the whole of New York City." Almost 40 percent of the total was not a small share for one organization among many. Even after four years of Jagjit's efforts the League had only 21 Indian members from Greater New York City.

Checker has been blamed for several things, sometimes undeservedly. His place like that of Bajpai in the history of the Indian experience in the United States has to be recognized. He was among the first Indians in New York to recognize the emotional associations of the name "India League" and he was its first president. The first conference on Indc-American trade and trade treaty was held during his presidency. He brought Indian and American merchants together for the first time to discuss their common problem *vis-a-vis* trade with India. His aggressive personality undoubtedly alienated several ambitious but less aggressive public workers like Haridas T. Muzumdar and Ramlal Bajpai until he met his match in Jagjit Singh.[75]

The contrast in personalities, maybe even in the degree of dedication to the cause, is illustrated by the story behind the birth of *India Today*. The League obtained its newsletter only after Jagjit joined it, and only because he and not Checker offered to commit himself. Anup Singh wanted a League bulletin, but there was no money. Here is the remainder of the story as told by Jagjit Singh:

> So we both went to Baldwin. Anup Singh introduced me to him: This is Mr. J.J. Singh. He is a businessman; he has just joined the India League. Then Anup Singh said: Mr. Baldwin, I have talked to you about this before, we want to start a bulletin for the India League of America. He said: Yes, Anup, I have told you many times, the bulletin needs money, printing cost, this that, unless you have some funds I would advise you not to do it because you cannot do it. I kept on listening to all this. I did not know Baldwin, I wanted to hear what he had to say. And then, at one stage, I just looked at him and said: Mr. Baldwin, I will steal, beg or borrow, I will guarantee one year's issue of India League's bulletin. Now Baldwin had not met any Indian to talk like that to him. I still remember his typical face. He looked at me, where has this man sprung up from. That sort of attitude. Incidentally, we have been such thick friends ever since. I said: Yes, Sir, one year, I guarantee. After that—he said: After that you will be all right because once you start then it will catch on by itself. If you can do that, fine; Anup, go ahead. So I told Anup Singh. I have guaranteed you a start—because he was Editor and was going to write. So that is how we started *India Today*.[76]

By early 1940 the League was in the hands of Jagjit Singh, Hemendra Rakhit, and Anup Singh. Checker's ouster from its presidency had been the first step in pursuit of a plan—to make the League a faithful supporter in America of the activities and policies of the Indian National Congress and to create a strong bloc of American opinion in support of the League. Hemendra Rakhit brought to the League his long experience as member of the Hindusthan Association of America (H.A.A.) since 1915, as editor of its journal, *The Hindustanee Student*, for several years, as an M.A. in history from Wisconsin and as a wellsettled importer in New York. He was concerned over the fate of Indians abroad, over anti-Indian propaganda in America, and over the Hindu exclusion legislation of 1917. Although he did not joint the India Chamber of Commerce, he favoured the Chamber's objective of obtaining a treaty of trade.[77]

Rakhit had discovered the essentials that build a strong organization several years before Jagjit established the Hazara Congress Committee in 1920. An organization he insisted must "put right men in the right position" and "must equip itself with . . . its monthly magazines and its press." For an Indian organization in America he considered the support and sympathy of American citizens "vital" to its growth.[78]

Rakhit and Jagjit entered the League together, presided over its fortunes together, and together brought about its orderly end twenty years later. Jagjit found him a "useful, helpful and delightful worker" and thirty years later he remembered the "loyalty, devotion and cooperation" he had received from "one of the most decent human beings you could meet."[79]

During the first eight years of the revived League (1940-1947) the hearts of its officials and those of the Indian residents throbbed in unison. The cause of India's freedom was close to the residents' hearts. They applauded Jagjit's pressure tactics in Washington, his campaigns in the press, and his debates over the radio networks.

Praise for the League leadership materialised as cash. During these eight years, although the League was never rich, neither was it what it became in November of 1949, when Jagjit Singh reported to his Executive Committee that "after many years, the League finds itself in a financial predicament, . . I have today made a loan of $500 to the League's funds."[80]

Money had continued coming during those eight decisive years. After the immigration law had been enacted and the British withdrew from India the following year, people generally concluded that the mandate of the League had run out. The League continued to exist for another twelve years but only "as a social agency for fraternal relations with Indians and Americans; it can have no other role," was Roger Baldwin's assessment five years before the League finally closed its doors. He had been the League's treasurer since 1943 "with little to do except to examine the contributions from Indians which kept the League solvent." The League had not only won "a substantial base in the contributions of well-to-do Indian businessmen resident in New York" as Baldwin testified, but also from Indians resident in California as well as Detroit and Chicago.[81]

A study of the few surviving documents bearing on the League's finances leads to several interesting conclusions. A significant conclusion can be that a biracial composition operates under an unwritten process of checks and balances that contributes to integrity in financial management and a healthy competition in scarifices and restraint.

The League's activities were never dictated by a small clique of big donors although the largest and relatively consistent donors were Indians among whom Jagjit Singh, Rakhit, S.S. Sarna and Moosa H. Rawjee were the most prominent. Big American donors were Richard J. Walsh, Emanuel Celler, and Henry Luce with a $500 donation made by the International Ladies Garment Worker's Union. Indians alone could not have financed the League's expanding activities and services.

Contributions from Indian industrial magnates were spasmodic, reluctant, and generally less than expected. There is nothing in the record to indicate that the League's finances were ever mismanaged. This is where the National Committee for India's Freedom was alleged by Jagjit Singh to have fallen short of his standards in respect of handling public funds. Moreover, this Committee which had no American office-bearers received $2000 from Sardar Vallabhbhai Patel sometime after October 31, 1947. By then India was independent and Patel was wearing two hats, one as the chief of the organizational wing of the Congress and the other as India's Deputy Prime Minister.[82]

The League membership had increased from that "unlucky number" in 1940 to 81 in the first half of 1942 and to 115 two years later. Public donations were a larger source of income than membership dues and subscriptions to *India Today*. For 1942 the three figures respectively were $8268.06, $549.41 and $258.20.[83]

India Today was not only the League's mouthpiece, it was also its showcase. Well-edited, informative, "newsy" and punctual, the four page monthly bulletin reflected the efficiency, the knowledge, and the single-mindedness of the missionaries behind it. It had been Jagjit's first donation to the League; it became the sharpest sword and the most pointed pen in pursuit of its objectives.

The League's biracial membership brought within its fold several Americans for whom support of India's cause had been a pride of their earlier careers. They converted the Indian question into an American question and their experience, friendship and contacts into league's assets. When liberals, "the salt of the American earth" became League's supporters, American labor, blacks and church groups were not far behind. Their support was vital in the achievement of repeal of Indian exclusion.[84]

In 1940 there were two Americans on the League's Executive Committee; the following year there were none. In March 1942, although the Executive Committee continued to be exclusively Indian, an Advisory Board of eleven Americans, six Indians, and one Chinese was added to the League's administrative set-up. Two months later the League "expanded the executive Committee to fifteen by taking in the American officers of the Friends of India's Freedom [sic] and others." Four Americans—Rev. John Haynes Holmes, Rev. John Holmes Smith, Mrs. Frances Gunther, and Roger Baldwin—were thus brought into the Executive Committee.[85]

The appointment of Lin Yutang as an honorary president of the League in September 1943, just when repeal of Chinese exclusion was moving through Congress, marked a step forward to Jagjit Singh's new plan to universalize the objectives of the League. This plan took concrete shape in the League's new constitution adopted early in 1944, which included "The ultimate freedom of all colonial peoples with a democratic world order" as an objective and opened League's membership to "all persons living in the Western Hemisphere." In March, Baldwin told Watumull, "The other night we revised the structure of the League."

The Advisory Board (now called the National Advisory Board) was expanded to include nine Indian and 35 American members. The Executive Council now had four Indians, nine Americans and one Chinese. After Labor Day 1944, Pearl Buck was announced as another Honorary President of the League. Jagjit Singh was happy, now that the League had been "transformed into a predominantly American body."[86]

This was not his single-handed achievement. Several factors had contributed including what Baldwin called the "already settled American attitudes to the spirit of 1776. . . and to the sense of the dramatic in the novel Gandhian tactics. [so that] Liberals, pacifists and missionaries became propagandists for values transcending mere nationalism." In his assessment, "No other nationalist cause found such a response in the United States.[87]

What the League's treasurer said in 1953 was almost the echo of what its president had told Mahatma Gandhi's son eight years earlier: the League, he wrote to Devadas, "is becoming the most prominent and powerful organization for the cause of India that has ever existed in this country. Look at our letterhead today. Some of the outstanding liberals and leaders of public opinion are members of our Advisory Board."[88]

Other supporters included the church groups that had seen the new Asia and sought to distance themselves from Western imperialism. Jews and blacks saw in the Indian residents' demand for immigration law reform the struggle of a racial minority for equality and justice. Isolationists and the Irish fraternized with the League's anti-British stance. Finally there were Americans who extended the logic of their country's war against Fascism and racism to include British rule over India and Asian exclusion at home.[89]

American colleagues sometimes served as conduits for contacts with Administration officials, Senators and Congressmen. Jagjit met Vice President Henry Wallace with a letter of introduction from Louis Bromfield. A P.S. to the letter mentioned "the smoke house on our farm here which is built of the bricks of your grandfather Cantwell's house which was torn down here recently." A few months later Jagjit told a friend that Vincent Sheehan, now a Captain in the Air Corps, "is trying hard for me to see Harry Hopkins.[90]

For some of them membership in the League was part of their life's pilgrimage through liberal causes. Dorothy Detzer worked for 20 years for Women's International League For Peace and Freedom. Walter White became secretary of the National Association for the Advancement of Colored People. In 1928 both had campaigned against Senate confirmation of Judge John J. Parker of Kentucky whom they suspected of being opposed to the interests of blacks and labor. Both became members of the League.[91]

Jagjit Singh carried the accession of Americans to the League beyond the formality of paying membership dues: "It is another thing for the same guy to sign on the dotted line. I most unashamedly wish to boast that I managed to get the largest and most important number of Americans to sign on the dotted line," he told Devadas.[92]

In September 1942, fifty-seven prominent Americans had signed on behalf of the League a full-page advertisement in the *New York Times* urging President Roosevelt and Chiang kai-shek to use their good offices between the British Government and the Indian National Congress. This was one of Jagjit's major achievements in the propaganda war against Britain. Venkataramani and Shrivastava assess it as the "most substantial manifestation of sympathy for India's cause" at the time and declared it had "attracted substantial attention," Jagjit's boast was justified. He felt "accepted" by his American friends and colleagues.[93]

The columns of several liberal journals became available to the League because some of its officials and members were in a position to influence their policy. Richard J. Walsh, chairman of the League's Executive Committee, was the editor of *Asia and the Americas* and head of the John Day Publishing Company. *Unity* was the organ of the Rev. John Haynes Holmes' Community Church, *Call* of Norman Thomas and of the Socialist Party of America. Bruce Bliven was the editor of the *New Republic* and *Time* was sympathetic because Henry Luce, its owner, was Jagjit's friend and also a member of the League's Advisory Board.[94]

The support of several associations was enlisted for India's cause by some of their officials becoming closely associated with the League. Pearl Buck's East and West Association, the Post-War World Council of Norman Thomas, the N.A.A.C.P. and Fellowship of Reconciliation, the organizations of blacks and sympathetic whites, the League for Industrial Democracy with Rev. Holmes and Norman Thomas among its major officials, the Socialist Party of America, the People's Mandate of Washington, D.C, lent resources in support of the League's propaganda campaigns.[95]

Between 1940 and 1943 Jagjit Singh built the League. In the light of later history these years prove to have been, for the League and Jagjit Singh, years of preparation to play their role as the emancipators of the Indian community in the United States.

American members of the League, the Congressmen, the Senators, and the journalists, all these valuable assets collected in the course of its propaganda mission helped to have the anti- Indian immigration laws repealed. In his efforts on behalf of Gandhi, Nehru and the Indian National Congress, he never received U.S. official endorsement for what he asked. In the matter of immigration and naturalization he got everything for which he lobbied. Those activities had brought to his "vehicle", the League, in addition to its pocket constituency of American adherents, a body of floating American opinion, including that of the Roosevelt and Truman Administrations. When the decisive moment for action came, this segment of opinion, disposed to be favourable to India, though unfavorable to the Indian Congress demands in the midst of War, was willing to say "yes" to the cause of the Indo-American community because of the same War.

Those battles are worth our study not as battles fought for his Indian leaders but as periods of crisis management in 1942 and again in 1943 which revealed Jagjit Singh as a man of deep inner resources.[96] He strengthened the bonds of affection with his American colleagues and developed contacts with his compatriots and their organizations which later carried him and the League to victory in its fight for immigration and naturalization rights. It was during these years that he found the two future sponsors of his bills—Clare Boothe Luce and Emanuel Celler.[97]

On August 8, 1942 the All-India Congress Committee (A.I.C.C.) adopted what has become famous as the "Quit India" resolution demanding "the withdrawal of the British power from India" and promising that "Free India will become an ally of the United Nations." Next morning all Congress leaders including Gandhi and Nehru were arrested.[98]

He had spent an evening with Henry and Clare Boothe Luce at their home in Greenwich, Connecticut. Henry was sure the British would not arrest Nehru. "How can the British do that?" he had wondered, "the same thing which I had been feeling" recalled Jagjit years later. Back in town at midnight he bought the paper and "there was the news on the front page that Gandhi and Nehru were all arrested."

The date had advanced in India. In New York it was still August 9. He sent a telegram to Henry Luce "What I apprehended has happened."

He was angry.[99] He withdrew five thousand dollars from his bank to spend on the campaign against the British—probably the largest single wager by an Indian against the British Empire outside of India. "I was lucky enough to have enough money." This withdrawal "was the original sum I took out. I took out much more later on."[100]

He was infuriated at "that s.o.b. Churchill" and "these thick-headed selfish, whiskey-blinded Englishmen" five days before the police swoop upon the Congress leaders.[101] On August 7 he had suggested that Henry and Clare Luce arrange for a deputation "to wait upon the President with a request to intermediate before it is too late." On August 9 he received a telegram from Pearl Buck. She had already made representation to the President and sent "a long personal letter" to Mrs. Roosevelt, in response to his request on August 8 to organize a deputation.[102]

In one fortnight (August 6-20)[103] he conferred with eight colleagues and held one meeting of the League, met five high officials and five officials of other organizations, and readied the August issue of the *India Today* for publication. For four of those days he "planted" himself in Washington, D.C. where he "had a long talk with Col. Louis Johnson" and "met various people" at the Press Club, and also Senators Tom Connally, Thomas of Utah, La Follette of Wisconsin and Pepper of Florida. Robert Sherwood of the Office of War Information was a conduit to reach the President's ear and a note alongside his name remarked "(very important)".

In this fortnight he also met over twenty-five journalists. These makers of public opinion taxed as well as sharpened Jagjit's qualities. His personal charm, his salesmanship, his tireless persistence that hardly ever became a nuisance, and his statesmanlike translation of the demands of the Indian Congress into American national interest won him journalist friends who, though reluctant to criticize Britain, were the convinced enemies of Japan and, therefore, aware of the need to conciliate Indian nationalist opinion.[104]

The crisis of 1942 left the League stronger than ever before. No American hostility had rubbed off on the League or on its president. Jagjit had in fact made new friends among high officials, Congressmen, Senators, and journalists.

In 1942, he had failed to have the Indian leaders released from prison. In 1943 when the most devastating famine of the century fell upor Bengal how well will he fare when his conscience called upon him to have his compatriots released from the threat of "Death by Hunger?"[105] The official estimate of deaths because of starvation was one and a half million but "responsible nonofficial circles" put the death-toll at three million. Venkataramani holds Churchill to a "substantial burden of responsibility"[106] for the famine. In the United States it did not arouse much concern except in circles that Jagjit Singh had brought into close association with the League during the last four years.

Jagjit Singh went to Washington in October 1943 where he called upon several Senators, Congressmen, and State Department officials. He "did not find anyone to take up the cudgels for this cause." In response to the request of many for some data about the famine, he laboriously brought together facts and arguments with Sidney Hertzberg's help and published his report on the famine. It proved to be timely, informative, and effective as "the only detailed report available." The League distributed it widely. The International News Service issued a release based on the report to 800 newspapers and "was editorially commented upon most favourably by dozens of newspapers."[107]

Although Jagjit Sigh was not told, Mrs. Roosevelt passed on his report to the President whose "instinctive response" was: "This is a matter which the new UNRRA can *properly* take up." The British delegates to the UNRRA conference and its president, Dean Acheson of America, however, believed quite the opposite of Roosevelt's reply to his wife.[108]

Jagjit came to Atlantic City to lobby the delegates to the UNRRA Council. As the result of his efforts, delegates from China, Chile, Mexico, South Africa and Australia agreed to vote for relief for India, if the Indian delegate brought up the matter before the Council. As an obedient servant of the British, the Indian delegate, Sir Girja Shankar Bajpai, did not raise the matter on the floor. Britain and the United States Administration had apparently decided to let the starving Indians die. Even President Roosevelt forgot his earlier view of the UNRRA obligations.

"It seemed a hopeless cause to all but the President of the India League, J.J. Singh," observes Dr. Venktatramani. "An incurable optimist and an indefatigable worker, he was spurred on by the faith that somehow and through somebody the situation would be reversed and American help would not be denied to his country." Having failed to convert the American government to his viewpoint, he decided to appeal to its financier, the House of Representatives, whose "right over appropriations were preserved" although the UNRRA Agreement was not the kind of a treaty "requiring approval by the Senate." He wrote to all members of the House Foreign Affairs Committee seeking their help. One of its members, Karl Mundt (R-SD) offered to listen to his tale of woe. Jagjit, though hardly recovering from "an acute and painful attack of neuritis," rushed to Washington to meet the Congressman. He gave him all information, learned from him the art of lobbying in Congress, and established a lasting friendship sealed by shared victory in battle. Congressman Mundt was not the first American legislator to bring up India in the House, but he was the first to get from it the legislation he proposed.[109]

He had proposed that the language of the Agreement be amended so as to make UNRRA relief available to "any area important to the military operations of the United Nations which is stricken by famine or disease." The Committee did not agree. Mundt, thereupon, brought his campaign to the full House where in two speeches he presented the arguments fed to him by Jagjit. The speeches convinced many, but it was lobbying that converted conviction into votes.

Being a Republican, Mundt may hope to get several Republican votes. The House, however, was controlled by the Democrats. The Administration was Democratic; its policy was under attack. Unless Democrats voted for it, Mundt's amendment was doomed. The Mundt-Jagjit coalition had to lobby or the coalition would lose.

Robert Shaplen described Jagjit's hike to victory:

> Engineering its (amendment's) passage was a far from easy task. He (Mundt) recommended that (Jagjit) Singh do his persuasive best to line up Congressmen behind the amendment. Each morning at nine, Mundt would meet Singh and draw up a list of Congressmen for Singh to visit, briefing him on their political inclinations, likes, dislikes, and idiosyncrasies. "I'd kind of give him a little lowdown and off he'd go, like a shot," Mundt says, "I took a lot of kidding about it in the cloakrooms. The boys began asking me about 'that big Indian your soothsayer (getting him mixed up with Sioux

> Indians of Mundt's home State)'. Singh would complete his rounds by noon and would report back to Mundt before the House went into session. Mundt, circulating in the cloak-rooms and on the floor would then press for the conversion of those of his colleagues who were showing a sign of being softened up by Singh. As the days passed, it began to look as though Singh's cause had a chance.[110]

Not quite. It needed help from another ally that Jagjit Singh had been building up over the years. Just three months earlier two great labor organizations, the American Federation of Labor (A.F.L.) and the Congress of Industrial Organizations (C.I.O.), had "after consultation with" him voted $100,000 for famine relief in India. He called in James B. Carey, Secretary of CIO to help him lobby the Democratic Congressmen. Eighteen liberal Democrats were convinced. "Carey's intervention proved to be of decisive importance." "We have broken your Democratic ranks." Mundt told Sol Bloom, the chairman of the House Foreign Affairs Committee. Bloom checked with his colleagues and discovered that Jagjit indeed had cut the ground from under him. He let the amendment pass the House without opposition. In February the Senate approved the bill as amended, and the UNRRA Council later adopted it as part of the Agreement.[111]

Not a single grain of wheat reached India as the result of Jagjit Singh's victory in Congress. Only a country's Government could get the UNRRA wheels moving by officially requesting relief. The Government of India never made such request in spite of public demand in India.

Nevertheless in terms of the future of the Indian community in America, the League's effort in connection with the famine carried significance. Jagjit emerged as the community's outstanding leader and the League, its most prominent organization.

The League had been able to concentrate its efforts on the famine issue because earlier in the year it had successfully scotched a frontal attack by two misinformed but widely-read columnists. Just when the League was preparing to celebrate the India Independence Day in the evening, the morning papers carried Drew Pearson's column Merry-Go-Round alleging the League as being "used as an umbrella" by isolationists, pro-Nazis and America Firsters. This charge was followed on January 29 and 30 by two cleverly phrased vicious columns by Waverly Root. Also rumours were let afloat that the officers of the

League were about to be arrested and that the League's offices were to be raided and the League's telephone wires were tapped."[112]

The League warded off the threat to its existence and emerged not only unscathed but with its morale raised higher. Jagjit Singh could report to the League's annual meeting in enthusiastic terms:

> "It was because we were becoming effective and our work was beginning to tell that the opponents of India's freedom did their darndest to crush the League and its Executive Committee members . . . We challenged our opponents and I went" to the Department of Justice and asked them to examine the League's papers.
>
> "Well friends, I am happy to inform you that we had a thorough investigation by the F.B.I. agents (out of which) we came out with flying colors."

It was with those high spirits that Jagjit Singh, though sick at the time, went to meet Rep. Mundt. This action was part of his campaign to "keep on fighting with both fists."[113]

Considering the number of his opponents, Jagjit Singh needed more than two fists. Mighty powers were ranged against him—the British Government, the Democratic leadership in the House, the House Foreign Affairs Committee, Dean Acheson and Herbert Lehman, Director General of UNRRA. He beat them all. In the process of victory, he and the League captured the headlines. This was nothing new. The Indian community in America was accustomed to seeing itself in the headlines—as targets of abuse, as unwelcome immigrants, as carriers of disease and repulsive customs, as Hindu conspirators, and as violators of American laws. Never had an Indian resident been the hero of admiring columns or addressed crowded press conferences or been recognized in such top-level periodicals as *Time* magazine, the *New York Post* or the *New York Times*. Never before had an Indian resident obtained from the Congress a law which the White House and the majority party in Congress were initially unwilling to enact.[114]

There was a message of hope in this success. By determined efforts Congress had been persuaded to adopt an amendment. Next time it could be a whole bill. Jagjit counted the Mundt Amendment, in spite of its "death by starvation," among the three major legislative achievements of the League and of his own thirty-three years residence in America.[115]

There are in the League papers about two dozen letters of praise for Jagjit Singh from both Indian and American friends (not counting the laudatory articles that appeared in the contemporary press) about his "thundering blitz" at the UNRRA parley and his work in the capital as the League's "Washington Diplomat." They congratulated him on his success, admired his courage—Mrs. Pandit's younger daughter called him a "superman"—his patriotism, his "pushing and go-getting" or expressed amazement "what a job you did in Washington. And all alone," wrote Louis Fischer. Looking at the publicity his work released, Rep. Will Rogers Jr. of California inquired "Who's your press agent?" The key members of the League recognized publicity as the best gain, "an asset to India," "The ground work for" success in Washington, and as an "achievement of which we are really proud."

Although he probably received some help from Taraknath Das's contacts in the State Department and the lobbying by G.J. Watumull, Rep. Will Rogers Jr. and Delegate Joseph R. Farrington from Hawaii, several friends including Louis Fischer, Richard Walsh, Pearl Buck, Godha Ram Channon and Rep. Eberharter gave the credit for the achievement to Jagjit "alone" or "almost" to him alone. The Nobel laureate had reason to confer that honor on the League's president—"because I know you have done ahead in spite of criticisms to do what you thought was right." Her husband knew something more personal—"because you told me the day before you went, with what slim hope and real humility you started for Washington . . . after the comparative failure of your stout efforts at Atlantic City."[116]

Before we turn to the League's next crusade, a passing reference may be made to the split among the Indian activists that took place in the summer of 1944. The National Committee for India's Freedom established in October 1943 in Washington, D.C. to "work under its (the League's) jurisdiction" became an independent entity with Indians only as its members. Its leaders were Dr. Syud Hossain who had the longest record as an Indian nationalist lecturer in America; Dr. Haridas T. Muzumdar, the most devoted Indian follower of Mahatma Gandhi in America; Dr. Krishnalal Shridharani, the author of *My India, My America* and *Warning to the West*; and Dr. Anup Singh who left the League and the editorship of *India Today* to become the Secretary of the Committee and one of the editors of its *Voice of India*. Syud Hossain was the chairman of the Committee.

The lines were drawn. It was the Ph.D.'s versus Jagjit Singh, "the intellectuals" versus "the businessman", four egos versus one super ego, jealousy versus well-earned financial success and name-recognition.

This episode is not material to our purpose except that it offers another instance where Jagjit's character as a man, a patriot, and an organizer shines brighter than that of his Indian rivals. The strongest evidence in his favour is that not even his worst critics ever accused him of immoral conduct or of questionable handling of the League's funds or laying the Indian community to personal tribute.[117]

Jagjit Singh's efforts to bring relief to the starving people back home brought him and the League appreciative name–recognition, public applause and valuable contacts. These gains proved to be the last-minute and strategically the most valuable additions to their weapons system just when the circumstances developing during the later half of 1943 were about to force the League and its President to declare their thirty-month war on Indian exclusion.

Notes and References

1. Robert Shaplen, "One-Man Lobby," *The New Yorker*, March 24, 1951, 38. This source will hereafter be cited as *The Profile*.
2. Fern Marja, "India's One-Man Lobby," *New York Post*, 31 July 1946; Mary Braggiotti, "A Voice for the 400 Million," ibid., 9 August 1943.
3. His given name was Jagjit Singh, Jag = world; jit, more accurately, jeet = conquer, subdue; Jagjit = one who has achieved victory over (or subdued) the (allurements of) the world. Singh which means 'lion' is a suffix for all Rajput and Sikh male names with no organic connection with the meaning of the rest of the name. Jagjit means "the world conqueror" but Jagjit Singh *does not* mean "the lion who conquered the world." It simply indicates that the "world conqueror might be a Sikh. The full form of his name appears in a document in the Roosevelt Library. Hyde Park, dated in 1937, probably the first official American document bearing his name. It is "Sirdar Kumar Jagjit Singh." The correct form of the first word in the name is;

   Sardar = the man whose function is to march at the head of the contingent, the leader. This title the Sikhs earned for their leading role in war in northwestern India in the eighteenth century. This term is now an honorific prefix when addressing a Sikh male.

   "Kumar" or "Kunwar" used to be the title and prefix to the name of the male heir to a Hindu ruler. Its use with Jagjit Singh's name indicates two things: firstly that the was the eldest son (in fact he was the only son) and secondly that the family claimed aristocratic status. Among the two terms Mrs. Malti Singh prefers "Kunwar."

The last part of his name should be "Ahluwalia" which Jagjit probably never used but is shown in his second Passport. It is not a subcaste. The term shows that his ancestors belonged to this Sikh warrior group—one of the twelve *Misls* which together fought against the Mughal rulers and the Afghan invaders during the eighteenth century. The name of the group (*misl*) became part of the family name and a basis for its elitist claims. The park (Baag) in Amritsar where the massacre of April 1919 took place was named after one of these *misls*—the Jallianwala.

The founder of the Ahluwalia *misl* was Jassa Singh Ahluwalia (= belonging to, or of, Ahlu, a village near Lahore). His family profession was brewing wine, hence his earlier name Jassa *Kallal*. In 1748 he obtained supreme command of the forces of all 12 *misls*, unitedly known as Dal Khalsa. When his forces occupied Delhi he even sat on the Mughal throne for a few hours until the democratic protest became vocal. He was a big tall man. His breakfast included two pounds of butter and a good quantity of sugar. "He could devour the meat of half a goat at one meal," writes Dr. Hari Ram Gupta. *A History of the Sikhs*, 3 vol.; Simla, 1952, Vol. 1, 51, fn. 1.

In India, Sikhs are frequently addressed as "Sardar ji" (sometimes as Sardar Sahib) so that Jagjit Singh would be "Sardar Jagjit Singh ji."

In this dissertation an attempt has been made to refer to our hero only by the name his parents gave him. Somewhere along the line Jagjit dropped "kumar" and abbreviated his name to "J.J." obviously under the influence of gradual Americanization.

Jagjit Singh's bio-data is attached to the Transcript in the Nehru Memorial Museum & Library (see fn. 4) and there is a biographical sketch in the brochure published on the occasion of his seventieth birthday celebrations in New Delhi on October 5, 1967.

4. Shri J.J. Singh (interviewee), recorded by Dr. Amit Kumar Gupta and Dr. S.R. Bakshi (interviewers) November 30, 1970, 1. NMML, New Delhi, India, Oral History Project. This document will hereafter be cited as *Transcript*. In a friendly exchange of letters with India's Ambassador, B.K. Nehru, Jagjit challenged His Excellency—"Let me see you tear the check up. You are not a Pathan—you are a bloody Kashmiri Brahmin." The letter ended with the threat that if the Ambassador did not visit him in New York before leaving for India "there will be one Nehru less in this world." Jagjit Singh to B.K. Nehru, Washington, D.C., January 15, 1953; I.L.A. Papers. At the time of Jagjit Singh's birth the Districts that were later grouped together by Lord Curzon to form the North-West Frontier

Province were part of the Panjab. The separation took place in 1901. Technically therefore, Jagjit was born a Panjabi, Lovat Fraser, *India Under Curzon & After*, London, 1911, 61; "My five, six generations are Sikhs," Jagjit, Transcript of his Interview with Dr. Naraynan, 20.

5. *Transcript*, 102, 19-20. Jagjit Singh contributed several articles to Indian and American periodicals, wrote numerous letters to editors, compiled a brochure on the Indian famine of 1943-1944, presented a memorandum at the March 1945 Hearings, and represented three Indian newspapers at the San Francisco Conference of 1945. They all illustrate his qualities of observation, analysis, and expression. A collection of his articles was published in 1947 as *India and America.*
6. R.C. Majumdar (General Editor), The History and Culture of the Indian People; *Struggle for Freedom*, Bharatiya Vidya Bhawan, Bombay, 1969, 292; *Transcript*,2 .
7. *Transcript*, 3.
8. Ibid., 4, 5-6, 10; Jagjit Singh, "Mahatma Gandhi—Some reminiscences," *The Hindustan Times*, New Delhi, 27 April 1969. His incarceration, *The Profile*, 47. Jagjit Singh's speech at the N.Y.C. Town Hall meeting, September 29, 1942, 3-4, I.L.A. Papers.
9. Participation in the Gurudwara reform, his speech at the N.Y.C. Town Hall meeting, September 29, 1942, I.L.A. Papers.
10. These credentials opened the way to his first contact and "long, long talk" with Pearl Buck, Jagjit to Pearl Buck, June 15, 1942 and Pearl Buck's reply June 25, 1942, I.L.A. Papers.
11. Friendship with Dewan Chaman Lal, *Transcript*, 11, left India, 14; H.K.S. Malik mentioned in Jagjit, "Mahatma Gandhi-Some reminiscences."
12. *Transcript*,23, 24.
13. Fern Marja, "India's One-Man Lobby," *New York Post*, 31 July 1946.
14. *Transcript*, 25; *The Mysore Economic Journal*, January 1926; 20.
15. Ibid., 19, 21; *Transcript*, 27, 28; *New York Times Index*, April-May-June 1926, 496-497: On October 9 *The New York Times* ran the caption, "Philadelphia Fair Never Had Chance" : among the reasons for failure was rain on 86 out of 130 days.
16. *Transcript*, 28; *New York Times*, 8 October 1926, 1.
17. *The Hindustanee Student*, January 1926, 7; *Transcript* 25-27.
18. Ibid., 28; entries on Jagjit's Passport.
19. *Transcript* 28; Mary Braggiotti, "A Voice for the 400 Million" *New York* Post, 9 August 1943; *The Hindustanee Student*, May 1927, 10; *Time*, February 28, 1944; Rep. James G. Fulton to J.J. Singh, November 19, 1946; I.L.A. Papers.
20. *Transcript*, ibid.; *Time*, ibid.; *The Profile*, 49; Anne Z. Bose, "Sudhindra Bose; Portrait," *Modern Review*, November 1948; 365.

On April 16 he was at the students' reception, on May 10 he was in London getting his visa to re-enter the United States, on June 6 he was admitted at New York. Passport entries; *Transcript*, 29.

21. *Transcript*, 29-30.
22. *The Profile*, 49.
23. Ibid., 50; *Transcript*, 31; Jagjit Singh's Bio-Data dated 1946, I.L.A. Papers; S.A. Waiz (Ed.), *Indians Abroad Directory* Bombay, 1934, 571; India's Trade Commissioner H.S. Malik, New York to C.N. Sharples, Undersecretary to Government of India, Department of Commerce, D.O. letter No. 45, dated November 10, 1939, File 325-X/39, 1939, External Affairs, National Archives of India; Braggiotti, "A Voice."
24. *The Profile*, 35, 49; *Transcript*, 29, 30. The second of the two venturesome ideas does not seem to have been very original. Blanche Watson wrote to N.S. Hardikar several years before Jagjit had reached America; "I wonder if you remember me. If the name has slipped out of your mind as names do, perhaps you will know the wearer of the India shawl coat whom you used to meet at the Rand School," Blanche Watson, New York to N.S. Hardikar in India, July 7, 1922; Hardikar Papers, Subject File No. 1, 1922, NMML; Jagjit had a shop outlet in Toronto also. Once Suzanne Goutal fell sick, "I had planned to leave New York (for India) on November 17th but the French woman who takes care of my place of business was suddenly taken ill and I had to postpone my trip. I expect her to return to work in another week or so." Jagjit Singh, New York to George E. Jones, 22 Feroz Shah Road (rear), New Delhi, India, November 4, 1946 I.L.A. Papers.
25. *The Profile*, p. 50; he had his turban and beard "for two years," *Transcript*, 37. If the years are counted from his arrival in New York which was in April 1927, he may have removed his hair in the summer of 1929 before he was hit by the Depression. Jagjit's was a multi-sided personality. Most of the time he was more than what people called him or he liked to be called—a Sikh, a Punjabi, A Hindu, an Indian, a New Yorker, an American, Oxford-educated, a businessman, a journalist, a playboy. He seems never to have been proud of being born in Rawalpundi or of being a Punjabi or an Ahluwalia. He claimed to be Pathan and so on. One might question his claim, to be a Sikh and a Pathan at the same time. The Pathans of the North-West frontier had been conquered, subdued and ruled over by the Sikhs. Politically there was no love lost between them. See also Har Dayal, "India in America," *Modern Review*, July 1911, 3.

He called the Sikhs "my community," in his letter of March 7, 1941 to Roy Howard and to President Roosevelt, March 10, 1941, 5; he asked for a "representation of the Khalsas on our (League's) Advisory Board; letter to Ajmer Singh, June 21, 1944. He claimed all the high qualities attributed to his community : "I am a six-foot tall Sikh and can hardly see my way to turning the right cheek when the left one has been struck," he wrote to Mahatma Gandhi in 1931. Even Sikh babies are supposed to roar louder than babies of other races and communities : Rep. D.S. Saund had just started addressing a public meeting when Jagjit with Malti and the baby "had to leave abruptly." The letter of apology told the story. "The reason was this : my wife is still feeding our infant son and she had to get back for the 10 p.m. feeding, otherwise *this young sikh [sic] would have brought down the roof by his yelling,*" J.J. Singh to Saund, House Office Building, Wash., D.C., February 1, 1957, emphasis added. In one public speech he called the Sikhs "my people," New York City Town Hall Meeting September 29, 1941, 1.

26. *Transcript*, 76-78; the first "Treaty of Commerce" visa on his Passport is dated July 16, 1932. It seems the American Consuls were admitting aliens in the 1930s not according to the letter of the law but by the spirit of the United States. Jagjit remembered his benefactor's name. Not all beneficiaries did. "I do not remember his name but without him I would not be here tonight," said Hollywood producer Billy Wilder while accepting the 1988 Irving award for "consistent quality of production." In 1934 his visa had expired and he had to leave for Germany and eventually probably for a gas chamber. He could produce only his birth certificate and the passport. He asked the U.S. Consul at Mexicali to let him stay. The Consul asked him what he did for a living "I write movies," Wilder replied. The Consul looked at the insufficient documentation, thought for a moment and then extended his stay. "Write some good ones" he urged the young man. "I have been trying ever since" the aged producer told his T.V. audience on April 11, 1988.

27. Jagjit Singh, *India and America*, New York, 1947, 9; "America : Going "Wet Again." Typed manuscript in India League Papers; one of his favorite night spots was Copacabana, 10 E. 60th St. which promised "the danciest music" Advt. on *The Profile*, 42; M.K. Vellodi, Hyderabad, Deccan to Jagjit Singh, New York, May 21, 1951, 3, I.L.A. Papers.

Some Indian residents thought Jagjit Singh had "moved ahead a little too far and too fast" towards Americanization, although an American assessment was that he had "established himself as the principal link between numberless Americans" and India and "had also made himself a most industrious interpreter of Americans to his fellow-Indians." *The Profile*, 35, 38.

An absence of open hostility; Jagjit "Singh made enemies as he made friends, even among Indians devoted to the same ends. But they were only enemies who disliked his drive, his ego and his monopoly of Washington politics in India's behalf"; *The Reminiscences of Roger Nash Baldwin*, Oral History Branch Office Trustees of Columbia University in the City of New York, Chapter VI, 429; he started drinking, *Transcript*, 70, 71, "My drinking is caused by Mahatma Gandhi and Nehru," 72.

28. The interdepartmental note on Jagjit's request says, "Ordinarily, the State Dept. would not suggest that a man of this sort meet the President unless he comes through the Embassy" still James Roosevelt made the said promise. Requests made by Chamanlal in 1935, Yusuf Mehrali in 1938, Baburao Patel and Mubarek Ali in 1939 had been rejected so were probably also requests made earlier by Sailendra Ghose and Dr. S.L. Joshi. Roosevelt Library Papers, NMML, New Delhi.
29. *Roosevelt Library Papers* in the NMML; Anup Singh to J.J. Singh, New York, September 7, 1937, I.L.A. Papers. There are among the League Papers three essays on American affairs of the early 1930s. They show his keen insight. The titles are : "America - Going 'Wet' Again," "America's New Blue Eagle - NRA" and "America - On the Road to Recovery."
30. *The Profile*, 50; *Transcript*, 31.
31. Roosevelt Library Papers, NMML, New Delhi.
32. Jagjit Singh, "Mahatma Gandhi," *Hindustan Times*, April 27, 1969; *Transcript*, 33; *New York Times*, 10 July 1931, 21, not the "front page" as Jagjit remembered; the *Reminiscences of Roger Baldwin*, Chapter VI, 421; Peggy Lamsen, *Roger Baldwin : Founder of the American Civil Liberties Union : A Portrait*, Boston, 1976, 146; extracts from Jagjit's letter are in *Collected Works of Mahatma Gandhi*, Vol. 47, New Delhi, 1971, 118-119.
33. *Transcript*, 31; *The Profile*, 38.
34. *Transcript*, 31, 37, 42, 43, 45. By "Das Gupta" he most probably means Kedar Nath Das Gupta, the founder of the Threefold Movement and the World Fellowship of Faiths. Haridas T. Muzumdar had his own doubts about him : "One problem remains unsolved : Where did Mr. Das Gupta get all the gold coins deposited in his bank vault ? On his death, as I understand it, the U.S. Government impounded all the gold coins—were they English pounds sterling ? — since this country had gone off the gold standard." *America's Contributions to India's Freedom*, Allahabad, 1962, 35.
35. *Transcript*, 32, 37, 39-40, 44; *The Profile*, 38, 40. Jagjit Singh was not alone in his disappointment with the nature and extent of the Indian nationalist activities in America towards the beginning of the 1940s. "An American" writing in a Calcutta monthly expressed his confidence that provided India's cause is properly explained it will receive American popular support but "India's cause has not been well presented or represented," he complained. Other weaknesses : there is no official Congress representative in America and no organized educational efforts have been made. Propaganda is limited to the "small group of liberals, intellectuals, and up-to-date clergymen," Indians speak to a limited audience, suffer

from a "feeling of inferiority and apologeticism"; "appear to be pleading for sympathy"; "lack firmness, conviction and positiveness that comes with a just cause." It seems that the anonymous writer had not yet heard of the India League, *India To-Day* or of Jagjit Singh, but he was pleased with the work the India Welfare League was doing to help the Indian immigrants; *Modern Review*, November 1940, 573, 574.

36. Dhan Gopal Mukerji's work was published by E.P. Dutton & Co., New York, 1928 and Saund's by the Pacific Coast Khalsa Dewan Society of Stockton, California, 1930, *The Hindusthanee Student* coverage was mentioned in *Modern Review*, February 1928, 244. A Hindu preacher Swami Amkar is also said to have written a reply to "Mother India," Wendell Thomas, *Hinduism Invades America*, New York, 1930, 184.
37. *Transcript*, 36, 42.
38. *India Today*, February 1941; *The Profile*, 40; Lajpat Rai's associates : Baldwin, *Reminiscences*, 412; Rev. Holmes in Alan Raucher, "American Anti-Imperialists," *Pacific Historical Review*, 1974, and Norman Thoman : Lajpat Rai, Lahore to N.S. Hardikar, New York, May 19, 1020, N.S. Hardikar Biography, 15, Hardikar Papers; at one time the India Home Rule League "claimed a peak of 900 dues paying members (Americans and Indians) with branches in at least ten cities"; Alan Raucher, Ibid., 49. Shridharani's assessment is closer to Jagjit's time, "India's nationalism received the greatest encouragement in the years 1937 and 1939. The efforts of the Indian volunteer interpreters were beginning to tell," *My India, My America*, 512.
39. See fn. 19.
40. Jagjit Singh on Gobind Bihari Lal, *Transcripts*, 47; Surendranath Kar; Dr. Bhupendranath Datta, "In Memoriam of Surendranath Kar, M.A. (California)", *The United States of India*, San Francisco, February 1924, 5, 6. The intellectuals, the members of the so-called "Brain Trust" were also each other's competitors for praise and earnings. Ramlal Bajpai to Jagjit Singh, March 13/14, 1941, I.L.A. Papers.
41. See fn. 29 for Anup's appreciation of Jagjit Singh's speech; Nehru's autobiography had already come to America and had been reviewed by Vincent Sheean, Transcript of Sheean's Oral History interview, NMML, 1, contact with Krishna Menon, *Transcripts*, 85.
42. *Transcripts*, 62.
43. Minutes of the meetings of Indian businessmen in New York held on March 4, 1938 invited by the Committee of Three, Flyer of the Indo-American Association for a dinner proposed for April 23, 1938, I.L.A. Papers.
44. The text of Jagjit Singh address, I.L.A. Papers.
45. "I talk emotionally as it is; I am an emotional person in that way." *Transcripts*, 71.

47. Haridas T. Muzumdar, *America's Contributions to India's Freedom*, Allahabad, 1962, 20, 21; his interview on September 22, 1977, NMML, New Delhi, India, Oral History Project, 42, 60, 62; for Krishnalal Shridharani : Muzumdar, *America's Contributions*, 27, 28; *Asia and the Americas*, September 1941, 457; Krishnalal Shridharani, *My India, My America*, New York, 1941, 33-35, 50, 72; for Syud Hossain : Muzumdar, *America's Contributions*, 12, 13; *New York Times* : Current History, Vol. XVI, April 1922, 82; Dr. Taraknath Das to Lala Lajpat Rai, January 11, 1926, 4, NMML, Acc. No. 512; Anup Singh's lecture tour is mentioned in *India Today*, May 1944, 4.
48. Age calculations based on references scattered in published and unpublished materials. For an account of some of Jagjit Singh's Asian Indian colleagues and contemporaries see Appendix II.
49. Interview on the phone with Mrs. Vivian Thind, July 25, 1984.
50. Dalip Singh Saund, *Congressman From India*, 12; *Biographical Directory of the American Congress 1774-1961* Washington, D.C. : U.S. Government Printing Office, 1961, 1563; *New York Times*, 24 April 1973 44; 4; Haridas T. Muzumdar, *America's Contributions*, 28-29; Saund to Jagjit Singh, New York, May 27, 1949; Jagjit Singh to Saund, February 1, 1957, I.L.A. Papers; *The Hindustanee Student*, January 1925, 7. January 1926, 7; S.S. Chawla, "Rep. Dalip Singh Saund," Dinanath Varma, "Recollections of a Friend," *The Tribune*, Chandigarh, December 7, 1957; Harold S. Jacoby, *A Half-Century Appraisal*, 23. My interview with Marian Z. Kosa (Mrs. Saund) over the phone on March 17, 1984. Saund was a helpful contact in California for the India League's "Washington, D.C. branch"; Ramlal Bajpai to Jagjit Singh, September 24, 1942, 2, I.L.A. Papers.
51. Ramlal Bajpai to J.J. Singh, New York, March 14, 1941; *The Hindusthanee Student*, September 1915, 6; November 1915, 23; January 1917, 23; September 1918, 14; January- February 1927, 8; September-October 1927, 15; India Political Council Papers in India Chamber of Commerce of America File, I.L.A. Papers. *Indian Review*, Madras, February 1934, 120; N.S. Hardikar, Oral History Project Interview, NMML, New Delhi, 17; *Young India*, New York, March 1918, 14; Alan Raucher, "American Anti-Imperialists and the Pro-India Movement, 1900-1932," *Pacific Historical Review*, Vol. 43 (1974), 100, fn. 35; Haridas T. Muzumdar's Oral History Transcript, 87; Muzumdar, *America's Contributions*, 37, 38; *House Hearings, March 1945*, 70.
52. Hemendra Kishore Rakhit; born 1887 probably in Dacca District, Bengal; came to America, 1912; graduated from University of Wisconsin; active in Hindusthan Association of America and Editor of *The Hindusthanee Student*; an associate of Lala Lajpat Rai in the India Home Rule League of America; lifelong friendship with Ramlal Bajpai; one of the earliest

members of the India League of America; president of the League, 1940, 1941; partner Sogani & Co., Inc. of New York; returned to India about 1962.

The Hindusthanee Student, September 1915, 12; April 1916, 6-7; January-February 1918, 21, 23; February 1925, 2; March 1925, 6; December 1928; 12; *Young India*, March 1918, 14; James Campbell Ker, *Political Trouble*, 434; *Modern Review*, July 1938, 584-586, 594.

53. R.C. Majumdar, *Struggle for Freedom*, 342.
54. *The Profile*, 49; "For the past several years, because of my preoccupation with international politics, I completely neglected my business. Now having gotten married and the expected addition in the family, etc., makes it compulsory for me to take some interest in my business," Jagjit Singh, New York to Walter F. Wanger, 4376 Sunset Drive, Los Angeles 27, California, November 2, 1953. Three days later his first child was born. *The Profile*, 41; Roger Baldwin notes that Jagjit Singh "devoted his time, money and tactical skills to the (League's) job," *Reminiscences*, 429.
55. *Transcript*, 31; Muzumdar, *Contributions*, 28; Syud Hossain's mileage : his speech at the Foreign Policy Association Conference, Philadelphia, February 27, 1926; Syud Hossain to Sir Akbar Hydari, Hyderabad, Deccan, February 25, 1941, Syud Hossain to M.J. Stevenson, July 14, 1930, Syud Hossain Papers, NMML.
56. Muzumdar's *Transcripts*, 63, 84; Muzumdar, *Contributions*, 41.
57. On Krishnalal Shridharani : Muzumdar, *Contributions*, 28, Jagjit Singh's *Transcript*, 40; on Anup Singh, *India To-Day*, May 1944, 4.
58. Krishnalal Shridharani, *My India, My America*, 513, emphasis added. There was no rebuttal from Jagjit Singh at the time. Readers of *India To-Day* were rather invited to get autographed first edition copies of the book from the League's office. *India To-Day*, October 1941. The following month a review found scope for "minor disagreements," ibid., November 1941.
59. *Transcript*, 75, 76, D. No. 2519-X/39, External Affairs with H. Dayal's notes dated February 17 and April 19, 1946, National Archives of India; "Summary of the Activities of the India Chamber of Commerce of America Inc.," 1, I.L.A. Papers; the question asked in the Indian Legislative Assembly about the Indian merchants' disabilities in America more than three years before the establishment of the India Chamber was probably prompted through Magan Dave's efforts, Waiz, *Directory*, 566, *Indian Review*, May 1934, 236.
60. J.J. Subject File No. 7, 1937-38, J.J. Singh Papers, NMML, *The Profile*, 40; *Transcript*, 62-63; *The Tribune*, Lahore, December, 17, 1937. It is possible that Jagjit Singh was exchanging views with Taraknath Das over the trade treaty question. A year before Jagjit visited India. Das had written an article suggesting the treaty as a relief for Indian businessmen in the

United States, *Modern Review*, February 1937, 151-152, the article is dated New York, December 8, 1936. The merchants' disabilities and hardships, File 401 (64)-X/38, File 325-X/39, File 202-X/41 External Affairs, National Archives of India; Jagjit Singh's statements, *Statesman*, Calcutta, January 25, 1939, *House Hearings, March 1945*, 86.

61. *Transcript*, 78-83; Dr. Narayanan's interview with Jagjit Singh, 9, 10; *Modern Review*, November 1938, 584-594; B.V. Mukerji, Secretary Indo-American Association of Commerce to President, Singh & Singh Co., July 15, 1938, I.L.A. Papers; *Senate Hearings on S. 1595*, 33; the state Department document is in the Roosevelt File in the NMML; Jagjit Singh's words, "This is America and we are doing nothing wrong," *Transcript*, 83 are significant. Checker might have prevailed over Jagjit and the merchants in the back alleys of Lahore even if they were "doing nothing wrong."
62. *Transcript*, 80-83; officials of Checker's Association are named on the stationery of B.V. Mukerji's letter to Jagjit in fn. 61, the Minutes of all preparatory meetings mentioned here are in the I.L.A. Papers.
63. Jagjit Singh's letter to the County Clerk, the Clerk's reply and other documents are in the India Chamber of Commerce File; Muzumdar, *Contributions*, 41, gives wrong date but remembers "lengthy debates"; *World in Brief*, New York, July, 1, 1938; the quotation is from Jagjit's *Transcript*, 83; several Indian businessmen located in New York City did not join the Chamber, for instance, Hemendra Rakhit, Heeramaneck, K.N. Ghose, C.S. Thakore, N.R. Chowdhury, B.V. Mukherji.
64. Jagjit Singh, "Mahatma Gandhi," *The Hindustan Times*, 27 April 1969; there was probably a temporary revival of respect for India's Prime Minister on his visit to the United States in 1949, *The Profile*, 53-55; Checker had given a fair fight. He was forgiven and accepted as a colleague in the League. In 1943, however, he suddenly resigned probably in the hope of starting an exodus from the League following an adverse column by Drew Pearson. He was immediately replaced on the Executive Council by S.S. Sarna who rejoined the League as a challenge to hostile columnist. Jagjit commented; "Just as it was most condemnable for any member to leave the League when it was under attack, it was most commendable for Mr. Sarna to offer us active support and cooperation at that juncture." Jagjit Singh's report to the League executive Committee on the work done in 1943, 1, I.L.A. Papers, *India To-Day* dates this meeting December 12, 1943. Checker applied for membership again but was not accepted.
65. H.S. Malik to Sharples, fn. 23 above, Jagjit Singh, "Mahatma Gandhi," *Hindustan Times*, April 27, 1969; an instance of the Indian merchants' patriotic motivation : Magan S. Dave was about to present a paper on the problem of the trade treaty at the India Chamber meeting on October 27, 1938. Haridas T. Muzumdar, general secretary, passed on to Dave a

written instruction that said, "When you are called upon to speak, you point out that the demand for the Trade Treaty has more than monetary and commercial motives : we want the Trade Treaty so that Indian businessmen are treated as merchants and not as visitors or tourists. It is a matter of national honor." Handwritten note, I.L.A. Papers.

66. *India Trade Bulletin*, July 1938, and "Summary of Activities of the Indian Chamber of Commerce of America," I.L.A. Papers.

67. *New York Times, Journal of Commerce* and *New York Herald Tribune* all of October 28, 1938; meeting with Nehru, *Civil and Military Gazette*, Lahore, January 17, 1939; meeting with Congress legislators, ibid., February 2, 1939; meeting with Sir Aubrey Metcalfe and other Government of India officials and also U.S. representatives in India, *Civil and Military Gazette* of both dates; consultations with Indian Chambers of Commerce, *The Tribune*, Lahore, December 27, 1938, January 19, 1939; *Hindusthan Standard*, Calcutta, January 6 and 7, 1939; *The Hindustan Times*, New Delhi, January 7, 1939; *The Statesman*, Calcutta, January 8, 1939; Sir Aubrey Metcalfe's support of Jagjit Singh, 325-X/39, External Affairs Department, National Archives of India, Sir Aubrey's Note of March 21, 1939. Jagjit started his press campaign the day he landed in India; *Sind Observer*, Karachi, December 15, 1938, *The Tribune*, Lahore, December 17, 1938; Jagjit Singh's statement, *House Hearings March 1945*, 86.

68. *Civil and Military Gazette*, Lahore, February 2, 1939; the Trade Treaty issue is discussed in Chapter VII; *Washington Post*; March 30, 1939; *New York Times*, March 31, 1939; "Summary of Activities of the India Chamber of Commerce," Transcript of Narayanan's interview with Jagjit Singh, 11.

68. H.S. Malik to C.M. Sharples, fn. 23 above; Jagjit's statement in *The Statesmen*, Calcutta, January 25, 1939; similar argument by Ramlal Bajpai : "About 95 percent of the business between India and U.S.A. is directly in the hands of British merchants," *Modern Review*, July 1938, 595; the Government of India interdepartmental correspondence is in the same 325-X/39 File as H.S. Malik's letter.

70. Baldwin, *Reminiscences*, 429; *India Trade Bulletin*, July 1938, 7, India Chamber of Commerce File; *Washington Post*, March 30, 1939; *The Profile*, 40; *Civil and Military Gazette*, Lahore, January 17, 1939; *Transcripts*, 86, 88; The Anup Singh incident I.L.A. Papers; also see Normal Buchignani, Doreen M. Indra, with Ram Srivastava, *Continuous Journey, A Social History of South Asians in Canada*, McClelland and Stewart Ltd., Toronto, 1985), 92.

71. *Transcript*, 88-90; Transcript of interview with Dr. Narayanan, 11, Muzumdar, *America's Contributions*, 41, 43; the offices held by Jagjit Singh, Anup Singh and Hemendra Rakhit are mentioned in the issues of

India Today for April 1940, May 1940, January 1941, December 1942; Anup Singh's resignation was announced in the issue of June 1944.

72. *The Profile*, 41.
73. Muzumdar, *America's Contributions*, 42; *Transcript*, 91; *Modern Review*, 1939, 181, note the speeches made by Anup Singh and Lin Yutang; *India Today*, May 1941, 2, the major concern of the meeting held "in the home of Mr. Checker" was the "strangely distorted reports about India"; the documents mentioning the various activities of New York organizations are in the India League Papers.
74. *Transcript*, 79-80; Bulletin of the American League for India's Freedom, July 1938, "Local Events"; the objective of the India League of America was printed on the front page of *India Today* every month; in the summer of 1939 Bajpai as chairman of the India Political Council wrote to President Roosevelt seeking his "expression of faith" in regard to India's fight for freedom, Venkataramani and Shrivastava, *Quit India*, 13.
75. H.W. Boulter, "July 4th and January 26th," *Modern Review*, September 1939, 344-347. Mrs. Boulter was probably referring to the India League of America. Both she and Anup Singh were associated at this time with the India League and not the India Political Council, the only other "recently" established Indian organization in New York, the dinner-conference proceedings are in *Modern Review*, November 1938, 584-594; for Tagore's birthdays, ibid. July 1939, 181, note the political tone of the speeches delivered by Anup Singh and Lin Yutang.
76. *Transcript*, 87; Interview with Dr. Narayanan, 10; Jagjit Singh, New York to Louis Bromfield, Malabar Farm, Lucas, Ohio, March 25, 1942; Jagjit gave the same argument in his letter to Herbert Matthews, Hotel Cecil, New Delhi, October 9, 1941; also see Jagjit Singh to Louis Bromfield, November 7, 1940; as of December 6, 1943, the total membership of the League was 111; there were over 50 Indian members from New York City, Detroit, Chicago, Los Angeles, and San Francisco; there was one Chinese, all others were Americans. Checker's activities concerning famine relief and immigration reform are mentioned in the following chapters.
77. *Transcript*, 91.
78. *Hindusthanee Student*, November 1915, 10-12; October 1915, 16; April 1916, 6-7; January-February 1918, 21-22; *Modern Review, November 1938, 584-586.*
79. *Hindusthanee Student*, October 1917, 25; January-February 1918, 20.
80. Annual elections of office-holders of the League were published in *India To-Day*. The first quotation is from the President's Report for 1943 in the India League Papers and the second from *Transcript*, 89, 90.
81. Unsigned circular of November 1949, to "Dear Colleague"; "Statement of Cash Receipts and Disbursements" for 1949, January through November 14, shows that it was Jagjit Singh who made the loan.

82. Baldwin, *Reminiscences,* 430, 429, 428.
83. Although Jagjit Singh objected to a few features of the National Committee's financial report, he does not seem to have noticed the contribution of a foreign official to an Indian organization in America. He was well aware of the implications as he told Bromfield :

    "In short, we have not a single Indian who is financially very well off, and who can be looked up to as a benefactor, upon whom we could, all the time, depend for financial aid.

    "We cannot get any money from India, not only because there are restrictions placed by the Government of India against monies being sent out of India, but if we were to accept any financial aid from any other outside source other than the United States of America, we will be considered 'agents for foreign principles,' and we do not want that." Jagjit Singh to Louis Bromfield, Lucas, Ohio, March 25, 1942, I.L.A. Papers.

    Jagjit's contributions to the League finances. He contributed "generously to the support of the League, his only dependent." By early 1951 he had given to the League "about $5000" *The Profile*, 35, 41; Moosa Rawjee usually paid $1000 a year. A similar sum was paid by Emanuel Celler in 1950; J.J. Singh to "Dear Colleague," December 8, 1950.
84. The figure for League members in 1942 is from "The Major Activities of the India League for the First Half of 1942," the figure 115 is from a typed statement "Members in Good Standing—Paid and With Signed Cards." That 115 was the "Total membership as of Feb. 29th 1944" written in Jagjit's hand, p. 4 of the statement. There were sixty-eight American and one Chinese members. From Greater New York there were twenty-one Indians and forty-four Americans. The three dollar figures are from page one of a tabulation titled "India League of America Jan.-Nov. Receipts."
85. Roger Baldwin's Foreword to Muzumdar, America's *Contributions*, vii, emphasis added; Baldwin's *Reminiscences*, 429; Muzumdar, ibid., 43, the quotation is from Venkataramani and Shrivastava, *Quit India*, 335.
86. *India To-Day*, March and May 1942; "Major Activities of the India League for the first half of 1942," India League Papers; League as the successor to the Friends of Freedom For India, Taraknath Das's Address on August 4, 1946, 9, I.L.A. Papers.
88. Baldwin, *Reminiscences*, 430.
89. Jagjit Singh to Devadas Gandhi, New Delhi, April 13, 1945, Subject File No. 10, NMML, New Delhi.
90. "After all, if Indians fight for the freedom of their country, that is the least one can expect from them, but when Americans give their wholehearted support in working for the cause of India's freedom, I cannot help but feel most grateful to such Americans." Jagjit Singh presenting his Report of League's work for 1943 to the Executive Committee.

91. Louis Bromfield to "Dear Mr. Vice-President," August 3, 1942; Jagjit to Herbert L. Matthews, Hotel Cecil, New Delhi, October 9, 1942.
92. Tyler Abel (Ed.) *Drew Pearson Diaries 1949-1959*, New York, 1974, 444.
93. Fn. 89 above.
94. Venkataramani and Shrivastava, *Quit India*, 292; two years later more than twice this number of Americans (127) signed a League appeal for release of Congress leaders, *India To-Day*, August 1944. The 55 who signed this advertisement were :

Louis Adamic
Trustee, Common Council for American Unity, N.Y.
Roger N. Baldwin
Director, American Civil Liberties Union, N.Y.
Bruce Bliven, Editor, "The New Republic," N.Y.
Clare Boothe Author, War Correspondent, Conn.
Mrs. Georges Bridges
Civic Leader, Ala.
Louis Bromfield
Author, Pulitzer Prize Winner, Ohio
Van Wyck Brooks
Author, Literary Critic, Conn.
Pearl S. Buck
Nobel Prize Winner, Pa.
John Chamberlain
Author and Literary Critic, Conn.
Wm. Henry Chamberlin
Journalist, Mass.
Stuart Chase
Author, Economist, Conn.
Chris L. Christensen
Dean, College of Agriculture, University of Wisconsin, Wis.
Georage S. Counts
Former President, American Federation of Teachers, NY
Dr. Tyler Dennett
Former President, Williams College, N.Y.

C. Halliwell Duell
Publisher, N.Y.
Dr. Sherwood Eddy
Former YMCA National Secretary in India, N.Y.
Dr. Charles K. Edmunds
President Emeritus, Pomona College, Calif.
John Erskine
Author, Education, N.Y.
Dorothy Canfield Fisher
Author, Vt.
Prof. Charl J. Friedrich
Harvard University, Mass.
Clinton S. Golden
Asst. to President, United Steel Workers of America, Pa.
Samuel Grafton
Columnist, N.Y.
Dr. Frank P. Graham
North Carolina, N.C.
John Gunther
Author, N.Y.
Henry I. Harriman
Former President, U.S. Chamber of Commerce, Mass.
Shelby M. Harrison
General Director, Russell Sage Foundation, N.Y.
Arthur Garfield Hays
Attorney, N.Y.
Lillian Hellman
Playwright, N.Y.

Prof. William E. Hocking
Harvard University, Mass.
John B. Hughes
Radio Commentator, Calif.
Fannie Hurst
Author, N.Y.
Paul Kellogg
Editor, "Survey Graphic," N.Y.
Dr. Frank Kingdon
President, Union of Democratic Action, N.Y.
Freda Kirchway
Editor and Publisher, "The Nation," N.Y.
Alfred M. Landon
Former Governor of Kansas, Kan.
Prof. Max Lerner
Williams College, Mass.
Prof. Robert M. MacIver
Columbia University, N.Y.
Bishop Francis H. McConnell
Former President, Federal Council of Churches of Christ in America, N.Y.
Ada P. McCormick
Civic Leader, Ariz.
Esther Morgan McCullough
Civic Leader, Vt.
Dr. Felix Morley
President, Haverford College, Pa.
Clarence Poe
President, Progressive Farmer & Southern Ruralist, N.C.
Prof. James B. Pratt
Williams College, Mass.
Josephine Roche
Former Assistant Secretary, U.S. Treasury, Colo.
Prof. Fred. L. Schuman
Williams College, Mass.
Prof. Robert L. Schuyler
Columbia University, N.Y.
William L. Shirer
Author, N.Y.
Rabbi Abba Hillel Silver
The Temple, Cleveland, Ohio
Upton Sinclair
Author, Calif.
Herbert Bayard Swope
Publicist and Journalist, N.Y.
Norman Thomas
Chairman, Post War World Council, N.Y.
Richard J. Walsh
Editor, "Asia," N.Y.
Prof. Fred J. Wampler
Virginia College of Medicine, Ca.
Dr. James P. Warbasse
President Emeritus, Cooperative League of U.S.A., Mass.
Walter White
Executive Secretary, National Association for the Advancement of Colored People, N.Y.
Dr. Mary E. Woolley
Former President, Mt. Holyoke College, N.Y.

95. Contributions from members of the India League such as Dr. Anup Singh and other Indian nationalists were almost a constant feature of *Asia and the Americas, New Republic*, and *Unity* throughout these years. Other friendly journals were *Amerasia* and the *Nation*, see for instance, *India To-Day*, April 1940. The *Call* raised its voice for India both during the Quit India crisis of 1942 and the famine of 1943.

96. For People's Mandate see Jagjit Singh to Miss Mabel Vernon, Director of People's Mandate, Hay-Adams Hotel, Washington, D.C., September 3, 1942 and November 3, 1942 to her at Hay Adams House, Washington, D.C.; for Fellowship of Reconciliation see its 2-page flyer titled "India's Cause" in the India League Papers; N.A.A.C.P.'s support for repeal of "Oriental exclusion" formed part of the agenda of a seminar held under chairmanship of Thurgood Marshall which Jagjit attended.

97. Jagjit Singh, "America—Going 'Wet' Again," 3; Emanuel Celler's words, "The stenographers said he had oomph"; when he returned to his shop after his first haircut and shave, one of the girls "rushed up and shrieked, 'you handsome dog'." *The Profile*, 44, 50; "sorry I missed you on television, but I will bet all the ladies in New York are now in a dither having seen your smiling countenance." Emanuel Celler to Jagjit Singh, July 11, 1950.

Pearl Buck and Henry Luce paid him tribute at his farewell in 1959; Mundt's praise was in a message on Jagjit's seventieth birthday. Rakhit quoted Rep. Celler on the occasion of the farewell.

Jagjit Singh's article "India's Publicity Abroad" written in September 1948 explains his methods and achievements in this field. His visits to Washington, D.C. to lobby for "meditation" in 1942, for famine relief in 1943-1944, and for the Luce-Celler bills in 1944, 1945, and 1946 were some of the major events of his life. The League addressed scores of letters to prominent Americans inviting them to become members of its Advisory Board (renamed the "National" Advisory Board in 1944). The India Independence Day Dinner on January 26, 1945, in New York was sponsored by about 400 Americans and about 900 persons mostly Americans came for the dinner. The League's propaganda efforts were paying off in terms of human materials although financially the dinner left behind a deficit.

The authors of *Quit India* pay the well-deserved credit to Jagjit Singh for understanding the need for new techniques of publicity to win American sympathy for India at a time when America was the ally of India's oppressor, Britain. "No longer could the old tactic of twisting the British lion's tail or describing the horrors of imperialistic domination serve to rouse American audiences. Among the Indian(s) in the United States, they conclude, "no one realized it more clearly than J. J. Singh," 291.

98. *The Profile*, 40. This problem, why the League did not take up the question of immigration and citizenship sooner than it did forms part of the Chapter VII. His major campaigns such as those in relation to the Cripps Mission and the Quit India movement of 1942, his defense of the League against the attacks of hostile journalists in 1943, the struggle against UNRRA and the silent settlement in 1944 of the rift between the Indian activists,

although of some biographical interest, have only been briefly discussed in these pages with a view to understanding Jagjit's strategy as an organizer and to trace the gradual growth of the League as an organization. Both of them were being trained and equipped to fight the legislative battles of 1944, 1945, and 1946 which repealed Hindu exclusion.

99. R.C. Majumdar, *Struggle for Freedom* 635, 639, 640; Venkataramani and Shrivastava, *Quit India*, 133, 262- 263, 264, 265. The full text of the A.I.C.C. resolution of August 8 is in Pattabhi Sitaramayya, *History of the Indian National Congress*, 2 vols., New Delhi, 1969, Vol. 2, 343-346.

Over a hundred thousand persons were arrested, convicted and detained without trial, R.C. Majumdar, *Struggle for Freedom*, 655; as to the number of deaths, here is Jawaharlal Nehru's estimate: "Popular estimates place the number of deaths at 25,000 but probably this is an exaggeration. Perhaps 10,000 may be nearer the mark." Quote in ibid.

Most of Jagjit's political friends in India were arrested, including Dewan Chamanlal, Yusuf Meharali, Asaf Ali (who five years later would come here as India's Ambassador), Mrs. Aruna Asaf Ali, and Jayaprakash Narayan.

100. *Transcript*, 54, 71. A chronology of his engagements from August 6 to 20, written in his own hand and with no erasures says: "Aug 6th Luces," "Aug 7th Telegrams Luces Pearl Buck," "Aug 9th check Telegrams." This shows that he stayed with the Luces on Aug. 6, a fact confirmed by his telegram of the following day. This and the telegram of the 9th are both extant but we don't have the one mentioned in his New Yorker Profile, which said, "I won't say I told you so but now I need your help," *The Profile*, 42. He was also not their "weekend" guest. August 6 was Thursday. Arrests were made on the morning of August 9 which would be late evening of August 8 in New York. Jagjit was not at the time returning from his visit to the Luces; *Transcript*, 55; he called August 9 "a day of infamy in the history of Britain in India," *India To-Day*, August 1943, 2.

101. Transcript, 54.

102. Jagjit to Frances Gunther, August 4, 1942, I.L.A. Papers

103. Telegram to Mrs. Henry R. Luce, Upper King Street, Portchester, New York, August 7, 1942, I.L.A. Papers.

104. Both the handwritten and typed parts of the chronology of his engagement and activities in New York and Washington, D.C. mentioned above in Fn. 100. He attempted to meet Senator La Follette through his sister's husband. He also met Sir G.S. Bajpai. Opposite the columnist Raymond Clapper's name he wrote, "wrote the column." On August 22 he held a press conference in Washington, D.C. and sent telegrams to Lin Yutang and Lauchlin Currie, President Roosevelt's Administrative Assistant,

I.L.A. Papers. Currie later helped in the passage of the Luce-Celler bill. Jagjit's interview with Dr. Narayanan, 23.

105. His main thesis was as follows:

The Japanese conquered Burma because the Burmese people joined the invaders against Britain who refused to promise them freedom after the war.

India is now the United Nations' supply base, the base of military operations for the recovery of Burma and also the supply route to China.

The lives of thousands of "American boys" would be lost unless the people of India are won over as enthusiastic fighting allies.

The United States must mediate to secure from Britain promise of freedom for India after the war. This would convince the Indian people that they are fighting for their own freedom rather than for the preservation of the British Empire. India has become America's business.

India's freedom is no longer an ideological issue, it is now a matter of stern military necessity for the recovery of South-East Asia and to keep China in the war. Jagjit Singh to William Randolph Hearst, Publisher, Wyntoon, California, February 20, 1942; to Raymond Clapper, c/o Scripps-Howard Syndicate, 1013 Thirteenth Street, Washington, D.C., August 31, 1942; to Ludwell Denny, c/o Scripps-Howard Syndicate, same address, same date; to George Parker, same address, same date; to Westbrook Legler, c/o *World Telegram*, 125 Barclay Street, New York City, September 5, 1942; same to Arthur Krock, c/o *New York Times*, Albes Building, Washington, D.C. September 8, 1942; to Herpert L. Matthews, Hotel Cecil, Delhi, India, October 9, 1942; Jagjit Singh's letter to Wm. Philips Simms quoted by Simms in his column "Orient Awakening" in *N.Y. World Telegram*, July 9, 1943; to Miss Marion Carter, Program Director, Town Meeting of the Air, Town Hall, 123 West 43rd Street, New York, N.Y.; August 31, 1944; to William Phillip Simms. Scripps-Howard Syndicate, 1013-13th Street, N.W., Washington, D.C., September 21, 1944.

The best enunciation of the thesis, however, was in the full-page statement signed by 55 Americans, published in the New York Times of September 28, 1942. The text of the statement was repeated in *India To-Day*, September 1942. Mary Braggiotti's Shihouette of Jagjit Singh in *New York Post* of August 9, 1943 under the caption "A Voice for the 400 Million" weaves his biography around his war-time strategy, the first time that the two had been the subject of a column in a major American newspaper.

One of the most direct and brief enunciations of his strategy was in a letter he wrote to a labor leader requesting that he (Jagjit) "may have the honor of addressing the (forthcoming C.I.O) convention on the Indian situation." The letter proceeds: "I may add here that I would only discuss this question from the viewpoint of its utter importance to the United States and to the ultimate victory of the United Nations, and my talk will not be in any way anti-British or such that may create ill feeling between the United States and Great Britain.'' Jagjit Singh to Mr.Clinton S.Golden, United Steel Workers of America, 1500 Commonwealth Building, Pittsburgh, Pa., October 29, 1942.

106. Caption of an article on the famine in *Time* magazine, February 8, 1943, mentioned in M.S. Venkataramani, *Bengal Famine of 1943; The American Response*, Delhi, 1973, 5, fn. 9. This source will henceforth be referred to as *Famine*.
107. Ibid., 6, viii.
108. Jagjit Singh's report to "Dear Members" on the work of the League for the year 1943, 7, hereafter cited as *Jagjit Singh's Report 1943; New York Post*, November 16 and 17, 1943; *PM*, November 16, 1943. His *Famine in India* was published in New York, October 27, 1943.
109. *India To-Day*, November 1943, 3; *Jagjit Singh's Report 1943*, 10; *Famine*, 42 (emphasis added).
110. *Famine* 47; Dean Acheson, *Sketches From Life: Of Men I Have Known*, New York, 1959, 124, 125; *Jagjit Singh's Report 1943*, 10.
111. *The Profile*, 43-44
112. *India To-Day*, November 1943, 3; another $100,000 had been donated later. *Famine* 62; Carey's intervention *Famine*, 52; "Mr. Carey, National director C.I.O." was one of the persons on Jagjit Singh's list during his visit to Washington, August 1942.
113. *The Newark Star-Ledger*, 26, 29 and 30 January 1944; *Jagjit Singh's Report*, 1943, 3.
114. *Jagjit Singh's Report*, 3, 11.
115. Jagjit Singh's assessment as to his "great achievement": "This is the first time in the history of the relationship between India and America that the Congress of the United States had adopted such an attitude and has suggested interference in India, notwithstanding the opposition of the British Empire," Jagjit Singh to Mumtaz Kitchlew, 17 Palmer House Arcade, Chicago Ill., February 18, 1944, I.L.A. Papers.

Instances of unflattering headlines about Indians in earlier years–

29 September 1910, *San Franciso Chronicle*, 3- column spread, Hindoo Immigrants Have Hookworm Disease: Dr. Glover's Discovery Stems Tide from India.

1 October 1910, *Survey*, The Hindu, the Newest Immigrant Problem.

24 January 1914, *San Francisco Examiner*, Turn Hindus Back, Says Secretary Wilson.

14 February 1914, ibid., Caminetti Defi Given to Wilson: Commissioner Scores Adm. Policy and Says Asiatics Must be kept out.

18 July 1914, *Literary Digest*. Sikhs Besiege Canada.

116. Jagjit Singh's speech on the occasion of the Farewell Public Meeting, February 11, 1959. 2, item 3.

117. Pandit daughter's letter from Wellesley College, dated March 2, 1944, also advised him "try not to rush around doing the work of ten men." Mumtaz Kitchlew, Chicago to Jagjit, December 3, 1943; Rakhit's complement in his letter to Jagjit Singh, August 27, 1943 (?); G.J. Watumull, 937 Malcolm Avenue, Los Angeles 24, Calif., February 1, 1944; Louis Fischer, 237 Madison Avenue, New York, March 3, 1944; Will Rogers Jr., House of Representatives, Washington, D.C, to Jagjit. March 1, 1944, Pearl S. Buck, Perkasie, Pa. to Jagjit, March 21, 1944; Richard J. Walsh to Jagjit, March 20, 1944; Herman P. Eberharter, House of Representatives, February 29, 1944; Ramlal Bajpai, 1753 Q St. N.W., Washington, D.C., November 30, 1943. A student from Berkeley wrote, "It is inspiring to know that there are men like you to voice India's problems to this country." Theresa Loeb to Jagjit Singh, December 12, 1943.

    Mrs. Frances Gunther's two letters, December 15, 1943 and February 18, 1944; Sher M. Quraishi's letter March 1, 1944; William Ernest Hocking's March 2, 1944; Louis Johnson's, February 29, 1944; Anne O'Hare McGormick's February 14, 1944; "WASHINGTON DIPLOMAT" is Rakhit's phrase, in an undated letter of these days to Jagjit Singh.

118. Jagjit Singh to Devdas Gandhi, April 13, 1945, I.L.A. Papers.

6

STRUGGLE AGAINST STATELESSNESS

"These Hindus were considered as white persons when they were granted certificates of naturalization. . . . (they) had every reason to believe that the same were legally granted. They took the pledge of allegiance, and they undoubtedly had every reason to suppose that the Government of the United States would not retract its pledge of protection to them."

— WILLIAM C. CRONMEYER, Attorney,
Senate Hearings Dec. 1926, 39

In March 1945 Jagjit Singh introduced into the record of the House hearing on the Luce, Celler and Dirkson bills, names of India League officials and of members of its National Advisory Board. Among them were those of Godha Ram Channon, Dr. Sudhindra Bose, Hemendra Rakhit, Profulla Chandra Mukerji, Roger Baldwin, Norman Thomas, Rev. John Haynes Holmes and Haridas T. Muzumdar.[1] Adding Dr. Taraknath Das, Gobind Behari Lal and Ramlal Bajpai to the list would bring together part of the galaxy of heroes who by their sufferings or endeavor or both wrote the history of the 40-year-long struggle of the Indian community to achieve a status of equality in the United States and freedom for India from British rule. They included some of the earliest veterans of the struggle still active, still in the United States and except for Sudhindra Bose, who died just one month short of the goal of legal equality, all were destined to outlive the legal "stigma" here and the political stigma in India.

The India League inherited the tradition of the struggle against American discriminatory laws both in its objectives as well as in personnel. It turned out to be a long agitation with its immediate issues changing from time to time but always consistent in its ultimate objective of achieving elimination of disabilities based on "race" or national origin.

The agitation had been pioneered and it continued to be dominated over the years by a small group hardly exceeding a few dozen students, political exiles, English-educated young men. They had awakened to the burdens of their race, color and the country of origin by the harsh treatment their countrymen received in Canada and the United States. They began to sympathise with those Asian elements—Chinese, Japanese and Islamic—who supposedly were eager "to teach the color-phobe and 'democratic' Americans a lesson in return for the American laws of exclusion."[2] The writings of Sant Nihal Singh, Lajpat Rai, Taraknath Das, Basant Kumar Roy and of several others helped create not only the anti-British ideology of Gadar but also a conscious ethnic identity based on resentment against immigration laws for which they held Britain and its Anglo- Saxon allies, including the United States, responsible.

These pioneers were Indians and nationalists already. What they saw and read about the fate of Chinese and Japanese immigrants made them Asians. The violence of racist abuse, America's support of British imperialism, and its imitation of the immigration policies of the British colonies made them angry. Their study of the American Revolution and the widening support they received from American friends made them hopeful.

Adding up all these qualities we find a leadership that believed in America, demanded and worked for the freedom of India, and sought full equality for Indian immigrants on the basis of reciprocity and human rights. In respect of the personal accomplishment and educational qualification of its individual members, this tiny group of intellectuals, students and merchants was probably one of the finest among the ethnic groups, white, black or Asian, in America.

Some scholars have expressed doubts about the intensity and volume of the Indian community's effort to improve its legal status in the United States. They recognize that the Gadar as well as the subsequent Indian nationalist activities within the United States had a dual—an Indian as well as an American—purpose. They have, however, failed to follow this conclusion to the shores of the Indian Ocean. They have searched only in America for evidence of the community's effort to gain a respectable status in their adopted country. Most of the affort, however, lay in India—the bloodshed, the martyrdoms, the court trials that took place in order to force Britain into a corner from where it would be reluctant to support the American exclusionists. When most of the effort went uncounted and unrecognized, the sum total was bound to be negative.

According to Bruce LaBrack, the Gadar Party "continued to affect the thinking and actions of many Sikhs but as a source of improving their living conditions in the United States the Ghadar had no impact nor was it designed to."[3] He approves of Jacoby's opinion that

> Many of the concerns of the East Indian associations were rather parochial in the sense of being rather closely tied to situations in India such as its independence or involving various reform movements . . . What appears to be lacking is a concern over the conditions of their life in America . . . there is little evidence of any general agitation for changes in their social or legal status in America, at least until the late 1930s.[4]

Regarding this alleged lack of evidence, LaBrack testifies that "Since there were numerous occasions when these groups could have registered protests or given testimony, it seems strange that there is not more evidence of such activity in the public record."[5]

As to the reasons for the comparative absence of such activity he argued that

> many of the East Indians, Sikhs included, did not originally plan to stay in the U.S., they were not immediately concerned with immigration or alien land laws. By the time they had decided to stay it was either too late to protest or they had come to terms with the restrictions. For some it was all rather incomprehensible, something done to them by some remote authority through a process they did not understand. Being aliens, many felt they had little "right" to protest. Others were illegals, liable to deportation if they became too visible or vocal.[6]

The Indian immigrants' Mexican marriages and other measures to side-track the Alien Land Laws and the determination they invested in developing American agriculture which have been discussed in previous chapters disprove the scholars' allegation that the immigrants did not show serious "concern over their conditions of life in America."

As to any favorable results in terms of changed American or British policies, they were not visible immediately or even in one generation. The opponents were too deeply entrenched to be pushed back easily or early. Nationalist forces in India in the 1920s and the early 1930s were still in the process of recruitment, reorientation, and consolidation. The Gadar leaders' thesis that the immigrants' efforts should be directed both against British imperialism and American racism, however, proved to be historically correct.

The allegation of parochialism can be leveled at almost all ethnic groups for being "closely tied to situations" in the home country. The Irish, the Germans, the East Europeans were "parochial" too. The WASP's of the United States themselves have almost never been *loosely* tied to situations in Britain, Canada and Australia. In fact this Anglo-Saxon "parochialism" was at the root of the troubles the Indian immigrants had to face in India, in America, and in the British Colonies.

LaBrack's conclusion that the Indians "had come to terms with restrictions" is based on comparative absence of any Indian agitation of the type usually undertaken by European immigrants that sponsored bills, organized petitions, and lobbied in Congress. Indians once mounted such an agitation in 1913-1914. They would mount another in 1926. The major effort of the Indian community, however, was to seek salvation in America by attempting to weaken British power over India. The community considered all enthusiasm, money and lives spent towards achieving that goal as good investment towards achieving a status of equality in America.

Some of the immigrants may not have had a clear understanding of the American constitutional process by which their disabilities were enacted. Their leaders, however, did understand those processes. LaBrack himself testifies that the Indian leadership consisted of "sophisticated. . . university intellectuals." Similar cases of less-informed masses and well-informed leadership were common among the European immigrants also, especially among those who came from despotically oppressed peasant communities of Eastern Europe and Ireland.[7]

It is true that some immigrants did not plan to stay permanently in the United States. Those who did, started the struggle to make their stay legally more comfortable soon after they arrived. Probably as early as 1907 some of them made representation against rejection of their applications seeking naturalization. Taraknath Das's naturalization was delayed till 1914 only by "several legal battles."[8]

Scholars have recognized that the Sikh immigrants had held the British responsible for the insults and hardships they had to endure in Canada and the United States. They also recognize the Gadar as an effort towards the liberation of India. A few have also depicted it as an Indo-German conspiracy of "the enemy within." Hardly any writer has consistently maintained the connection between the origin of the Gadar and the history of the Gadar. They unconsciously merge it into the general stream of India's freedom struggle as if it were born in India without any lineal connection with American or Canadian racism. The origins of the Gadar lay not in the atrocities of the British rule over India but in the grievances of the Sikhs as immigrants in North America.

The intellectuals who were leading the Gadar Party sought a revolt against Britain as the alien ruler over India. For the Sikh immigrants, however, the concepts of republicanism and self-determination meant little. To them the denial of family reunion, rights to citizenship, and to landholding were the causes that stimulated rebellion. Their British overlords had denied them the right to protection in a foreign land. But for their grievances as immigrants their conversion into rebels would not have been easy or even probable.

LaBrack is aware of the cause and effect relationship between the Indians' complaints as immigrants and the growth of the Gadar Party. The Gadar, he says, reflected the politics of India and "also the conditions under which Indians were laboring abroad" that "the reality of racism and discrimination" helped to make them revolutionaries so that the Gadar Party became "a platform for their assertion of human rights."[9]

On several occasions, the Sikhs referred to their troubles as immigrants as reasons for turning against Britain. For instance, several former soldiers among the immigrants adopted a resolution in a gurudwara meeting of October 3, 1909 to stop wearing their medals and uniforms. One of the reasons offered was the "deplorable conditions of our countrymen in India and other parts of the world, especially in the British Colonies."[10]

A Supplement to the *Gadar* issue of February 1914 accused the British of having "leagued themselves with the Government of

Australia, Canada and South Africa to prevent Indians from entering these countries and now wish to ask the American Government to prohibit Indians from coming to America."[11] The Gadar, therefore, has to be considered a part of the Indian community's struggle to obtain a better status as lawful residents of the United States. The energies and sacrifices expended in the Gadar effort should be credited to the agitation against American discrimination. Probably no other American ethnic community except the American Indian and the black has paid such a heavy price to obtain a status of equality in the United States. The number of Indian immigrants executed, shot, and imprisoned during the course of the Gadar uprising was, in proportion to their numbers, almost comparable to what the American blacks had to suffer during the first half of the present century including the lynchings.

The question can be raised : Why did the Indians go the hard way? They could have avoided having to make those sacrifices by seeking redress of their American grievances in America and of Canadian grievances in Canada. This question would be relevant only on the supposition that there were only two parties to the dispute—the immigrants and the host country. That supposition is not correct. Britain was as much to blame as the host countries. America was not treating the Indian immigrants well partly because the British colonies including Canada were not treating them well, and Canada did not treat them well because Britain was not treating Indians well in India. The Gadar thesis reflected sound logic—the basic cure lay in India.

> The British rulers devised every conceivable means to keep India isolated. To make this isolation complete it was necessary that the peoples of India must not have the opportunity to migrate as free men in a free world on the basis of equality.

This is how Taraknath Das, one of the makers of the ideology of revolt, summed up the British policy while celebrating its defeat in 1946.[12] Had Britain refrained from instigating or encouraging the American exclusionists as it was doing during the earlier decades of the century, Indian immigrants would have had a better bargaining position against hostile legislation. The settlement offered by the restrictionists to white immigrants—literacy and quota—could possibly have been obtained for Indian immigrants too on the basis of their common Caucasian origin. Because of British collusion with exclusionists, the settlement instead of being reached in 1917 or even in 1924 could be reached only decades later.

Scholars have not adequately recognized the fact that unlike the immigrants from Europe, those from Asia were the victims of the worldwide Anglo-Saxon bloc, the "white peril" holding Asia (except Japan) under its imperialist control and denying equality to all Asian immigrants. Their struggle for justice in America had, therefore, to be directed both against the Anglo-Saxon bloc as well as against the American exclusionists.

These Asian immigrants had a common interest in weakening the "white peril." But the homelands of the Chinese and Japanese immigrants being sovereign states could not go to war against the Anglo-Saxon alliance to secure equality and justice for their nationals abroad. Moreover, China was too dependent upon the Anglo-Saxon powers for protection against Japanese aggression for almost fifty years. It had, therefore, to swallow its nationals' exclusion from America like other unequal treaties. Even the more independent Japan had to swallow the Alien Land Laws, the *Ozawa* ruling, and the exclusion of 1924. Even though it may have been eager to fight the United States, it could not go beyond raising the question of racial equality at the Paris Peace Conference, an effort which the Anglo-Saxons rendered futile. The best Japan could do was to nurse its grievances for a reckoning at a later date. Indians were the only immigrants from a major Asian country who were untrammelled with diplomatic restraints of a sovereign state. They declared "Open War" upon Britain, the most powerful member of the "white peril" alliance, their oppressor at home and the instigator of oppression abroad. Their immediate provocation was the immigration problem; their ultimate objective was to obtain a just solution to the problem. Whether it was the Gadar trying to incite a mutiny in India or the Friends of Freedom for India and the India League engaging in anti-British propaganda in America, the Indian nationalists were in fact all the time and in both countries engaged in a lobbying campaign for an immigration and naturalization bill.

As in all lobbying, their intention was to win supporters against the opponent's policies, to force him to change his policy, and failing that to throw him out of office at the "next elections." In the context of Indian politics the Gadar 1915-1917, Martial Law 1918-1919, the Non-Cooperation movements 1921-1922 and 1931-1932, the elections of 1936-1937, the Quit India uprising of 1942, and the elections of 1945-1946 were a part of these lobbying campaigns and "next elections." A change in British policy was discernible after the elections of 1936-1937, and finally it conceded freedom to the Indian immigrants two years before it conceded freedom to India. The Gadarites had started winning supporters in India by their sacrifices. Their successors in America widened their contacts and support by continuing to beat the nationalist drum in America for thirty years and by winning American friends. The head of the nationalist movement in India (Mahatma Gandhi) sent his letter of congratulations on the enactment of the immigration and naturalization bill to the chief lobbyist (Jagjit Singh) through an American friend of India (Louis Fischer). The man who delivered the keynote address at the victory celebrations was a former Gadarite—Dr. Taraknath Das. The Gadar thesis had come true. The nationalist struggle had forced a change in British policy. American exclusionists had been left without British support.

There was also another reason why Indians had to fight their battle both against their rulers at home and their host country, unlike the immigrants from Europe who lobbied or agitated only in the United States. The Indians were not treated as Europeans were. There undoubtedly were several similarities between the Anglo-Saxon hostility to Indian Immigrants and to those from southern and eastern Europe.[13] Both were equally unwelcome as "cheap labor"[14] who were brought in by greedy steamship companies. Both were accused of being "strike-breakers"[15] and threats to the Anglo-Saxon standard of living.[16] Soon these economic arguments took on racial tones and the alleged "mongrel-bloods" of southern and eastern Europe became threats to the purity of the Nordic blood.[17] Madison Grant even called for not just restriction but exclusion of the "Alpine Mediterranean and Jewish breeds as the only means of preserving America's old Nordic stock."[18]

The Teutonic alliance—Britain, the British Colonies and the United States—was using the weapons of exclusion and restriction to reserve the empty spaces of the world for its own people. The victims were the people of Asia and of southeastern Europe. But the United States at the same time drew a deep distinction between the white and the non-white races. This is where similarities between the legal status of Indian immigrants and that of the European immigrants ended. The host country agreed to a limited partnership with the non-Nordic ethnic groups of Europe. The limits of partnership were registered in the immigration quotas. For Asians it was exclusion from partnership and common citizenship in America. For the white races Americans were only restrictionists, for the Asian people almost all Americans were exclusionists. In the settlement of 1924 virtually all Asians were excluded while no European ethnic group was denied a quota or the right of citizenship.[19]

There were also other dissimilarities. The intended targets of the literacy test enjoyed strong American support including some big business organizations "which lobbied continuously in Washington against proposed restrictive measures" and from "the older immigrant element."[20] "What gave effectiveness to the opposition" was the fact that they were voters whose increasing numbers "forced" the Republican Party "to take their wishes into account."[21] Indians, on the other hand, had no American support worth the name and they were not voters either. As pointed out by Roger Deniels, historians have agreed that there was "something that set them (Asian immigrants) apart from the tens of millions of other immigrants who came here." Edith Abbot discovered that Asian immigration involved "very different problems" while Carl Wittke characterized it as "a brief and strange interlude."[22] Dissimilar situations dictated to Indians dissimilar strategies that were not always confined to lobbying in Washington.

Which European government ever asked the United States government to mistreat its emigrants, to deny them the privilege of immigration or ever acquiesced in the denial to them of rights available to other immigrants ? Indian immigrants at a very early point in time decided "to set their own house in order" before they could expect to get equal rights abroad. Starting with the Gadar, they continued to pound at British sovereignty over India until that linchpin of white racist imperialism started to behave better from the mid 1930s. This achievement of the Indian activists' was worth hundreds of miles of footwork in the corridors of the American Congress. No wonder that so many former Gadarites and their associates were on the India League's letterhead.

Scholars like Edith Abbot who excluded a discussion of Asian immigration from their works may, in a way, have been right. They had set out to write on immigration to America not on the New World extension of the age-long conflict between the East and the West. The story of European immigration to the United States too got occasionally distorted by the old hoslitities of the Jews and the Gentiles, the Irish and the Anglo-Saxons, the Catholics and the Protestants. But they were settled within the fraternity of Western culture. Immigrants from Asia aroused hostilities of race, culture and color which the white fraternity was not willing to terminate.

Both sides recognized the gulf and its implications. "The immigrants have against them their skins and the fact that they come from Asia" wrote Sant Nihal Singh in 1908."[23] The Californian exclusionists had decided on white exclusiveness about half a century earlier. Living abroad, the Indian immigrants were forcefully made aware, in the words of Taraknath Das, that "Indians, because of their race and color i.e., being Asiatic and also brown men are not worthy to enjoy full civic rights in the United States of America."[24] Indian immigrants in North America absorbed this Asian perspective not from books but from personal sufferings often endured in common with other Asians in Canadian cities, on California's farms and, in American universities. The Gadar rebels picked up Asia on their way to India. This wider view is Gadar's contribution to India's freedom struggle. One of the honorary presidents of the India League was the Chinese writer, Lin Yutang, and one of the most dramatic testimonies at the 1943 hearings for repeal of Chinese exclusion was that of an Indian, Dr. Taraknath Das.

Three years later this professor of world politics summed up the historical thesis of the struggle just concluded. Fortified by his forty-year association with the struggle and as one of its leading originators, ideologists and prosecuted participants, his summation carries weight. It is the authentic voice of all those who worked for India's freedom and for improving the immigrant's legal status from the Indian community's base in North America.

> One phase of the struggle for Indian freedom, is based upon the desire of the Indian people of remove all obstacles which thwart them from asserting their mastery in their own home . . . . The other and larger phase of the struggle was that Indians must have the same right to participate in human endeavors in all parts of the world without any hindrance and on the basis of equality. Thus one may point out the often overlooked fact that the struggle for Asian independence and the movement

> for free immigration of Asians are two aspects of the same great movement. I may also emphasize the point that as Indian Freedom has a very close relation to Asian Freedom, similarly the right of Indians to have equal human rights in America and other lands has also very close relation with the efforts of other Asian peoples for the acquisition of the same rights.[25]

The struggle for "equal human rights in America" had been waged, as we have maintained, both in India and the United States. The part of the struggle which was waged in the United States whether directed against Britain or against American immigration laws developed a character all its own dictated by the Indian community's assets and liabilities as well as the climate of public opinion surrounding it. We have to grasp the various facets of the character of that struggle in order to appreciate the historical development of the struggle itself.

Indian organizations directed this struggle through their newsletters, the public press, from their own or borrowed platforms and in later years over the radio as well. Indian nationalist leaders' birthdays, other nationalist anniversaries and visits of Indian dignitaries were put to good use.[26]

The voluminous writings of Lajpat Rai, Sudhindra Bose, Taraknath Das, Haridas T. Muzumdar and the articles contributed by Basant Kumar Roy and Surendra Karr have lasting value as specimens of vehement sincerity that pervaded their patriotic fervor. The contributions of Anup Singh and S. Chandrasekhar to Indian and American periodicals are among the earliest attempts to piece together the history of Indian immigration to North America and to investigate the problem of naturalization. Krishnalal Shridharani's three works interpreted the Indian and Asian arguments to American readers in terms of American national interest. The outstanding work immediately concerned with the cause of the immigrants was Rajani Kant Das's little monograph. It is historically important as the major contemporary corrective to the Canadian and Californian views of the Indian immigrants' social and economic personalities. So is the Burjor Report though on a smaller scale.[27]

The people, who wrote, debated, lectured, organized associations, and fought the long-drawn propaganda war against Britain on American soil, were highly educated individuals. They were also elitist. None of them came from aristocratic families, but they ranked high in the socioeconomic scale even by American standards. Consequently they brought a bourgeois moderation to the solution of their American problems. We have already seen how Ramchandra, in his letter to the *New York Times*, and Sudhindra Bose, in his testimony at the Congressional hearings, were ready to accept restricted immigration at the cost of the Indian farmers and laborers. This moderation now as well as in the 1940s may also have been dictated by the Indian leadership's "beggars-cannot-be-choosers" realism.[28]

Once exclusion from immigration had become the law in 1917, no Indian organization attempted to reopen the question until the India League started to campaign for repeal in 1944. Verbal protests against exclusion, however, continued. For instance Sailendra Ghose complained that the immigration laws of the United States had become "more restrictive with the growth of America as a world power"[29] and the organ of the Friends of Freedom for India quoted with approval a labor leader's opinion that "our exclusion laws are unfair and unjust to our brothers of the Orient."[30] Yet for over one generation there was no organized voice calling for the repeal of the Barred Zone or for the grant of a quota to Indians. Indians continued to suffer the pain and the insult of those laws—professor Surrendra Nath Das Gupta in 1926, Rabindranath Tagore in 1929, Anup Singh in 1938.[31] On the Pacific coast hundreds of immigrants remained separated from their wives and children. Instead of demanding the right to family reunions, emphatic disclaimers were announced by Indian activists and their friends of any intention to seek a liberalization of the immigration part of the Act of 1924. Senators Reed and Copeland, the India Chamber of Commerce, and the India League all found this precaution necessary in order to soothe the nerves of the exclusionists.[32]

It was not just their nerves but also their determination with which the Indian leaders had to deal. From the 1920s the American people were in no mood to relax Asian exclusion or to liberalize the quota system to benefit even white immigrants.[33] When America was saying "no" to China and Japan, what chance did the citizens of a dependent India have in those years ? Indian leaders understood this situation. Moreover, except for the national insult implied in the exclusion laws, and the restrictions on merchants resulting from the absence of treaty of trade, the Indian intellectuals were getting from the restrictive immigration laws whatever advantages they had hoped for. Students, scholars, and preachers were coming and the "laborers" were not. In its immigration clauses, the Act of 1924 was working beautifully as the instrument of Indian middle-class urban professionals. The recovery of the right to citizenship, however, was always agitating their minds because it involved their interests as closely as those of the farmers. Citizenship rights would have cancelled the effects of immigration restriction for those who received them and their families.

As was done by other disadvantaged groups such as the blacks, the working classes, and women, the Indian immigrants too appealed to what Sant Nihal Singh called "the Spirit of America," the higher principles enshrined in the Declaration of Independence and the Constitution. They never tired of reminding America of its reputation as the land of freedom and democracy with the implication that racist discrimination was un-American.

While appealing to the United States to extend to them courtesies becoming a tolerant host, the immigrants themselves tried their best to fulfill the obligations of loyal and understanding guests. Their published writings leave no doubt as to their love for the United States. Several immigrants served in the American defense forces in both World Wars. Even when the United States was clearly acting against their interests, the immigrants' resentment was expressed in restrained phrases—"In doing so (i.e., while expressing resentment) the etiquette and rule of hospitality [are] scrupulously observed" the Gadar Party journal asserted in 1920.[34]

In October 1919, Taraknath Das arrived in New York after completing his term in the Leavenworth Penitentiary. He was thirty-five and was returning to a changed and a changing world. The Gadar objectives had suffered defeat in America, India, and South-East Asia. Indian exclusion had become a legislative fact. World War I had enlarged and strengthened the British Empire, and General Dyer had massacred people in Amritsar. The white nations had rejected Japan's proposal to abolish racial discriminations. The United States appeared eager to wean Britain away from its Japanese alliance.[35]

Although dejected at having failed in its attempt to use Britain's war to India's advantage and defamed by adverse publicity over the San Francisco trial, the Indian community continued to improve its economic strength and to maintain its nationalist aspirations. The farmers were expanding the area under cultivation. They made good money during the war. Their donations to Indian causes continued. Several Sikhs went to India to participate in the gurudwara reform movement.

Writing in 1922 Dr. Rajani Kant Das observed that the Indian residents on the Pacific coast

> are energetic and successful. Some of them have become fairly educated and acquired some degree of business success. The knowledge of the country and the success in life have made them conscious of their condition. They feel more than ever the injustice of the social, political and industrial discriminations under which they have to live.[36]

Lala Lajpat Rai left the United States soon after Taraknath returned from Leavenworth. His assistant, N.S. Hardikar, left in 1921. They left behind a cadre of dedicated young workers like Ramlal Bajpai, Hemendra Rakhit, S.S. Sarna and Basant Kumar Roy. Of the former Gadarites, Sailendra Ghose and Profulla Mukerji were already actively engaged in nationalist work in the East, while Godharam Channon organized the Hindusthan Welfare Association in California. Future leaders such as Syud Hossian, Haridas T. Muzumdar, and Dalip Singh Saund came in the early 1920s.

Thanks to the contacts established by Lajpat Rai, the community had gained the support of a valuable segment of American opinion. Roger Baldwin, Norman Thomas, Rev. John Haynes Holmes and Robert Morss Lovett had established the Friends of Freedom for India to protect Indian immigrants from executive arbitrariness. Taraknath and Sailendra Ghose extended their contacts among the Irish-Americans and organized labor. These were the seeds of strength which would bear fruit two decades later under more favorable Indian, American, British, and world circumstances.[37]

Indian students were content with the "deal" they got under the Acts of 1917 that permitted them to earn their way through college. Still exclusionist forces, organized labor, the United States Government, in fact the American people in general, remained unconvinced of the advisability of extending the privilege of citizenship to any Asian people. The Indian community itself, weak in numbers, divided by vast distances, disunited internally by antipathy among Hindus, Muslims and Sikhs, hardly received any morale boosts from home after the withdrawal of Gandhi's first Disobedience Movement in February 1922.

The Gadar enthusiasts had argued for India's freedom as the cure for the immigrants' hardships. Dr. Rajani Kant Das had imagined that probably Indian nationalists "can retaliate economically" by organizing boycott of a discriminating country's goods.[38] The Gadar effort failed. Dr. Das's suggestion never became a practical proposition. The United States remained firmly committed to its racist policies. Britain had suppressed three uprisings—German, Gadar and Gandhi.

When the veterans of the Gadar started coming out of American prisons in 1919, they discovered some outstanding debts still waiting to be paid. For Taraknath they called for cancellation of his United States citizenship and deportation to India.

Some people are never able to escape their creditors particularly when the creditors have their collection agents all over the world. Taraknath had two loves in life—love of India and love of learning. He had come to America to satisfy both passions. It was his dream that "India some day should have a Republic . . . and if it is a crime I plead guilty before you" he told the Senate Committee on Immigration in December 1926.[39] But Britain would not let him run away from his obligations of loyalty to the Crown. Consequently the Anglo-Saxon bloc came down so heavily upon him as to give him the distinction of being probably the most harassed Indian patriot in America. In 1908 he had been forced to resign his American civil service job because the Canadian authorities objected to the anti-British writings in his journal *Free Hindusthan.*[40] A year later he was discharged from a military training course because as master of the Philippines, the United States had a common interest with Britain in keeping their Asian subjects ignorant of the art of war.[41]

In 1911 the British Ambassador suggested to the U.S. Government that Das should not be naturalized as an American citizen. In 1914 he was naturalized over the objection of the U.S. Bureau of Naturalization. He told Robert Morss Lovett that once his apartment in New York had been searched without a warrant by Sir George Denham, head of the British police at Calcutta with the complicity of local authorities.[42] At the Gadar trial Britain secured for him the longest of all sentences pronounced. On his release he was threatened with loss of U.S. citizenship and deportation to India. A judge saved him from this double disaster.[43]

Three years later, the *Thind* decision, considered by some of its victims as another instance of Anglo-Saxon bias against all Asians, rendered both Das and his wife Mary stateless persons. It also placed the question of naturalization at the top of the Indo-American community's agenda. National dignity and naturalization were the two objectives on which all Indians—elitist, farmers and factory workers—were of one mind. From 1923 the community was constantly at war with the *Thind* case ruling.

Next to his arrest and conviction in the Gadar affair the years 1924 to 1928 were the most troubled in Taraknath's life. He had completed his doctorate and had become rich by marriage in 1924. He was forty and was preparing to "start my life as a scholar"[44] combined with political work among Indian students when the blow fell. The *Thind* ruling was declared to have retroactive effect so that all naturalization certificates granted to Indian civilians were rendered liable to cancellation.

The total number of Indians naturalized was at least 69. By December 1926 when through Taraknath's efforts the matter came before the Senate Committee on Immigration, the situation stood as follows :

Naturalization cancelled by District Courts	40
Naturalization not challenged (being soldiers)	10
Cases still before courts	13
Rejected by the Supreme Court (Bhagat Singh Thind)	1
Left uncontested (Thakur Dev Sharman)	1
Not accounted for (Nainsinh L. Thaker)	3
Deceased	4
	69[45]

None of the 40 cancellations had been appealed to the Supreme Court. By December 1926 it was too late to appeal so that a favorable decision in a lower court in any of the 13 pending cases "even if sustained by the Supreme Court [could] furnish no relief" to these 40 former citizens.[46]

When the government filed suits, the District Courts had no option but to cancel the naturalization certificate because of "the binding precedent" established by the Supreme Court.[47] Under the decision as interpreted by Taft, it was held "that such certificates are void because under the law there was no authority to grant a certificate to anyone but a white person and that Hindus do not come within that description."[48] American authorities told Taraknath Das that he "was never an American citizen *ab initio*."[49]

Cancellation orders poured out from the Courts in alarming numbers, denaturalizing over sixty percent of the total in four and a half years. Thirteen Indians whose cases were still before the courts and two others whose naturalizations do not seem to have been challenged, were the only civilian American citizens of Indian origin left. They were citizens still, but they were scared because the naturalization law was now definitely against them. Cancellation of their own certificates seemed not far away. Scared they well might be because they stood to lose a great deal including their ability to make a living as professional men."[50]

These people had renounced their British citizenship when they swore allegiance to the United States. Although he was under no legal obligation to do this, Taraknath Das (in British eyes the "well known Indian agitator" even before the Gadar trial), had probably as a gesture of defiance told the British Government that "I . . . hereby give up and renounce my British citizenship."[51] Under Section 13 of the British Nationality and Status of Aliens Act of 1914, British nationality once voluntarily renounced could not be automatically recovered. If their certificates of American citizenship were cancelled, these people would become stateless persons. In Das's case under the short-lived Cable Act, his America-born wife was faced with possible loss of her own citizenship for having married an "alien ineligible to citizenship."[52]

A scholar of American nationality law and Sudhindra Bose's colleague at the University of Iowa summarized the Indians' predicament in these terms :

> The practical effect is that of a retroactive decision depriving them of a status which some of them obtained years ago in reliance upon the decisions of respectable judicial tribunals. They have adjusted their social and business affairs on the justified adoption that they were American citizens . . . They now find themselves still subjects of the country allegiance to which they had been led to renounce. It may well be surmised that their disappointment is poignant.[53]

Soon disappointment turned into alarm. It seems that the U.S. Government was determined to enforce the consequences of the *Thind* decision upon Indians to its utmost extent. The month after the Iowa article was published, the State Department told Sudhindra Bose that no passport would be issued to him. Two years later he revealed that "American Government authorities have repeatedly told me that they do not want us the Indians in the United States."[54]

America did not want them. The government of their own country did not want them. The British prevented Bose from visiting India in 1925 on the "convenient excuse" of "the question of naturalization," although American authorities offered him the necessary facilities to proceed to India. As Taraknath Das told the American Society of International Law, any Indian who swore allegiance to the United States "rendered himself for all time to come, an alien to the British Government" and as an alien he "cannot enjoy the right to return freely to the land of his birth." The British Government of India could, therefore, legitimately refuse entry to any Indian who had accepted American citizenship particularly if they had been an "agitator" like Das or Bose. In the summer of 1928 Bose was permitted to pay a brief visit to India but could not obtain any assurance from "the tin-gods of Simla" that he would be allowed to come again.[55]

What these resistors valued most about American citizenship was the feeling of emancipation from British control and the victory over American racism it symbolized. For instance Sudhindra Bose "born a British *subject* . . . probably thought be could be free by becoming an American *citizen.*" Conversely, according to Taraknath Das the British authorities did not want Indians to enjoy greater rights in America than they did in the British Colonies.[56] Indians valued American citizenship as a trophy. They had in most cases struggled hard to obtain it. Shankar Gokhale twice rejected the British request to renounce his American citizenship. As punishment for oburacy "he was dismissed [from his college job] with orders to leave immediately."[57]

The seven leading figures in this group that decided to challenge the cancellations included one scientist, two engineers, two university teachers, one economist. Five of them were Ph.D.'s; two had been imprisoned as revolutionaries and all were Indian nationalists. They would not easily let go of what they considered vital to their careers, personal status, and political emotions.

It was uncertain how long the court delays would keep their citizenships and passports alive. They could be saved only by a change in the law, getting Sutherland overruled to save the men and the Cable Act amended to save their wives from statelessness.

The struggle to achieve these objectives started immediately. Sudhindra "felt this blow keenly" and "promptly took up his pen" in defence of Bhagat Singh Thind."[58] This defence appeared in an Indian journal. He characterized the Supreme Court ruling as a "slap at India" which casts a "lurid light " on the "workings of the racial psychology of the West . . ." and "to unspeakable injury of Indians, crudely and boldly along the line of skin color."[59]

In the same article he quoted a Japanese journal's suggestion that "the Japanese (who had been similarly hit) must try to acquire the right, either by a revision of the laws or by concluding a treaty of naturalization with America." That Britain would want a treaty that would benefit the Indian residents was not to be expected. A "revision of the laws," therefore, became the community's theme. The "American nation" should amend the old statute "if it has the courage to be fair to the Indian," challenged another Indian critic of the *Thind* ruling.[60] Prof. D.O. McGovney whose help Sudhindra seems to have recruited to draw the attention of scholars and legislators to the serious jeopardy to which the ruling had exposed the whole community, urged Congress to naturalize the resident aliens.[61] Over three and a half years later, Chief Justice Taft also agreed that the remedy lay with the Congress. The "Hindus who received certificates," he wrote to the Secretary of Labor

> and who acting on the assurance that they had become American citizens have lost the citizenship of Great Britain and are really without a country and without allegiance to any government. It would seem to me that such a situation calls upon Congress to right the matter . . . There might well be special legislation on the subject to meet a real injustice.[62]

Like Bose, Taraknath Das also had started expressing his injured feelings in print. From the time of the *Thind* ruling to the Supreme Court's upholding of S.G. Pandit's plea four years later, there appeared in the *Modern Review* of Calcutta over fifty-five articles and editorial notes complaining about American naturalization policy and Anglo-Saxon anti-Asian racism. Most of the elaborate and scholarly contributions came from Sudhindra, Taraknath and Mrs. Mary Das. Das's study of the problem of citizenship now as a victim and later as a scholar made him a recognized authority on the subject in the 1940s when his expertise proved useful in the fight against the exclusion laws.

Dr. Das also read a paper before the American Society of International Law in April 1925 with the American Secretary of State Charles Evans Hughes presiding. He explained how naturalized Indians and their wives were threatened with statelessness following the Sutherland ruling.[63]

The farmers also took defensive action against the Sutherland ruling immediately. At least ninety-five of them including a naturalized citizen approached the British Government "to secure mitigation of the hardships likely to result from speedy enforcement" of the California Land Laws. The British Embassy requested the U.S. Secretary of State to allow the farmers enough time to dispose of their properties.[64] Beyond this, the cooperation of the farmers was limited to acts of self-preservation. When they were approached "regarding the need to lobby for citizenship they had argued that earning their livelihood was the first priority and the corporations [a device to escape the mischief of the land laws] were set up."[65]

The organizations and the contact established earlier by Lala Lajpat Rai and Sailendra Ghose paid dividends now. Dr. E.R.A. Seligman of Columbia University and president of Society of Ethical Culture (1908-1921) had helped Lajpat Rai by arranging his lecture engagements.[66] One of the members of the Society was Alfred W. Martin. Both became vice presidents of the India Society of America established in 1924 by Hari G. Govil of New York. Rev. John Haynes Holmes was the president. It was here that Taraknath found the intermediary to reach the ear of Chief Justice Taft. Martin, a student of comparative religions and in the estimate of the Chief Justice, "a gentleman of the highest standing" talked to him "with reference to the injustice that he conceives to have been done" to Das. Meanwhile Das had also persuaded Justice Harlan Fiske Stone, Charles E. Hughes and Senator William E. Borah that "some kind of relief measure should be passed by Congress."[67]

Sailendra Ghose, national organizer of Friends of Freedom for India and a "colorful scholar and revolutionist," persuaded Senator Royal S. Copeland to introduce a bill in the Senate and lobbied in Washington, D.C. where he met Senator Hiram Johnson, chairman of the Senate Committee on Immigration and some of its other members.[68] Dr. and Mrs. Taraknath Das had "extended interviews" with the Secretary of State, the Secretary of Labor, the Asst. Attorney General and various other high officials including the Commissioner of Immigration.[69] Professor S.L. Joshi, Profulla Mukerji and Taraknath himself kept the Indian students well-educated on the major issues of immigration and citizenship by addressing their conventions and encouraging them to take active interest in the struggle.[70] Further help came from two other American sources. Roger Baldwin's American Civil Liberties Union announced its "support of Congressional measures to determine the eligibility of immigrant Hindus to citizenship and to restore citizenship to American women married to Hindu aliens."[71] American missionaries working in India issued a statement protesting against the hardship caused to the Indian immigrants.[72]

Senator Royal S. Copeland (D-NY) introduced his bill S. 4505 on June 24, 1926. It proposed to include Hindus in the category of "white persons" so that the Hindu residents of the United States would thereby become eligible to citizenship. It was argued that the Dillingham Immigration Commission had included them in "white race" in its *Dictionary of Races*.[73]

The Senator himself "did not see any chance" for his bill. The high officials to whom Dr. and Mrs. Das had talked plainly told them that "they would not approve of any legislation classing the Hindus to be eligible to American citizenship." The California Joint Immigration Committee strongly protested against the Copeland bill and urged its defeat.[74] The Copeland episode was the second attempt by the members of the Indian community to get relief from Congress. Like Sudhindra's attempt in 1913, this one was also thwarted by the California exclusionists.

The third attempt was made through Chief Justice Taft and Senator Reed. Finding that the climate of opinion was not yet ready to naturalize all the approximately 3000 Indian residents, this attempt was directed at saving the already naturalized Indians and their America-born wives from the consequences of the Sutherland ruling.

Profulla Mukerji "sought the assistance of Pennsylvania Senator David Reed who was sympathetic to the cause of Indian citizenship."[75] As mentioned earlier, Alfred Martin brought the hardship cases of Dr. Das and his wife to the attention of the Chief Justice. Das followed this up with a letter and a personal meeting. Taft was persuaded that the fallout from the Sutherland ruling amounted to a "grave injustice" which called for some Congressional action to "right the matter."[76]

With this weighty recommendation in their favor, Dr. and Mrs. Das were assured by the high officials and members of the Cabinet that "the Administration would not oppose any bill validating the citizenship of those Hindus who were naturalized." On December 7, 1926 Senator Reed (R-PA) moved a Joint Resolution S.J. Res. 128, proposing that naturalizations existing prior to the Sutherland ruling be "ratified and confirmed" and those persons be "declared to be citizens of the United States." As for their U.S. citizen wives, it was provided that no such woman "shall be deemed to have lost her citizenship by reason of her marriage to any of said persons."[77]

The Senate Committee on Immigration under the Chairmanship of Hiram Johnson held hearings on the Resolution. Several Indians including Taraknath Das, Profulla Mukerji and Vaman Ramchandra Kokatnur gave testimony. Swami Yogananda of the Vedant Mission sent a New York attorney to represent him and Barbari [Darbari?] Rampal.[78] The Indian witnesses sought to impress the Committee with their academic, professional and technical qualifications. Senator Reed commented in support that "these 69 men include a larger number of talented people than the 69 people taken at random through the country."[79]

Chairman Johnson believed that "as an apparent gross injustice has been done [I] would have no objection to remedial congressional action *if thereby the present Japanese situation would not be interfered with.*[80]

Taft's recommendation did mean a great deal to him. He and his colleagues recognized the justice of the Indians' complaint as well as the emotions involved in the fact that while the Japanese retained the citizenship of their motherland, the Indians were left without a country. He disagreed with the California Joint Immigration Committee that no special action was needed to help Dr. Das and his fellow-sufferers. About the Japanese he was of one mind with the California exclusionists and the American Federation of Labor.[81]

The California Joint Immigration Committee did not approve of any Congressional action to "generously grant favors" to Indians because they had been found by the Supreme Court to be legally ineligible to naturalization and, therefore, earlier decisions in their favor were erroneous and illegal. It held that the persons adversely affected by the 1923 verdict should not resent their loss because "they suffer no wrong in the matter any more than wrong would be suffered by him who had enjoyed for some years the possession and revenues from a property erroneously awarded to him by one court but who was forced to relinquish it on final decision. If there be wrong in this matter it has been suffered by the citizenry of the United States in the conferring of citizenship on those not entitled thereto."[82]

The Committee argued against Congressional action for also another reason. It sought to assure the Indians that "there is little occasion for alarm on their part" because of the recent favorable decision in the *Pandit* case. It hoped that most of the Indians including Taraknath Das had similar cases, which, of course, was not correct. The Committee repeatedly expressed the opinion that the *Pandit* ruling was "good law" and hoped that the Supreme Court would uphold Pandit's plea of *res adjudicata.* In that event these Indians would remain citizens. So why enact special legislation through Congress to benefit them and thereby encourage the Japanese to demand similar treatment ? Moreover, the Committee gave assurance that "If the Hindu cases are permitted to rest" on the *Pandit* case decision "we will cease to make issue." In other words the Committee would accept any Supreme Court decision in favor of Pandit's plea with good grace.[83]

Nearly 400 Japanese in Hawaii had been deprived of their naturalization certificates under circumstances resembling those that the Reed Joint Resolution sought to remedy in favor of the Indians. If Congress were to declare these Indians American citizens, the Japanese would quote this action as a precedent for similar relief or allege discrimination, even though they had not been rendered stateless because of their dual citizenship under Japanese law. Even a Congressional declaration that its action in favor of the Indians would not be used as a precedent "would not amount to anything."[84]

Chairman Johnson claimed to know that "somebody in the House was going to tack on to this resolution the Japanese-Hawaiian naturalizations." He confessed himself "quite sympathetic" with the Reed resolution, but at the same time he repeatedly told the Committee that "would this establish a precedent for the admission of Japanese I should very vigorously and emphatically oppose it."[85] Several members including Copeland and Reed agreed with him over the extended implications of the Joint Resolution. But for their reluctance to provide the Japanese an argument to reclaim their naturalization, the Senators might have reported favorably on Senator Reed's proposal. Instead it died in committee.

Senator Copeland and Mrs. Taraknath Das held the United States government responsible for this third failure of the Indian immigrant's cause before Congress.[86] The fact of the matter, however, seems to be that since the spring of 1924 the American Government, the House and the Senate, and indeed almost the whole nation were determined not to yield to the Japanese any concession in matters of immigration or citizenship. The exclusionists had succeeded in misinterpreting the Japanese Ambassador's "grave consequences" letter of April 10 to achieve their objective of excluding the Japanese from immigration as "ineligible to citizenship." Naturalized Indians and their American wives became the victims of U.S.-Japanese antagonism. Mrs. Das was disappointed. She saw no prospect of securing justice in a world in which "there are in existence double standards of international morality . . . one for the superior White-men and the other for the Asiatic." She looked forward to "the dawn of a new era . . . when the Asiatics will be able to demand and extract recognition of equality in matters of human rights, as human beings."

For the immediate present the hope for men now lay in a favorable verdict from a court and for women, in the fight which Mrs. Das was carrying on to get the Cable Act amended. She had dated the words quoted above February 21, 1927. Exactly three weeks later a decisive court action came, far sooner than she had expected.[87]

When the Justice Department began its offensive, suits had been filed against all civilian naturalized citizens for the cancellation of their certificates in the light of the Sutherland ruling. The government contention was "that such certificates are void because under the law there was no authority to grant a certificate to anyone but a white person and that Hindus do not come within that description." The certificates were, therefore, according to the Government attorneys, "illegally procured" in that the beneficiaries were high-caste Hindus of Aryan blood and not white persons.

The offensive did not meet with much resistance. Some of those whose cases were pending before the courts in December 1926 could have, like Profulla Mukerji, obtained extensions permitted under the law. Akhay Kumar Mazumdar, Shankar Lakshman Gokhale, Sakharam Ganesh Pandit and John Mohammed Ali decided to fight it out in the courts.

Mazumdar who had been naturalized in 1913 (207 Fed. 115) lost his certificate in the District Court in December 1923 (296 Fed. 173) and in the Circuit Court of Appeals in June 1924 (299 Fed. 240). In both these courts he had been defended by S.G. Pandit.

John Mohammad Ali had received his naturalization papers in June, 1921. Four years later he tried to defend them by the plea of "res adjudicata" and of not being a Hindu but an Arab resident of India (7 Fed. (2d) 728). Both pleas were rejected. After the Supreme Court had acted on the *Pandit* case, Ali tried to benefit from that decision by filing an appeal in his own case (20 Fed. (2d) 998). The Court rejected it for being filed too late.

S.G. Pandit, a Sanskrit scholar, Hindu preacher, Lajpat Rai's colleague, and an American attorney, and S.L. Gokhale, a college principal in India and an engineer in the General Electric plant at Schenectady, proved to be tough litigants partly because they valued U.S. citizenship and partly because they had good attorneys. Pandit had himself and his law partner Lucius K. Chase; Gokhale had Emanuel Celler and Louis Marshall. In the 1940s both Pandit and Celler were in the India League.[88]

Pandit had been naturalized in May 1914. The suit to cancel his certificate was probably the earliest one launched by the Justice Department after the *Thind* ruling. The District Court struck down all the defenses he offered except that of *res adjudicata*. The Court recalled that at the hearings in 1914 the examiner of the Bureau of Naturalization had contested Pandit's right to naturalization, cross-examined him and his witnesses, and filed a brief in support of the Bureau's objection. After the Court decided in Pandit's favor the examiner had made a full report in writing to the Government authorities in Washington, D.C. and nothing was done thereafter "to change, modify or reverse the said judgment" for over nine years.[89]

The District Court concluded that

> Upon the record a clear issue of fact was raised. The United States and defendant had their day in court. The question of fact was distinctly put in issue and directly determined by a competent court having jurisdiction.

The Court upheld Pandit's plea of *res adjudicata* and refused to cancel his naturalization. The Government took the case to the Circuit Court of appeal.

This Court was even more emphatic in Pandit's support. "The issue in the trial court," it observed, "was clearly an issue of fact." The defendant asserted a status, "free white person," within the meaning of the naturalization act. This status the court determined as a question of fact in considering the evidence presented and after the issue was fully briefed and argued. The court erred in its conclusions." But the Circuit Court pointed out that "the term 'erroneous' is never used by courts or law writers as designating a corrupt or evil act."

The Court also explained that "The foundation of the doctrine of *res adjudicata* or *estoppel* by judgment is that both parties have had their day in court." It also quoted a Supreme Court opinion that

> a judgment granting a certificate of naturalization is a final judgment. The correctness of the findings to support the judgment does not affect it. [The grant] cannot be impeached by showing that it was based on mistake of law.

The issue of the defendant's right to citizenship having been "directly determined by a court of competent jurisdiction, not having been modified or reversed, cannot now be disputed" ruled the Circuit Court. Pandit had retained his citizenship so far. The Pandit case immediately became a cause celebre. This was in November 1926.

The California exclusionists recognized it as an alternative to Congressional action that might result in helping the Japanese. This ruling might possibly save twelve other Indians whose cases were still in the judicial pipeline. But this breach in the Act of 1924 was to them a lesser evil than what might follow upon the adoption of the Copeland bill or the Reed joint resolution.

They had also, as already mentioned, characterized the *Pandit* case judgment as "good law". At least one District Court did not agree with this view even after the Supreme Court had finally conceded victory to Pandit by denying the United States petition to reopen the *Pandit* case in March 1927. Here is a case of conflict inside the American judiciary that had significant consequences for Indians.

While denying John Mohammad Ali's motion for not having been "seasonably filed,"[90] Judge Tuttle made two critical comments on the Circuit Court opinion in the *Pandit* case. He cited a Supreme Court ruling in their support.

> 1. "It is settled law," the Judge wrote, "that in a suit by the United States for the cancellation of a certificate of citizenship . . . the previous decision of the court granting such certificate is *not . . . res judicata*."[91]
>
> 2. "In view of the decision of the Supreme Court in *United States v. Ness*" the opinion of the Circuit Court of Appeals "*cannot be regarded as authoritative*."[92]

Two years earlier in August 1925, while cancelling Ali's naturalization certificate, the Judge claimed to have acted under "settled law" that the issuance of a certificate of citizenship is "merely a grant . . . of a political privilege conferred by the government upon the petitioner alien purely as a gratuity and subject to . . . the right of the government to insist upon a cancellation of such certificate, if found to have been illegally procured." Two Supreme Court rulings were cited in support, namely *Johannessen v. U.S.* (255 U.S. 227) and *U.S. v. Ness* (245 U.S. 319).[93]

The Judge also maintained that the right of the government to insist upon a cancellation is not barred by lapse of time. "It is elementary" he wrote, "that the doctrine of laches does not apply as against the government, when suing in its capacity as a sovereign and asserting Governmental rights" and cited *Chesapeake and Delaware Canal Co. v. United States* (250 U.S. 123).

On the support of two cases, United States v. Ginsberg (243 U.S. 472) and U.S. v. Ness, Judge Tuttle defined "illegally procured" a certificate procured when the holder is not a "free white person" as decided by Sutherland. All certificates of naturalization procured by Hindus would, therefore, be judged "illegally procured."

The cases of Akhay Kumar and Pandit had been originally heard in and appealed to the same two federal courts in California. In the former case, however, "the question of *res adjudicata* was not presented or considered." As a result Akhay lost his certificate in both courts, but Pandit who pleaded *res adjudicata* retained it on appeal. Akhay lost his case on the same arguments that Judge Tuttle used to cancel Ali's naturalization.[94] His view that the *res adjudicata* plea is not applicable to naturalization cases and the alleged non- authoritative nature of the Circuit Court of Appeals ruling in Pandit's favor have been mentioned above. One set of courts upheld all of Pandit's contentions—definition of "illegally procured," doctrine of laches, United States "sovereign" right to cancel naturalization any time while the other set rejected them all, one of the sets turning 180° when presented with a plea of *res adjudicata*. This is what we call the rift in the American judiciary that helped the Indians.

The Circuit Court of Appeals decision in the *Pandit* case had been delivered on November 1, 1926. Three months later the Solicitor General petitioned the Supreme Court for a writ of certioraris to the Circuit Court. Towards the third week of February Mrs. Das expressed her fear that the Supreme Court docket being "very full," the legal point called *res adjudicata* would be fought out "at some future date, possibly about two years from now." Instead the Supreme Court action came in three weeks.[95] On March 14, 1927 it denied the Solicitor General's request without opinion. Pandit retained his citizenship. Within ten days the Department of Labor (which included the Bureau of Naturalization) issued a recommendation to the Department of Justice that "authorized the respective United States Attorneys to discontinue suits which had been instituted to cancel naturalization of certain Hindus and which had the status of pending cases." This saved another eleven naturalizations including those of Taraknath Das, Profulla Mukerji, and Sudhindra Bose. Gokhale, too, could have claimed back his citizenship under this procedure, but he insisted on fighting it out.[96]

The Government had filed suit for cancellation of his citizenship in a New York District Court that upheld the request in August 1926. Gokhale appealed to the Circuit Court of Appeals and pleaded *res adjudicata.* In May 1928, more than a year after the Supreme Court's action in the *Pandit* case, the Circuit Court rejected Gokhale's appeal. However, the Supreme Court granted *certiorari* on October 22, 1928, and in less than a month reversed the lower court's decisions. The District Court was directed to dismiss the bill of complaint and its judgment and that of the Circuit Court of Appeals were vacated and set aside.[97]

March 20, 1908 may have been the first time an American court agreed to grant naturalization to Indians. (There were two on the same day.) The Supreme Court pronounced its verdict in the *Gokhale* case on November 19, 1928. The history of Indian naturalization during these twenty years was shaped by three influences—proper adherence to the law, Anglo-Saxon racism, and finally an intention to avoid "grave injustice." There was one aberration along the way, that of the *Thind* case ruling.

At least fifty-nine civilian Indians had been naturalized in sixteen states by what we regard as the proper interpretation of the law of the pre-Sutherland years. The Sutherland interpretation of the law in the *Thind* case established an anti-Indian precedent. The cancellations that followed were proper under this interpretation.

The *Pandit* case and its sequelae were exceptions. They were contrary to the intentions of *Thind* and other Supreme Court rulings.

They were not the law. The exclusionists called them "good law" but intended to use them as good riddance. This goal is obvious from what V.S. McClatchy wrote to Senator Hiram Johnson in November 1926—"As we understand it, this (i.e., the recent Circuit Court of Appeals ruling in Pandit's favor) would not in any way conflict with permanent bar to Hindus in the future . . ."

Exclusionists were willing to let a few Hindus escape the Sutherland net, if they could thereby preserve the net from a possible Congressional mishandling. If the *Pandit* ruling were to pass Supreme Court scrutiny, "we will cease to make issue," McClatchy had promised. If the *Pandit* case rulings were "good law," then McClatchy's Joint Immigration Committee should have characterized the cancellations as "bad" law. It never did.

The courts hearing the "Pandit case seem to have been influenced by the "able and enlightening manner" in which he may have presented his case as he had done for his client Mohan Singh a few years earlier.[98] He was a Ph.D. from an Indian University. He had "by becoming a citizen lost his inheritance in the old country and his social status." The inheritance included his family home worth $30,000 and other properties valued at from $100,000 to $250,000. If he lost his citizenship, he would lose the license to practice law and his wife, a white American citizen, would become a stateless person and lose her 320 acres of land in the Imperial Valley. These considerations might have influenced the judges.

Had the Supreme Court agreed to reopen the case, Pandit's fate could have been different. The Court, however, had decided probably under Taft's recommendation, to narrow the area of "grave injustice" and at the same time to maintain "our rule of rigid exclusion."

The fate of the white American women who were threatened with statelessness might also have helped convince the Justices that the Sutherland ruling had overshot its brown target. Mrs. Taraknath Das had personally explained her case to Chief Justice Taft, while Justice Harlan Fiske Stone might also have been apprised of her possible loss by Dr. Das. Sakharam Ganesh Pandit, Profulla Mukerji, and Dr. Kokatnur also had white American wives. Sudhindra Bose married Anne Zimmerman after his citizenship had been reassured, while T.D. Sharman's citizenship had never been challenged.

Taraknath Das married Mary K. Morss in May 1924 after the process of cancellation of certificates had started. The newlyweds must have been surprised to learn that they had married into statelessness. Mrs. Das's family had lived in America since 1700, and she was born in South Carolina. Now she found herself "the American-born wife of a Hindu who today is a woman without a country." Her plight aroused considerable interest in academic circles.[99]

Both husband and wife swung into action. Mrs. Das and her sister enlisted the aid of the National Women's Party of which she was a founder-member. They obtained a memorial signed by 2500 women calling for a law validating the citizenship of women rendered stateless by marriage. Their efforts, as we have seen, failed to produce favorable results immediately because, as Mrs. Das complained "of the spirit of anti-Asianism of the American legislators and public."

In 1930, however, the Cable Act was so amended that an American woman was not to lose her American citizenship unless she wished to renounce it. "One may claim that in this case American women became the beneficiaries of the struggle for retaining American citizenship by Indians" and their American wives," commented Dr. Das.[100]

We have traced the campaign of resistance and recovery that these men and women organized and the support they gathered in the course of that campaign. The experience they gained in facing this crisis at the midway point between their arrival in America and the enactment of the legislation of 1946 would be a valued asset in the campaign of the 1940s. Many of the leading organizers of resistance would again be on the front line under the banner of the India League that would succeed the Friends of Freedom for India, while Jagjit Singh would succeed Taraknath Das.

The campaign had been conducted in Congress, among the people and in the law courts. All along it was a salvaging operation. Most of the cargo was lost. Only about a dozen of the threatened citizenships were saved. The exlusionist forces proved how well-entrenched and how determined they still were. They still considered Asia a peril.

The little that was saved by the campaigners came mostly as the result of the differences of opinion that developed inside the American judiciary. Its head, Chief Justice Taft, roundly held the Sutherland ruling responsible for "a grave injustice." Two courts in California ruled that S.G. Pandit had not received his naturalization "illegally." Even the exclusionists and later the Supreme Court accepted these rulings as "good law."

There was also the emergence of a feeling in the highest quarters that too inelastic an insistence on a good thing can sometimes become a dehumanizing fetish. Taft believed "that the admission of a few Hundus [sic, to citizenship] would not at all break down our rule of rigid exclusion." Some nineteen years later, five weeks before his death, President Roosevelt urged that "There can be no real danger that this small number of [proposed 100] immigrants will cause unemployment or provide competition in the search for jobs." These were, initially, small breaches in the exclusionist wall. It is said that exceptions prove the rule. They also start nibbling at the rule. But isn't this the way how liberty widens ?

Notes and References

1. Hearings before the Committee on Immigration and Naturalization, House of Representatives, 79 Cong., 1st sess., on H.R. 1584, H.R. 173, HR 1624, H.R. 1746, H.R. 2256, H.R. 2609; Bills to Grant a Quota to Eastern Hemisphere Indians and to make them racially eligible for naturalization, March 7, 8, 13, 14, 1945. U.S. Government Printing Office, Washington, 1945; 96. This Hearing shall henceforth be cited as *House Hearings. March 1945.*
2. Basant Kumar Ray, "The Orient and the World Peace; From an Oriental Point of View," *Open Court*, Vo. 27 (1913), 623; also his "The New Nationalism in India," ibid., Vol. 31 (1917), 165 where he explains the ideologies of the various 'sections' of the New Nationalists including those who advocate the establishment of the "United States of India" on the line of the "great and glorious" American Republic.
3. Bruce Wilfred LaBrack, "The Sikhs of Northern California : A Socio-historical Study" (Ph. D. Diss. Interdisciplinary Social Science in the Graduate School of Syracuse University, December 1980), 115.
4. Ibid., 118.
5. Ibid.
6. Ibid., 121.
7. This question of the masses and their leaders came up in the course of the Luce-Celler bill debate in the House on October 10, 1945; "Mr. Ellis. I would like to know if the gentleman has any evidence or information that the masses of Indians or the masses of Chinese are interested to any great extent in this subject ? Mr. Johnson of California. Frankly I do not think they are, but their leaders are, and the leaders are the ones who disseminate the information and mold the opinion of their people." *Cong. Record*, 79th Cong., 2nd sess., October 10, 1945, 9537.
8. Sant Nihal Singh, "Indians in America," *Modern Review*, March 1908, 207; Taraknath Das's "Address delivered on the occasion of a dinner given

on August 4, 1946 at Ceylon India Inn, New York City, in celebration of Indians winning the right to become American citizens and also to honor Sardar J.J. Singh," 2. Henceforth this document from the India League of America Papers, Sapru House, New Delhi shall be cited as Taraknath Das, *Address*.

9. LaBrack, *The Sikhs of Northern California*, 120, 122, 124.
10. Quoted from Taraknath Das's *Free Hindusthan* from September-October 1909 in J.C. Ker, *Political Trouble in India 1907-1917*, Delhi 1973, 229.
11. Ker, *Political Trouble in India 1907-1917*, 126; other instances of Sikh discontent arising directly from the immigration problem are on 231, 232, 233, 236, 237; *Burjor Report*, 16; Srinivas R. Wagel, "Secret Woes of Vassal India," *New York Times*, 30 October 1915.
12. Taraknath Das *Address*, 3.
13. Jones, *American Immigration*, 256, 257, 258.
14. Ibid., 295; Higham, *Strangers in the Land*, 89.
15. Jones, *American Immigration*, 251.
16. Ibid., 257.
17. Ibid., 266.
18. Ibid., 268.
19. "Even Adolph Sabath of Chicago an immigrant Congressman and the leader of the fight against a discriminatory quota system, announced himself in favor of excluding the Japanese," Daniels, *Prejudice*, 98.
20. Jones, *American Immigration*, 261.
21. Ibid., 262.
22. "Westerners from the East : Oriental Immigrants Reappraised," *Pacific Historical Review*, Vol. 35 (1966), 373-383, 375; Jones, *American Immigration*, 249.
23. "Indians in America," *Modern Review*, March 1908, 208.
24. Taraknath Das *Address*, 2.
25. Ibid., 3. He had expressed similar views in *Modern Review*, August 1925, 227; March 1926, 349-350.
26. Speeches on the radio often brought interesting comments from listeners.

    "You *are* an eloquent speaker . . . I speak not only for myself but for every human being within range of your voice." Dr. Harry C. Bricker, Chairman, American Free World Association, Brooklyn Branch to Jagjit Singh, February 21, 1944; "while you may be dialectically amusing to an unenlightened audience, I feel that for real amusement we can look to more competent comedians." Sender's name illegible, to Jagjit Singh, October 20, 1942; "We heard you over the radio on Town Meeting. You were good ! We recognized your rich voice immediately." James Callahan, to Jagjit Singh, February 11, 1946. Visitors often came on invitations—"Our little group sponsored the tours of distinguished Indian patriots." Roger Baldwin, *Reminiscences*, Chapter VIII, 416.

27. Whenever the students had money enough to publish it, *The Hindusthanee Student* continued to provide fresh news of happenings on the campuses. Its issues have enabled us to piece together the student careers of several important members of the Indian community. The *Burjor Report* is a delightful description of the early years of Indian immigration but it was not public property till only recently. Burjor was not a British spy. He merely asked that his report be kept confidential. If a spy at all, he wrote like a patriotic reporter.
28. The elitism of Indian students, intellectuals, and businessmen has been discussed in Chapter IV.
29. *The Dial*, New York, August 23, 1919, 145.
30. *India News Service*, December 20, 1919. Sudhindra Bose once termed those laws "stupid," *Modern Review*, March 1927, 326.
31. For Professor Das Gupta, *Modern Review*, fn. 26; for Tagore Chapter IV, Anup Singh incident Chapter V.
32. Senator Copeland's assurance that his bill will not bring more Hindus into the country, *New York Times*, 25 June 1926; Senator Reed's was a tiny effort to declare less than 60 Indians American Citizens; Jagjit Singh's press statement in India published in *The Statesman*, Bombay on January 25, 1939, File No. 287-X/39, External Affairs, National Archives of India; S.R. Zaman, Additional Secretary, Govt. of India. Commerce Department wrote on December 17, 1941 about the view generally held in his Department : "the repeal of the emigration laws so far as they affect Indians in America was a forlorn hope"; Sir Feroz Khan Noon, Labor Member of the Viceroy's Executive Council wrote in Minutes dated May 14, 1942; "After all the U.S.A. is a white man's country, and if they wish to keep out Asiatic people, then I do not see how in justice we can thrust ourselves upon them." Both these documents are from the National Archives of India.
33. E.G. Mears, *Resident Orientals*, 117; "But the war also set the American thinking more seriously about immigration. His experience with alien enemies, his discovery through war activities of the persistence of racial traits, his realization of the delay in Americanization, and his closer acquaintance with racial colonies' societies and press, are transforming racial detachment into positive antagonism. His faith in automatic assimilation has given way to apprehension. He too has become distrustful of the wisdom of past immigration policies." Frances Kellor, "Future Immigration," *North American Review*, Vol. 214 (July-December 1922) : 15.
34. *Independent Hindustan*, San Francisco, November 1920, 51.
35. Andre Siegfried, *America Comes of Age*, New York, 1927, 323. J.Z. Hodge, "The United States of India," *North American Review*, Vol. 214 (July-December 1921) : 460.

36. Das, *Hindusthani Workers*, 116-117.
37. Robert Morss Lovett, *All Our Years*, New York : 1948, 157, 158.
38. Das, *Hindustani Workers*, 117.
39. Hearings before the Committee on Immigration United States Senate, 69th Cong., 2nd sess., on S.J. Res. 128 providing for the ratification and confirmation of the naturalization of certain persons of the Hindu race, December 9, 1926, Washington, D.C. : 1926, 25. Henceforth to be cited as *Senate Hearings December 1926*.
40. *Senate Hearings, December 1926*, 25, 26.
41. Ronald Spector, "The Vermont Education of Taraknath Das : An Episode in British-American-Indian Relation," *Vermont History*, Vol. 48 (1980) : 89-95.
42. *All Our Years*, 157; *Modern Review* for December 1925, 701 carries an extract from an article in *The New Republic*, including this sentence : "We have no doubt that underlings in the administration today are as much flattered at receiving a suggestion from London as they were seven years ago, and as eager to show their subservience."
43. *Senate Hearings December 1926*, 24.
44. Ibid., 23.
45. Dr. Mohammad Sulaiman, one of these forty, recovered his citizenship in 1934. *Indian Review*, Madras, April 1934, 263. The official figures as published in the *Senate Hearings December 1926*, 1, 2, 6 and 7 are not accurate. On p. 2 Dr. Kokatnur has been included in the list twice, Gokhale's case was still pending, so was in all probability that of Dr. Mohammed Sulaiman. Part of the reason for this high number of uncontested losses was that several had moved away from the United States—"Sudhindra Bose : Portrait" by Anne Z. Bose, *Modern Review*, November 1945, 371. Several lost because they "did not have sufficient means and influence to fight their cases up to the Supreme Court of the United States," *Modern Review*, August 1927, 192; also see ibid., October 1927, 440. Among those who lost their certificates was Ram Nath Puri one of the earliest revolutionary associates of Taraknath Das. Another was S.R. Mandal, an active member of the India League in the 1940s.
46. *Senate Hearings December 1926*, 13.
47. George W. Gold, "The Racial Prerequisite in the Naturalization Law," *Boston University Law Review*, Vol. Xv (1935) : 465.
48. Chief Justice Taft to Secretary of Labor, October 19, 1926 in *Senate Hearings, December 1926*, 3.
49. Taraknath Das to Taft, October 18, 1926, in *Senate Hearings December, 1926*, 4.
50. For privileges lost with the loss of citizenship, see the Circuit Court of Appeals decision in favor of S.G. Pandit, *Senate Hearings, December*

1926, 11. The quotation is from Taraknath Das's paper published in *Modern Review*, July 1925, 44; also see ibid., October 1927. 440.

51. Home/Political July 1916, No. 74 Deposit : Correspondence Relating to Naturalization of Indian agitator Taraknath Das, National Archives of India, New Delhi; Dignan believes there was a calculated reason why Das informed the British of his American citizenship—to remind the British "of his immunity as an American citizen before he left Berlin in March 1916 on a Far Eastern mission aimed at receiving Japanese and Chinese support for the Indian revolutionary schemes." Don K. Dignan, "Hindu Conspiracy," *Pacific Historical Review*, Vol. 40 (February 1971), 76.
52. *Senate Hearings December 1926*, 8; Taraknath Das, "Some Stateless Persons in the United States of America," *Modern Review*, July 1925, 44; Sailendra Ghose in *New York Times*, 25 June 1926.
53. D.O. McGovney, "Race Discrimination in Naturalization," *Iowa Law Bulletin*, Vol. VIII, No. 3 (March 1923) : 146.
54. *Modern Review*, July 1925, 44; December 1925, 745.
55. Ibid., December 1925, 745; July 1925, 44; June 1927, 760-761 for the devious ways British authorities barred him from visiting India; August 1928, 230, emphasis added.
56. Taraknath Das *Address*, 7.
57. *Senate Hearings December 1926*, 39; Taraknath implied he won his naturalization after prolonged litigation, his *Address*, 2.
58. *Modern Review*, November 1948, 371.
59. Ibid., June 1923, 691, 695.
60. Ibid., July 1923, 119.
61. *Iowa Law Bulletin*, March 1923, 131, 154, 216- 231.
62. *Senate Hearings December 1926*, 3, also 41 for the Committee's estimate of the recommendation.
63. "Some Stateless Persons in the United States of America," *Modern Review*, July 1925, 43-45.
64. James K. Fisk and V.S. MaClatchy to Senator Hiram Johnson, *Senate Hearings December 1926*, 43-44; Surendranath Dasgupta, "Indians in the United States," *Modern Review*, July 1924, 15-19.
65. Karen Leonard, "Punjabi Farmers and California's Alien Land Laws," *Agricultural History*, IV (October 1985), 9 and fn. 19.
67. Martin was a frequent speaker at Indian cultural functions. He was the author of *Seven Great Bibles*, New York : 1930; Taft's opinion was expressed in his letter to Secretary of Labor, October 19, 1926, *Senate Hearings December 1926*, 3; Justice Stone and Senator Borah in Taraknath to Taft, October 18, 1926; *Senate Hearings December 1926*, 4.
68. On Sailendra Ghose, *The Profile*, 38; Copeland's bill, *New York Times*, 25 June 1926; *Hindustanee Student*, September-October 1926, 7; Transcript of Dr. Narayanan's interview with Jagjit Singh, 10; Muzumdar,

Contributions, 38, 39. Ghose also engaged attorney Kronmeyer to represent Gokhale at the *Senate Hearings December 1926*, 29.

69. *Modern Review*, April 1927, 464; *Senate Hearings December 1926*, 23.
70. Taraknath's address to students. *Hindustanee Student*, January 1925, 3; Joshi's address, ibid., January 1926, 8; Mukerji's talk, ibid., September-October 1927, 13; student's dramatic performance to collect funds for the struggle, ibid., September-October 1926, 7; November 1926, 12; dinner to honor Senator Copeland, ibid., May 1927, 11; New York Times, 5 May 1927.
71. *New York Times*, 16 June 1926.
72. *Hindustanee Student*, May 1926, 12.
73. Mary K. Das, "True Status of Hindus Regarding American Citizenship," *Modern Review*, April 1927, 464, 465. The Copeland bill died with the end of the Congress session on March 4, 1927.
74. V.S. McClatchy to Hiram W. Johnson, November 30, 1926; same to Hugh White Adams, November 20, 1926, *Senate Hearings December 1926*, 17, 18.
75. Maxine P. Fisher, *The Indians of New York City*, New Delhi 1980, 15; Senator Reed had also been sympathetic to the Japanese; Roger Daniels, *Politics*, 100; also opposed quotas being based on the 1890 Census, Constance B. Schulz, *Samuel Dickstein*, 18; *Modern Review*, April 1927, 464; *Senate Hearings December 1926*, 24.
76. Taft to Secretary of Labor, October 19, 1926, *Senate Hearings December 1926*, 3.
77. *Modern Review*, April 1927, 464; *Senate Hearings December 1926*, 23, 24; text of Reed's Joint Resolution, 1, 2.
78. *Senate Hearings December 1926*, 37-38.
79. Ibid., 32.
80. V.S. McClatchy to Hiram Johnson, November 30, 1926; *Senate Hearings December 1926*, 17. Emphasis added.
81. Ibid., 17, 19, 47.
82. *Senate Hearings December 1926*, 43, 44.
83. Ibid., 17, 18, 44.
84. Ibid., 17, 18, 19, 20, 42, 43, 45; Daniels, *Politics*, 148, fn. 33.
85. Ibid., 20.
86. *Modern Review*, April 1927, 464, 465.
87. For the whole incident of the "grave consequences" letter, Daniels, *Politics*, 100-103; "The Americans at Bataan and Iwo Jima would admit there have been rather "grave consequences." Rep. Judd of Minnesota, *Cong. Record*, 79th Cong., 1 sess., 10 October 1945, 9511; the whole nation's support of the anti-Japanese policy, Daniels, *Politics*, 105, Indians suffered because of U.S.-Japanese antagonism, Taraknath Das *Address*, 8-9.

88. Biographical information on Pandit is in 15 Fed. (2d) 285, *Young India*, New York, August 1918. An India League of America document ticks him as one of the "members in good standing" in December 1943. Also see Muzumdar, *Contributions*, 30, Mohan Singh case 257 F 209 where Pandit appeared for Mohan Singh, *Modern Review*, 1908, 313 has a very early reference to his activities in the United States.
89. *Senate Hearings December 1926*, 11, 12.
90. Ali Case 20 F (2d) 998, 999.
91. Ibid., 999-1000. Emphasis added.
92. Ibid., 1000. Emphasis added.
93. 7 F (2d) 728.
94. U.S. v. Akhay Kumar Muzumdar, 296 F 173, 176, 178, Akhay Kumar Muzumdar v. U.S., 299 Fed 240, 242.
95. *Modern Review*, April 1927, 462; *New York Times*, 6 February 1927, U.S. Reports 273, October Term 1926, No. 870.
96. *Modern Review*, August 1927, 192 (Rabbi Carl White to Senator Copeland, May 21, 1927); February 1928, 243; May 1927, 637.
97. 26 Fed. (2d) 360; S. Ct. of U.S. October term 1928, 591; 278 U.S. 591, 49 S. Ct. Reporter, October term, 1928, 30, 662-663; No. 361; "won't make issue," *Senate Hearings December 1926*, 44.
98. 257 F. 209, 209.
99. *New York Times*, 27 March 1927; J.W. Garner, "Denationalization of American Citizens," *The American Journal of International Law*, Vol. XXI (1927) : 107; E.G. Mears, *Resident Orientals on the American Pacific Coast : Their Legal and Economic Status*, Chicago : 1928, 112-113.
100. Taraknath Das *Address*, 10.

7

EQUALITY ACHIEVED

Bombay July 6, 1946
Dear Singh,

Our mutual friend, Mr. Louis Fischer tells me that your persistent labours were solely responsible for the passage of the Indian Immigration Act. I congratulate you on your successful labours. You will, perhaps, oblige me by sending me a copy of the Act.

— M. K. GANDHI

There was a time when Indians landed on American shores able to exercise all the rights of immigrants under the law. Exclusionists, however, had demanded that the law be changed. In the course of just a few years, the law was changed and the Indians found themselves living in America not by right but on sufferance. Their status had become one of "perpetual alienage."[1] From 1924 onwards it was the Indians' turn to demand that the law be changed. A new age began. Roles were reversed. Exclusionists, once the advocates of change, became the defenders of the status quo. Meanwhile, Americans continued living in India under rights obtained by their country over a century ago without reciprocal obligations.[2]

The story of Indians' demands before Congress started with Senator Copeland's bill in 1926[3] and ended twenty years later in the acceptance of their demand for a quota and the right of citizenship. It took at least six Congressional hearings, one Indo-American treaty negotiation, and a war that brought America's armed forces to north-eastern India to reach the goal. It was not easy to convince Americans, indoctrinated as they were, by several decades of anti-Asianism, that to naturalize a few thousand Indian residents and to permit a 100 Indians to enter the country every year, was not a high price to pay to win friends and customers in India.

In 1924 the exclusionist forces had obtained through Congress the immigration and nationality system of their dreams. Their spokesmen claimed the system to have been designed "for the protection of the nation" and inspired by a "great principle." The principle was that of "Asiatic exclusion." Rep. A Leonard Allen (D-LA) compared the whole structure to the levees of his state. "In Louisiana," he retorted to Mrs. Clare Booth Luce during the House debate on her bill, "we have levees and we know what happens to the people behind the levees when you blow up the levees."[4]

Senators Copeland and Reed had, as we know, expressed to Mrs. Taraknath Das their sense of pessimism as to the possibility of securing from Congress or the Administration any relaxation of the restrictive code. The watch on the levees continued for several more years.

It ended, as we will see, in 1946 in a compromise between Indian nationalism and American exclusionism. Threatened by the alarming distortions of these two ideologies—that of nationalism by Japan and of exclusionism by Germany, the American people decided to dilute their exclusionism in order to distinguish it from the German practice. Indian nationalists on their part attempted by the moderation of their demands to offer assurance that their nationalism was the product of Gandhi's spinning wheel, not of the Tokyo textile mills. Moderate American exclusionists reached an accommodation with moderate Indian nationalists. The accommodation was sealed with cheers and high-sounding platitudes, but it was merely an attempt to give the war-baby a peacetime date of birth.

A member of India's brain trust lamented that the Indian community in the early 1940s was

> isolated and hemmed in by legal restrictions. Some (members) would like to go to India, marry and return to their adopted land, some would like relatives in India to come here and share the American way of life . . . . India's nationals, in spite of their important contributions are still ineligible for citizenship in the United States.[5]

Indians resented the "noneligibility" label as a hindrance to their full participation in American life. "These farmers," Mubarek Ali told the

Senators of the Immigration Committee; "have turned their backs on their old homes and have not been given the opportunity to enjoy freedom." Taraknath Das included in this "freedom" the enjoyment of "full civic rights" and "to break up isolation" of the Indian and the American people. Dr. Muzumdar asked the House Committee, "Shall we enable them to participate in the civil, political and social affairs of this country or shall we let them remain on the periphery of American life?"[6]

At the start of the India League's campaign for a quota and citizenship in 1944, indeed a week before Rep. Emanuel Celler introduced his first bill in the House, two highly educated Indian residents wrote a joint letter to Jagjit Singh. The letter represents a new point of view regarding the acquisition of American citizenship that most leading Indian activitists proved by their later conduct, to have also been their point of view. Here is the relevant portion of the letter:

> Personally we—not one of us [sic]—have no intention, whatsoever of ever becoming American citizens. We wish to remain & die Indians. We are eager, however, to change our status from a subject of England to that of a citizen of Free India. We are pledged to work unremittingly towards that goal. But we do recognise the great international prestige that will come to our people by having lifted from our brows the present stigma re [sic] our ineligibility for American citizenship. And also we recognize the immense value that that prestige can be to us in our immediate struggle with the english [sic] to get our Independence of and from them.
>
> With these thoughts in our minds you have our fullest support in your present venture.[7]

Anup Singh, Shridharani, and Syud Hossain left for India in the late 1940s. Jagjit stayed on for over a decade without seeking naturalization. Ramlal Bajpai died here an Indian citizen. Watumull, Haridas T. Muzumdar, and Dalip Singh Saund became U.S. citizens.

Value systems had changed. A certificate of American citizenship was no longer valued as a patriot's certificate of release from British authority. Achievement of eligibility to naturalization, however, remained part of the struggle for civic equality and national self-respect. Kitchlew's and Sinha's declaration of self-denial was as good an indication of patriotism in the 1940s as Taraknath's fight in the courts first to obtain and then to retain his certificate of naturalization in earlier decades. In both periods, as the letter implies, the community's struggle for equality in America remained closely tied to the patriotic agitations in India.

The Gadar thesis, however, had been reversed because the national movement in India had unexpectedly outdistanced the community's progress towards equality in America. The link between the two was, of course, still considered valid by the Gadarites' political descendants.

These descendants seem hardly to have relaxed in their efforts to regain the right to citizenship. The results of their efforts appear as bills before Congress from 1926 through the 1930s, proposing to legislate their relief. It may not be far wrong to assume that behind each bill there was an active though anonymous Indian who had succeeded in converting a Congressman or a Senator to his view of the argument. We will return to this part of our story later in this chapter.

Although the Act of 1917 denied Indians the right to come as immigrants, it provided that if the members of the "excepted classes" such as professors, businessmen and students, maintain their status for five years "they were no longer members of the deportable classes. So they were legally here."[8] This was an advantageous loophole in the law.

By a new law enacted in 1935 veterans of the First World War even of ineligible races were declared eligible to naturalization. Bhagat Singh Thind and several other Indians became citizens under this law.[9]

During the Second World War the Nationality Act of 1940 was amended by the Second War Powers Act of 1942 to confer citizenship on noncitizens serving honorably in the U.S. armed forces provided that they had been "lawfully admitted to the United States, including its territories and possessions." "Slightly less than 50" Indians had been naturalized under this Act by April 1945.[10]

In 1937 and 1938 three organizations were founded in New York City, not to add further to those others already working for India's freedom, but distinctly to seek solutions to their hardships as legally disadvantaged alien residents. These organizations were the India League of America, the India Chamber of Commerce and the India Welfare League. During the next nine years these three dominated, though they did not monopolize, the Indian community's agitation to gain the status of legal equality.

We will first deal with the major concern of N.R. Checker's Indo-American Association of Commerce, a Division of his India League and with the "central feature" of Jagjit Singh's India Chamber of Commerce, namely to improve the legal status of Indians who had come to the United States to establish their businesses.[11]

This priority is deserved because the agitation created by these two organizations was the first to be listened to in high quarters. The Welfare League's plea was heard two years later. It was the first time the British and the United States governments started negotiations to implement a scheme intended not to *restrict* Indian citizen's privileges in America but to *expand* them. Surprisingly enough the initiative for the talks came from the Government of India. This fact is historically significant. Twenty years of nationalist effort following the San Francisco Trial and the Gadar executions, were starting to show good results in 1937. The good habit took hold. Eight years later high officials of the Government of India would call the Luce-Celler bills "our Bills."[12]

It is safe to say that from 1937 onward the British government, both of London and New Delhi, were on the side of their Indian subjects in America on matters concerning only immigration and naturalization. The inter-governmental negotiations being confidential—secrecy becoming even more vital because of America's excessive demands—much room was left for misjudging the British position. For instance, even a year and a half after New Delhi had committed itself to have the merchants' disabilities removed by concluding a treaty, public opinion declined to forget "that the Government of India in the past neglected to protect the interest of Indians abroad" and threatened that "it is now not possible to permit the continuance of such a state of affairs." The External Affairs Department assured the correspondent that "the primary object of such a treaty is to secure greater facilities than at present for Indians wishing to enter the United States for purposes of trade." Whosoever else may have been mellowed by such assurance, Jagjit Singh never was. This "influencer" of Indian opinion in the United States continued to believe almost to the end of his life that the British did not want this treaty because that would mean more Indian businessmen in America and more contacts between Indians and Americans.[13]

His and N.R. Checker's organizations sought the removal of the merchant's hardships by satisfying a requirement under Section 3 of the Act of 1924 that the country of origin have a treaty of commerce and navigation with the United States. In that case instead of being admitted "temporarily for business or pleasure" under Section 3 (2) of the Act, they could enter as treaty traders on a Treaty of Commerce visa under Section 3(6) of the Act. In this latter case they could bring their wives and unmarried children under 21, and would be entitled to build permanent offices and reside permanently so long as they maintained their status as treaty traders. The United States had such treaties with China, Japan, Thailand, and some 40 other countries.[14]

The Government of India's first effort in favour of removing restrictions on Indian traders came under consideration in 1935 "but on the advice of the British Ambassador at Washington the question was not pursued." The next time India's official machinery was set into motion by Indian businessmen of New York City. They met in deputation Sir Feroz Khan Noon, later India's Labor Member who was visiting the United States on official business in 1937. He heard the story of their hardship. Officials of the U.S. State Department told him that the remedy lay in a treaty of trade. Immediately he urged upon the Government of India the desirability of such a treaty. It will be, he was convinced, "definitely a great advantage to the people of India to have given to them the rights which the Americans enjoy in this country without any reciprocal responsibilities." In July the Government of India not without some hesitation suggested to the Secretary of State for India the need for concluding an India-United States trade agreement. This was several months before Jagjit Singh campaigned for it in India in the winter of 1937-1938.[15]

The next two years were full of activity directed towards this goal. Jagjit and Checker both visited India to meet officials and public leaders. Questions were asked in the Indian legislature. The Indian Chambers of Commerce urged the Government of India to start negotiating the treaty.

From 1937 when they were first contacted by Feroz Khan Noon to October 1939 when they finally submitted the draft treaty to the British Ambassador in Washington, the officials of the U.S. Department of State continued to upgrade the terminology to describe their view of the purpose of the treaty. Starting with "no matter how few the clauses." as they told Sir Noon in 1937 , it became a "comprehensive treaty of commerce and navigation" in May, 1938. The next month they defined their goal as being to place India-U.S. relations on a "modern footing." The draft itself came with the ambitious title, "Treaty of Establishment, Commerce, Navigation and Consular Rights between the United States and India." Six months later there came a supplementary note adding to and revising the draft. Clearly the United States had its eyes not on the Indian merchants alone.[16]

For the merchants the draft conceded "everything that the U.S.A, can give under the U.S.A. Immigration Act 1924 . . . . all that is required (and certainly all that we are likely to get)." In return for this concession that, it must be noted, did not require any change in America's basic policy of Indian exclusion, the draft demanded American partnership with Britain in the economic exploitation of India.[17]

For instance, the most-favoured-nation treatment was defined as "treatment accorded to the most favored third country including the United Kingdom of Great Britain and Northern Ireland." This treatment was demanded in exploration for and exploitation of mineral resources including oil. "National" treatment was demanded in the ownership of stock of domestic corporations and in manufacturing as well as in coastal trade. The treaty was to apply not only to British India but also to the Indian States. American Consulates were to be set up at several places including the capital.[18]

The price asked for that solitary concession to the Indian merchants proved so unacceptable that after two years of thorough examination of the treaty, the Viceroy's Execution Council on June 17, 1942 unanimously decided to terminate further negotiations. The decision was phrased diplomatically as "negotiations be postponed till after the war." The Secretary of State for India, instead of using the British Embassy to convey the decision to the U.S. State Department deputed two Indians to explain why the treaty could not be negotiated during the war. He was at pains to give Americans the impression that the decision to suspend negotiations was purely an Indian decision unstained by considerations of British economic interests.[19]

It indeed *was* an Indian decision made in India, by the Indian members of the Executive Council with the full consent of their British colleagues. Behind them stood their Departmental Secretaries who declared its acceptance, in the words of one of them, as "an act of economic suicide on the part of this country."[20]

By the time the draft treaty had reached New Delhi in February 1940, Britain was at war not only with Germany but also with the Indian National Congress. To placate moderate nationalist and anti-

Congress elements, Britain was forced to make promises of constitutional changes after the war and to expand the Viceroy's Executive Council immediately. This expansion raised the number of non-official Indian members from three to eight in the summer of 1941 and to eleven a year later.[21]

The new appointees strengthened the hands of Sir Feroz Khan Noon and Sir Ramaswami Mudaliar who were already in the Council. They were all British appointees. They were not British stooges. Their first major recommendation, for instance, was for the release of all prisoners convicted of participation in Gandhi's recent nonviolent, anti-war protest movement. The Viceroy, Churchill, and the British Cabinet, accepted the recommendation fearing resignations.[22]

Under such changed political climate, British privileges, in which the American draft demanded a share, were no longer guaranteed their former life expectancy. After the war they were bound to become Indian privileges. For all practical purposes from 1941 when the expanded Executive Council was put into place, the sharing could only be with the people of India.

This episode of infructuous treaty negotiations is the first landmark in the final phase of the struggle that ended in 1946. The character of the American terms, the reaction to them of the Indo-British officialdom, Indian public, and British official support of the Indo-American community are the four highlights of this episode. These highlights with their implications determined the history of the struggle for the next four years.

America would not grant even a minor concession to the citizens of an excluded nation except at an excessive price. The terms it offered to India reflected, in part, its present and future economic ambitions in Asia.[23] This is a sobering footnote to the efforts of Jagjit Singh and his compatriots in America who were seeking American official help in India's freedom struggle. The British attitude reflects the changing equation inside the Viceroy's Executive Council that had been brought about by the war and the increasing radicalization of the nationalist movement. This fact will influence the fate of the Indian bills before the U.S. Congress. Indian public opinion, although seriously concerned over the merchants's hardships, would not purchase relief at a humiliating price. These are the various conclusions one can draw from the views recorded by Indians and British members of the Executive Council with which the Viceroy himself agreed. We start with the Law Member, Sir Syed Sultan Ahmed :

> While I fully agree . . . that a large number of concessions have been made by America, I think the *quid pro quo* are highly objectionable and might lead to economic strangulation of this country . . . It seems to me that if we accept this Agreement, there will be an outcry all over the country that we have gone and sold this country to America. I feel that America is taking unfair and undue advantage of the help that we are receiving from her during the War and it is our duty to resist this attempt . . . the least that we should do is to publish this draft Agreement and wait for the reaction of the Press and the Public and we must further wait till the Autumn session of the Assembly. If we on our own responsibility accept the Agreement, I am afraid this will be made a major political issue in this country, and we might find ourselves in serious troubles.[24]

Sir A. Ramaswami Mudaliar, Commerce Member:

> If national treatment in the economic field is extended to American citizens the "result will be that India will be compelled to maintain an 'open door' policy to all foreigners . . . No country in the world could voluntarily accept so humiliating a position."
>
> These objections must be examined in the light of the strongly expressed views of the Indian commercial community which has voiced in no uncertain terms its opposition to any measure which might be described as an attempt to facilitate the "joint exploitation" of this country by the United Kingdom and U.S.A. . . . the public will consider itself deliberately misled and India's war effort will suffer a grievous set-back if we are now to accept the terms of this draft Treaty.
>
> While superficially reciprocal the draft treaty seeks to weigh the scales against India and in favour of U.S.A. The reciprocity secured by the treaty is deceptive and illusory.
>
> Granting national treatment to America "is a principle so utterly at variance with our present policy . . . that it would be improper for the present Government, knowing that constitutional changes are impending to subscribe to the principle so as to commit both itself and succeeding Governments."[25]

In a letter to Sir Mudaliar, the Viceroy enumerated the various reasons why the draft treaty was unacceptable:

> 1. The fact that the United Kingdom was included in the draft as a most-favored-nation raised very large constitutional issues.
>
> 2. Generally the American demand to get in on the ground floor and obtain privileges, the concession of which to United Kingdom was already subject to criticism . . . and it was in any case inopportune for India at present to undertake obligations for the future when constitutional changes were in prospect and (perhaps most important of all).
>
> 3. The United States were seeking under cover of reciprocity to obtain from India economic advantages of immense value in return for concessions to Indians in America of small scope.[26]

Sir Olaf Caroe, Secretary of the External Affairs Department and member of the Executive Council, noted that the United States' offer to Indians in America was "of small scope and in any case not covering emigration or immigration" and with a much needed touch of humor he proceeded to explain: "In other words to quote the old adage with America in place of ancient Holland,

> In matters commercial
> The fault of the Dutch
> Is giving too little
> And asking too much.[27]

Sir Feroz Khan Noon was willing to concede several American terms including most-favored-nation treatment in order to get the treaty that, he argued, "definitely confers upon Indians a large number of rights which they do not enjoy now in the United States."[28] His arguments, however, failed to reassure his colleagues about the hostile public reaction, if the American terms were to be accepted.

The merchants' cause was lost also because in the view of several Council Members and Secretaries, the war had made it of less immediate significance by cutting off shipping and trade.[29] Although Jagjit Singh would not have disagreed with this last conclusion, he and possibly others were left with an erroneous judgement as to the Government of India's role in this whole affair.[30] This judgement was left uncorrected because the Indian Government had declined to take non-official Indian commercial opinion into confidence or to publish the American draft as suggested by some members of the Executive Council.[31]

In this climate of hardened opinion that nothing favourable could be expected from Britain or its minions, Jagjit Singh and Ramlal Bajpai planned to give a hostile reception to Sir Noon, the Indian merchants' best friend, when he visited the United States in March, 1941. "We must do all we can to counteract Sir Feroz's propaganda trip," Jagjit Singh suggested to Ramlal Bajpai.[32]

We now return to America to examine how the rest of the community fared in dealing with the discriminations which needed new laws rather than a new treaty for their elimination. The most obvious route pursued over the years and the one that proved most fruitful was to find Congressional sponsors and win the support of the Administration.[33] The other was to institute a test case and carry it to the Supreme Court thereby offering it an opportunity to revise its earlier ruling.[34] In both routes the community relied upon its big gun, the Caucasian origin argument presented through American scholars of repute whose authority would, it was hoped, silence the exclusionists.

The third route was to sponsor bills for the naturalization of an individual Indian as was done by Rep. G.A. Dondero (R-MI) for the relief of Dr. Kameshwar Nath Kathju, an eminent scientist.[35] And lastly Haridas T. Muzumdar planned in 1939 to persuade the House Immigration and Naturalization Committee that was at the time engaged in codifying the nationality law to add Indians to the list of ethnic groups entitled to become naturalized citizens.[36]

With regard to sponsorship of bills seeking naturalization, the Indian residents of Michigan were somehow better able to win the support of their Congressmen than those of New York or California.

Rep. George D. O'Brien (D-MI) introduced H.R. 10736 in 1938 to "amend section 2169 United States Revised States, being Title 8, section 359, U.S. Code." Justice Sutherland had relied upon this Section in his ruling against Thind. Rep. Rudolph G. Tenerowicz (D-MI) sponsored two bills in 1939 — H.R. 6798 on June 12, 1939, to amend the same Section 2169 and H.R. 4996 for admission to citizenship of aliens who came prior to January 1, 1930. Rep. John Lesinski's bill HR 7110 was probably introduced to help India Welfare League's efforts in 1939.

None of these bills except probably HR 7110 reached even a Committee hearing stage. Some died even before they had been introduced because Rep. Samuel Dickstein, Chairman of the House Immigration and Naturalization Committee "discouraged it when they (the sponsors) rang me up." He also told the Committee, "they (the Indians) have been here quite a number of times."[37]

From 1924 the Japanese spokesmen kept their attack on exclusion alive on both sides of the Pacific. A few American businessmen tended to suggest a revision of the law to help foster trade. The Japanese politicians, on the contrary, by their aggression against China further strengthened the resistance of the exclusionists and alienated the forces that may have wished to include the Japanese residents in any favourable revision of the law.[38]

The Indian community, however, benefited from this widening breach between America and Japan. The superficial community of Asianism that in the American practice had for three decades bound India and Japan together in a fraternity of disadvantages, started to loosen. India was now seen as a distinct entity entitled to be judged on its own merits and not how the Japanese residents may react to that judgment. The arguments resembling those that clouded Senator Hiram Johnson's willingness to help the Indian citizens in 1926 were not presented at the hearings in 1939. Any possible Japanese reactions were no longer of decisive concern.

The Japanese launched their war in Manchuria in September, 1931. One calendar year before this, Hitler's National Socialist Party had emerged as the major party in the German Reichstag. Midway between these two tragic events, on March, 4, 1931 began the promising age of Samuel Dickstein as the Chairman of the House Immigration and Naturalization Committee.[39] Dickstein's advent is significant as much for whom he replaced as chairman as for the new attitude he brought to the chair. Indians may have remembered Albert Johnson as the instigator of anti-Indian violence in his State of Washington; immigrants knew him as the father of the Act of 1924 and Dickstein a Jew must have been aware of his anti-Semitism.[40]

Both Chairmen contributed forewords to Sidney Kansas' work on American immigration law in 1927 and 1936 respectively. While Johnson pointed out the need to "survive overpopulation," "to regulate the inflow of aliens," "for the further restriction of immigration" and quoted Washington out of context, Dickstein emphasized the need for the study of the law of naturalization and immigration. While still in the New York State Assembly in 1921, he, an immigrant Russian Jew, who had grown up on the lower east side of the City, had protested against Johnson's sweeping restriction bill and quota calculations based on the 1890 census.[41]

This "energetic, aggressive and indomitable" opponent of propagandists of Nazism was by the logic of his ethnic sympathies conditioned to welcome a more tolerant and less racist immigration policy.[42] In Dickstein, Indian representatives found a sympathetic listener who, being a Jew, was also anti- British over the Mandatory's policy in Palestine. With him and Emanuel Celler on the Indians' side, the network of Jewish organizations also ranged itself behind them.

Both these New Yorkers had taken their seats in the House of Representatives thirteen days after the *Thind* ruling. Celler became aware of the ruling as Gokhale's Attorney in 1928. Dickstein learned of it from Indians in 1939, not from his colleague and friend. This may indicate the insignificance of Hindu identity in the general scheme of things even among active politicians whose political careers subsisted on the votes of the foreign-born.

Indian workers lived in Dickstein's constituency. Being nonvoters their Congressmen owed them no I.O.U.'s. Indian activists, who owed him so much, suffered a surprising loss of memory. Haridas T. Muzumdar both in his book-length account and in his oral history testimony consistently called him "Goldstein." Jagjit Singh remembered him as "this chap from New York, he was the Chairman of the Hearing committee . . . Congressman Celler spoke to him (about supporting his bill) because they were both from New York, both were Jewish."[43]

One evening in the early thirties Muzumdar "happened to be seated by the side of" Congressman Emanuel Celler at a banquet in New York. He talked to him about the injustice of the denial of citizenship to Indians.

> He listened gravely to my story and told me that he would be glad to introduce a Bill to the effect, when we were ready . . . . Next I saw Mr. Bruce Bliven, Editor of *The New Republic* . . . and recounted the story of the injustice. He asked me to write a letter to the editor of *The New Republic* explaining the situation. But in terms of the Gandhi philosophy I felt a crusade in the press was not yet called for.[44]

He felt himself better prepared for the "crusade" in 1937. "At the suggestion of Ramlal Bajpai" the Hindusthan Welfare Association, better known as India Welfare League, was established to seek the right to naturalization. Their immediate constituents were the Indian laborers of the New York east side who, as noncitizens, were at a disadvantage in the job market. Most of them were Muslims. Mubarek Ali Khan was elected President. In June 1939 "in the name of this organization we went to Washington, D.C."[45]

During just the first year of its existence, the League strengthened its organization by adding several Americans to its Executive Board and advisory committee. It also discovered active workers so that Mubarek Ali could boast to President Roosevelt's Secretary, Stephen T. Early, that the League had "obtained more than 5000 signatures . . . . in the form of a petition to Congress and the President of the United States." The League later started its own newsletter *New India.*[46]

Reaching Washington they contacted the press and lobbied members of the House Immigration and Naturalization Committee including Dickstein and Asa Leonard Allen (D-LA). *The Washington Post* flashed on its front page that a professor [Muzumdar], a chemist [Bajpai] and an auto mechanic [Mubarek Ali] would appear before the committee. For the first time an Indian organization had been granted a hearing before a Congressional committee to present its demand for naturalization.[47]

In his testimony Ramlal Bajpai pointed out that the denial of the privilege of naturalization to Indians appeared to be incongruous for a country known as the haven of free institutions and an asylum for the oppressed. This denial had relegated them to a "permanent alien status" that was proving "demoralizing and devastating." He suggested that Section 2169 should be amended so as to expressly include the Indians at present resident in the United States.

Father John M. Cooper of the Catholic University, Washington, D.C. told the Committee that "All our data seems to show conclusively that the Hindu people are members of the white race" and this conclusion, he said, is "accepted as almost a first principle." The other expert Harry L. Shapiro, Associate Curator, American Museum of Natural History, New York City and Lecturer, Columbia University, testified that "The great majority of the reliable" anthropologists classify Indians as "members of the Caucasian family."[48]

Dr. Muzumdar urged Dickstein whose committee was engaged in codifying a comprehensive nationality law to "remove some of the existing discriminations against natives of India." The way to do this, he suggested, was to add Indians to the list of ethnic groups eligible to American citizenship in the proposed Section 303.

Mubarek Ali Khan told the Committee that his organization represented the Indian workers who "being non-eligible for citizenship they cannot get any kind of a job even W.P.A. or P.W.A. . . . they have been outlawed because they are not recognized as Americans."[49]

Paul Scharrenberg, representing the American Federation of Labor, did not "like to see any opening anywhere [for the Asians], not even to give them a foothold . . . . not to permit the smallest loophole in our present immigration restriction law . . . ." Muzumdar replied to every objection raised by Scharrenberg, denied any intention "to open your question of immigration" and claimed that "Our concern is merely that those who are already here " be enabled "to participate in the civil, political and social affairs of this country."[50]

Chairman Dickstein had granted the deputation a hearing because they had petitioned the committee seeking relief. He advised them to persuade a Congressman to sponsor a bill on their behalf to enable his committee to proceed through the normal channels of legislation. Rep. John Lesinski (D-MI) introduced such a bill in July (H.R. 7110). Mubarek Ali claims the bill was given a hearing in January 1940. Anyway it died in Committee with the end of the 76th Congress.[51]

The June 1939 hearing was the beginning of the education of Samuel Dickstein in the Indian question. It was here that he learned of the *Thind* case and also that several Indians had been naturalized prior to that decision.[52]

Representatives Noah Morgan Mason (R-IL) and William Robert Poage (D-TX) asked helpful questions and generally supported the Indian side of the argument. They continued to be friends of the Indian cause. Rep. Allen (D-LA) on the contrary was never convinced of the desirability of granting American citizenship or an immigration quota to Indians.

The India Welfare League had been established by two Indian Hindus to help the Indian workers of New York City, most of whom happened to be Muslims. Dr. Muzumdar, one of the two Hindu founders, emphasized the "Muslim" designation as well as his deliberate intention of keeping the direction of the League in Muslim hands.

> So we [he and Ramlal Bajpai] organized the Hindusthan Welfare Association. And I *had* one of the Muslim gentlemen become President and another one Vice-president. Ramlal and I said we would act as Secretaries or something like that. 'This is your organization', we told them.

This was good work in the true way of Gandhi's secularism, a well-intentioned effort to associate Indian Muslims in every aspect of political agitation.[53]

Some American observers almost immediately recognized its advantages :

> The Indian people themselves have been too divided along communal and economic lines to organize for any effective action. Only recently has any sort of united activity been carried out . . . The India Welfare League—a non-communal organization . . . has been organized and has devoted itself to a nationwide campaign for citizenship rights.[54]

The League continued to agitate for citizenship rights, but did not long retain its inter-communal character. It became a Muslim organization with a Muslim flag on its letterhead almost indistinguishable in later years from the India Muslim League of America demanding India's partition. Both in its demand for citizenship for residents only and in its approach to India's political destiny, the Welfare League acted as divisive influence in the Indian community in America. All these years Mubarek Ali Khan was the national president of the League, in later years also becoming secretary of the India Muslim League of America.[55]

Who was this new star Mubarek Ali Khan who deservedly claimed credit for himself and his League for "the first active and fighting" demand for citizenship "that Congress had heard for many years" ? Three independent documents give us three facts about his pre-1939 career.

In 1938 he was Roger Baldwin's colleague as member of the India Political Council in New York City. *The Washington Post* called him a "former automechanic." He seems to have already earned considerable influence within the Indian Muslim community in New York City. In July 1940 the British Consul General in New York responded to an inquiry from the Government of India regarding the whereabouts of an Indian Muslim. The Consul found him out "through the good offices of Mubarek Ali Khan" and he also made that person pay right away the sixteen dollars he owed to somebody in Calcutta.[56] He had gained the influence over the Muslim workers by what he claimed to have been his efforts on their behalf, such as seeking, jobs, visiting Washington, meeting high officials during the years of high unemployment. As president he claimed to have made his Welfare League a relief organization. Jagjit Singh knew of other methods that Mubarek Ali allegedly used to collect people around him and also to earn money.

He remembered him as a man "with no ethics," who "used to carry on gamblings, dances in Brooklyn." When Indian sailors would jump ship "he would keep watch on them—(make them go to his gambling dens) on the threat that if they did not, he will report them to the Immigration authorities." "So he is not a good man" Jagjit said. Further, he "started taking money from Indians on the West Coast and told them—he was a smart operator—that he would get a bill passed in Congress which would entitle them to own their lands." "He kept on collecting money on this excuse." Jagjit used to meet Mubarek Ali "but I was not impressed by his behavior, things that I heard about him."[57]

Mubarek's actions were not always straightforward. At the hearings on his bill S. 1595 in September 1944, Senator Langer introduced his first witness, Mubarek Ali, saying : "I would have the record show that Mr. Khan's father was Municipal Council Secretary of Interior of India and his brother is a major general; put that all in the record." Mubarek Ali offered no amendment to what the Senator said. The Government of India asked its Intelligence Bureau what it knew about these "impressive connections." The Bureau replied that "the information is obviously not correct." An Undersecretary in the External Affairs Department commented, "Mr. Mubarek Ali Khan has been gilding, if not inventing, his relatives."[58] At the April 1945 hearings on his bill S. 236, the Senator gave his protege another impressive brother : "I might add that Mr. Kahn's [sic] brother . . . is a delegate to the San Francisco Convention, appointed. The brother of the man who is here." Again Mubarek did not correct the Senator.[59]

Among the documents introduced into the record on behalf of the Welfare League at this hearing is one captioned "Background of Mubarek Ali Khan." Though in the third person, the style is Mubarek's own. This document of 25 lines contains five hyperbolic statements, two claims that need independent confirmation, one claim to university education contradicted eleven lines later, and a confession of probable illegal entry into the United States.

The style of the confession reveals the style of the man :

> Background of Mubarek Ali Khan
>
> Born of noble family—Chutri—Chutries being ancient rulers which are still ruling in the interior of India.
>
> 1914, Khan educated in Agra University, majoring in economics, and later went to China and to Europe to study the social conditions of the common people.
>
> 1916-17, Served in World War I and became prisoner in Germany, remained there until 1919, the purpose being to learn the language and the people.
>
> 1920, October 15, Came to the United States as a seaman because the House Secretary for India, in London, England, who was also an Indian, refused to issue a passport to Khan for the United States. However, Khan was desperate and determined to visit the promised land. Finally he succeeded.
>
> 1921. Went to night school, New York City, to obtain some English education. Same year organized India Labor League of America for the betterment of working class and farmers in this country.
>
> Khan's exile from India was due to his desire for India's freedom and his people. This has been his inherent longing from childhood to the present day.
>
> 1937, October 27. India Welfare League Inc., a humanitarian organization, was organized for the social contact and welfare for the Indian nationals residing in the United States.
>
> Khan was first leading party amongst Indian leaders in this country to unite against Japan.[60]

In December 1943 the League made its second attempt to regain citizenship rights, but this time it was pursued by a rival. The Welfare League's bill—Senator Langer's S. 1595, sought citizenship for Indians resident in the U.S. before July 1924. The India League's bill—Rep. Celler's H.R. 4416, in addition to naturalizing the about 3000 resident Indians—would also remove the national stigma implied in racial ineligibility to citizenship and denial of an immigration quota. Mubarek Ali who insisted on the Langer bill, in G.S. Bajpai's opinion, "for purely selfish reasons" turned against every supporter of the rival bill except the British Government of India and the U.S. Administration. For years he railed against the India League, Jagjit Singh, Rep. Celler "the Ph.D.'s and XYZ's" ending up as a Muslim Leaguer demanding partition of India.[61]

His frustration lay in finding "that I was the only Muslim; the rest all Hindus opposing Senator Langer's bill, after all my hardships for a long six years for them to come into the picture at the last moment" (and) complicating the entire works."[62] He started accusing the India League of being endorsed in the American Congress by "reformed and unreformed isolationists" and supported by a "handful" of Indians who came to America "for transient and propaganda purposes," unlike the farmers and laborers who came "with the intention of making it their home." He asked Emanuel Celler whether by his bill he intended to bring here more "lecturers," more "emotional blackmailers," more "authorities" on India and more businessmen [63]

Celler passed on these letters to Jagjit Singh who confronted Mubarek Ali and extracted a "humble apology" from him. As to the letters, he pleaded ignorance. "I was not the author or writer of these letters and my signature must have been forged." For the objectionable article published in his *New India Bulletin*, he blamed a colleague who "has been trying to ruin the reputation of the India Welfare League and myself." He promised to "be more careful in the future." As regards his resolve "to free my people," he assured Jagjit Singh, "I am not one of the 'Barking Dogs,' but mean action."[64]

His apology does not seem to have included assurance of better public conduct in the future. A year later, *The New India Bulletin* accused the American friends of India of "encouraging the Hindu Congress Party to obstruct the Muslim League" and advised them to keep "hands off" India's problems and "mind their own business" because these Indian parties "do not need any legal advisers," a reference to Rep. Celler.[65]

He termed Celler's bill "a Mixture Bill and Business Bill" and forecast that in case it were enacted "Indians could not come to this country for perhaps another 25 or 30 years but only merchants and exporters and importers will be benefited." This was not a very balanced interpretation of the bill. In view of the merciless Hindu-Muslim controversy raging in India at the time and injected into the affairs of the Indian community here by Mubarek Ali and his Muslim associates even distortion could earn him partisan applause.[66]

Another way of earning applause was to decorate oneself in borrowed feathers. From the end of June 1945 he started adding "Dr." before his name. When questioned by a reporter which university conferred this degree upon him, he explained, "At our citizenship Congressional hearings Senators and Congressmen used to address me by 'Dr.' so I too adopted it."[67]

In the fall of 1946 he announced the coming publication of his autobiography bearing the modest title *Lincoln of India*. The book seems never to have been published.[68]

There were two sides to Mubarek Ali's public character. He did admirable work for years nursing his Muslim constituency in the east and the west, and spending months in arduous travel in 1944 visiting the scattered colonies of Indians in several states.

His fulminations against non-Muslim Indian nationalists are understandable in the context of the situation in the mid-1940s when such outbursts had become the accepted way of rallying Muslim opinion behind a Muslim leader or his cause. The India League spokesmen, however, never replied to him in kind. On the contrary, they took constructive note of the situation. In a memorandum prepared in August 1944, Richard J. Walsh, Chairman of the League's Executive Council, included a new item in the "Suggested Program for the India League of America"; "1. make special effort for relations with Muslims in New York and elsewhere." The India League president although recognizing "the duty of all Indians to expose imposters amongst us" left its performance to others.[69]

Senator Langer introduced his bill on Indian citizenship on December 15, 1943. The same day he launched a one-man filibuster on an unrelated piece of legislation. According to an eyewitness, the Senator "ranted and raved and pounded and roared" so that it became a "humorous, disgraceful, saddening spectacle all rolled into one." So was the India Welfare League. Celler called it "rather a selfish organization. They seek to feather their own nest, and I think they do a woeful injury to their own people and in my humble estimate they should bow in shame."[70]

The North Dakota Senator's other filibuster, his bill S. 1595, came very close to succeeding. Of all the Indian organizations working as rivals to the India League, the India Welfare League became Jagjit Singh's chief Indian competitor in Congress. Its president knew enough English to serve him as a lancet and enough tact and energy to captivate a leading U.S. Senator. The Mubarek Ali-Langer alliance weaned away nearly all Muslim support from the India League and fought against it for years almost on equal terms.

There had been three bills before the House in 1939 proposing naturalization of Indians resident in the United States—H.R. 7110 of Rep. Lesinski introduced on June 12, H.R. 6798 and H.R. 4996 both sponsored by Rep. Tenerowicz. The fourth proposal was the petition brought to Rep. Dickstein by Mubarek Ali and his two colleagues. The petition and probably H.R. 7110 received the House Committee hearings. Except for this legislative courtesy all four attempts were infructuous. Still Mubarek Ali was justifiably left with the proud memory of a well-conducted first attempt.

During the next three and a half years from about February 1940 to the beginning of May 1943, he was busy helping Indian workers, occasionally seeking support in favor of his naturalization project, and watching Indian political developments.[71] After Pearl Harbor opened the avenues both of employment and naturalization by joining the armed forces, Mubarek submitted to the Secretary of War a list of names of "sons of Mother India who wish to defend America." The object was to gain citizenship "by our fighting for the common cause."[72]

He was still a worshipper of "Mother India," a Hindu concept. This would soon change. Three months previously he had received from Mohammad Ali Jinnah a letter in support of his citizenship campaign and "by separate parcel all the [Muslim League] literature that is available and which might be useful to you." It proved very useful indeed to the sender. In 1942 at a time when Jagjit Singh and the India League were angry at the British, Mubarek was angry with the nationalists. His appeal was to "Unite Against Japan" with Britain. "We must fight for victory—fight for the lives of our people; after victory we will talk about freedom," he promised. He had thus put himself directly in opposition to the India League two years before the battle of the bills was joined at the Congressional hearings. He also adopted a Muslim flag as the insignia of the Welfare League.[73]

We are now approaching the opening shots of the battle, the last chapter in the Indian community's struggle for equality. That chapter opened in the second half of 1943 with certain initiatives taken by Mubarek Ali Khan and Senator Langer including the sponsorship of his bill S. 1595.

Much of the story of the Mubarek-Langer joint effort lacks mutual corroboration. It seems however that the India Welfare League addressed an open letter to every member of Congress in May, 1943. Among the many sympathetic responses Mubarek professes to have received was one dated November 18 from Senator Langer inviting him to Washington, D.C. for an interview. He kept the appointment at which the Senator seems to have given him some assurance because on December 4 he told Jagjit Singh that "we definitely expect . . . shortly" the introduction of a bill.[74]

In February, 1944 about two months after introducing his bill the Senator, accompanied by Mubarek Ali Khan, visited the "West coast Indian colonies gathering material to support his bill." Both were back east where Langer was announced to "be present" and Mubarek Ali to "report on his recent visit to the West" at a public meeting scheduled for March 5 in Jersey City.

On February 21 G.H. Watumull sent Jagjit Singh a telegram from West Los Angeles, California, saying :

> Senator Langer now visiting West coast Indian Colonies gathering material to support his bill. We missed him here. I understand one Mr. Mubarek Ali is traveling with and guiding him. Who is he ? Can we trust him ? Somebody reported from Imperial Valley he kept many Indians from seeing Langer whom he should have contacted there. It is reported they have gone north.
>
> Telephoned [Godha Ram] Channon to be on lookout. This Indian citizenship matter vitally important. Wish you all Anup [Singh] [Syud] Hossain had informed us. Watumull.

Copies were sent to Anup and Hossain.

Suspicion had been aroused and an alarm bell sounded on the West coast. The East was warned that the "citizenship matter vitally important." In other words, the East coast Indian organizations were told to get active and snatch the initiative from Langer and Mubarek Ali in the "citizenship matter." There was resentment in the words "Wish you all . . . had informed us," a virtual accusation of having let down the guard.

In four days the India League Secretary called a meeting of the Executive Committee "to consider the citizenship matter" and a week later the first Celler bill was in the Congressional legislative mill. On March 15 Saund's organization held a public meeting in Los Angeles. Mubarek lost the initiative. A fortnight later he wrote his first angry letter to the bill's sponsor, Rep. Celler.[75]

It may seem as if the India League was hurried into the struggle for citizenship by the telegram from the west. In fact, the League's mind had already been made up by the character of the Langer bill. The East did not have to ask who Mubarek Ali was or could he be trusted. He was not important. The League had looked at the bill and decided it had to be opposed. Its origin from people of the negative reputation of Senator Langer and Mubarek made the decision more determined.

The issue of eligibility to citizenship had never been far from the League's agenda. "To improve the civic status of the Indian community" was one of its objectives. In October, 1940 it had submitted to the U.S. Government a memorandum on status of Indians in America. The January, 1941 issue of its newsletter complained of the Sutherland ruling, and in August it published a research article on the citizenship problem by Taraknath Das.

A League document of 1942 included repeal of Asian exclusion among items on "The Political Platform of the India League of America." The Walsh Memorandum of August, 1944 suggested that the League "should not hesitate" to work for "bills for Indian immigration and citizenship, landownership laws and other discriminatory measures." By this time, of course the League was deeply committed to the struggle.[76]

For years its president, however, had never been committed. "I had no interest" in the naturalization and immigration affairs. "I was a businessman." "I was in a different category." The thought [of improving the legal status of the Indian community] came later to me because I lived in different circumstances." It seems that Jagjit Singh did not identify himself with the legal disabilities of the vast majority of Indians in America until probably 1942 when the pressure of the nationalist movement made an organizational and psychological expansion advisable. What he had attempted to do in 1938-1939 had been for the benefit only of his own class.[77]

Early in 1943 the State of California enacted another anti- alien land law. Jagjit Singh complained to India's Agent-General, G.S. Bajpai who promised to make inquiries. In June the representatives of California Indians requested Jagjit "to plead with the authorities in Washington" over the new law. Friends within the League, among them Pearl Buck and her husband Richard J. Walsh, advised that "this was not the proper time for us to create any agitation in Washington and that all such efforts at this stage would be more or less futile."[78]

Already busy treading on California exclusionists' toes in the summer of 1943 over the proposal to repeal Chinese exclusion, those friendly advisers may have been reluctant to further exasperate the conservative forces. Shying away from one "agitation," the League was soon drawn into another by the news of the famine in India that kept it busy through the remainder of 1943 and the first two months of 1944 until a few days before the Watumull telegram.

It seems almost certain that the usefulness of Indian organizations would have been seriously questioned had they not followed the repeal of the Chinese exclusion laws with a similar demand on behalf of their own country. Several prominent associates and officials of the India League had worked for the Chinese repeal. That achievement worked for them as an "incentive" and the League was theirs as a "vehicle" to reach the Indian goal.[79] Before they could hope to reach this goal, the India League's supporters had to deal with Indians who did not want their bill to go far enough to erase the national stigma or to provide for an immigrant quota.

Mubarek Ali Khan, as we know, was working hard among Indians to gain support for his objectives. In one of his letters to Jagjit Singh, he conceded that Congress had "OK'd Exclusions' end" for the Chinese and promised that the soon-to-be introduced (Langer) bill "will wipe out the injustice towards Indian nationals who like China, are also nationals of the United Nations" [sic]. In his second letter, a month later, he claimed that "Our policy is vindicated" in the light of the end of Chinese exclusion.[80]

The provisions of the Langer bill, however, contradicted the Welfare League President's assertions. His "policy" both in 1939 and in 1943 had been to agitate for far less than what the Chinese had asked for and obtained from Congress in November, 1943. When he first saw what the North Dakota Senator had proposed, Roger Baldwin warned Jagjit Singh, "This is a very bad bill . . . . This is not eliminating stigma from the Indian nation."[81]

It took even Jagjit Singh a study of the Indian Welfare League's bill and of the "immigration difficulties" to appreciate Baldwin's alarm. The land-starved farmers of the West, however, were not easily persuaded to resist the attraction of the catchy idea "half-a-loaf is better than no loaf." Even a year after the Celler bill, clearly providing for the racial eligibility of *all* Indians to U.S. citizenship had been introduced, Dr. Saund had to vigorously expound the inadequacies of the Welfare League's proposals to disenchant his coreligionists and fellow-farmers from half-measures and disruptive strategies. His chief argument was that unless all the Indian people were made eligible to U.S. citizenship, landownership by Indians would always remain suspect in the eyes of the American people and the law officers.[82]

The representatives of Muslims of Arizona, Texas, California, and Washington resolved to demand (July 27, 1944) "no longer to be excluded *from entry into the United States of America* and from asking citizenship." But Mubarek Ali did not join them in asking for the "whole loaf." Instead he was joined by the India Association for American Citizenship whose president, N.R. Checker was driven mostly by personal pique against the India League and its president. He was also supported, initially at least, by Drs. Hossain and Anup Singh.[83]

Jagjit has testified that the officials of the League "had been questioning the awfulness of the immigration law for years." But the Langer bill "made us aware of the danger more so than it had been before." He and his colleagues decided "that India League cannot afford this kind of bill to pass through (Congress)." After several meetings of its Executive Committee in February, 1944, the League decided to dissociate itself from Mubarek Ali's plan and to initiate an immigration bill that would repeal racially insulting legislation.[84]

A decision to support the India Welfare League's bill would have meant a break with the nationalist character of the earlier Indian protestations against discriminatory laws. It would also have violated a major plank in the India League's recently proclaimed "Political Platform" which argued that *discrimination against Oriental peoples on racial grounds can be righted only by repeal of the exclusion acts.*"[85]

Friends and associates of the India League who had testified in favour of the repeal of Chinese exclusion would certainly have been very inconsistent had they not pleaded for similar favor for India.

Taraknath Das in his testimony had considered it "necessary that quota system and equal privilege for citizenship be given to the Chinese *and other orientals.*" Attempting to make the Chinese relief a precedent, he pleaded that quota and citizenship rights be granted to the Chinese "and then the same measures be extended to *other peoples.*"[86]

Indians on the West coast, particularly those in California would be the most numerous beneficiaries of repeal just as they had been the most numerous victims of exclusion legislation.[87] In the struggle for repeal their leaders played their part as effectively for equality as the whites of California had played theirs years ago as a "barrier" against Asia.[88] Being tied to their farms far away from the legislative center, the West coast leaders were unable to provide personal direction on the spot. They provided almost everything else—the prodding, the single-minded support for the Luce-Celler bill against the Langer bill, and complete confidence in Jagjit Singh's leadership. They also gave what the India League wanted most from California, namely, "large monetary contribution."[89]

Except for Haridas T. Muzumdar's India Welfare League, no Indian effort to protect or reclaim equality of legal status had originated on the East coast. The Sudhindra Bose deputation, the Gadar, the *Thind* case, the *Pandit* case, the Dr. Pandia's exploratory mission to Washington D.C., the *Samras* and the *Karam Chand* test cases all started in California. Even the India League campaign represented by the Celler bill of March 1944 had its roots in the organized initiative from the leaders of the California Indian opinion.

In all their previous efforts, including the two test cases of the early 1940s, the Indians of the West coast, according to Saund "had suffered so many hardships and had been knocked about so much that it was very difficult for them to believe that there was a chance of our winning."[90] But towards the end of 1943, hope and enthusiasm took a new birth among the California Sikhs.

The repeal of Chinese exclusion laws brightened their hopes. The passage of the Mundt amendment was interpreted as the dawn of a new era—"The days are gone when only the British power worked." Donations for famine relief in India showed the people's will to support a good cause. The Langer-Mubarek tour of the West in February, 1944 added the suspicions about the tourist's designs to the objections to the tourists' bill. The Langer bill persuaded the more watchful patriots that in order for the immigrants' cause to be really good, the demand for grant of mere citizenship for the resident Indians must be substituted by a bill providing the total repeal of Indian exclusion laws.[91]

The India League's organizational efforts in 1943 included keeping "close contact with Indian community in California." The famine relief and the UNRRA episode provided occasions when several prominent Californians such as Bagga Singh Sunga, Ajmer Singh, Dr. Jagan Nath, and Watumull became interested in the affairs and the fortunes of the India League. Godha Ram Channon became a member of its National Advisory Board. The West coast developed confidence in Jagjit Singh's leadership.[92]

This was happening at a time when Dalip Singh Saund and his friends including Bagga Singh Sunga started a campaign of their own to gain equality of status for Indian immigrants. "Part of our plan," Saund explained later, "was to furnish financial assistance to some leading Indians in New York urging them to make contacts with the members of Congress and other officials and friends of India to rally support for our case."

They started raising a fund to which Sunga and Saund contributed "both money and time." They made several trips to all parts of the state, wrote and mailed out "thousands of circular letters" that "had to be carefully and patiently lettered by hand with black ink in the Punjabi language and then printed by offset." Hard work paid off—"support began to come in from all quarters," Saund claimed in his autobiography.[93]

In the legislative and the propaganda struggle that followed, all the traditions, the experience, and most of the human resources of the Indian community were ranged behind the India League. The experience gained in fighting the British propaganda for 40 years, the organizational skills, the methods of lobbying, and of "influencing the influencers" during the Quit India crisis of 1942 and the famine crisis of 1943 all contributed to its legislative victory of 1946.

Among human resources the League's assets included the university educated brain trust, some of the earliest Indian residents of America, the Gadarites, the ideological descendants of Lajpat Rai and Rev. J.T. Sunderland, the defendants of the Gadarites' civil rights, the Indian merchants, the latest Indian arrivals, and American attorneys who once had Indians as their clients. The Indian nationalist movement helped the League's cause on two continents : in India by converting the Government of India into a supporter of the Luce-Celler bills and in America by enabling Jagjit Singh to win the support of six important figures of the literary and the publishing world, Lous Bromfield, Louis Fischer, Pearl Buck and her husband Richard J. Walsh, publisher of *Asia*, Henry Luce of *Time*, *Life* and *Fortune* and his wife Clare Boothe.

It was the most significant agitation ever launched by the Indian community in the United States. Better supported than the lonely H.A.A.-Khalsa Diwan deputation led by Sudhindra Bose in 1914, better organized than the Gadar, it was neither the forlorn hope of political orphans nor a punitive march mounted by desperate men who felt cheated of their dreams.

American liberals gave important support and served as intermediaries with the American people. They were attracted to the Indians' cause by American and/or Christian inspirations. For Roger Baldwin it was a "feeling for minority rights." The pacifists were attracted to Gandhi not through Buddhism or Vaishnavism but through what appeared to them as a close resemblance between Gandhian teachings and the Sermon On the Mount. Some of them were not even color blind or may have, like all good intermediaries, brought in the color argument to underscore the mutual Caucasian courtesy of same color, same treatment. For instance in her attempt to awaken her audience to this courtesy, Pearl Buck mentioned that Mrs. Vijaylakshmi Pandit had told her "that her own grandmother had red hair, didn't you?" Mrs. Pandit replied, "Yes." Pearl Buck: "And blue eyes."[94]

These liberals were the middle class, patriotic Americans who happened to have better eyesight than many of their contemporaries. They, therefore, saw sooner than others that the white racist game of the first half of the century was over. Henry Luce believed, however, that America could still make the twentieth "The American Century" by discarding "any and all forms of isolationism," and working "in terms of a vital international economy and in terms of an international moral order." Asian exclusion had been interpreted by some as "an integral part of the American attempt at international isolation." Repeal of Asian exclusion was part of a liberal effort to inaugurate America's world leadership—economic leadership through Asian trade and moral leadership partly by Asian conversion to Christianity.[95]

Among other segments of American opinion that welcomed a widening of the perimeters of racial toleration were the organized labor, the blacks, and the Jews. The helpful intervention of C.I.O. Secretary James B. Carey on Jagjit Singh's behalf during the UNRRA debate was an instance of how significantly American labor had come to sympathize with Asian problems. Phillip Murray, C.I.O. president became a member of India League's National Advisory Board in 1944. Walter P.Reuther (international vice-president of the U.A.W.-C.I.O. in 1942) and Jagjit Singh maintained a personal friendship for years after the crises of the 1940s were over.[96]

The India League had developed a close working relationship with many of the centers of black political activity. Walter White, executive secretary of NAACP, was in contact with Indian activists as early as 1938. Later he was a member of the League's National Advisory Board. Rev. Holmes Smith was at one time a member of the Executive Committee. Both the Fellowship of Reconciliation and the NAACP supported the cause of India's freedom. The latter at a session attended by Jagjit Singh resolved to support repeal of Asian exclusion because of its effect on the Orient "on American democratic pretensions." Thurgood Marshall presided over the session.

Soon after Emanuel Celler had introduced his bill, Sir G.S. Bajpai told his Government in New Delhi that the U.S. "State Department felt that Celler was not the sponsor whom they would have chosen because he was left-wing Jew and extreme Zionist and a supporter of freer immigration generally, a cause which was most unpopular." A year later in another telegram Bajpai expressed the fear that "some of our supporters may be suspected of backing us in order to push passage of the Indian Bill as precedent of more liberal immigration policy in respect of Jews and other aliens."[97]

This was an instance of anti-Semitism among some high American officials. Indians had supported the Chinese repeal "as precedent of more liberal immigration policy in respect of" Indians. Celler indeed wanted more trade with India and also to serve the interests of the minority to which he belonged. Repeal of Asian exclusion spelled a revolution in American policy in which numerous have-nots including Jews and blacks believed and hoped to benefit from. Indians benefited immensely from the Celler-Dickstein combination and the Jewish organizations that backed them. India pocketed the gains but Pandit Nehru's pro-Arab policy was later a disappointment for Emanuel Celler.[98]

Indians appeared before the Congress in split ranks, as two separate "schools of thought." The opponents of the bills sponsored by the India League, however, could never match its resources. Mubarek Ali's bill never received endorsement from the Government of India nor from the United States Administration. No American newspaper editorial came out advising that the Langer or the Lynch bill was the farthest that the country should go. Despite all the personal rivalries between the India League and the D.C. based National Committee, the latter's officials Anup Singh, Krishnalal Shridharani, and Haridas Muzumdar testified at the Congressional hearings that the Welfare League's bill should be amended to conform to the provisions of the India League bills.[99]

The Indian community's fight for legal equality was, therefore, in fact a united effort except for the discord injected into it by the followers of the Muslim League of *India*. They opposed the Luce-Celler bill because its Indian supporters were the followers of the Indian National Congress. But when this bill gained strength, they too rallied behind it. From July, 1945 they virtually disappeared from the battle of the bills.[100] All Indians were of one voice against racial insult. Several organizations joined hands to achieve victory. Taraknath Das acknowledged the valuable services of a "large number of devoted American friends" including those who sponsored bills and "above all the Indian workers and businessmen on the Pacific Coast" as well as Jagjit Singh's "co-workers." The only individual he named was Jagjit Singh whom other contemporaries hailed as a "one-man lobby." Similarly Mahatma Gandhi, as informed by Louis Fischer, held Jagjit "solely responsible" for the passage of the Act. Twenty years later Emanuel Celler "remembered well" Jagjit's "ingenuity and wise ministrations" during the fight over the bills.[101]

These two qualities—ingenuity and wise ministrations—helped him during the 930 days of the most successful campaign of his life.

He educated himself in the immigration problem for which he had not cared until he was challenged by the Langer bill. He had already become an expert in what President John Adams had called "touching some springs and turning some small wheels" to win the legislators' votes.[102]

Interpreting India's case in terms of American national interest is an instance of his flexibility in tactics, as was his refusal to beg for equality of status as a reward for being America's fighting ally. He claimed equality rather as the right of a proud people. "Why are we not considered good enough to stay in your country?" he demanded to know. "We just don't want to be considered inferior," he said.[103]

The Welfare League arguments in favour of the Langer bill were presented by its President Mubarek Ali several times including his testimony at the Senate hearings. He complained that Indian residents had been deprived of the blessings of freedom in a free country, although they had lived here for over two decades. They had, he claimed, helped in the agriculture development of lands "where all was mud and sand" before. Being law-abiding people, members of the Caucasian race, and "doing more than their part to serve in the war effort," they were entitled to the privilege of naturalization. As a fling at the India League bill, he told the Senators that "our problem is not what you all hear about the quota bill or the bringing of some more immigrants from India, because we do not wish to take the candles to the church and leave our homes dark."[104]

Mubarek Ali was thus categorically rejecting the validity of the Chinese, the Indian nationalist, the Korean and the Filipino demands. His contentions were pedestrian, his ambitions limited to a few Indian farmers in the West, some workers in Detroit and New York City. Only about a thousand of them might have qualified for citizenship.[105]

Jagjit Singh's canvas was vast. It extended to the destiny of nations, to the shape of the world to come, the fate of Empires, the freedom of the people of Asia and to the universalizing of the principles of democracy. It linked American immigration and naturalization favors to the global issues of political, cultural, and economic traffic between nations. The bill provided for racial eligibility to citizenship and a token annual quota of immigrants, provisions not significant as to their numerical impact but in Mrs. Luce's view, their psychological effect may well have been out of all proportion to the number of their Indian beneficiaries.

For America she felt "It is seldom that a nation has the opportunity to obtain so great a profit at so little cost." The bill, instead of being an American grant became an instrument of international exchange, a preamble to an Indo-American compact for a hoped-for immediate future. As such it gained the support of all American elements that looked to Asia for trade, for evangelization, for partnership against international communism and of those who were eager to make a repetition of Nazi racism impossible. As a result we see in the pages of the congressional hearing a parade of American liberals, businessmen, church missionaries, war veterans, labor leaders, and representatives of Jewish organizations urging the passage of Luce-Celler bill.[106]

On the Indian side those two provisions were cherished as symbolizing the fulfillment of the martyrs' dreams and vindicating the nation's honor. They also proved to be historically significant in the finality of the solution they offered. Once enacted they would provide for all that the Indian community needed to work out its political and economic destiny in the United States. Among the legally admitted Indian residents, no have-nots would be left to clamor for anther struggle under another League.

The repeal of Chinese exclusion seems to have made the case of India its "logical consequence." All arguments that prevailed in the case of one Asian member of the United Nations were claimed to be equally pertinent in the case of India. The validity of this similarity of arguments was accepted by the *New York Times* even before Celler had introduced his bill and by the *Los Angeles Times* and *Asia and the Americas* soon after.[107]

The Chinese emancipation indeed served "to emphasize the continued existence" of restrictions on the nationals of India.[108] Whites, blacks, South American Indians, veterans of every race, and now the Chinese were qualified to be citizens, so why not Indians, the argument ran. India was not the only member of the United Nations barred from the privileges of quota and naturalization. The opponents' argument, that China deserved a better deal as an independent sovereign nation since India was just a British province, was cancelled out by the British support for the Indian bills.

Both China and India benefited from a growing American consciousness about making and keeping friends in Asia. The people of

Asia had been excluded from the benefits available to others because they were Asians. In the 1940's they were admitted to these privileges because they were Asians. The character of American awareness of Asia and Asians had changed.

The war dissolved the West's former advantages of one-sided power. Wendell Willkie called for "new ideas in the machinery of our relations with the peoples of the East." Whether it was Cordell Hull's desire to have the son of Thailand's Prime Minister admitted to West Point or his effort to "build up" China into the rank of the major powers, both actions reflected a new type of American awareness of Asia. So was Justice Frankfurter's attempt to persuade Churchill "to assure India of its eventual independence" in the interest of the "new international order."[109] Taraknath Das advised that "if this war is for world unity and world freedom then the United States cannot practice double standards of international morality . . . one for the whites and the other for the Asiatics." Krishnalal Shridharani had expressed the hope that "the Anglo-Saxon" will "rise to the grand occasion of the war and that he will do justice to the East gracefully and during the period of grace."[110]

At the time when Rep. Emanuel Celler introduced his bill (March 1944), five forces were seeking relief for Indian immigrants. They included public opinion in India, Dr. Dalip Singh Saund's associates in California, the India League of America in New York, the Government of India, and the United States Department of State. All five wanted relief through a bill in Congress. None of them felt satisfied with a bill of the Langer variety. The Celler bill was the confluence where those five channels met. It did not just represent the India League's reaction to the inadequacies of the Langer bill. It was an attempt to topple the next big domino of Asian exclusion.

The Indian Merchants' Chamber had urged the Government of India to represent to the United States Government the need for passage of necessary legislation with a view to enable Indians to acquire citizenship rights in America. The Chamber "understood" that the Government had "already taken up the question with" the U.S. Government and that the "matter was under consideration." In February, 1944 the Indian Legislative Assembly was officially assured that the government was greatly interested in the matter and that its Agent-General, G.S. Bajpai having made representation to the U.S. State Department had been informed that the latter would examine the possibility of having legislation introduced. Indians in California and New York, heartened by the Chinese legislation and disappointed at the Langer bill, were looking for sponsors. "We shall redouble our efforts from New York to get a resolution drafted for introduction in Congress, and to arrange for a hearing on it" Baldwin assured Watumull a couple of days before Celler sent his draft bill to the Department of Justice.[111] The American support for the bill, the extent of which would have been unimaginable only a couple of years earlier, was vocalized by a nationwide educational campaign conducted by the leaders of the Indian community. Taraknath Das, the patriarch of the community both in age and in personal suffering under the unequal laws, had researched the Indian problem for over 35 years as a journalist, a victim, and a scholar. For the last twenty years he and his equally talented wife had contributed articles to Indian and American journals and most recently to *India To-Day* and the *Voice of India*. Krishnalal Shridharani's two masterly works had presented the Indian and the Asian point of view to American readers. Jagjit Singh and Anup Singh studied the history of the community in order to formulate realistic solutions.[112]

After the League decided to go to Congress, the Indian brain trust started writing in several American journals. The Californians raised the tempo of their publicity at the direction of Jagjit Singh who also sent a circular letter to newspaper editors requesting them "to comment editorially on this vital matter." He claimed to have canvassed all the forty-eight states and to have received 1300 replies. Public meetings were held in New York City, Washington D.C., and Los Angeles. *India To-Day* and the *Voice of India* were put to effective use as interpreters of the nationalist opinion on the Luce-Celler bills and to keep the readers informed of their progress in Congress. Rep. Emanuel Celler explained the purpose and content of his bill in two "Extension of Remarks" in the Congressional Record.[113]

Before the year 1944 ended the League's bill had been endorsed by Jewish public opinion, and the Methodists, the Federal Council of Churches, the New History Society, the Post- War World Council, and the American Civil Liberties Union. Americans in India signed a statement of support. The Congress of Industrial Organizations (C.I.O.) committed itself to India's freedom from Britain and later expressed that support on behalf of the Luce-Celler bill.[114]

Members of the Indian legislature pressed the demand for "reciprocal treatment" and wished that Indians should cease to be treated as "prohibited emigrants." The official spokesman in reply pledged the Government of India in favor of the "enactment of a measure giving exactly the same treatment to Indians as had already been accorded to China" and categorically rejected the Langer bill saying that it is "not what we here should like or wish."

The Shiromani Akali Dal, the largest political organization of the Sikhs, sent President Roosevelt a telegram urging the grant of citizenship to Indians. The U.S. State Department notified Rep. Emanuel Celler and Samuel Dickstein of its "sympathy with the broad purposes of the proposed legislation." Several segments of American public opinion extended a helping hand by adopting resolutions and publishing favorable comments.[115]

Jagjit Singh repeatedly claimed to have lined up "powerful Americans" to appear as his witnesses at the Congressional hearings. Looking at the support the League was receiving for its bill from the peoples and the Governments of the countries, a professional observer of the public pulse, Henry Luce, became "confident of its passage." But when the long-awaited Congressional hearings were announced, neither the League nor its witnesses were ready.

In May it had been expected that hearings would take place "soon." This did not happen. Twice Rep. Celler "assured" Jagjit Singh that they might take place after Congress reassembled in September. Instead it was the rival Langer bill that got a hearing. Then Celler fixed his hopes on "after elections." Dickstein fixed November 15 for the hearings, but they were called off at the League's request. "We were given only one week to line up our witnesses to testify," Jagjit Singh complained in a press release.

In fact as long as five months previously, he had convinced himself that "If Congress adjourns till after Labor Day, then there is hardly any chance of the bill going through in this Congress." This conclusion he never really gave up in spite of Celler's repeated assurances. His witnesses also may have reached the same conclusion and may, therefore, have relaxed in their preparedness for the hearings, particularly when these were proving to be elusive and assurances proving to be wrong.[116]

The reasons for this apparent organizational failure were lucidly explained by Dr. Saund to his compatriots in their native language. The introduction of bills had been delayed. Consequently hearings could not be obtained during the decisive months of May and June. The Justice and State Departments sent their endorsements to Chairman Dickstein very late. 1944 happened to be an election year. Members were concerned with their election. More than half were absent. The September session was spent mostly on the G.I. bill debates. Therefore, according to Saund, "Jagjit Singh in consultation with Luce, Celler, Dickstein and the Assistant Secretary of State decided that no action is necessary before the new Congress assembles in January." This setback probably delayed the enactment of the bill by several months and it invited taunting criticism from Mubarek Ali ridiculing "our so-called patriotic Indian leaders" [who] "are not too enthusiastic about any legislation but certainly are champion talkers."[117]

This, however, was not a year of wasted effort. The supporters of the Luce-Celler bill almost took over their opponents' hearing and with unexpected help from official quarters and Senator Harold H. Burton (R-OH) virtually destroyed the chances of the Langer bill getting out of the Committee.

The Attorney-General Francis Biddle had written to the Committee Chairman, Senator Richard B. Russell (D-GA) that "no reason is perceived, however, why a line of demarcation should be drawn as of July 1, 1924" and objecting to the proposed grant of exemptions from "requirements imposed on all other applicants for naturalization by existing law." Edward J. Shaughnessy of the Immigration Service amplified his superior officer's views with further arguments. The Attorney- General and his subordinate official thus knocked out two of the three major constituents of the Welfare League's proposals. No Congressional Committee would ordinarily recommend favorably any bill, the basic premises of which were denied by the Administration. Shaughnessy also told the Senators that "if you pass the House bills (the Celler and Luce bills) you would not want the Langer bill, because the greater includes the lesser."[118]

In contrast to the deficiencies of the Langer bill, Shaughnessy repeatedly brought up the advantages of the Luce and Celler bills which, it may be noted, were not the subject of the present hearings. He too like the Attorney-General failed to see "where the term July 1, 1924 has any particular significance." The Luce and Celler bills, he pointed out, have no limitation of dates, nor do they provide for grant of naturalization only to those Indians who came from India.[119]

Senator Burton said that if the Langer bill were passed in its present shape "limiting it to those who came before July 1, 1924, it would not only not eliminate this discrimination (the one imposed by the *Thind* case ruling), it actually would confirm the discrimination by legislative act [implying that] "the Congress was in agreement with the Supreme Court, and expressly prescribes after that date East Indians cannot be naturalized." And moreover "for the first time" Congress would be "really confirming the Supreme Court's decision, as of July 1, 1924, instead of overruling it." He further argued that if good will were one of the reasons for the bill and we pass it, "I am afraid we have not been helping good will."

The supporters of the Langer bill expressed unconcern with the Senator's arguments. Joseph Tenner, Counsel for N.R. Checker's organization, for instance, told the Senators that these "3000 are not interested in the interpretation of what happened in 1923. They are interested in themselves."[120]

Checker, Tenner and Mubarek Ali all testified but most of the time was taken up by Shaughnessy, and by three other critics of the Langer bill, namely Anup Singh, Jagjit Singh, and Krishnalal Shridharani. They advocated the provisions of the Luce and Celler bills and placed on the record documents supportive of the India League objectives. All of them pleaded that the Langer bill be amended to conform to the provisions of the Luce and Celler bills. Taraknath Das, who was unable to appear in person, submitted a written statement supporting the nationalist position.

Mubarek Ali was not happy at the argument getting out of his hands. When Shridharani urged that the Langer bill "be readjusted to resemble" the bills pending in the House, he intervened calling Shridharani one of the "newcomers" who "have no experience of their country brothers and only interested in themselves." Addressing the Senators he asked, "Gentlemen, I wish you would not consider this gentleman's statement." Six weeks later in an open letter to Dr. Anup Singh he accused him, Jagjit Singh, and Shridharani—"two Sikhs and one Hindu"—of trying "desperately to oppose and wreck the hearing" and calling their bills "a dream which you should know will never come true."[121]

The hearing itself ended with an understanding expressed to the Subcommittee on behalf of the Welfare League and the India Associate for American Citizenship that the Langer bill would not be amended. Both wanted the committee to act as soon as possible on that bill. They also announced that they were "in favor of" the Luce and Celler bills.[122]

This was a victory for the Indian nationalists. The Langer-Mubarek-Checker coalition on the other hand had weakened its standing with the U.S. Government by insisting upon special privileges. The Government of India had not come to its help at all. Senator Burton had exposed the coalition's disregard for equality of legal status. The official representative of the Immigration Service had made no secret of his preference for the Luce and Celler bills over the Langer bill and finally most of the public support the coalition secured was for all the bills not for S. 1595 alone. The Government of India's secret service assessed the situation correctly. In a report on Mubarek Ali it wrote that his activities in favor of citizenship rights for Indians had been "overshadowed by those of J.J. Singh who reaped the credit for any success which the campaign had."[123]

The Senate Subcommittee issued no report on the Langer bill. All bills died with the 78th Congress. Elections to the 79th Congress were held on November 7, Dr. Saund was pleased at the results. Los Angeles "will support our bill . . . Their election is a special news for us," he announced.[124]

Three types of bills were introduced in the 79th Congress : (1) Those providing for both a quota and racial eligibility to naturalization. These were the Luce, Celler, and Everett M. Dirksen (R-Ill.) bills in the House, and Joseph H. Ball (R-Minn.) and Arthur Capper (R-Kans.) bills in the Senate; (2) Providing for naturalization of Indian residents prior to July 1, 1924. This was the Lynch bill in the House; (3) Those providing for the naturalization of *all* Indian residents of the United States. These were the Powell bill in the House and the Langer bill in the Senate. Senator Langer's earlier concern for the pre-1924 residents alone had now been taken by Rep. Walter A. Lynch (D-NY).

The hearings were scheduled to start on March 7. N.R. Checker invited the India League to "formulate plans and procedures" to be followed at these hearings in order "to avoid the unpleasant situation that occurred" at the hearings on S. 1595. India League seems to have declined to cooperate and declared its opposition to both the Langer and the Lynch bills.[125]

The March, 1945 hearings were remarkable in several respects—in the breadth and intensity of American and Indian popular support for the Indian nationalists' bills, the friendly concern with which they were followed by the Government of India, the backing received from the highest quarters of the U.S. Government including the President, and the almost total absence of opposition from public witnesses.

The nationwide range of the documentary evidence backing the demands of the India League amounted almost to the dimensions of an overkill. It shocked the Congressional remnants of the age of exclusion. Sudhindra Bose might have remembered the lonely one-page memorandum he had left with the Committee in 1914. He might also have seen not a Raker, a Church or a Camille but Jagjit Singh dominating the hearings, the first Indian spokesman whose pleas were honored by the Congress and the country. Jagjit made history with honors in March, 1945.

The first witness properly enough was Celler himself. Emanuel Celler (D-N.Y.) as a Congressman for over twenty years in 1945 had seen "a lot of causes a-borning and a-dying." He might also have added "undying." As a cause, immigration existed before he came to the Congress, enveloped him as soon as he came and continued to claim his attachment for thirty years so that he "had become identified with the subject." Two of the causes he had witnessed "aborning" were India and Zionism. He cared about them "passionately." Both appeared to him "assertions of independence." Together they became two lodestars which he pursued through two successful Celler bills, one in 1946, the other two years later.[126]

He called his Indian bill "One of my most successful endeavors in the Congress." He could also call it his first successful attack on the Act of 1924 that had been enacted over the protests of Representatives Sabath, Dickstein, LaGuardia and his own to block or curtail the influx of "Orientals," "wops," "dagoes," "Hebrews," "hunkies," and others. Sabath guided the Celler bill through the House. LaGuardia sent a letter of support to Jagjit Singh, while Dickstein fought for his friend's bill in the Committee as well as in the House.[127]

Celler told the Committee that "these bills do for the native(s) of India what you have heretofore done for the natives of China." To grant Indians "our allies" an immigration quota would, in his view. "rob the Axis of their most telling barbed weapon in the battle of psychological warfare."

During the two years of his promotion of India's cause his major theme had been America's trade. "India is a huge untapped reservoir for American goods," he declared. The connection between these bills and trade was goodwill. "The purpose of his bill," he confessed, was to "create goodwill between India and the United States primarily for enlargement of our foreign trade." That was one of his reasons for opposing the Lynch bill—"It would not reach the purpose of my bill," because leaders such as Nehru, Tagore, Gandhi, and Mrs. Vijaylakshmi Pandit would continue to be barred. Hence the "Grant of citizenship to those already here would not create goodwill in India at all." "We must increase our exports remember that" he cautioned all Americans.[128]

Jagjit and India had been befriended by Henry and Clare Boothe Luce in the critical days of 1942. In November Mrs. Luce was elected to the House as a Republican. "We just have to have a champion of India in the House," he wrote to her and suggested she become "India's Pearl Buck." He was not trying to persuade her to shift her literary talent to the interpretation of Indian life but to become closely identified with the cause of India, maybe even including the repeal of the exclusion laws as the author of *The Good Earth* was doing for the Chinese. In March, 1944 she introduced her bill to give the India League's campaign a bipartisan and a conservative character.[129]

She highlighted the restrictive provisions of the bill and justified them on principles of exclusionism. Mindful of " our national, racial and cultural composition" she favoured a low quota because she had "no wish to see my country flooded by peoples" whom it "would be impossible for us to assimilate." She justified her proposed legislation "not so much (as) an immigration bill as a diplomatic and political measure against our present and future enemies." Her purpose was "primarily to help keep India in the columns of our democratic allies."[130]

Mrs. Luce's statement, which in her absence was read by Celler, pointed out that Indians are legally classified "by us as undesirable residents, along with our enemies, the Japanese." Such treatment amounts to "a continued affront to the pride and self-respect of a valuable ally," she believed.

She too highlighted the advantages in trade, saying "Next to Russia and China, India offers us the greatest potentiality for foreign trade during the rest of this century."[131]

The first witness from the church was Dr. Walter W. Van Kirk, secretary of the Federal Council of the Churches of Christ in America. He came to present the views of the Executive Committee of the Federal Council as embodied in a resolution. It was weighty support because the Executive Committee which adopted the resolution was composed of "25 of the larger and more influential (Protestant) denominations of the country." Dr. Van Kirk also reported that resolutions of support had been adopted by seven other religious bodies, that there were opinions of personal support expressed by executive officers of nineteen organizations and by seventeen city and State Councils of churches, and letters of support from editors of many religious publications.

The reasons for support were that "racial discrimination. . . does violence to the Christian view of one humanity under God, is contrary to the democratic principles upon which this country was founded and to proved scientific facts." In reply to Rep. Allen's question, Dr. Van Kirk confessed that he favored repeal of exclusion laws against all Asian countries with which America was at peace. "This insufferable discriminatory legislation must be removed," he concluded.[132]

The next witness from Protestant church was Miss Sue Weddell, executive secretary of the Foreign Missions Conference of North America and secretary of its India Committee. The Conference, she told the committee, consisted of 123 foreign mission boards and agencies in U.S. and Canada doing work overseas. Of these, 58 were doing work in India and made up the membership of her India Committee. Explaining a part of Dr. Van Kirk's statement of the previous day, she testified that the seven bodies which took formal action represented approximately 20,000,000 church members and nineteen other boards and seventeen councils representing almost the total Protestant membership of 40,000,000 in the United States.[133]

John B. Chevalier, secretary, American Asiatic Association put into the record the names of 150 members of the Association that included "chiefly men whose names are well known as managing important business interests in the Far East" including India. He presented the Association's resolution recommending quota and naturalization rights for Indians.[134]

The major argument in favor of trade came from V.A. Dodge, president, Dodge & Seymour of New York who had visited India on business "15 or 16 times" since 1897, the last time in 1936. In his estimate, the Indian businessman "is a man of as fine honor as anyone I have ever done business with . . . He is a man I respect and I dislike to feel that he is discriminated against."[135]

The United States Government's support was presented to the committee by Francis Biddle, the Attorney General, appearing before the committee and through five letters all addressed to Committee Chairman Dickstein and made part of the record. One of the letters was from President Roosevelt.

The earliest of these letters, the one from Acting Secretary of State Joseph Grew, states that "the Department views with favor the passage of" Rep. Celler's bill H.R. 173. Its enactment, he believed, would remove "an outstanding inequity in American immigration and naturalization law and one which causes bitter resentment against the United States by the people of India."[136]

The Attorney General's own letter also endorsed the purpose of H.R. 173 because the present provisions of the law "seem to me to be unwise and unfair." The quota of just 100 per annum he thought," is a sufficient protection to this country against excessive immigration from India." The number of Indian residents of this country who will be eligible for citizenship will not be large because their total number "does not exceed 3896."[137]

In a second letter Joseph Grew informed Dickstein that the State Department "has now received strong representations in support of this legislation" from Sir Girja Shankar Bajpai on behalf of the Government of India and that the American Commissioner to India, New Delhi had warned the Department that "sentiment in India may preclude the extension of reciprocal trade treatment to the United States in the absence of such legislation."[138] Grew's third effort was a statement on his behalf brought to the committee by George V. Allen, chief, Division of Middle Eastern Affairs, Department of State. Referring to India as a "prominent member of the United Nations, the statement complained that "existing barriers against Indians contained in our immigration legislation" hinder efforts to defeat Japanese propaganda and to bring the people of India "into full and enthusiastic cooperation with us in the war." Grew also pointed out that "Declarations such as the Atlantic Charter are unimpressive when no Indian can be naturalized as an American citizen or immigrate into the United States."[139]

On March 13, Chairman Dickstein put in the record President Roosevelt's letter to him dated March 5. Historically the letter has significance as being the first ever signed by a President in support of the Indians' demand for legal equality in the United States. The President regarded this legislation (as proposed in the India League bills) "as important and desirable" [which] "will help us to win the war and to establish a secure peace." India, he said, has rendered "great services" in the war. The existing laws, he observed, "provoke ill-feeling, now serve no useful purpose and are incongruous and inconsistent with the dignity of both our peoples." Looking at the quota of only 100 immigrants a year he saw "no real danger that this small number" will cause problems in search for jobs.[140]

Francis Biddle in the course of his testimony told the committee that H.R. 173 (Celler's bill) "is the bill that on the whole we prefer in the Department." "India is a great and a rising market," he said, adding that "Industrial development in India has grown amazingly fast during the war." He also explained at some length what India had done as fighting ally. The bill seemed to him to be a "wise measure and one that will help our relations from every point of view, and these fellows deserve it."[141]

March 13 was the day which Jagjit had been waiting for. He came to testify and brought a prepared statement with him. He also brought with him resentment for the insinuations that Rep. Allen (D-LA) had been making against India and Indians. With further help from Allen, he was able to pierce the fog of British propaganda and to offer statements—quoted elsewhere already—arising out of the anguish of decades—"We just don't want to be considered inferior" and to ask "Why are we considered not good enough to stay in your country?"

Jagjit Singh started his statement with a rebuttal to Rep. Allen's remark on the first day of the hearing that the good treatment Americans receive in India was the courtesy of the British Government. "It cannot be said that Indians have anything to do with it," Allen had said.[142]

"I can assure you, Sir," Jagjit said, "that when India becomes free we will be able to accord you even a heartier welcome and greater courtesies," because "your past history, your great men. . . your struggles for your liberty are a great inspiration to us in our country."[143]

Next he took up another Allen remark that "the followers of Gandhi are not cooperating at all" in the war.[144] Jagjit accused the "very well organized, well sustained, well financed British propaganda in this country" for creating that impression. "It is not the people of India who are not cooperating... it is the British imperialists who stand in the way," he asserted. Allen interrupted him asking whether the British "frowned on the Indians taking part in the war? is that the substance of your statement?"[145]

At this interruption Jagjit Singh went deeper into his argument than he probably intended to and won at least one supporter in the committee. He replied "not only frowned, but they have definitely discouraged it . . . I am not at all impressed with that figure [of 2,000,000 volunteers in the Indian army] . . . we should have at least 10,000,000 in the armed forces today."

"It does not," he continued, "suit the British to have more Indians in the armed forces" fearing that they "might learn the art of killing" and thus no longer be "quite such nice kind of people to deal with."

"Mr. Allen, Mr. Chairman, the witness is making a very interesting statement and I would like to pursue it just a little further."

"What outward acts do the imperialists do to prevent Indians from taking part in this war?" he asked.[146]

In his reply Jagjit came out with his master hit.

> The people of India wanted this war to become popular in India, as a people's war, so that the man in the street would feel that he was fighting for something. The people of India were asked to fight for the freedom of Czechoslovakia, Belgium, Luxembourg, and so on and so forth, but when the people of India asked, 'How about our freedom?' they were locked up in jail, beaten up or shot at. Therefore, the man in the street just couldn't make sense out of this war. He couldn't understand what he was asked to fight for. Now, if the British had really wanted the people of India to be back of this war they would not put a man like Nehru, the anti-Fascist, anti-Axis, great disciple of democracy, in jail. They would have given him a job recruiting men for armed services, the job of creating propaganda in favor of the Allied cause. But what did they do? They take a man like Nehru on the 9th of August, 1942, and throw him in jail, and today, at this moment, a great

> man who should be sitting in the conferences at Yalta and San Francisco, is rotting in jail in India.
>
> Mr. ALLEN. In other words, if Nehru had had the proper backing and encouragement on the part of the British imperialists, he probably could have organized with ease an army of ten or fifteen million men?
>
> Mr. SINGH. Yes, sir. In other words, what I am trying to suggest is this: that if you are finding any fault with our lack of war effort, then the blame lies at the door of the British imperialists and not on the Indians.[147]

Replying to Rep. Dalliver's question whether "the resentment toward the British imperialists will carry over toward the whole white race," Jagjit assured him that the people of India "have begun to draw the line of demarcation between white and white" so that "the moment an Indian saw the uniform and recognized that it was a United States Army Officer, his attitude changed . . . and by passing this bill you will increase that good will." He warned the Committee, however, that "there is a tremendous amount of excitement in India at the present moment about this bill—it is a front-page news. . . . They are watching this as a test case of the professions of democracy and equality, and the Yalta Conference and the San Francisco conference and the new world order."[148]

A few minutes later, Rep. Allen attempted to trick him with a compromising temptation. He suggested "granting to Hindus, Indians, in the United States, a quota equal to as many Americans who become citizens of India" because "you want the stigma removed, you are not interested in numbers?"

Jagjit answered, "I don't know how that question crops us, Sir." This reply saved him and the League from an embarrassment. Rep. Mason revealed the intended trap. Allen's suggestion, he said, "was only a hypothetical question, because we would have to change our entire quota system and scheme, and change it for other nations too . . . So that was just a hypothetical question to see what was in your mind, I imagine."

"Mr. Singh. Very interesting. All of Mr. Allen's questions are very interesting."[149]

In the course of his remarks Jagjit Singh emphasized the need for better trade relations several times. The passage of this bill, according to him, will encourage trade in many ways. "Even some of your obsolete machines will be very good for us" he assured them. "So you have a beautiful market, an excellent market for unloading a lot of your machinery after the war."[150]

Rep. Edward Oscar McCowan (R-OH) referred to the statement made at the hearings "not by this gentleman, however," that Indians should be given these rights on account of participation in the war. To his mind, he confessed that the statement "carries no argument whatever. They either are or ought to be fighting for their own country," he suggested. Jagjit agreed with him. "I don't think," he replied, "we want this bill to be passed as you would give candy to a child. . . . I agree with you, Sir, that that point is a little too much emphasized."[151]

Jagjit earned praise for his performance, at least from one member of the panel.

"*Mr. Mason*. I think this witness, Mr. Chairman, has proven to be not only the most spectacular but the best witness we have had, not even excepting Mr. Celler himself.

"*Mr. Singh*, Thank you, sir."

"*Mr. Celler*. I agree with you (Laughter)."

Mason was also enthusiastic about selling old machinery to India. He was from Illinois "probably the greatest machine tool center in the world" with about 10 billion worth of machine tools to "be dumped into the ocean" or else disposed of. "And so, for selfish reasons, if I can encourage better relations, I am for it" he announced.[152]

At the end of his remarks Jagjit mentioned that "the American Legion is not against this bill. They have done nothing about it," and he presented a letter from the national commander of the legion. Rep. Allen, taken by surprise, asked "A letter from the national commander of the American Legion?," and wanted to have it read. The commander had written to Jagjit Singh that neither the national conventions nor the executive committee of the Legion had authorized support of this particular legislation and "it is not within my authority as national commander to provide for representation in its behalf . . . ."[153]

The American Federation of Labor was also shown to be not really opposed, but only after a little argument and a little drama. Lewis G. Hines, Legislative Representative of the A.F. of L. appeared to testify against the Luce-Celler bill. He was reading into the record a resolution committing the Federation to remain "unalterably and actively opposed to the lowering of our immigration standards which would permit an influx of the improverished people to our country."

While some members were arguing with Hines over the interpretation of the resolution, Jagjit Singh handed a telegram to the Chairman who read it and asked Hines the date of the resolution he was reading.

The date was November of last year, but here in the telegram the President of the A.F. of L. stated "I would be complelled to give said (Luce-Celler) bill careful thought and study before making any comment regarding our attitude toward the legislation." "Isn't that inconsistent with your statement here?" Dickstein asked Hines who replied, "Not at all," but the Chairman and Rep. Mason agreed that the "telegram from Mr. Green is a telegram on this specific bill which says they have not gone on record either for or against."[154]

Immediately following the Hines fiasco, came the positive testimony of the other wing of the labor movement, the Federation's rival, the C.I.O. Its Director of Education and Research, Kermit Eby, told the Committee that "our position on the Celler-Luce bill is exactly the same as it was on the Chinese Exclusion Act. We think it is fair. We think that the benefits would be extraordinary."[155]

Except for the representative of A.F. of L. whose testimony was cancelled out by the Federation President's telegram, no witness appeared in opposition to the Luce-Celler bill. There, however, were seven letters that Dickstein made part of the record. One was from the president of the American Coalition, three from Junior Order United American Mechanics, two from Daughters of America, and one from a New York resident, all urging defeat of the proposed legislation. They covered two pages in print.[156]

On the India League's side were the President of the United States, his two Cabinet Departments concerned with such legislation, the Agent-General for India and the overwhelming Protestant Church support mentioned in the testimonies of Dr. Van Kirk and Sue Weddell. The documents filed in the record by Jagjit Singh and Emanuel Celler indicated support of two Nobel Prize winners, Albert Einstein and Pearl Buck, prominent Americans, such as Roger Baldwin, Norman Thomas, Rev. John Haynes Holmes and Walter P. Reuther, one past national commander of the American Legion, publisher Henry Luce and Richard J. Walsh, Indian intellectuals, Taraknath Das, Sudhindra Bose, S. Chandrasekhar, and prominent American organizations, the American Civil Liberties Union, and the Fellowship of Reconciliation. Americans who sent letters of personal support were spread over 30 states, the District of Columbia, and Hawaii. They included 80 educaters, 63 Christian and Jewish religious leaders, 32 writers and publishers, 39 businessmen, and 49 persons prominent in other fields.[157]

Even the sponsor and supporters of the rival bills, Representatives Walter A. Lynch (D-N.Y.) and Adam C. Powell (D-N.Y.), Senator Langer, Mubarek Ali, Joseph Tenner, Haridas T. Muzumdar, and Ramlal Bajpai included support for the Luce-Celler bill in their statements. Indeed they almost gave up on their own bills as soon as the other bill got support from the highest official in the land. Mubarek wrote in his statement that since

> the Attorney-General and the President of this country and the Secretary of State have been kind enough to do full justice to India at this time .... As far as we are concerned, the hearings are over. We hope justice will be done.

While Senator Langer was giving his statement, Chairman Dickstein told him that the President had sent a message asking for both quota and naturalization and that the State Department had endorsed the principles of both the Celler-Luce and the Lynth bills. The Senator replied, "I do not know that .... I am glad to hear that. That will obviate the necessity of my going any further, I take it" and ended his statement right there. Langer and Mubarek had started it together and now they ended it together although they would make a final effort the following month.[158]

From the Washington-based National Committee for India's Freedom, only Haridas Muzumdar appeared as a witness on behalf of the Lynch bill, although he also supported the Celler-Luce bill. Dr. Anup Singh sent a written statement through Emanuel Celler. Syud Hossain never appeared at a hearing nor contributed a written statement.

Krishnalal Shridharani's contribution was a magazine article on Indo-American trade possibilities that Celler introduced into the record, but there was no statement from him this time. The National

Committee's direct help in the common cause came in two respects—it persuaded Senator Arthur Copper to introduce his S. 505, a bill identical with other India League bills and secondly its newsletter *Voice of India* continued to publish the news about the progress of the bills.[159]

Samuel Dickstein did real service for the Luce-Celler bill. As Chairman of the committee he asked questions in order to draw out answers helpful to the bill and at one point even explained its advantages over the Lynch bill. He also used hearings on other bills to laud the benefits and posibilities of the proposed repeal. In August 1945 for instance, he attempted to educate a member of the exclusionist McClatchy family that "things have changed since 1926 . . . We are going to try to build a new world" and that two Presidents had sent him messages favoring the grant of a quota to India. To another hostile witness he explained how India "will be one of our greatest customers in postwar, so much that it will keep our factories and workers busy for the next many years."[160]

Open hearings concluded on March 14. Tuesday, March 20, was set for an executive session to vote on the bill. That day the Committee met, debated, and tabled it. Emanuel Celler immediately complained to the President. Sir G.S. Bajpai informed New Delhi. The Government of India called this development "unfortunate."[161]

The New Delhi Government's interest in the legislation had been continuous and sincere. It was to also prove decisive. Without this interest even the American Presidents may have wavered. Both New Delhi and London had compulsions that made this legislation a "most important case." They had to keep the moderate and business interests on their side that on the question of national honor were as insistent as the jailed and gagged extermists.

The Indian Government's and people's advocacy was directed solely toward the passage of the Luce-Celler bills because they alone covered the needs of the Indian people. The Langer and Lynch bills were America's business. The moderate leaders, not being in jail, could express their demands through the press and from the floor of the legislature. The Government, being itself anxious to promote the cause, could afford to give honest assurances, although public opinion often continued to be skeptical of official good faith.[162]

India's Agent-General in Washington had been keeping New Delhi posted on developments and supplied it with copies of bills and of hearings. Proceedings of the hearings on Langer's S. 1595 had been studied in the External Affairs Department with interest. In January, 1945 Sir Bajpai was asked whether progress was likely to be made now that the Presidential and Congressional elections were over. The Agent-General sent texts of all bills introduced in the 79th Congress, attended all hearings, and passed on to New Delhi the U.S. State Department official's concern over the sponsor of the India League's bill being a "left-wing Jew."

The March hearings were studied in detail by the Secretaries in the External Affairs Department. It was noted that the war argument "has not been well received in many quarters" in the Congress, that Representative Allen appeared to be "the bitterest opponent of these bills on the Committee although he is, of course, supported by others" and that Jagjit Singh "puts his case cleverly, using the probable commercial advantages to accrue to the U.S. as his *principal* argument."[163]

The U.S. Government support that was expressed at these hearings gave encouragement to India's official representative but also posed a challenge for him. "The State Department statement was strongly in our favor," Bajpai told New Delhi. The Attorney General, he said, "made a forceful speech" and "we are especially indebted to him for having persuaded the President to send letter to the Chairman of the Committee, supporting India's claims." He assessed that a "good beginning has been made [but] vigilance on our part essential to ensure that possible set backs do not produce relaxation of effort on the part of administration." Consequently he could not relax in his own efforts.

Earlier, during his career as a high official in the British-Indian administration, Bajpai had been publicly criticized for lack of sympathy for the interests of Indian emigrants, once by Mahatma Gandhi himself.[164] When he was sent to Washington D.C., the India League newsletter mentioned him as "an expert on the status of emigrated Indians" and hoped he would "render great service by safeguarding the interests of the nationals of India in this country."[165]

His actions during the Cripps and the Quit India crises earned him the reputation of being "very diligent in carrying out the desires of his British masters." In matters concerning immigration, however, the "desires" of the British were made in India and by Indians. He, therefore, brought to the purpose of the Luce-Celler bill the same diligence which he brought to his other official performances, which may have been distasteful to the nationalists.[166]

He started helping as soon as Indians in America started helping themselves. After Senator Langer returned East from his tour of the Indian colonies in the West in March 1944, Bajpai invited him to a lunch at his official residence. To the Senator's surprise the Agent-General was "wholeheartedly in support of this (S. 1595) bill." By the end of June, however, as Bajpai wrote to Mubarek Ali, that support had been extended to "bills now before Congress" that also included the Luce and Celler bills.[167]

Sir Girja's acceptance of the nationalist position on immigration and naturalization did not waver even under severe challenges to him both as an official and as a father. In August 1944 India League's friends in Congress proposed to declare him "persona non grata for endeavoring to "influence the views of the American press regarding India." At about the same time his eldest son, Uma Shankar seems to have rebelled and become Jagjit Singh's protege. "He has torn himself away from the official atmosphere of his father and is determined to serve India," Jagjit told Ambassador William Phillips. There was gallantry on both sides, however. Recognizing that the father also continued "to serve India," the League President gave him credit "for securing this letter (of March 5, 1945) from the President . . . I must say that at least in this instance Sir Girja has been of great help."[168]

The Agent-General was due to leave the country on his entitled leave. Attorney General Biddle advised against it—he might be required to inspire a few editorials or to convince opponents and wavering supporters about the united demand in India when the bill came to the Rules Committee "composed of reactionary Democrats" and on the House floor. Lord Halifax also advised him to stay because "Should bill fail here during my absence, both Government of India and I might come in for criticism in India for my absence," Bajpai told New Delhi.[169]

He decided to "postpone" his leave, convinced that process of legislation through *both houses* would be over soon though not in ''less than two months''. It took more than seven times that long. In his next telegram six days later the Agent- General reported : "Immigration and Naturalization Bill has struck its first major SNAG."

At the executive session held on March 20 a combination of Southern Democrats and isolationist Republicans spearheaded by

Robert Ramspeck (D-GA), the Democratic Whip, voted 10 to 6 to table the bill. The Government of India saw in this maneuver the hand of the U.S. Government to force New Delhi to revive negotiations on the treaty of trade. It also blamed the propagadists visiting the United States who "harping on subordination . . . tend to cause India to be taken on their own valuation." Anti-Semitism, absence of any pronouncement directly from the British Government in support of the bill, the possible American impression that the bill did not represent a *united* Indian demand, may have been among the factors which persuaded some members to vote with the exclusionists.[170]

Reaction in India was bitter. "Is this a foretaste of things to come at San Francisco ?" asked the *Free Press Journal* and commented that the vote of the House committee "reflected only racial antagonism." The business community expressed "keen disappointment" that might lead to "unfortunate repercussions" in regard to America's attitude towards "problems of racial equality." At a meeting of his Executive Council the Viceroy of India drew attention to the subject saying, "he realised the dropping of the proposed bills had caused disappointment in India."[171]

Emanuel Celler and Jagjit Singh, though somewhat shaken and embarrassed by the unexpected blow, declared their determination to pursue the fight. Particular care seems to have been taken to keep California active and optimistic by intensifying close personal contacts.[172]

The existence of a strong opposition to the repeal of Indian exclusion cannot be denied although luckily that opposition had not registered itself prominently in the record of the hearings. The A.F. of L. and the veterans were neutral; California, the former home of anti-Asianism, was virtually silent. The magic lay in the insignificance of the quota figure that made the repeal arithmetically a formality. The bill would be released from the committee once the supporters of the formality—the President, the Government of India, and the British Government, reiterate their determination so as to wean away from the exclusionists the moderate colleagues they had won over temporarily to their side.[173]

It took over three months to bring the bill back into the legislative process. Several people helped. Celler appealed to two Presidents, both Roosevelt and Truman appealed to the truant legislators; Biddle and Grew continued to recommend support for the bill. The Government of India's Agent-General Bajpai did much foot work and deserves credit fc· helping to revive the bill. He alone was in touch with all three Governments—the Indian, the British, and the United States—on this issue. His plan was ready the day the bill was tabled. It was helpful that India had its own official representative in Washington during these two critical years and that the official was an Indian. A British Ambassador would have lacked the motivation of personal involvement. Had it not been for President Roosevelt's death and the problems that the new Administration was having with the Congress in other areas of foreign policy, the crisis would probably have ended two months earlier than it did. Several days may also have been lost because Lord Halifax waited for a printed copy of the Hearings before putting the British endorsement of the bill in writing.[174]

The day the bill was tabled, Sir Girja met Attorney General Biddle who advised him to see the Secretary of State and the President if necessary. Clearly Biddle was hinting that the matter had become more a subject of foreign policy than of mere immigration. The Agent General took the hint and never saw Biddle again while the crisis lasted. He did see the Undersecretary of State and also explored with Ambassador Halifax the "possibility of invoking support of His Majesty's Government."[175]

He met Grew on March 24 who assured him of the Department's "continued and active sympathy" and told Bajpai "confidentially" that he had recommended to the President a fresh initiative in the matter." The Undersecretary indeed had written to the President a day before Bajpai saw him, and he was "quite definite" that it was not necessary for Bajpai to see the President.[176]

The President had already been apprised of the tabling the day it happened. Emanuel Celler wrote him a letter marked "Personal and Confidential" addressing him as "Dear Franklin" and signing as "Mannie." He complained against Congressman Ramspeck (D-GA) "who apparently was the spearhead of opposition." He assured the President that being the Democratic whip in the House he "would hearken to some importuning from your goodself." He also suggested that Speaker Rayburn and majority leader McCormack "be informed of your views." The president wrote to Ramspeck but probably never had time to contact the Congressional leaders. He had, however, "fully concurred" in the Grew memoranda. Bajpai thought of asking Truman for help just three days before he succeeded Roosevelt. "As a Southern

Democrat . . . he may be able to influence conservative elements" in his Party, he hoped.[177]

In mid-April he invited Edward J. Shaughnessy to lunch and told him that "as soon as the printed hearings on the House bills are received, Lord Halifax will send a letter to Dickstein showing that the British have no objection to the principle involved [in the bills]. At the end of April Bajpai wished to start canvassing support of the House Committee members, but Speaker Rayburn advised him through Dean Acheson to let hostility to the bill calm down for another "two or three" weeks. A significant step toward that process was taken on May 3 when Halifax sent his letter to Acting Secretary of State, Joseph Grew. He assured him on behalf of His Majesty's Government in the United Kingdom that it "would welcome enactment of a law on the lines of the Bill as a gesture of friendship to India which had played, and is playing, so important a part in the war."[178]

From now on matters started to move forward because this was the letter that American offical and non-official circles had wanted to see—a letter of endorsement from His Majesty's Government.

Representative Allen had raised the issue at the hearings asking Attorney General Biddle : "Are we liable to run into a little confusion with Great Britain ?" and thinking he had stepped upon sensitive diplomatic ground he added : "Perhaps you would prefer not to answer that." "Not at all" replied Biddle, "I think Great Britain would welcome this." But he had nothing concrete from "Great Britain" to show the committee. Celler tried to help saying : "The *British Government in India* favors the legislation" but that apparently was not enough.

The issue also came up at the hearing on Langer's bill S. 236. Senator Maybank wondered "why anyone would presume that England would not [endorse the East Indian bills in the house]?" Shaughnessy explained to him that when dealing with the Chinese exclusion "we were dealing with an independent nation whereas India is a possession of Great Britain. You see the difference ?" The Senator was still sure "they [the British] would not dare interfere." But some Congressmen, however, would modify the existing law only after receiving an assurance from Britain. According to Dickstein's version of what took place in the execution session, the bill was lost in the committee "solely upon" the feeling "that this legislation might embarrass the British Government."[179]

The Halifax letter acted as a propelling force on the U.S. Government. It persuaded Attorney General Biddle to broach the subject of the India bills with the new President for the first time. He sent him a copy of the Roosevelt letter and suggested that the President write a letter to Dickstein "urging the passage of the bill" and added, "I believe a word from you to the House leaders would insure it."[180]

President Truman took up the matter from where his predecessor had left it in his letter of March 5. He told Dickstein of his "agreement with the position set forth in that letter." This "gracious intercession" as Bajpai called it, was followed three weeks later by securing an "O.K." from Ramspeck. The Speaker too seems to have been "talked to" on bahalf of the President so that by mid- June he was "actively in our favor." Dean Acheson summed up the situation for Bajpai—"prospects of our Bill in the House are quite hopeful." The New Delhi Government sent its Agent-General a letter of appreciation for his efforts.[181]

At an executive session on June 14 the committee heard Mrs. Luce and Ambassador William Phillips and then reversed itself, voted 9 to 6 to report the bill to the House for favor of passage. Five members signed a Minority Report that Congressman Allen wrote. It bore the imprint of his style of reasoning and included all his arguments against bills that "further break down our immigration laws." The number two officer in the External Affairs Department, New Delhi, commented : "The minority adhere strictly to an obvious ignorance of the most elementary facts about India, even though prepared to express their views on the question with so much emphasis."[182] Whatever the depth of their ignorance the opponents had placed the fate of the bill in serious jeopardy for several months. Both Celler and Jagjit Singh issued bold fighting statements, but there was a limit to the fighting either one could do. Not Celler but only a President of the United States and a Democratic President could convert Ramspeck. For Jagjit Singh it must have seemed like a national insult that the key to the situation lay with a hated former Viceroy of India now the British Ambassador in Washington. He would probably have been embarrassed to learn that the Halifax letter was the result of Bajpai's efforts. His own presence in California for the San Francisco Conference, however, had enabled him to establish new friendships and maintain the morale of the Indian community over the stalled citizenship issue.[183]

When the stalemate was resolved. the League morale was high. London. New Delhi. and Washington were on its side. and the opponents in the committee had been defeated. Chairman Dickstein now sided with the India bill more openly, Jagjit Singh's friend, Ambassador William Phillips, had sopken "very strongly" in bahalf of the bill in the executive session of June 14. His name carried much weight.[184]

Meanwhile a hearing on the Langer bill S. 236 had taken place on April 26 and had ended without advancing the prospects of its success. Besides Mubarek Alis' alleged "selfish" reasons, there might have been a more valid motive for insisting on this hearing. At the hearings held in March, Mubarek, Langer, Lynch, and Powell all had testified to the effect that their bills had to be kept alive in case the Celler bill were not enacted. The heavy support this bill received gave them faith. When the bill was tabled, their faith was shaken. Demand for "half a loaf" had to be revived, hence the hearing. Bajpai thought that "nothing willl come of this move. Full Senate Committee will probably reconsider Langer's bill and then decide to postpone decision" until the House decides about the Celler bill. In fact this was the last time that the Congress attended to any legislative proposal that conflicted with the India League bill.[185]

Several months previously, the Attorney General had warned Sir Girja that the House Rules Committee was dominated by "reactionary Democrats" who might keep the bill there "either through active opposition or reluctance to get on with it." H.R. 3517 the Luce-Celler bill was to come before the rules committee on September 25. To ward off the possibility of delaying tactics, Emanuel Celler wrote to Charles G.Ross, President Truman's secretary suggesting that the Speaker and the Majority leader be informed that "this is an Administration bill." The President replied "you discuss the matter" with those two House leaders "and I will speak to them at the next meeting of the Big Four."[186]

The Rules Committee, however, reported favorably the motion for consideration by the House. G.S. Bajpai felt there was "good reason to hope that motion will be adopted." He also told New Delhi that the "plan" was to bring the bill to the House floor between October 8 to 10 "when all its supporters are likely to be present."

The date selected was October 10. Already on October 2 India League had sent to every member of the House a memorandum in favor of the bill for his or her consideration and support. Jagjit sent a few notes to help Rep. Fulton prepare his speech and met Rep. Noah Mason a few days before the debate.[187]

When the debate opened, 285 members were present. Some Indian princes were in the gallery. Six members of the committee including two signers of the Minority Report were absent.[188] The opening volley was fired by the veteran Congressman Adolph Joseph Sabath (D-IL), an immigrant from Czechoslovakia who had led the fight against exclusionists and restrictionists in 1917 and 1924.[189]

Knowing from experience that opponents would "create an issue and shout" about standard of living, wages and competition for jobs, Sabath forewarned the House that "their opposition to the pending measure is due to unwarranted and unjustificable prejudice." He inserted a statement he had obtained from Edward J. Shaughnessy explaining that this bill was not as broad as the Chinese bill, quoted two opening parapraphs from Jagjit Singh's memorandum submitted at the hearings and "a petition signed by many outstanding American citizens . . . all of whom urge and endorse the enactment of this legislation."

Noah M. Mason (R-IL), the ranking Republican on the committee, expressed himself "wholeheartedlhy" in favor of this bill "for the same reasons" as he favored the Chinese bill. He drew attention to "the effort Stalin is making today through his Communist agents" in China and India. "We must do what we can to offset his efforts in these two countries" he advised. The Cold War had begun. Both India and China need to buy machinery and machine tools "which we can supply." He forecasted that "these two countries constitute the greatest potential market for American goods for the next 50 years."

Rep. Dirksen (D-IL), sponsor of one of the India League bills, offered five categories of reasons why he favored adoption of the bill. The moral reason—to lift the stigma of inferiority in order to develop good will; the economic reason, the great trade opportunities with India and "they have the money with which to buy." The political reason : India is going to have her freedom some day. America has friendly diplomatic relations with her, "why not promote it by the development of further good will ?" he suggested. The fourth reason was ethnic. "The Indian is a Caucasian," he said. The last one was language. English was the accepted language of the Indian legislature and he was "amazed" at the number of people in India who spoke the English language. The "confraternity of language" was, therefore another reason why he pleaded for adoption of the bill. "Finally, permit me to say they are people of culture . . . . some of the finest things that have ever been written upon the parchment of ancient literature come from India."

Rep. Dickstein briefly described the history of the bill after President Roosevelt wrote him the letter of March 5. He urged the passage of the bill not only in the interest of our trade but "also, it could be one of the finest gestures we could make toward millions of people."

Edward O. McCowan (R-OH), a member of the Committee, opposed the bill saying he was scared of the trade argument : America "opened Japan up for trade about 1854. We sold her everything with which to make war, from gas to scrap and got it shot back at us . . . Shall we start that with India ?" he wondered. He also argued that the right to enter a country or to become a citizen is a privilege and, therefore, "no injustice and no discrimination can be correctly charged." As regards the proposed quota of 100, he asked, "Do you remember the story of the break in the dyke ?" He wondered, "Why do we always have to be doing something for other countries to keep them sweet ?" This bill proposed to admit only 100 but "It may be only a hundred for another, then another, and again another" and finally "a law that will let the deluge in" he forecasted.

Nobody was planning a deluge, but the bill's opponents were not always wrong. Rep. Allen, for instance, was correct in most of his counterarguments. Mrs. Luce had to admit that the war argument no longer applied after the war ended and that the supposed trade benefits argument was "nonconclusive." She also agreed that if too many Asians were permitted to enter the country, they could "undermine our way of life, our living standards, our form of religion."

Allen was right though often blunt. "India," he said, "is nothing in the world but a province of Great Britain." The Celler bill, he pointed out, "was approved by the British Ambassador. The British will not give the Indians or Hindus what they want, but they tell us to do this." About help in the war, Indians should be under "everlasting gratitude to us because India was saved from the Japs largely through the effort, the toil, sweat and blood of American manhood."

Instead of bringing the Indians here in order to lift the stigma of inferiority, "Send the Gospel to them" he advised. In response to Dirksen's "moral reason," he urged that "we go to the greatest force this world had ever seen for right and morality—the Gospel of Christ—it will establish a bond of friendship for our country that will stand the tests of wars."[190] He reminded the House that the bill had been tabled by 10 to 6, but resurrected after "all the pulling and the pressure and wirepulling and everything else that could be done" only by 6 to 9. He urged his colleagues to "read between the lines."

Allen's major concern was to preserve the exclusion laws. The number in the quota was not the issue. "It is the principle . . . . I tell you my friends when you break down the principle you have gone far. They argue that this number is small and they will lull you to sleep with that argument . . . and if you want the wall to crumble down and let them come in, go on and do it but it is not going to be done with my vote," he told the House.

Although Allen was concerned with the laws of the past, Mrs. Luce drew the members' attention to "years ahead" when, according to experts on the Far East including Owen Lattimore, a great deal of "shopping" will be going on among the Asian people for an "ideology which promises them most in terms of their own economic and spiritual security." She believed that in "a very important way" Soviet Russia "appears to offer an advantage over us and that is the vital matter of racial discrimination." She called this fact "a most potent fact in the world," and concluded that "the colored peoples of Asia . . . will be inclined, all other forces being equal, to do their idological shopping in Moscow." If that should happen, India "with its vast potential industrial power, India, with its rich soul and unexplored fund of spiritual power . . . might be lost for all time foreseeable to the family of free, liberty- loving nations."

She warned that America had lost her former "moral leadership" in Asia and was coming to be viewed "as a nation of dollar imperialists . . . of hypocritical coexploiters . . . [and as a country which] does not practice what it preaches abroad." The loss of this leadership, she characterised as "a very great tragedy for our nation" but the leadership could be regained if "we stick with principles instead of trying to follow expediency."

Contrary to Allen's view of the "principle" *established* earlier in the century, Mrs. Luce believed that a principle had in fact been *abandoned.* By establishing Asian exclusion the "principle we abandoned . . . was a great American principle, perhaps the greatest of all that "all men . . . are judged alike not only in the eyes of God, but in the eyes of Uncle Sam . . . [and] the Hitlerian principle that we put in its place, was the principle of racial discrimination." She urged that this principle existing within the quota system must be removed. In case this is not done "we will turn over a billion of the world's population solidly against us."

Emanual Celler attempted to underline the conservative nature of his bill. There was already a quota for India. Not one person is to be added to that quota. The less than 4000 Indian residents "are already assimilated here, they are a part and parcel of our life" and only a small number "probably only 50 or 60" will come in yearly. But this he wanted to "underscore and emphasize"—passage of the bill will create great psychological and economic benefits for America and remove a "sinister bar" that has existed against them for years. Failure of passage "would involve a terrible and terrific let-down in India."

Rep. Bennett (R-MO) was afraid that "the camels" nose was under the tent." The Chinese law had "let down the bars" and is now being used "as a precedent for the Indians." Advocates of this policy, in his view "are travelling with the same crowd of no-good do-gooders and downfallen-uplifters who think this country should be run as a free-lunch counter for the whole world."

He advised that we should not "let floods of people come into America with alien ideologies and with the avowed intention of overthrowing this Government" and further he aked "Why should our war heroes have to compete [for American jobs] with foreign people whose necks they have saved ?"

George Anthony Dondero (R-MI) told the House about a discussion he had the previous day with a high American official just returned from India. The official he said, was "very much disturbed" at the "deep penetration" that an ideology opposed to democracy had obtained in the Orient. "For the reason" and from what he learnt from the debate, Dondero said, "I am going to support this bill." He also described, to the surprise of some members, his failure so far to obtain the naturalization of Dr. Kameshvar Nath Kathju.

Gearhart (R-CA) invented a novel reason for opposing the bill. The quota for India would only be 75 for a population of 400,000,000 whereas Great Britain's quota was 65,721 for a population of only 45,000,000. Instead of promoting friendship the bill, "will operate, I verily believe, just to the contrary [because the Hindus] are going to see the very thinly veiled insult which it carries."

According to the House majority leader McCormack (D-MA), there being no area of the world "more important to the United States at the present time than the Far East" the attitude of the people of India toward the United States is therefore of "direct and important concern to my country." However the principle of racial discrimination in American immigration laws is "most bitterly resented [there] and makes us highly vulnerable to anti-American propaganda." Instead of Japan "some other country or countries for their own interests are using it against our best interests at the present time." He professed to make this statement "not only as my personal opinion but on the authority of the officials of our Government."

John M. Robsion (R-KY) intervened saying that Indians

> were not very much in the war. It was Mr. Gandhi who sat down in the grass and agreed that they would not fight, even though the Japanese threatened to come in there and take their country .... Now, what can we get out of a country like that? he wondered.

Leroy Johnson (R-Calif.) was from "the part of the country that has 95 percent of these Indians" and was elected to represent Stockton where the Sikhs had their religious center. He did not profess to favor the bill for trade or to help Indians or the Hindus but because on this occasion "Congress has a chance to pass a law which may be very minor in its significance at the time but which may have tremendous significance in the future."

He thought "there might be another great war brewing in the future" the seeds of which were planted by Japan. "It is the seed of revolution and war against the white man and against imperialism" he said. The seed had not hurt America but "It is taking root" in some parts of Asia. The American policy with reference to the Philippines—the policy of giving political freedom to a racial, geographical, or economic unit when it shows that "its people can handle their own affairs"—is a "very humane policy . . . the model every country that has an imperial system ought to follow." The war may not come during our lifetimes but our

> grandchildren may live in a day when this great racial war will develop. The white race constitutes a very small fraction of the people of the earth. They would have no chance against a billion or two billion black, yellow and brown men if they were properly armed and industrialized. To avoid this, it seems to me, is the basic reason for this law.

Looking at the cost of the last war in men and money, he expressed his opinion frankly that "the white race cannot stand any more wars like this." "A racial war," he continued, "would be deadly, more bitter, more vicious than any war the world has ever seen." But war can be avoided by means of "a small and friendly gesture that will not injure us." That gesture was provided for in the bill—allow them a quota to enter America. Thereby "we can plant the seed of friendship now which in the future will be a valuable thing to us." He knew that Indians living on the Pacific coast "cannot be amalgamated and they will not be amalgamated," but the bill will indicate to the people "out in the Orient that the American white man is not going to discriminate against him because of color or race." He concluded with the belief that "this law will pay big dividends in the long future ahead of us."

Dickstein intervened saying he had not intended to quote but called attention to the fact that Ambassador William Phillip had "urged upon the Committee that it is very essential for the interest of this country that the pending legislation be passed."

Frederick Smith (R-OH) joined the debate while the bill was being read for amendment under the five-minute rule. Probably to arouse curiosity he asked for unanimous consent to speak for an additional five minutes. He announced his intention to vote against the bill not on racial grounds but for what he called "other reasons." One of the reasons he gave was "a movement that is being undertaken in India to communize that country." He had discovered a pamphlet that proved it. He told the House that "it was difficult for me to obtain a copy of this pamphlet as apparently it is being suppressed in the United States." He did not say by whom and why.[191]

This communist movement seemed to be unique as regards the soil from which it was growing. "The mevoment does not spring from the bourgeois or the working people." he said. "It is fruit of the industrial leaders of India," among whom he named seven of the top men in the industrial, commercial and the financial world of India. He called J. R. D. Tata, head of the Tata industrial empire, as "one of the top leaders of this communist movement at the present time."

Probably the pretense for Smith's allegation was that they were *planning* an economic program under the leadership of the central government of an India expected to be free soon, and planning is communistic. It was a good try to turn the House against the bill. Celler told Smith he had "unitentionally made an agregious error," because that would be equivalent to saying that J. Pierpont Morgan or Edward Stattinius were communists.

Walter H. Judd (R-MN) delivered a brilliant oration in which like McCormack and Johnson before him he connected the terms of the bill to America's enlightened self-interest in the sphere of world politics. According to him the Act of 1924 that made race the basis of exclusion made war between America and Japan inevitable "if we were not willing to change it." He called it "an utterly needless slap in the face." The Japanese Ambassador warned there would be "grave consequences." "The Americans at Bataan and Iwo Jima would admit there have been rather "grave consequences." In his opinion the results sought by the Act of 1924 "could have been achieved by legislation such as we are considering today."

He asked the House "to look at the good results on the other side"—the Filipinos treated on basis of racial equality stood by America in the war. The effect of 1943 Act on Chinese morale was "extraordinary." "There are," he said, "a billion people in Asia . . . in the process of diciding whether to go with the communists or with all the nonwhite people, or with the democracies. Which way they go depends largely on our wisdom and our justice. Let us not be the ones who draw the color line and force them into that bloc," he pleaded.[192]

Charles Marion La Follette (R-IA) was "astounded" that anyone would assume that "a resident of India *ipso facto* is a communist." To him that assumption was "the most tragic and silly" red herring "that has been drawn across this legislation." He also roundly took to task those [presumably former America Firsters and isolationists] who thought Japan would never go to war with the United States and "should now arize and criticize Gandhi." He hoped that his fellow legislators will understand the fact that by this bill "we are removing a stigma which we as a white people and Caucasians . . . inflicted upon other Caucasian peoples too long ago."

After a few more speeches the Committee of the Whole House rose. the Speaker resumed the Chair and the bill was read the third time. At this stage Rep. Allen offered a motion to recommit and demanded a division which he lost by 47 to 99. He objected to the vote on the ground that no quorum was present. The Speaker agreed. Absent members were notified. The question was taken again and the motion to recommit was lost by 83 to 207 with 141 not voting.

The Speaker put the question on the passage of the bill. John Rankin (D-MS) asked for a division. The House refused the request and passed the bill with voice vote which the India League thought was "overwhelming." If all those who voted 'Nay' on the motion to recommit favored the bill's passage, then clearly the bill had been adopted by almost 70 percent majority.

Of the 21 members of the committee, 12 voted 'nay', 5 voted with the 'yeas' and 4 'not voting'. Ramspeck was among the 12. From the California delegation of 23, only one voted to recommit, 4 'not voting', 16 voted 'Nay', 2 were absent. Both sponsors of the limited bills, Walter A. Lynch and Adam C. Powell Jr. voted 'Nay'. One of the Congresssmen who voted 'Nay' was Lyndon B. Johnson. Representative Mundt and Lesinki were absent, but several other Congressmen who had been attracted to India and the India League in recent years were present to help the bill's passage. Among them were Walter Judd (R-MN), James G. Fulton (R- PA), Carl Anderson (R-MN), Jerry Voorhis (D-CA), Louis Ludlow (D- IND) and Vito Marcantonio (D-NY).[193]

The next stop for the bill was the Senate. Here the Immigration Committee was, according to Jagjit Singh, "the proverbial graveyard of all such bills." and according to Bajpai's information, "both slow and unfriendly." The committee held up the bill for over seven months. "Five or six weeks" more and the bill would have been dead and would have had to be brought back to life in the next Congress.[194]

Six members of the committee were from the South. Five of them had supported repeal of Chinese exclusion. One of them, Senator Charles O. Andrews (D-FL) had not only sponsored the bill, but had become its "chief advocate in Committee and on the floor" of the Senate. But the world situation had since changed. The Senators looked upon India from a different perspective. The war was over. Chinese repeal had been accepted by the Southern Democrats as a war measure. Senator Russell (D- GA), Chairman of the Committee, had visited China, discussed the matter with Chiang Kai-Shek, and learnt how strongly the Chinese wanted this action. He had met President Roosevelt who may have asked him to help the bill. He was also presumably influenced by his esteem for Senator Andrews.[195]

Another important factor had been the attitude of the American Legion. Its California branch adopted a repeal resolution with the help of Col. Louis Johnson, formerly President Roosevelt's personal representative in New Delhi, past national commander of the Legion, and a close friend of Jagjit Singh. The Legion's national convention did not adopt a resolution of support, but neither did it come on record as opposing it—a situation similar to the one Jagjit took advantage of at the Luce-Celler bill hearings a few months later.[196]

At its national executive committee meeting, however, after hearing Senator Russell on behalf of repeal and with the helpful activity of Louis Johnson, the repeal resolution was adopted. This action of the American Legion "proved an important factor in obtaining the support of a few hesitating Senators."[197] Jagjit Singh, as we shall see later, attempted to use his friendship with Louis Johnson to win Senator Russell to the side of the India bill.

The Chinese and the Indian bills had several features in common. Both had disarmed conservative legislators and traditionally exclusionist organizations like the veterans and labor by asking for small quotas only. They were supported by the U.S. Government and the governments at home and had been approved by the House. The Indian bill, however, labored under grave disadvantages. The war having ended, it could no longer be pushed as an emergency measure. The Indian repeal would, therefore, be a deliberate post-war decision to continue the American retreat from Asian exclusion. Apparently Senator Russell was not agreeable to accepting this situation.

Richard B. Russell was in his thirteenth year as a Senator, more as a Southerner than as a Democrat. "I am not ashamed of being a southern Democrat," he once confessed on the Senate floor. "I am proud that I am a southerner and I glory in the history and traditions of the people of the South. However, there are times when I do not boast very loadly about being a Democrat." In recent years he had fought for the southern agenda—to get rid of the Fair Employment Practices Committee and to keep the poll tax.

These qualifications added to the chairmanship of the Immigration Committee promised to make him a more destructive opponent of the bill than Rep. Allen had been in the Committee and the House.[198]

Pressures from several directions were being built up to persuade the reluctant Senator to move the bill out of the committee. Bajpai had told New Delhi in October that while the Senate Immigration committee was "unfriendly," there were the President and Secretary of State "on credit side," and "I am trying to enlist active support of both." Celler also felt that enlisting support had become necessary. Hardly two weeks after the passage of his bill in the House, he found cause to complain to the President that the bill was "apparently having hard sledding in the Senate," that the Chairman, "may be loath to act" and consequently, he was afraid that the bill might "be stymied unless something is done by your good self." The President wrote to "Dear Dick" that the passage of the bill was "necessary to help our foreign policy in the Near East." But Russell wouldn't budge.[199]

In December an editorial in *Christian Century* complained that even after two months the Senate Committee on Immigration "has made no sign that it knows this action [passage of the bill] by the House requires any action by the Senate." It warned that "unless pressure is brought to bear on the Committee . . . there is grave danger that the bill will be allowed to die in Committee."[200] In January Undersecretary of State Dean Acheson and George V. Allen of the State Department appeared before Senators Burnet R. Maybank, James O. Eastland and Homer Ferguson, all members of the Immigration Committee and urged passage of the bill.

The lack of progress was also becoming a matter of concern for Indian legislators. P.N. Sapru, a member of the Council of State, asked the Indian Government in February "the steps, if any, they have taken to press on the United States administration, the desirability of passing the Celler bill at an early date ?" He was told that the Agent General "continues to represent" to the U.S. Government "The importance to Indo-American relations of the early enactment of the Bill." There was a similar question by Seth Gobind Das in the Legislative Assembly.[201]

Definite progress was recorded in March when the bill was referred to a Subcommittee consisting of Senators Maybank, Eastland, Ball, and Ferguson with the young and relatively new member Senator Fulbright acting as it Chairman. The Subcommittee held a hearing on

April 15. Mrs. Luce, Rep. Celler, and Dean Acheson appeared in favor of the bill. Attorney General Tom Clark sent a letter approving it. Celler later learned that the subcommittee "reported the bill favorably to the full committee." *India Today* reminded its readers that the main hurdle had yet to be overcome. In a private letter, Jagjit Singh named the hurdle. He told his friend James Callahan that Senator Russell "is not in favor of this bill, and of course we expect that he will try and stall it . . . . However, we are marshalling our forces and are trying to bring as much pressure upon Senator Russell as possible."[202]

What could have been more "possible" than the President himself? The day after Jagjit's letter to Callahan, Emanuel Celler informed President Truman of the sub-committee's favorable action and reminded him "to contact Senator Russell and others of the Immigration Committee to the end that they may accept this bill, which is in a sense an Administration bill since it seeks to carry out Administration policy." The President did the best he could. "I had a conference with Senator Russell," he wrote back, "and it was not a very satisfactory one. I have also discussed the matter (of the bill) with the Leaders of the Senate, Senator (Alben W.) Barkley and Senator (Kenneth) McKellar. Both of them have agreed to discuss the matter with Senator Russell . . . he is the stumbling- block."[203]

He had accepted the repeal of Chinese exclusion "during the stress of war" and "as an exception to our restrictive immigration laws" when "it was strongly implied that it would not be considered as a precedent for other legislation." From this standpoint the Senator must have felt himself justified in defying President Truman's wishes and holding on to whatever was left of Asian exclusion.[204] In less than a month, however, the Senator came around and decided to place the subcommittee report before the full committee. He admitted later that the forces back of the bill were "great" but which ones forced him to change his stance he did not reveal. Several forces were at work.[205]

The two Senate leaders may have "discussed the matter" with him. He had seen his southern colleagues, James O. Eastland (D-MS) and Burnet R. Maybank (D-SC) with members of the Fulbright subcommittee permitting the bill to be reported favorably without even a minority report. This may have indicated a mellowing of the opposition and also that in the eyes of some of the Senators who had supported the repeal of Chinese exclusion, the arguments for repeal were as valid during the war as after it. The Senator's own inner conviction to which he later confessed in the Senate that "there was much to commend favorable action" on H.R. 3517 may have restrained him from letting the House-approved bill die in the Senate Committee.[206]

Jagjit Singh had obtained from Col. Louis Johnson a letter on this subject addressed to Senator Russell. In case this letter was ever used it may have at the least warned the Senator that his friend was seriously interested in the bill's passage.[207] Finally we have to take into account Jagjit Singh's claim that Russell agreed to bring the bill before the full committee when during a face to face confrontation he accused the Senator of sitting on the bill and thus not giving its proponents a fair fight. If his claim can be substantiated, this particular lobbying venture of the man who made a successful career out of such ventures, can be called the most decisive of all. By accusing a southern aristocrat of violating the code of chivalry of his Cavalier ancestors, Jagjit allegedly provoked him into taking an action that he had declined to take even at the President's request and thereby precipitate the enactment of H.R. 3517. Russell's *Rajputi* maryada did the bill immense good. [See : Appendix IV.]

Whatever the pressures and from whichever side they came, the Senator at last submitted the bill to his Committee. On June 25, 1945, eleven days after the Senate had adopted the bill, Russell revealed that the bill had been reported to the Senate "over my opposition." Considering the fact that no other member of the Committee voiced opposition to the bill on the Senate floor he may well have been in a minority of one at the Committee meeting.[208]

The bill had been reported to the Senate on June 10. The proceedings of June 14 contain these words : "The bill (H.R. 3517) . . . was considered, ordered to a third reading, read the third time, and passed." The struggle that began exactly two and a half years ago with Senator Langer's sponsorship of bill S. 1595 ended in the Senate without debate with Langer, Fulbright, and Russell all absent. America had agreed to repeal an Asian people's exclusion even in peacetime.[209]

The bill H.R. 3517 and a bill to authorize the naturalization of Filipinos were passed by the Senate, one following the other, the same day on the call of the Celendar.[210] The Fillipinos were eager to have their bill signed by the President before July 4, the day their country was to become independent. In this hurry the legislators made a mistake which took a fortnight to rectify. It did not take the clerk of the Immigration Committee long to discover the mishap. Since both bills had amended the same section of the Nationality Act and the Senate had made no amedments in the House bills, whichever one the President signs last would automatically repeal the other one. Senator Joseph H. Ball (R-Minn.) who was steering the India Bill on behalf of the India League informed his fellow Senators that "in order to straighten out this angle" it was necessary "to reconsider the vote by which both bills were passed, to amend one of them so as to combine the two and then send them to the House for concurrence."[211]

The two bills were merged into one, the name H.R. 3517 was retained, the new title named both India and the Philippine Islands. The bill was presented to the President for his approval on June 29. He signed it on July 2 with Rep. John Lesinksi, Rep. Emanuel Celler, Jagjit Singh, and Anup Singh behind him with Filipino representatives. Jagjit Singh received the pen.[212] The text is in Appendix III.

Public Law 483, the official name of H.R. 3517 after it received the President's approval, did not grant official recognition to those Indians who had come after July 1, 1924 and therefore did not stop deportations.[213] It did not reverse the *Thind* decision. The naturalization certificates of those who had lost them in the sweeps that followed that decision were therefore never restored.[214] The mission that had recalled Jagjit Singh to public life—to get for the Indian merchants a status more stable than that of temporary visitors—was not realized.

Yet it was welcomed as an act of "simple justice—long overdue." The "first step" in Emanuel Celler's threefold plan for India and in Taraknath Das' estimate an "engagement in the battle for the abolition of discrimination against men."[215] Both he and Celler were looking to the future. For 3896 Indian residents there was now American citizenship in their future, and the anti-alien land laws were in their past. They now "could own land, secure passports, travel to India, bring over relatives from India" because under the new law wives and children of newly naturalized Asian Indians could come as nonquota immigrants.

The whole Indian community's future was assured. "Had not immigration and naturalization laws changed in 1946" Gary Hess has argued, "the East Indian community would almost certainly have eroded significantly perhaps to the point of extinction."[216] Right to naturalization, family unification, and the annual quota recognized the Indian community as a permanent part of the American population.

Jagjit Singh was honored at a dinner on August 4. Praise for him poured in from most of the well-known Indian residents of the United States during the last forty years. Indians in California promised to "remember forever (his) untiring efforts on their behalf."[217] He had worked hard for almost thirty months canvassing the immigration bills.[218] Immigration reform, however, was never the sustenance of his life. That was India's freedom. The Luce-Celler bill had to be sponsored and the Langer bill had to be resisted not only for their provisions, but also for their bearing on Indian national honor and pride.

Lack of equality for Indians in immigration law may have rankled in the hearts of Indian activists, but their first priority was to win India's release from British rule. At the eighth annual meeting of the India League in December, 1945 resolutions urging freedom for India and protesting against use of Indian troops in Indo-China and Indonesia were adopted, but there was no mention of immigration reform although the Luce- Celler bill was lying before the Senate. Again at the League's tenth anniversary in January, 1948 there were several speeches expressing joy at India's freedom but no reference was made to the Act of 1946. In his oral history evidence Jagjit Singh was neither asked nor did he volunteer to describe his struggle for the Luce-Celler bill. Yet it is Public Law 483 that ensures his place in history not his ten year propaganda campaign to educate American public opinion about the Indian National Congress struggle against British rule.[219]

The Act changed the daily lives and the economic fortunes of thousands of Indians. The glowing tributes they paid to Jagjit Singh and his associates indicate their recognition that something historically important had happened on July 2, which they and the coming generations would remember.[220] The Act also signified the desire of the American people and their government to welcome India, expected to be independent soon, as a democratic ally and a profitable trading partner. The Government of India expressed its "appreciation of the presistent and active support of the (United States) administration.[221] Sir Girija Shankar Bajpai regarded the Act as a "mark of American friendship" for the people of India "who are anxious to live on terms of the closest understanding with this great Western democracy."[222]

The press in India received the passage of the bill "with great acclaim," with leading newspapers commenting on it editiorially.[223] The *Hindustan Times* edited by Mahatma Gandhi's son hoped the Act "will usher in a period of increasing friendship and association economic and cultural, between the two peoples."[224]

In the course of years scores of arguments had been offered in favor of repealing the exclusionary laws. The argument that really turned the scales against the exclusionists in the case of China was not the sentiment of equality of man, nor the democratic traditions of American history, nor any special friendship for the people of China. China had to be kept in the war for America's sake. Repeal of Chinese exclusion was a psychological boost, a reward for a faithful ally, a token of regard for fighting the common enemy. A community of Sino-American national interests at a period of crisis had persuaded the legislators including convinced exclusionists like Senator Russell to vote for China because they wanted to vote against Japan.[225]

The grant of the right to citizenship to the Filipinos was a parting gift that had no ideological relationship with repeal of exclusionism. The gift was in recognition of the loyal help given to General MacArthur before he left and after he "returned."

America owed nothing to India. Repeal of Indian exclusion was in a class by itself. It is the key to a new American thinking on Asia. India was "nothing" to the United States except as a British possession. Rep. Allen was right in saying that America would get only that much Indian trade as Britain would permit. That India was one of the United Nations was a legal fiction made in England. The fate of the bill was, therefore, not determined by any military, trade, or political relationship between the people of India and the people and Government of the United States.

President Roosevelt had recognized that the time had come for discriminatory laws to go because they "provoke ill- feeling" and "are incongruous and inconsistent with the dignity" of the Indian people. Joseph C. Grew had characterized exclusion laws as an "outstanding inequity... which cause bitter resentment against the United States by the people of India."[226]

The Government of the United States was seeking an entente cordiale with the people of India. Its sight was on them not on the few thousand residents here or the rulers of India in London. Roosevelt's recommendation in favour of the Luce-Celler Bill may seem to have been a compensation for his failure or disinclination to "mediate" over the Indian question as suggested by the India League of America in 1942.[227]

President Truman believed that the passage of the bill was necessary "to help our foreign policy in the Far East" indeed, "exceedingly helpful in *clarifying* our Far Eastern policy."[228] The war was over. Japan had been occupied. The bill's enactment would "clarify" America's postwar policy in Asia and towards Asian people. There were, of course, some calculations about the Cold War. President Truman's endorsement of H.R. 3517 in the context of Far Eastern policy bears some resemblance to obligations accepted by the United States under the Doctrine enunciated by him—a recognition of American concern over the spread of communism in areas vacated by the British. Clearly the British were on the way to sharing power with the people of India. Therefore, not the British but the *people* could prevent a communist takeover in India. *Their* goodwill had become essential—in the eyes of Rep. Celler for more U.S. trade, in the calculations of President Truman, to win a democratic ally in the Cold War. War or peace, Asia had become important to the United States because the war for Asian hearts—even Asian territories—had really never ended. It was all, as Dr. Muzumdar said to a congressional hearing, "a question of trying to bring the thinking of the American people in line with the demands of the international situation."[229] The supporters of the bill had seen the future.

CONCLUSION

In America homogeneity of race and color was once treasured as a blessing indicative of a divine purpose. Gradually, however, it became apparent that ethnic individuality refused to yield to Anglo-conformity. German-Americans, Irish-Americans, Polish-Americans, and Italian-Americans and countless others kept their hyphens intact. They adopted some WASP mores but retained, as did the Anglo-Americans themselves, cultural and emotional links with countries of their origin.

In the face of this ethnic pluralism scholars wondered whether America was a melting pot, an orchestra, or a salad bowl. The immigrant and ethnic groups themselves proved by their deeds that pluralism held no threat to national unity. In basic loyalties they were all Americans. Timothy McCarthy, President Ronald Reagan's security guard seriously wounded during the assassination attempt on the President, in a statement on his own release from the hospital boasted, "It is great to be Irish." Dr. Taraknath Das, American citizen of Asian Indian origin saw no disloyalty in the greeting "Vande

Mataram"—hail to the Mother (India). No Asian Indian is known to have expressed disloyal feelings towards the United States in spite of disappointments over American policy on Indian freedom or the discriminatory legislation under which the community suffered.

Congressional hearings and the House debate on the bill to repeal Indian exclusion show the former slave states as the only refuge left for exclusionist ideology. Its adherents though no longer inclined to indulge in phrase-mongering of the type that had disfigured the pages of the Congressional Record three decades ago but had developed a few code words or phrases as shibboleths to conceal their hidden agenda.

But America had changed. Popular and Congressional majorities had gone over to the other side. Justice Sutherland's arguments against the Asian Indian claim to naturalization had disappeared from the vocabulary of Asian issues. California's delegation to the Congress, in earlier years the spearhead of Indian exclusion, had undergone an almost wholesale transformation. In 1946 Indian ethnics were accepted as members of the American nation exactly for the qualities for which they had been excluded—good workers, ambitious farmers, descendants of an ancient culture expected soon to take charge of their own country by a successful rebellion against the race brothers of the American WASPs.

White ethnics, blacks and American Indians were gradully accommodated under the parasol of the American nation. Asian ethnics too were brought in as the lessons of the Second World War started to permeate American psyche. This was, in part, a necessary adjustment to give credibility to America's new role as the leader of the "Free World." It was also a phase in the ongoing struggle to redeem the promise of equality with which the American nation began.

Notes & References

1. Ramlal Bajpai's phrase: "permanent alien status," as interpreted by Dickstein, "people without a country." *June 1939 Hearings*, 2, 3; Governor Osborn of Arizona considered it "tragic that these good people should forever be men without a country." S. 1595 Hearings 4; *Modern Review*, September 1944, 175; Point 2 of Tenner's Statement, *House Hearings March 1945*, 142.
2. "At present citizens of the United States have full rights and privileges to come to India, to stay in India and to trade in India as freely as they would

like to." Sir Chunilal B. Mehta, chairman of the Indian delegation to the Rye Conference, *Washington Post*, 14 November 1944; "We could come in when we wanted to, we could stay as long as we liked, and we could go out when we pleased." Statement of V.A. Dodge, President Dodge & Seymour, New York, at the *House Hearings March 1945*, 24.

3. Chapter VI, 31.
4. James K. Fisk and V.S. McClatchy to Senator Hiram W. Johnson, December 2, 1926, *Senate Hearings December 1926*, 43; Rep. A. Leonard Allen, House debate October 10, 1945, *Cong. Record*, 79th Cong.. Ist sess., 9525, 9529.
5. S. Chandrasekhar, "Indian Community in the United States," *Far Eastern Survey*, June 6, 1946, 149.
6. Mubarek Ali's statement, *S. 1595 Hearings* 37, Taraknath Das, *Address* August 6, 1946, 2. Muzumdar's statement at the *June 1939 Hearings*, 18.
7. Mumtaz Kitchlew and Tarani P. Sinha from Chicago, March 9, 1944. The letter is in Sinha's hand but had Kitchlew's signature above his. Sinha was a Professor at the Roosevelt University, Chicago. Less than nine months before he would have become "a citizen of Free India" Dr. Sinha died December 2, 1946, following a stroke while he was lecturing to his class. Haridas T. Muzumdar, *Contributions*, 32; *Voice of India*. Washington, D.C., December 1946, 374; K.L. Dikshit, a merchant in California expressed views similar to those of Dr. Sinha and Kitchlew. "There is a big difference between becoming a citizen and having the right to become a citizen" wrote Dr. Saund in 1944, California Newsletter 1, 17.
8. Statement of Edward J. Shaughnessy, Special Assistant to the Commissioner Immigration and Naturalization Service. *Senate Hearing on S. 236* April 1945, 19.
9. By the bill S.2508 signed by the President in June 1935 resident alien World War I veterans were granted the right to citizenship, *Cong. Record*, 74th Cong., 1st sess., June 10, 1935, 8977. A photocopy of his certificate was graciously supplied to the writer by Mrs. Vivian Thind. It is dated March 2, 1936. His color is given as "white" and complexion "medium"; P. Kodanda Rao, "Indians Overseas," *The Annals of the American Academy of Political and Social Science*, Vol. 233 (May 1944): 205. Ramchandra D. Shelke had been a veteran but was naturalized (in 1921) as other 68 Indians were, by the courts. His naturalization was sought to be cancelled. His name is listed among the pending cases, *Senate Hearings*, December 1926, 7.
10. *Senate Hearing on S. 236*, 19.
11. Jagjit Singh addressing the first annual meeting of the Chamber on May 18, 1939 characterized the conclusion of an Indo-American trade treaty as "the central feature of our activities," Minutes of the Meeting, 2.

12. Telegram from Halifax, Washington to Govgenext, New Delhi, No. 360, April 26, 1945; Telegram same to same, No. 498,, June 15, 1945, File 256-F.E/45, External Affairs 1945 National Archives of India.
13. P.L. Sodhbans to Secretary, Government of India, Commerce Department, New Delhi, January 28, 1939; C.A.G. Savidge to Honorary Secretary Indian Chamber of Commerce, Lahore, February 14, 1939, File 325-X/39, 1939. External Affairs, National Archives of India: Jagjit's *Transcript*, 78; In March 1942 a Government of India official had "stated frankly that the phrasing of the present draft Treaty calls on India to give so much in return for so little that the reaction of the commercial community could only be expected to be hostile." H. Weightman's Note in File 300-X/40 National Archives of India, 86 Notes. In 1945 avoidance of publicity about these treaty negotiatons became a deliberate decision of the Government of India as a result of a conclusion to that effect reached by the Commerce, External Affairs, Finance Departments and the Bureau of Public Information, *vide* a Note from the Office of the Secretary to the Executive Council of the Governor General, May 16, 1945, File 245-F.E/45, National Archives of India.
14. In July 1945 the number of such countries, according to a United Press of India report from Washington, was 44; File 246-F.E/45, 1945 External Affairs, National Archives of India.
15. Ambassador's advice, External Affairs Department Note dated February 8, 1939 on 17; File 310 (7)-X/39, 1939 External Affairs Department, National Archives of India, Feroz Khan Noon had arrived in the U.S. at the end of March 1937, *New York Times*, 31 March 1937, 6:3: his efforts mentioned in his Note of May 4, 1942 for Secretary to the Executive Council. Not without hesitation, S.R. Zaman's Note December 14, 1941, "In the earlier stages of the discussion it was doubted whether it would be wise to negotiate for a treaty at all" because India was already enjoying most-favored-nation treatment and having a favorable trade balance with U.S., thirdly during negotiations America might "ask for a price for what we are getting free." File 300-X/40 External Affairs, National Archives of India, 70 Notes: also N.R. Pillai's Note January 29, 1942, ibid., 77.
16. When Sir Feroz Khan Noon first approahced the American authorities in Washington in 1937 he was told that "If India were to have a trade treaty, *no matter how few the clauses*, that would legally permit the U.S.A. Government to give the Indians the rights that I claimed for them." Sir Noon's Note to Secretary Executive Council, dated May 4, 1942, 102-103 Correspondence, File 300-X/40 External Affairs, National Archives of India.

    A year later the State Department wanted a "comprehensive treaty" more elaborate than the proposed convention between U.S. and Australia. The Government of India insisted that "they would prefer that the proposed treaty should be as simple as possible": Brief for Sir Ramaswami Mudaliar, ibid., 141; the State Department handed the draft treaty to the British Ambassador on October 10, 1939. It was called treaty of "Establishment, Commerce Navigation and Consular Rights."

In April 1940 a supplementary note arrived which contained "additions to and revision of the draft." Ibid.

17. Additional Secretary Prior's Note, August 5, 1940, 11, 12; the quotation is from 12. Ibid., Notes.
18. The terms of the American Draft as briefly explained in H. Walton Moore of the Secretary of State Office London to Marquess of Lothian, British Ambassador in Washington, October 10, 1939; ibid., 4, 5, Correspondence.
19. Ramaswami Mudaliar from Washington to the Viceroy of India, January 3, 1943, ibid., 148-49 Correspondence.
20. Additional Secretary N.R. Pillai's Note, January 29, 1942, ibid., 79-80, Notes.
21. At the outbreak of the war in 1939, there were three Indian Members of the Governor-General's Executive Council. There was one Indian serving as India's High Commissioner in London. This post had been occupied by Sir Feroz Khan Noon since 1936. It was from London that he had come to the United States in 1937 when he met a deputation of Indians in New York.

    Five Indians were added in 1941 and three in 1942. Diwan Bahadur Sir Ramaswami Mudaliar became a Member in 1939 receiving Commerce and Labor portfolios. In 1941 Sir Noon returned from London and received the Labor portfolio. In 1942 Mudaliar became Member without Portfolio and Accredited Representative of India at the War Cabinet. Sir Feroz Khan became the Defense Member.

    Sir Syed Sultan Ahmed received his first appointment in the Executive Council as Law Member in July 1941.

    The Executive Council meeting of June 17, 1942 which decided to suspend treaty negotiations was attended by eight members and the Viceroy. Four of the members were Indians. The Law Member was not present but had instead sent a Note favoring suspension. The four were Mudaliar, Noon, M. S. Aney, Member for Indians Overseas, and Nalini Ranjan Sarkar, Member for Education, Health and Lands. Much of this footnote is based on *The Statesman's Year Book.* (New York, volumes for the years 1940 to 1943.)
22. R. T. Moore, *Churchill Cripps and India 1939- 1945*, Oxford : 1979, 41-42.
23. "American Imperialism is mainly of the economic variety." *Modern Review*, December 1924, Notes, 723; suspicions of America's economic

ambitions in India appeared to be widespread, for instance Pandit Nehru saw the American technical mission sent to India in 1942 "as an effort to exploit India." W. C. Mackett, "Some Aspects of the Development of American Opinion on India, 1918-1947" (Diss., University of Southern California, June 1957), 317.

The "Indian Congress Party was now talking of American imperialism 'more up-to-date and streamlined' based not on territory but on commercial supremacy." Mackett, ibid., 327 quoting a report in the *Los Angeles Times,* 12 April 1942; "We know what American aid means. It amounts in the end to American influence, if not American rule, added to British," Mahatma Gandhi quoted in ibid., 329; Gandhi's words are in *The Collected Works of Mahatma Gandhi* v. 76 Ahmedabad, 1979, 49; *Amerasia* of March 1946 published a G.I.'s letter saying that in India the United States is alleged to have intention "of eventually taking over the whole structure [Britain's India empire] by economic penetration." Quoted in Mackett, ibid., 459.

Sir Girja Shankar Bajpai accused the Indian industrialists—an "extremely reactionary and self-seeking" group who had spread the first rumors designed to discredit" the technical mission, expressing the view that "American imperialism was endeavoring to replace British imperialism in India and that as far as they were concerned, one was just as bad as the other." Memorandum of Conversation, by the Adviser on Political Relations (Murray), Washington, April 24, 1942, *Foreign Relations of the United States*, 1942, Vol. I, 641.

"The leading lights of American capitalism had many points of common interest with the captains of British big business. The one area of sharp disagreement that persisted was over Britain's reluctance to offer an "open door" with equal opportunities in colonial areas." Venkataramani and Shrivastava, *Quit India*, 10.

24. Note dated June 14, 1942; File 300-X/40, Secret, External Affairs, National Archives of India.
25. Mudaliar's Note dated June 5, 1942, ibid., 98-103 and Appendix 104-108 Notes. The quotations are from 100, 102, 105 and 107; in 1943 he "announced that if a force was raised to attack South Africa, he would enlist," Hugh Tinker, *Separate and Unequal*, 226.
26. Viceroy's letter, March 4, 1943, File 300-X/40 Secret, External Affairs, 154-155, National Archives of India.
27. Olaf Caroe's Note February 11, 1943, ibid., 125-126 Notes.
28. Noon's opinion May 14, 1942, ibid., 94-97 Notes. The quotation is from 94.
29. A sample opinion may be that of the Education Member of the Executive Council which he expressed at its meeting of June 17, 1942, that decided to suspend further treaty negotiations. He believed that the "benefits

conferred by the Treaty on Indians were not likely to be substantial during the war"; 120 Correspondence.

30. Jagjit Singh remembered several years later that during the war merchants could not increase exchange of goods, because shipping was difficult. The India Chamber had consequently become "a paper organization," *Transcripts", 86.*

31. The Law and the Home Members had suggested (the former in his written opinion) that the terms of the draft treaty be published. The Labor and Finance Members had opposed. File 300-X/40 External Affairs 118-120 Correspondence, National Archives of India.

32. The quotation is from Jagjit Singh to Ramlal Bajpai, March 20, 1941, Jagjit promised that the League's idea was to "do something in New York, Washington, Chicago, Los Angeles when he (Noon) will be in those cities." I.L.A. Papers. Four years later Jagjit discovered that Sir Noon's "propaganda" was not always contrary to India's national interests. Noon came as an official delegate to the San Francisco Conference. In a press conference he explained "India's governmental machinery and the voluntary character of India's important war contribution." Commenting on the press conference the New York *Post* observed that it "held a note of hope even to J. J. Singh."

    Ramaswami Mudaliar was chairman of the Economic and Social Council Committee of the Conference. He earned praise "as a learned and forceful speaker admittedly above the heads of most correspondents." One west coast newspaper stated that "200 correspondents hailed him as frank and unhesitating and "making the most honest reports of any committee chairman. . . ." Even J. J. Singh is quoted as saying: "He is one of India's finest minds. We hate to see a man like him on the other side." Round-up of American Press Comment on India, June 30, 1945, File 249-E.P/45, External Affairs 1945, 23, 24, National Archives of India.

    But as regards Sir Noon, Jagjit was not finished with him yet. At a press conference the honored knight was forced to admit in answer to Jagjit Singh's question that he was not the elected representative of the people of India. *India To- Day*, May 1945.

    It seems that some members of the Indian business community blamed the Government of India for the suspension of treaty negotiations. Sir Chunilal Mehta, leader of the Indian delegation to the Rye Conference, told a press conference that the suspension of negotiations "had surprised the American authorities (who) were willing and also prepared to conclude such a treaty with India." But Mehta could not be told why India suspended the negotiations; *Modern Review,* February 1945, 52; a slightly different version, *Washington Post*, 14 November 1944.

33. Suggestions by Chairman of the House Committee on Immigration and Naturalization Samuel Dickstein (D-NY) and Dickstein and Asa Allen (D-LA) at the *June 1939 Hearing*, 9, 13.
34. Two test cases were launched, the Samras case (Kharaiti Ram Samras v. United States 125 Fed., 879 and Kharaiti Ram Samras v. United States 317 U.S. 634) and the Karam Chand case. The former was rejected both by the District Judge and the Circuit Court on ground of racial ineligibility and by the Supreme Court because the application for certiorari was not made within the time provided by law. The Karam Chand case probably never reached its first court appearance before prospects of bills in Congress seemed to become promising.

    In 1939 a lobbying campaign in Washington, D.C. was launched at the behest of a politician from India, D.P. Pandia. The results were disappointing; R.K. Samras, "Hindus in U.S.A.: Attempt to Regain American Citizenship" *The Mahratta*, Poona, June 21, 1940; *Christian Century*, March 13, 1940, Mubarek Ali in *New India*, November 1944; Norman Buchignani et al., *Continuous Journey, A Social History of South Asians in Canada* Tornoto, 1985 for the Pandia episode, 92, 97.
35. Congressman Dondero's efforts, *Cong. Record*, 79th Cong., 2nd sess., October 10, 1945, 9532; for Muzumdar's plan, June 1939 Hearing, 7. Dr. Kathju was an eminent chemist who in collaboration with two American chemists had developed "green and other paints that cannot be told from surrounding vegetation even under infrared photography." He had come as a student from Kashmir in 1921, was hit by the Sutherland ruling after he had filed his first papers. He married an American citizen in October 1923. Rep. Dondero's persistence succeeded in the House. The Senate however, did not go beyond giving Kathju the status of a permanent resident. *The New Republic*, September 20, 1943, *S. 1595 Hearings*,, 39; *Cong. Record*, 74th Cong. 1st sess., August 20, 1935, 12908, 13827, 13960; ibid., 75th Cong., 1st sess., May 17, 1937, 4668, 4670, 4671, 4719,; ibid., 76th Cong., 1st sess., August 1, 1939, 10655; ibid., 79th Cong., 2nd sess., October 10, 1945, 9532.
36. Dr. Muzumdar's plan, *June 1939 Hearing*, 7.
37. Rep. O'Brien's bill, *Cong. Record*, 75th Cong., 3rd sess., 7453. Rep. Jenerowicz bills; ibid., 76th Cong., 1st sess., Index 7061 and 261 respectively; Dickstein's revelations. 1939 Hearing, 3; it may be of interest to note that Rep. O'Brien introduced a resolution in Congress to provide for recognition by the United States of the National Government of India, Venktaramani and Shrivastava, *Quit India*, 190.
38. The Japanese campaign against exclusion, *New York Times*, 24 May 1930; Japan "still feels deeply injured over what she regards as the affront of the statutory exclusion provisions of our 1924 Immigration Act. . . . But the lack of steel eliminates Japan as a war threat . . ." Discussions at the

Williamstown Conference as reported in *The Hindustanee Student*, September-October 1925, 14.

General James G. Harbord, Chairman of the Board of the Radio Corporation of America speaking at the annual dinner of Japan Society at Waldorf Astoria expressed the hope that the Immigration Act which, he said, placed Japan "on a footing different from other friendly nations" would be "removed through an informed American public opinion." *New York Times*, 31 March 1937.

39. Constance B. Schulz. *Samuel Dickstein: Congressional Investigator, 1934-1939* (M.A. thesis, University of Cincinnati, 1966), 21.
40. Violence against Indians, Chapter II, footnote 14; anti-semitism, John Higham, *Strangers*, 309-310.
41. Sidney Kansas, *U.S. Immigration, Exclusion and Deportation and Citizenship of the United States of America*, 2nd ed. New York; 1941; iii, v, vii; Schulz, *Dickstein* 14, 15
42. Rep. John D. Dingell, Address Before American Jewish Congress Extension of Remarks, October 9, 1939, *Cong. Record*, 76th Cong., 2nd sess., Appendix, 214.
43. *Transcript of Narayanan's interview with Jagjit Singh*, 22, 23.
44. *Contributions*, 39.
45. Ibid., 37; Muzumdar's *Oral History Transcript*, 67; the League was probably founded on October 27, 1937, *Senate Hearing on S. 236*, 22, "Background of Mubarek Ali Khan," it was certainly in existence on July 1, 1938, Hans Stefen Santesson, Secretary, India Political Council to Jagjit Singh, July 1, 1938, I.L.A. Papers.
46. Mubarek Ali Khan to Stephen T. Early, May 26, 1939, Franklin D. Roosevelt Documents, NMML; *June 1939 Hearing*, 14, gives the figures 28,000 for signers of the Welfare League petitions.
47. Muzumdar *Contributions*, 38; Muzumdar's *Transcript*, 87-88, *June 1939 Hearing*, 4, *Washington Post*, June 21, 1939, front page.
48. Bajpai's statement, *June 1939 Hearing*, 1,2; Father Cooper's statement, ibid., 3; Shapiro's statement, ibid., 6.
49. Muzumdar's statement, ibid., 7; Mubarek Ali's statement, ibid., 14.
50. Scharrenberg's statement, ibid., 15, 16; Muzumdar's response, 18.
51. *New India Bulletin*, July 1945, India Welfare League Petition of May 3, 1943; R.C. Lindsay to Viscount Halifax, London, August 22, 1939. File 325-X/39, External Affairs, 1939, 48, 49.
52. *June 1939 Hearing*, 12.
53. Muzumdar *Transcript*, 87, emphasis added; The Treasurer too was a Muslim, Muzumdar, *Contributions*, 37.
54. An American, "India's Cause in America," *Modern Review*, November 1940, 573; in August 1939 the Deputy Leader of the Congress Party asked a question in the Legislative Assembly which implied that denial of

citizenship was unjust and urged the Government of India to help those 3000 Indians to secure "the right to become American citizens under ordinary conditions." Question by S. Stayamurti, No. Q.S. 33, 14, 9.A. Mian Muhammed Rafi to the Secretary to the Governor-General (Personal), Simla, August 16, 1939, National Archives of India.

55. The letterheads and other literature of the Welfare League show that neither Ramlal Bajpai nor Haridas Muzumdar held any office in the League until 1945. In telephone interview with the present writer on June 7, 1987 Dr. Muzumdar said that "Many remarks he (Mubarek Ali) made at the Congressional hearings were offensive to my ears but I thought only of the common cause which was the citizenship of the Indian workers who could not get jobs."
56. Mubarek's claim is in a letter to Jagjit's Singh, June 13, 1944; India Political Council letterhead in I.L.A. Paper; File 632-X(4), 1940, External Affairs, Enquiry regarding the whereabouts of one Sheikh Rais Ali in New York; *Washington Post*, 21 June 1939, front page.
57. *Transcript of Narayanan's Interview with Jagjit Singh*,2, 3, 7.
58. *S. 1595 Hearings*, 36; Intelligence Bureau report File 256, E.F/45, External Affairs, 1945, 7-8 Notes and the Undersecretary's remarks, 8 Notes, National Archives of India; the Senators again gave him a high class father the following year, *Senate Hearings on S. 236*, 8,
59. Claim as to brother, *Senate Hearings on S. 236,* 10.
60. *Senate Hearing on S. 236*, 22. It was probably alumni like him who gave the Agra University its uneviable reputation as a school in the early 1940s—having majored in Economics he had to go to night school seven years later to obtain "some English education."
61. Bajpai's opinion, File 256-F.E/45, External Affairs 1945, Telegram No. 360 from Halifax, Washington to Govgenext, New Delhi dated April 26, 1945, 112 Correspondence, National Archives of India.
62. The first quotation *The New India Bulletin* August-September 1945, 5, the second Ibid., 4.
63. Mubarek Ali Khan to Emanuel Celler, March 21, 1944, April 9, 1944, I.L.A Papers.
64. Mubarek Ali Khan to Emanuel Celler, June 9, 1944; Mubarek Ali Khan to Jagjit Singh, June 9, 1944, I.L.A. Papers.
65. *The New India Bulletin*, August-September 1945, 3.
66. Ibid.
67. Probably the first published document he signed as "Dr." was his letter to the Viceroy Lord Wavell, June 29, 1945, *New India Bulletin*, July 1945; R. Chand to India League of America, April 28, 1947, I.L.A. Papers; for instance Senator Stewart referred to him as "Dr. Khan," *S. 1595 Hearings*, 31.

68. *The New India Bulletin.* August-September 1945, 8.
69. Jagjit Singh to R. Chand June 3, 1947; I.L.A. Papers.
70. Allen Drury, *A Senate Journal 1943-1945* New York, 1963, 27. Drury also calls the Senator "an odd character, the maverick of the Senate (whom other Senators watch) in half-amused, half-fearful silence as though in the presence of an irresponsible force." Ibid., Celler's remarks, *House Hearings, March 1945,* 9.
71. *Senate Hearings on S. 236*, 40, 41; Mubarek's own assessment of the significance of the Welfare League is hard to refute: "There HAD of course been frequent previous attemps led, at times by distinguished interpreters of India in the United States, but it remained for a poorly financed and a small organization like ours, an Indian workers' group to make the first substantial contribution to the story of the fight of the Indian nationals in the United States to regain the rights which they had lost through the Oriental Exclusion Laws." Mubarek to Jagjit Singh, June 13, 1944, I.L.A. Papers.
72. *S. 1595 Hearings*, 41
73. *Hearings on S. 236,* 39, 41, for the Muslim flag. Mubarek Ali's letter to Jagjit Singh, December 4, 1943 shows the flag but Bajpai's and Muzumdar's names are not on the letterhead.

    In his letters to Jagjit and Rep. Celler in the summer of 1944 there was the insignia but no Hindu officials. At the Hearings on S. 1595 in September 1944 Bajpai was introduced as Vice-President of the Welfare League. It seems that the insignia was removed from its stationery in the fall of 1944.
74. *The New India Bulletin*, August-September 1946, 6, 8; Mubarek Ali to Jagjit Singh, December 4, 1943.
75. The telegram is in the I.L.A. Papers, so also is Hemendra Rakhit's notice dated February 26 for the Executive committee meeting on the 29th. The phrase "citizenship matter" shows relationship with the telegram; Celler's Extension of Remarks, *Cong. Record,* 78th Cong., 2nd sess., Appendix A 1427; Mubarek to Celler, March 21, 1944, Los Angeles public meeting, Indian National Congress Association Newsletter, I.L.A. Papers.
76. "I think even before me, the first President (of the League) N.R. Checker and Mr. Rakhit, they were very aware of the cause (of immigration and citizenship)." Transcript of Narayanan's interview with Jagjit Singh, 6, one of the "primary objects" of the League as stated in its constitution was "To improve the civic status of the Indian community in the United States of America," which was reitereated in "Statement by the India League of America on False Charges Made by Drew Pearson," 3; *India To-Day*, October 1940, January, August 1941; the Walsh Memorandum reference is on page 2 of the Memorandum; the "Political Platform" is a two-page

document important by the fact that it defines the League's attitude towards America's Asian exclusion laws before the repeal of Chinese exclusion. The whole paragraph concerning immigration and naturalization deserves close attention:

> One injustice in American policy needs correction in relation to India and to the entire Orient, whose people are excluded from permanent residence in the United States and who, if here for exceptional reasons, cannot become citizens. This discrimination against Oriental people on racial grounds can be righted only by repeal of the exclusion acts. Such an action would have a profound effect on the relations of the United States and India, and indeed on the entire Orient, not only in the morale of the war, but in building the foundations of a democratic peace.

77. Transcript of Narayanan's interview with Jagjit Singh, 2. 8, his *Transcript*, 85, he was not unaware of the Indian immigrants' hardships in America, his statement, *The Tribune*, Lahore December 29, 1937.
78. Jagjit Singh to unknown, July 1, 1943, describing R.S. Dhillon's concern over a new law in California; T.B. Creagh Coen, First Secretary Indian Agency-General, Washington, D.C. to Jagjit Singh, April 3, 1943; *India To-Day*, April 1943.
79. Among those who gave testimony on behalf of the Chinese were Taraknath Das, Pearl Buck, Richard J. Walsh, Oswald Garrison Villard, and Rev. J. Henry Carpenter. The League was the "vehicle," Jagjit's interview with Narayanan, 6.
80. Mubarek Ali Khan to Jagjit Singh, December 4, 1943 and January 3, 1944, I.L.A. Papers.
81. Transcript of Narayanan's interview with Jagjit Singh, 3.
82. Ibid.; Dalip Singh Saund, "Citizen bill" *Hindustani Congress Association Newletter* 1-7; "Senator Langer's Bill," 7-9, both in Gurmukhi script.
83. The resolution, *Cong. Record,* 78th Cong., 2nd sess., August 14, 1944, 6871 emphasis added; Checker's Association formed, *India To-Day*, March 1944; Syud Hossain and Anup Singh were its "Washington Advisors," ibid., April 1944; letterhead of Checker, Tenner and Choudry letter to Jagjit Singh, February 20, 1945.
84. Transcript of Narayanan's interview with Jagjit Singh, 6, 5, 3 respectively.
85. See fn. 76.
86. Hearings before the House Commitee on Immigration and Naturalization to repeal the Chinese Exclusion Act, May and June 1943, 78th Cong., 1st sess., 37, 38, emphasis added. There was apprehension among some Indians that if every Asian nationality started asking for equality "there will be so many bills in Congress that it will be a mess . . . which may make our case tougher." G. J. Watumull to Jagjit Singh, June 20, 1944, I.L.A. Papers.

87. The Indian community in California during these years was wealthy, with an active social conscience motivated from its religious center at Stockton. Farming, religion, Indian patriotism, and an intense desire to secure the right to American citizenship were the four passions that dominated the life of the community. British intelligence that watched its political activities has documented for us the lecture tours of Indian extremists like Ataullah Durani, Rajani Patel, Kamaladevi Chattopadhyay, Abdul Waheed, and others. There were membership drives on behalf of the Indian National Congress and celebrations of Independence Day with mass meetings at the Labor Temple in Sacramento. Files 675-X/39; 75-G(4) 1940 Nos. 1-2; 278-X(40) Secret 1940, Nos. 1-25, all External Affairs, National Archives of India: Prof. K. R. Samras, "Attempts to Regain American Citizenship," *The Mahratta*, Poona, June 21, 1940. The opening paragraph testifies to their "feelings of respect and affection for the motherland."

88. "You can, by what you decide, be a barrier—or you can be a gateway to a new and better world, for us and for all peoples." Pearl S. Buck, "An Appeal to California," *Asia and the Americas*, January 1944, 23.

    Indians of the different parts of California were not equally interested in the Luce-Celler bills. "I do not know whether many members of your Associaion are interested in the India . . . Bill. Perhaps they are not as much interested as our countrymen in the Imperial Valley," Jagjit Singh to *The Hindustan Gadar*, San Francisco, October 15, 1945.

89. Jagjit Singh to S. Ajmer Singh, November 18, 1943.

90. D. S. Saund, *Congressman From India*, 74: Dr. Samras had almost similar doubts about the success of any effort to gain citizenship rights at least while the War lasted. "These matters," in his view, "are connected with international politics, which Dr. Pandia and his native supporters do not fully understand, and the international situation is too tense to warrant a drastic change in the official attitude toward the Hindus in the United States." *Mahratta*. Poona, June 21, 1940, 7; an American friend to whom Dr. Saund talked about his intention to start the citizenship campaign advised him to "have his head examined." It was wartime, the friend reminded him, when even minorities in millions "are not getting to first base," *Congressman From India*, 73.

91. The quotation from an article by Dr. Anup Singh, California Newsletter IV, the assessment of the Langer bill, see fn. 82.

92. "Close contact" with Indians in California was urged by the Walsh Memorandum of August 6, 1944; Jagjit Singh invited several West coast Indians to become members of the League's National Advisory Board, among them Dalip Singh Saund, Ajmer Singh of the Pacific Coast Khalsa Dewan Society, R.S. Dhillon of El Centro, G. J. Watumull, Dr. J. N.

Sharma, Jagjit Singh papers, Subject File Invitations to join Advisory Board, Nehru Memorial Museum and Library, letters of praise from Godha Ram Channon, December 1, 1943, February 26, 1944; from Dr. J. N. Sharma, November 15, 1943, December 6, 1943; from G. J. Watumull, November 28, 1943, February 1 and June 20, 1944; from Ellen Watumull, July 17, 1944; praise from Saund and Bagga Singh Sunga was expressed in their Newsletter.

Dr. Saund's chief associates in California were themselves officials of other active organizations who were supporting the India League's bill. Hindustanee Civil Rights Association, the Watumull Foundation, Hindustan Welfare Society, Indian National Congress Association, the Pacific Coast Khalsa Diwan Society all communicated their support to the House Immigration Committee, *House Hearings, March 1945* 133, 134; Emanuel Celler had high regard for these Indians of the West Coast, calling them "upstanding gentlemen, cultured, refined, educated, soft-spoken, thoroughly Americanized." *Cong. Record,* 79th Cong., lst sess., October 10, 1945, 9531. A delegation of leading Indians had waited upon Celler in Los Angeles on October 7, 1945, as arranged by the India League, Jagjit's telegram to Dr. J. N. Sharma, October 1, 1945 suggesting "deputation of Indians wait upon him and thank him. Also assure him California Indian community wholeheartedly backs India League's work."

93. Saund's own part in the struggle for equality was summarized later in pages 72-76 of his autobiography. The contemporary evidence of his activities is in the newsletters he continued to publish during the years when the bills were before Congress. The quotations are from *Congressman from India*, 74, 75. Dr. Saund himself and other western activists did not feel satisfied with their compatriots' response to the financial needs of the campaign in Congress. The India League and the Washington Committee continued to receive their contributions both for the nationalist propaganda and the citizenship bills although very often they had to be asked twice. The National Congress Association alone collected $15,000 for the citizenship work. The Washington Committee had received at least $2000 out of that amount till June 1945. Other documents testifying to monetary help from California: Jagjit Singh to Ajmer Singh, November 18, 1943; Dr. Jagan Nath to Jagjit Singh, December 6, 1943; Roger Baldwin to G. Watumull, March 5, 1944; Hemendra Rakhit to Bagga Singh Sunga, March 21, 1946; *Voice of India*, June 1945, 151. In 1946 Californians collected $27,599 for famine relief in India. Haridas T. Muzumdar wrote the very obvious fact: "The Sikhs, most of them unlettered farmers, are patriotic to their fingertips; and I understand they contributed vast sums of money to projects calculated to promote India'a freedom." *Contributions*, 34: The Indian National Congress Association

newsletters mention financial contributions in almost every issue. Donating money for patriotic causes was the California tradition going back several decades. The East-West alliance of the mid-1940s represents what Karen Leonard called "a coalition of the better educated, urban Indians and the Panjabi farmers to work for U.S. citizenship." "Panjabi Farmers and California's Alien Land Law," *Agricultural History*, No. IV, October 1985, 9.

94. Roger Baldwin's Oral History transcript "Indian Independence 1917-1947," 412, 430; Pearl Buck *My Several Worlds: A Personal Record* New York: 1954, 298; Pearl Buck's speech at the Independence Day Dinner, Commodore Hotel, New York City, January 26, 1945, I.L.A. Papers.
95. Henry Luce, "The American Century," John A. Garaty and Robert A. Divine, *Twentieth Century America: Contemporary Documents and Opinions* New York, 1968, 471; Asian exclusion as part of American isolationism, Statement of Nathan D. Perlman at House Immigration Committee Hearings on H.R. 3663 to Deny Admission to the United States of Certain Aliens and to Reduce Immigration Quotas, 79th Cong., 2nd sess., Part I, February, March 1946, 56.
96. For Carey's help, see Chapter V, 54-55, fn. 112. Walter P. Reuther's support in 1942, message on India Independence Day 1943, Jagjit's letter of introduction for Walter on his visit to India in 1956, his brother Victor's message of farewell on Jagjit's departure for India in 1959, Greater New York Industrial Union Council's resolution in 1942 in support of Indian freedom, A.F. of L. second Vice-President Mathew Woll's help in 1942 are documented in I.L.A. Papers.

    Victor G. Reuther joined the League's National Advisory Board in July 1944, *India To-Day*, July 1944; Jagjit Singh's Press Release of March 1, 1945, says Philip Murray has assured him that the witness on behalf of the C.I.O. shall testify in favor of the bill; Murray and Roger Baldwin were friends, Peggy Lamson, *Roger Baldwin*, 221.
97. Notes by Olaf Caroe, Secretary, External Affairs Department and H. Dayal, Deputy Secretary, dated March 25 and 26, 1945 respectively. Bajpai had first reported about Emanuel Celler in his telegram of March 15, 1944 and reiterated the U.S. State Department reservations on March 10, 1945, File 256-F.E/45 External Affairs, National Archives of India.
98. In a letter addressed to Jawaharlal Nehru, May 6, 1947, Celler wrote, "I note with keenest disappointment and sadness that you are supporting the Arab League in its demand for an independent Arab state in Palestine . . . . I assure you that your statement on Palestine will make no difference to Mohammed Ali Jinnah." Extension of Remarks, *Cong. Record*, 80th Cong., 1st sess., Appendix A2093.
99. "Indian rivalries irritated me; they seemed so personal and trivial." Baldwin, *Reminiscences*, 429; personal rivalries among other irritants had

brought about a split in late 1943. Discord between Jagjit Singh and Anup Singh took a nasty turn in the late summer of 1944 just when national affairs at home and the citizenship campaign here had started to heat up calling for mutual cooperation and single-minded effort. The Jagjit-Anup correspondence became recriminatory, eloquent, philosophical and at this distance in time, amusing. Jagjit to Anup, September 1, 1944: "Your last paragraph amuses me. Look who is talking. Don't put on that garb of innocence. People can see through it now. It does not suit you to preach when you are the guilty one. If you had not opened your big mouth and had not indulged in your favorite past time [sic] of scandal-talk none of these unpleasant developments would have taken place."

Anup's reply: "If I were aiming at wounding your feelings as you have obviously sought to do in your letter to me, I would lash out some biting but appropriate epithets without indulging like you in cheap language.... I know you will accuse me of "preaching" but I hope that even you will one day learn that unless the law of Karma is suspended for the duration a smear campaign always comes back with boomerang." September 4, 1944. I.L.A. Papers.

Even though angry at each other, both were conscious of their public responsibilities—as Jagjit told Watumull, "we must try and keep a united front where the Americans are concerned," August 25, 1944, Anup wrote to Gobind Behari Lal, "... the whole mess is utterly deplorable, and it's a pity that at a critical time like this when we should mobilize our meagre resources for national work, our energies should be dissipated in such matters," August 28, 1944; and Watumull advised everbody that "this personal criticism is a waste of everyone's time, energy and thinking. Due to the urgency of the present situation ... we should bend our concerted efforts to the promotion of India's cause.... And in this connection, of course, *the problem of citizenship for Indians in this country is also an issue*, to Jagjit Singh, September 1, 1944, emphasis added. I.L.A. Papers.

100. The Welfare League's newsletter *New India Bulletin*, July 1945, expresses opposition to the Luce-Celler bill and insists on the passage of the Langer and Lynch bills. In subsequent issues much space was devoted to the reiteration of Mubarek Ali's activities since 1937 and to Muslim separatist propaganda. In the March 1946 issue Mubarek Ali said, "We have all wholeheartedly favored the Luce-Celler-Powell-Lynch bills." In what he called his "interview" with President Truman he sought Presidential support for the Langer, the Lynth and (the Luce-Celler) Quota bills. August-September 1946 issue, 4. He claimed full credit for the passage of the Luce- Celler bill—"My job is done and thanks to the President of the United States who has kept his promises made to me during his interview with me on March 1, 1946 ... I deeply appreciate that I have

been enabled to gain for them (his countrymen) the desire to become American citizens . . ." Ibid., 6.

Mubarek Ali was never happy with the three officials of the National Committee, Anup, Shridharani, and Muzumdar for supporting the Luce-Celler bills. His remarks against Anup are in *New India Bulletin*, November 1944, against Muzumdar, ibid., March 1946, 9-10, and against Shridharani in *S. 1595 Hearings*, 50. The Muslim League of America had become, according to Jagjit Singh "hardly more than a paper organization," and he continued, "Neither the head of this organization nor its few members count in the Indian community in the United States." Jagjit Singh to George E. Jones, April 19, 1946. I.L.A. Papers.

101. *Taraknath's Address* of August 4, 1946, 1, similar remarks on pp. 10 and 11; Mahatma Gandhi to Jagjit Singh, July 6, 1946; Celler's Message on Jagjit's 70th birthday celebration.
102. Calculated from the day after the Langer bill was introduced December 16, 1943 to the day President Truman signed the Luce-Celler bill, July 2, 1946; Garry Wills, *Inventing America: Jefferson's Declaration of Independence*, New York, 1979, 95.
103. Attempting to win the C.I.O. to the side of India's freedom, Jagjit Singh asked to be permitted to address its forthcoming National Convention and added that "I would only discuss this question from the viewpoint of its utter importance to the United States and to the ultimate victory of the United Nations." Letter to Clinton S. Golden, United Steel Workers of America, Pittsburgh, PA, October 28, 1942, I.L.A. Papers. Jagjit Singh's refusal to ask for passage of the bill as reward for war services, Transcript of Narayanan's interview with Jagjit Singh, 21-22; *House Hearings March 1945*, 90; quotations are from ibid., 91, 88; the *Voice of India* too would decline to accept the passage of the bill as a reward for help in the war, October 1945, 182.
104. *S. 1595 Hearings*, 36-38; the quotations are from 37, 38 respectively.
105. Senator Langer's estimate, *Senate Hearing on S. 236*, 11.
106. *House Hearings March 1945*, 10, 11, the idea of Indo-American compact is in Rep. Celler's remark on p. 30.
107. The quotation is from Celler's Extension of Remarks, *Cong. Record*, 78th Cong., 2nd sess., Appendix, A1427; Anup Singh, "Discrimination Against India," *Voice of India*, September 1944, 11; Miss Sue Weddell's statement at *House Hearings March 1945* , 42-43; Anup Singh's statement S. 1595 Hearings, 19, "We have lifted the bars for the Chinese," The *New York Times* editorialized on February 8, 1944, " We can afford to do the same for the Indians. We can't afford to do otherwise"; the *Los Angeles Times* on March 21, 1944 argued that Indians deserve the same concession "for much the same reasons as in the case of the Chinese." The appreciation

that to "win this war the principle of world-wide legal equality of races will have to be recognized "had finally dawned upon American public opinion." The *New York Times* believed that "the Chinese, the East Indians, and the numerous African peoples" must be "completely convinced that we mean what we say by equality." Editorial, April 3, 1942, quoted in Gunnar Myrdal, *An American Dilemma*, New York, 1944, 1008. The support from the Editors of the *Asia and the America* was in its issue of July 1944,324.

108. *Baltimore Sun*, 22 February 1944.

109. Willkie quoted in P. Sitaramayya, *History of the Indian National Congress*, New Delhi: 1969, Vol. II, 393; Thai Premier's son, 77th Cong., 1st sess., House Report No. 1471 on H.J.R. 251, Admitting Anant Khittasangka to the Military Academy at West Point, December 3, 1941. Hull recommended the admission "as it is at this time particularly desirable to foster and maintain these relations (between Thailand and U.S.) at their previous high standard." The Report itself, four days before Pearl Harbor, said this: "In view of the extreme national tension now prevailing in the Far East, it is deemed wise and expedient by our Government to go to considerable length in cultivating the goodwill and friendship of those peoples who are inclinded to be in accord with our way of life"; Hull's effort to "build up" China, *The Memoirs of Cardell Hull* New York, 1948, Vol. II, 1583; Frankfurter, in Bruce Allen Murphy *Brandeis/Frankfurter Connection: The Secret Political Activities of Two Supreme Court Justices* New York, 1982, 279; Jagjit Singh's own awareness of Asia was reflected in several of his letters. His argument in 1944—the war on the continent will be over soon. Eyes of the world will then be turned toward our war with Japan, and on the whole continent of Asia. Jagjit to Theodore Granick of the Forum on the Air, August 31, 1944; to William Philip Simms, September 21, 1944. In a press statement May 10, 1945 on a British promise to grant self- government to Burma after the war, Jagjit said no country in Asia will believe in this declaration "so long as India is not free! India is the test case for all Asiatic peoples." I.L.A. Papers.

110. Statement at Hearings to repeal the Chinese Exclusion Acts, 37; *The New Republic*, May 22, 1944 referred to China as a country "whose aid had grown indispensable to victory." *House Hearings, March 1945*, 106; Shridharani, *Warning to the West*, Foreword, viii.

111. Secretary, Indian Merchants Chamber, Bombay, to Secretary, Government of India, Department of External Affairs, New Delhi, January 16, 1945 referring to his office letter of November 10, 1943, File 256-F.E/45, External Affairs 1945, 3 correspondence. The earlier letter is Serial No. 9 in File 379- X/43 External Affairs 1943, National Archives of India: *India To-Day*, April 1944, 2 for Indian Chamber of Commerce demand; Sir Chunilal Mehta, delegrate to the Rye Conference urged a U.S.-India treaty

providing for reciprocity in residence and trade and complained that American naturalization was unduly postponed. File 249-E.P./45, 1945 External Affairs: Round up of American press comments on India; *India News* (Los Angeles), April 1944, 3; Roger Baldwin to Watumull, March 5, 1944, I.L.A. Papers Emanuel Celler, Extension of Remarks, *Cong. Record*, 78th Cong., 2nd sess., March 7, 1944, Appendix, A1427.

112. Dr. Das's statement at Hearings to repeal Chinese exclusion Acts, 34 and written statement at *S. 1595 Hearings* , 28, 30.

113. Anup Singh, "A Quota For India Too," *Asia and the Americas*, April 1944, 157; S. Chandrasekhar, "Indian Immigration in America," *Far Eastern Survey*, July 26, 1944; Jagjit Singh to Sidney Hertzberg, April 3, 1944, Jagjit Singh to John Doe, May 1, 1944; *India To- Day*, April and May 1944, Jagjit Singh's Press Releases, April 13, May 4, 1944; Emanuel Celler's Extension of Remarks, *Cong. Record*, 78th Cong., 2nd sess., Appendix, A1347, A1427; Celler's speech at the New York Town Hall meeting April 13, 1944, ibid., A1833, A1835; League's claim to have canvassed all 48 states, *S. 1595 Hearings*, 21; *India To-Day* urged its readers to "spread the word around," April 1944.

114. Jewish support; Hayim Greenberg, "Justice for Asians," *Modern Review*, September 1944, 175-176; Methodists, *Modern Review*, July 1944, 15; Federal Council of Churches, the Post-War World Council, *India To-Day*, July 1944; the New History Society, ibid., May 1944; American Civil Liberties Union and Americans in India, ibid., September 1944; the C.I.O., ibid., November 1944.

115. Indian legislature, *India To-Day*, April 1944, *House Hearings March 1945*, 112-113; Akali Dal telegram was dated May 22, 1944. Roosevelt Library Papers 1943-1945, 110. Nehru Memorial Museum and Library; State Department support, *India To-Day*, July 1944; Sir Chunilal Mehta's statement suggesting Indian merchant community's exasperation at the bill's consideration "being postponed from time to time." *Modern Review*, February 1945, 52. Support from American organizations, *House Hearings March 1945*, 94, 110; *Hearings on H. Res.* 52 Part 3, July 3, 1945, 97, 109.

116. *India To-Day*, May, July, August, December 1944; Jagjit Singh to Henry Luce, May 31, 1944; Jagjit Singh to Sudhindra Bose, September 26, 1944; Henry Luce to Jagjit Singh, May 5, 1944; I.L.A. Papers, *The New Republic*, May 22, 1944 wrote that hearings are to be held "soon," *House Hearings March 1945*, 106; India League's Press Release, November 15, 1944.

117. D. S. Saund, "Citizen Bill," India Congress Association Newsletter; champion talker quotation, Mubarek Ali to J. D. Khan, Phoenix, Arizona, November 11, 1944; more taunting comments, H. Santesson to Rustam Khan n.d., *The New India Bulletin*, December 1944, 3, 4.

118. Attorney General's remark, his letter to Senator Russell January 21, 1944, *S. 1595 Hearings*. 8. Statement of Edward J. Shaughnessy, Special Assistant to the Commissioner, Immigration and Naturalization Service, Washington, D.C., ibid., 6-16, the quotation is from p. 12. Emanuel Celler had sent his bill to the Department of Justice, *Cong. Record* 78th Cong., 2nd sess., Appendix, A1427.
119. Shaughnessy's helpful remarks, *S. 1595 Hearings*, 8, 9, 11, 12, 13, 14-15; he rejected all exemptions proposed in the bills; the amended text appears on p. 36; also see *India To-Day*, September 1944.
120. Sir G. S. Bajpai called Senator Burton a "progressive," File 256-F.E/45 External Affairs 1945, telegram No. 79 from Halifax, Washington to Govgenext, New Delhi, dated January 27, 1945, p. 4. Correspondence, National Archives of India; *S. 1595 Hearings*, 9, 13, 19, 45; India League's request for permission to testify at the hearings, ibid., 21. A year later Senator Burton, a former mayor of Cleveland was appointed an Associated Justice of the Supreme Court.
121. *S. 1595 Hearings*, 50; India Association for American Citizenship, called this incident an "unpleasant situation"; its letter to Jagjit dated February 20, 1945; Mubarek Ali to Anup Singh, *The New India Bulletin*, November 1944, Mubarek did not at that time know that another "Hindu," Dr. Das had sent in a written statement against the Langer bill.
122. Tenner insisted on keeping the exemptions, *S. 1595 Hearings*, 16-18; support for Luce-Celler bills, ibid., 50-51.
123. G. C. Ryan, Assistant Director, Intelligence Bureau's Note dated February 20, 1945, File 256-F.E/45 External Affairs 1945, 7-8 Notes, National Archives of India.
124. Dilip Singh Saund, "Citizen Bill," *Indian National Congress Association* Newsletter, November (?) 1944, 6-7.
125. Letter to Jagjit Singh, February 20, 1945; Jagjit Singh's Press Release February 5, March 1, 1945; *India To-Day*, February 1945; File 256 F.E/45, External Affairs 1945 telegram No. 79 from Halifax, Washington to Govgenext, New Delhi, January 27, 1945, pp. 4, 5, Correspondence; Indian Agency-General Washington to Joint Secretary to Government of India, External Affairs Department, January 29, 1945, p. 7 correspondence, National Archives of India.
126. Emanuel Celler, *You Never Leave Brooklyn: The Autobiography of Emanuel Celler* (New York, 1953), Foreword VII, 94, 22, 99, the second Celler bill became P.L. 774 on June 25, 1948.
127. Ibid., 95, 81; *House Hearings, March 1945*, 93; his opposition to the Act of 1924, *New York Times*, 30 June 1926; Dickstein, Celler and Zionism, *Cong. Record*, 79th Cong., 2nd sess., November 15, 1945, Appendix, A5162, Riggs, *Pressures on Congress*, 141.

128. *House Hearings, March 1945*, 2, 3, 5, 6, 9: some writers observed that "Indian and American economies could complement each other," Kate L. Mitchell, *Far Eastern Survey*, June 6, 1945, 137. Vice-President Isthmian Steampship co. to Jagjit Singh, August 4, 1945, I.L.A. Papers.
129. Jagjit Singh to Mrs. Luce, January 20, 1943; Jagjit had to keep a balance of praise and appreciation even between her and Celler, Jagjit to Mrs. Luce, November 26, 1945; she asked for material for her speech at the University of Rochester where she intended to argue "from America's own self-interested point of view for why we should urge Indian freedom." Mrs. Luce to Jagjit, October 18, 1843; Mrs. Luce's Secretary to Jagjit, October 25, 1943; Mackett, *Some Aspects*, 399-400.
130. Mrs. Luce's speech at the India League of America public meeting at the National Press Club Auditorium, Washington, D.C. May 4, 1944, *S. 1595 Hearings*, 23.
131. *House Hearings, March 1945*, 10, 11.
132. Ibid., 13, 14, 15, 17.
133. Ibid., 33, 39.
134. Ibid., 17, 21.
135. Ibid., 23, 25, 28, 30; Mrs. Dodge had attended the first annual dinner of the India Chamber of Commerce, on July 25, 1938. I.L.A. Papers.
136. *House Hearings, March 1945*, 80.
137. Ibid., 80-81.
138. Ibid., 80, Sir Bajpai was indeed having a series of conversations with the State Department in January 1945, probably with Grew himself, in the course of which he expressed his belief that "India is entitled . . . to be treated as China's equal both as regards citizenship and immigration." He also assured New Delhi that "in recent conversations, at any rate, I have had no indication that the State Department view this matter differently."

    As regards the apprehension expressed by the American Commissioner about a "reciprocal trade agreement," a letter of the same date as the Commissioner's, expressed the view of three high officials, Bajpai, Secretary Olaf Caroe and Commerce Member Sir Mohammed Azizul Huque that the bill before Congress had with them a higher priority. "I am more than ever convinced," Olaf Caroe wrote to Huque, " that we ought to get the naturalization and immigration business out of the way before we tackled seriously any revival of negotiations for a commercial treaty." File 246-F.E/45, 1945 External Affairs: Treaty of Commerce and Navigation between the Government of India and the U.S.A., Bajpai's letter is at page 1, Caroe's on page 2 of Proceedings.
139. *House Hearings March 1945*, 59.
140. Ibid., 79.

141. Ibid., 50, 51, 52: Biddle had already given public expression to his views favoring "democratic equality of opportunity, irrespective of race," in a speech in 1943, Charles Gordon, "The Racial Barrier to American Citizenship," *University of Pennsylvania Law Review*, March 1945, 253, fn. 80. His interest in such reform continued as Chairman of Americans for Democratic Action. Point G of its "Draft Domestic Policy," dated April 9, 1949. One of the members of its National Board was Ronald Reagan.
142. Regarding the anguish of decades—"No one can talk to Indians and not feel the burning," Pearl S. Buck, "India Tomorrow," *India Facts in Briefs* The National Committee for India's Freedom, Washington, D.C., 1945, 68, her article in File M-1517-C/45, dated September 5, 1945, National Archives of India; *House Hearings March 1945*, 24; Jagjit's prepared statement was widely distributed, Rakhit to J. N. Sharma, March 8, 1945.
143. Ibid., 84.
144. Ibid., 48.
145. Ibid., 84, 84-85.
146. Ibid., 85.
147. Ibid., Richard J. Walsh had in *New Leader*, November 11, 1944, expressed his confidence that Nehru could become a key man in the conferences for framing a new world order, File 249-EP/45, 1945, External Affairs; Round-up of American press comments on India, 6, Indian National Archives.
148. *House Hearings March 1945*, 86.
149. Ibid., 89.
150. Ibid., 90, 91.
151. Ibid., 90. In his interview with Narayanan Jagjit attempted to make his argument wider and more eloquent than he did at the Hearings, Transcript of Narayanan's interview with Jagjit Singh, 21-22.
152. *House Hearings March 1945*, 89, 90. On the following day Rep. Mason said at the hearing, ". . . until yesterday I will say definitely I was in favor of granting the half loaf, but we had testimony yesterday that rather opened my eyes to one or two things that I had not thought of before, and today I am ready to grant the whole loaf," 142.
153. Ibid., 91, 92. This incident of the Legion's neutrality over exclusion has behind it the story of a friendship established over twenty-five years ago between the Sikhs of California and their attorneys Shaughnessy and Atherton of Stockton; *California and the Oriental*, 108. Warren H. Atherton's high regard for his clients as farmers must have been reinforced by several of them having been soliders. Atherton helped in the repeal of Chinese exclusion, Riggs, *Pressures on Congress*, 79. The Legion was neutral but Atherton himself was not: His written statement in support of Luce-Celler bill, *House Hearings March 1945*, 92-93; Langer's statement regarding Atherton, ibid., 149, and *Senate Hearing on S. 236*, 11.

154. *House Hearings March 1945*, 113, 114, 115. During the House debate on the bill on October 10, Rep. McCowen insisted on Hines's version, *Cong. Record*, 79th Cong., 1st sess., 9525.
155. *House Hearings March 1945*, 115.
156. Ibid., 129-131; The Majority Report on the bill noted that "practically no one appeared in opposition."
157. Support from several other organizations was also expressed in the course of House hearings on H. Res. 52, part 3, 97, 109.
158. *House Hearings March 1945*, 147, 150.
159. Shridharani's article, ibid., 116-120; Anup Singh's claims expressed in the Congress Association Newsletter are somewhat exaggerated. His claim that Syud Hossain proposed a resolution as a member of the India League to start a campaign for citizenship may be well-grounded.
160. Fred W. Riggs, *Pressures on Congress*, 141, instances of help, *House Hearings March 1945*, 7, 50, 63; Hearings before Subcommittee I of the Committee on Immigration and Naturalization, House of Representatives, 79th Cong., 1st sess., Pursuant to H. Res. 52, Part 4, 335-336, Part 5, 372. It was H. J. McClatchy that Dickstein was trying to educate.
161. Emanuel Celler to President Roosevelt, March 20, 1945, Roosevelt Library Papers, Nehru Memorial Museum and Library, for Bajpai's message to Government of India, see fn. 175 below.
162. Government of India's interest, Telegram 2837, March 23, 1945 from Foreign, New Delhi to H. M.'s Ambassador, Washington, File 256-F.E/45 External Affairs, 1945, Correspondence 12, H. Dayal's Note, January 1, 1945, Notes, 1. The Indian Council of State adopted a resolution recommending equality for Indians in America. Secretary External Affairs Department accepted the resolution in the name of the Government of India. "But it is still a matter of doubt whether the resolution will ever reach Washington; the Viceroy and the India Office in London will probably be reluctant to take a step which might be interpreted as intervention in American internal affairs." Hayim Greenberg, "Justice for Asians," *Jewish Frontier*, May 1944, reproduced in *Modern Review*, September 1944, 176; this deep-seated habit of distrusting the British in every facet of their policy which might prove helpful to Indians once gave Jagjit Singh wrong notions. "I am making good use of the position of Sir G.S. Bajpai," he wrote to the head of an Indian Association in California, "to help us in this (Luce-Celler Bill) matter. The Government of India is in favor of this bill and therefore Sir. G. S. Bajpai has to help." Jagjit to The *Hindustan Gadar*, October 15, 1945. I.L.A. Papers.
163. File 256-F.E/45, External Affairs 1945; Grant of citizenship and immigration quota to Indians in the U.S.A. National Archives of India. The emphasis is in the original.

164. *Collected Works of Mahatma Gandhi*, Vol. 74, Ahmedabad, 1978, 190; *Modern Review*, June 1928, 750.
165. *India To-Day*, August 1941, January 1942.
166. Venkataramani and Shrivastava, *Quit India*, 280, for an example of his services to the British cause, 187; Jagjit Singh's comments on Bajpai over the UNRRA affair, see Chapter V, fn. 120; however there were limits to his docility, *Quit India*, 289-290 on his reaction to the Viceroy's policy statement. Ramlal Bajpai in his letter of November 30, 1943 to Jagjit Singh expressed his "indignation at the unworthy role played by (G. S. Bajpai) who did not have the courage (during the UNRRA controversy) to display any interest in the people on whose money he has been living in this country."
167. *Senate Hearings on S. 236*, G. S. Bajpai to Mubarek Ali, June 29, 1944, ibid., 40; also see Feroz Khan Noon to Mubarek Ali, May 31, 1944, ibid., a more positive statement as to the Agent-General's inclination is what Celler told the Immigration Committee, "The Indian government has come out in favor of the Bill, and has indicated in no uncertain language that it would create a tremendous entente cordiale between this country and India." *House Hearings March 1945*, 30.
168. Rep. Calvin D. Johnson's H. Res. 629, 78th Cong., 2nd sess., August 30, 1944; in January 1945 the Agent-General was again under attack by the nationalists who this time charged that his office was engaged in propaganda hostile to Indian national aspirations and was more concerned with watching the movements of Indian visitors and students than in helping them to establish contacts with Americans. He asked that the Government contradict such statements "promptly and emphatically." "I am not unduly sensitive" he told the official concerned, "but feel charges of this kind if repeated frequently without contradiction will bring office of Agent-General and its incumbent into disrepute in India." Telegram from Prodrome, Washington, No. 30 to Gov-Gen. E.A. Dept. Jan. 12, 1945; Jagjit Singh to William Phillips, November 20, 1944; Jagjit to P. T. Chandra, and to Devdas Gandhi both on August 9, 1945. Uma Shankar who wanted to become a journalist, helped with *India To-Day* which drew a taunt from Jagjit's friend Obeid Rehman that the elder Bajpai had "bought over" the League, Obeid to Jagjit, August 18, 1944; credit to Bajpai is in Jagjit's statement of March 12, 1945 which was given to Reuters. Jagjit and Bajpai were on speaking terms often exchanging communications on the fortunes of the bill, for instance. Bajpai's telegram to Jagjit mentioned in Jagjit's telegram to Master Umrao Singh, June 12, 1945 and a letter mentioned in Jagjit to *The Hindustan Gadar*, October 15, 1945.

Credit for the President's letter should go to the Attorney General. Bajpai did not even know the letter was coming. He told his bosses in New

Delhi ". . . we are especially indebted to him (the Chairman of the committee supporting India's claims. Text of the letter not yet available but I shall endeavour to obtain a copy." Telegram No. 153 from Halifax, Washington to Governor General (E. A. Dept.), New Delhi, March 10, 1945, File 256-F.E./45 External Affairs 1945, National Archives of India, 81. Correspondence; Bajpai i.e. the Government of India got a copy of the letter only after the President's permission ". . . the Indian Agent General requested . . . to get a copy of this letter for him to send to his Government as he knew his Government would like very much to read the letter in the Indian National Legislature. Mr. Allen (of the State Department) wants Mr. Bohlen (Secretary to the President) to find out if the Agent General can have a copy for them to make public, or if not, can a copy be given him in confidence."—Typed notation—"C(harles) B(ohlen). OK F.D.R.," Roosevelt Papers, Nehru Memorial Museum and Library.

169. Telegram No. 203, March 14, 1945, from Halifax, Washington to Gov-genext, New Delhi.

170. *House Hearings March 1945*, 150, 151. The Government of India suspicion and the quotation, File 256-F.E/45 telegram No. 2837 of March 23, 1945 from Foreign, New Delhi to H. M.'s Ambassador, Washington, p. 85 Correspondence; Emanuel Celler objected to Olaf Caroe's allegation (made publicly in the Council of State) in a statement on April 2 and Jagjit Singh on April 10, Celler called Caroe's observations "utterly absurd." Jagjit Singh revealed that Mrs. Pandit's statement which had upset the External Affairs Secretary had not even been published in any American paper. In a press statement on June 8 Jagjit Singh held Mrs. Clare Luce partly responsible for the tabling of bill: "It was very unfortunate that Mrs. Luce was away in Italy when these bills came up for hearing . . . which deprived us of her active support. Mrs. Luce has a strong following among the Republicans and her presence at the time of the hearings would have greatly helped." In a statement issued on April 10 he revealed that three members of the Committee who favored the bill had failed to attend the March 20 meeting.

171. *India To-Day*, March 1945; *Newsindia*, London, April-May 1946, 6. This journal also saw racism in the Committee's decision; Statement of President, Federation of Indian Chambers of Commerce and Industry, April 3, 1945, Viceroy's observation was made at a meeting of the references and the decision to withhold official publicity, File 256-F.E/45, National Archives of India. In his letter of June 7, Celler told President Truman that the India Purchasing Commission was instructed to cease purchases of American goods" a loss to the extent of $9,000,000 a month.

172. Jagjit's telegram to Bagga S. Sunga (n.d.) with copy to Dr. (J.N.) Sharma, the latter's reply June 23, 1945; intention to keep on fighting, Jagjit's press

statements, April 10 and June 8, 1945; he professed to have met "scores of Indians" residing in California since his arrival in San Francisco to cover the United Nations Conference; his statement of June 8; Jagjit to Rep. James G. Fulton, April 2, 1945; Jagjit to Dhillon, July 11, 1945 with copy to Sharma and Sunga; to Sunga, June 11, 1945. Jagjit telegram to Master Umaro Singh, June 12, 1945; in April he had informed Godharam Channon, Sunga, Karm Singh, Watumull, J.N. Sharma of his desire to meet them in San Francisco, his letters dated April 17, 1945. I.L.A. Papers.

173. Roosevelt had called the quota "this small number," Halifax called the bill's provisions "a *gesture* of friendship" and Biddle wrote to Truman that the quota would be about one hundred a year, "yet I believe it important that bill should be passed," Letters of March 5, May 3, May 15, 1945 respectively. Emphasis added.
174. Edward J. Shaughnessy's statement, *Senate Hearing on S. 236, 3.*
175. Telegram Halifax, Washington to Govgenext, New Delhi, March 20, 1945, No. 227, File 256-F.E/45, External Affairs 1945, Correspondence, 84, National Archives of India; also Shaughnessy in fn. 174 above.
176. Acting Secretary of State Grew's letter to the President dated march 23, 1945, Roosevelt papers, Nehru Memorial Museum and Library, Telegram No. 247 March 24, 1945, from Halifax, Washington to Govgenext, new Delhi, File 256-F.E./45, External Affairs 1945, Correspondence, 86, National Archives of India.
177. Celler's letter to the President see fn. 161. The President wrote to Ramspeck on March 25 which the latter acknowledged on the 29th, Roosevelt Papers, Nehru Memorial Museum and Library; seeking Senator Truman's help, telegram No. 287, April 9, 1945 from Halifax, Washington to Foreign, New Delhi, File 256-F.E/45, Correspondence, 88, National Archives of India.
178. Telegram from Halifax, Washington to Govgenext, New Delhi April 26, 1945, Correspondence, 112, Halifax letter text in File 256-F.E/45, Correspondence 273, Truman Library Papers; *Cong. Record* 79th Cong., 1st sess., October 10, 1945, 9524.
179. *House Hearings March 1945*, 55 and 30, respectively. *Senate Hearing on S. 236*, 4. *Cong. Record*, 79th Cong., 1st sess., October 10, 1945, 9523. Rep. Allen did not agree with this version. Ibid.
180. Francis Biddle to the President, May 15, 1945, Truman Papers, Nehru Memorial Museum and Library, New Delhi.
181. William D. Hassett, Secretary to the President to Samuel Dickstein, May 18, 1945; G.S. Bajpai to President Truman May 28, 1945, handwritten note on "Memorandum for the President" by "S.I.R.," June 11, 1945; handwritten note initialled H.S.T. on the letter. Celler to Truman, June 7, 1945. The note says "Talk to Rayburn" probably an instruction to his

Secretary; File 256-F.E/45, telegram June 15, 1945, Correspondence, 277, appreciation for Bajpai's work. ibid., June 19, 1945, Correspondence, 278; Clare Luce telegram to Jagjit Singh, June 9, 1945.

182. Telegrams to the League from Mrs. Luce and Emanuel Celler, June 14, 1945; Jagjit's statement June 15, 1945, *India To-Day*, June 1945; *House Hearings March 1945*, 153; 154; Rakhit to Celler, June 15, 1945, Rakhit to all members of the League and Indians, same date, Jagjit to Celler, n.d. Majority and Minority Reports are in Report No. 854, 79th Cong., Ist sess., Rep. Allen's authorship of the Minority Report, *Indian To-Day*, September 1945,October 1945, comment on the Minority Report, Deputy Secretary C.B. Duke's Note, July 23, 1945, File 256-F.E/45, Notes, 30, National Archives of India.

183. On how Lord Halifax, as Undersecretary for the Colonies, in the early 1920s had thwarted the political welfare of Indians settled in British possessions, see Hugh Tinker, *Separate and Unequal*, 41, 42.

184. Just two weeks after the bill had been released from the Committee, Chairman Dickstein inserted in the Congressional Record several editorial comments favorable to the passage of the bill. *Cong. Record*, 79th Cong., 1st sess., Appendix, A 3574, A3575, A3578, A3588; William Phillips support, Mrs. Luce's speech, *Cong. Record*, 79th Cong., 1st sess., October 10, 1945, 9527; Dickstein, ibid., 9537.

187. File 256-F.E/45, External Affairs 1945, National Archives of India, Correspondence, 113.

186. Ibid., Correspondence, 82; Emanuel Celler to Charles G. Ross, September 22, 1945; President Truman to Celler, September 26, 1945 Truman Papers; Jagjit to Emanuel Celler, September 26,1945.

187. File 256-F.E/45, Correspondence, 355, National Archives of India; telegram Martha E. Cameron to Jagjit Singh, October 5, 1945; Jagjit Singh to "Dear Congressman," October 2, 1945; Jagjit to Congressman Fulton, October 6,, 1945 (2 letters, same date).

188. *Cong. Record*, 79th Cong., 1st sess., 9519, figures and names mentioned in the "Call of the House"; presence of princes pointed out by Congressman Gearhart, 9533. The debate covers 9519-9544. About 27 members particpated, 15 for, 12 against the bill; Jagjit's presence, Jagjit to Congressman Fulton's Secretary, October 6, 1945.

189. Rep. Sabath's experience had been a long one even ten years ago: "As an old member of this committee, for 24 years I have had a great deal of experience with the gentleman who preceded me . . . claiming to represent the Fraternal Patriotic Americans and the Junior Order United American Mechanics," *Hearings on H.R. 6795*, April 9, 10, and 11, 1935, 70.

190. Rep. Allen would send the Gospel to India rather than let Indians enter the United States. His colleagues John C. Kunkel and Jerry Voorhis too

believed in spreading the teachings of the Gospel but both voted for the bill. Four days after the House debate Kunkel in a speech denied that the Luce-Celler bill opens the gates to any flood of immigration from outside and believed that "The bill removes a legislative insult to a people and a race." *Cong. Record.* 79th Cong., 2nd sess., Appendix A4494.

191. The pamphlet Congressman Smith said he was quoting from was *A Penguin Special: A Plan of Economic Development for India*, published January 1944, the House debate of October 10, 1945, 9537. The Plan had also been published in *Hindustan Times*, New Delhi, January 29, 1944 under the caption, "Post-War Economic Development of India." In this connection Jagjit's remarks on the character of some speeches made in Congress during the India Food Bill debate in 1946 are of interest. Such debate, he wrote in one of his articles, "gives the chance to some irresponsible" and "one-hundred-and-ten percent Americans" to open their big mouths and heap ludicrous attacks upon us. "Is American Aid Necessary For India? I.L.A. Papers.

192. Rep. Judd's part in the repeal of the Chinese exclusion had also been significant: "His importance in bringing about the passage of the repeal law cannot be exaggerated," Riggs, *Pressures on Congress*, 191. An official of the Government of India paid Judd's speech a high compliment, calling it "interesting," File256-F.E/45. External Affairs 1945, 33 - Notes, National Archives of India.

193. Not all friends of India voted for the bill. Francis Case of South Dakota had spoken in favor of India in 1943, *Cong. Record*, 78th Cong., 1st sess., p. 4800. The India League had distributed copies of his speech. Congressman Boykin of Alabama had forwarded to President Roosevelt in February 1943 a telegram asking for release of Mahatma Gandhi. Roosevelt Papers, Nehru Memorial Museum and Library. Case was among the "Not voting" although he was present when the debate started. Boykin was absent but he had paired with Gorski who was "against" (Allen's move to recommit) *India To-Day*, October 1945; the League sent out a letter of thanks to Congressmen. Jagjit to "Dear Congressman," October 19, 1945. Rep. W.R. Poage (D-Tx) who supported the Indian witnesses at the 1939 hearings also voted "Nay."

194. Jagjit Singh to James Callahan, April 29, 1946. I.L.A. Papers

195. Riggs, *Pressures on Congress*, 79, 137, 143, 181, 182, 188, 189.

196. Ibid., 77-79.

197. Ibid., 79.

198. *Cong. Record*, 79th Cong., 1st sess., March 8, 1945,, 1902; Drury, *A Senate Journal*, 122-196, 238.

199. One-man Lobby, *The New Yorker*, March 24, 1951, 46; File 256-F.E/45, telegram No. 7541, dated October 13, 1945, National Archives of India: Congressman Celler to President Truman, October 23, 1945; President

Truman to Senator Russell, November 2, 1945; Jagjit Singh's own efforts to push the bill through the Senate Committee—his telegrams to Senator Ball, November 7 and 12, 1945, his telegram to Senator Russell, November 21, 1945.

200. "When Will the Senate Act on Indian Immigration?" *Christian Century*, December 12, 1945, 1376; Mackett, *Some Aspects*, 440; *India To-Day*, February 1946.

201. *The National Herald*, Lucknow, April 3, 1946; file 330(8)-F.E/45, External Affairs, 1946.

202. Hemendra Rakhit to Bagga Singh Sunga, March 21, 1946, Celler to President Truman, April 30, 1946; *India To-Day*, April 1946; Senate Report 1440, June 10, 1946; 79th Cong., 2nd sess., Jagjit Singh to James Callahan, April 29, 1946, I.L.A. Papers.

203. Emanuel Celler to President Truman, April 30, 1946; President Truman to Emanuel Celler, May 7, 1946.

204. *Cong. Record* 79th Cong., 2nd sess., June 25, 1946, 7458.

205. Ibid.

206. Ibid.

207. Jagjit had written to Col. Johnson in January that he would use the letter "on my next trip to Washington." Jagjit to Louis Johnson, January 31, 1946. We do not know when, if at all, the letter was actually used.

208. *Cong. Record*, 79th Cong., 2nd sess., June 25, 1946, 7458.

209. Ibid., June 14, 1946, 6918.

210. Ibid., 6918, 6919

211. Ibid., 6933; *India To-Day* November 1945.

212. The new title, *Cong. Record*, 79th Cong., 2nd sess., 7957; presented to the President, 8015; signed by the President 8299.

213. *The Voice of India*, September 1946, 324.

214. Dr. S.R. Mandal's telegram on the occasion of a reception dinner given in Mr. Singh's honor by the India Community in New York, August 4, 1946. It reads in part: "I was a citizen at one time but my paper was cancelled. Now I shall be able to regain it. Thanks to you." His name is in a Senate Hearing as "Sant Ram Mandel" naturalized by the District Court of San Francisco on June 10, 1920, *Senate Hearings, December 1926*, 1.

215. Press Release, Tuesday, July 2, 1946. Passage of India Immigration Bill First Step in Three Fold Plan: Statement by Congressman Emanuel Celler, Representative 15th Congressional district, N.Y.; Taraknath Das's *Address*, August 4, 1946, 1.

216. Gary R. Hess, "The Asian Indian Immigrants in the United States: The Early Phase, 1900-65" in S. Chandrasekhar (Ed.). *From India to America*, Ch. 2, 32.

217. These well-known Indians included Dr. Taraknath Das, Gobind Behari Lal, Bagga Singh Sunga, Mumtaz Kitchlew, Prafulla Mukerji, Haridas T. Muzumdar, S.S. Sarna, D.S. Saund and G.J. Watumull. The quotation is from Dr. J.N. Sharma's message.

218. His hard work is mentioned in several letters: Jagjit to Callahan, April 29, 1946 and June 11, 1946; to R.S. Dhillon, October 14, 1947, to George E. Jones, June 19, 1946; Hemendra Rakhit's report on League activities 1946, p.3. "Never again. With the kind of run-around you get in Congressional circles and from attractive but adamant secretaries in Congressmen's and Senators' offices, I feel I have done my job." Jagjit Singh quoted in Fern Marja, "India's One-Man Lobby," *New York Post*, July 31, 1946.

219. Jagjit Singh Oral History Transcript, "Main Points Covered in the Interview," other documents in the I.L.A. Papers. Jagjit Singh's own assessment of his nationalist work in the United States was accurate because it was realistic and modest. "I have never been foolish enough to think that what I or anyone else may do in this country will have any direct effect upon our freedom movement. But I do think that our work here has made the life of the British propagandist slightly uncomfortable and it has also been an incentive for English liberals in England to do more active and effective work. In short, though the frontal attack must come from within India, I believe we have been able to deliver a few flank attacks." Jagjit Singh to Mrs. Ammu Swaminathan, New Delhi, February 14, 1946, I.L.A. Papers.

220. Messages from Bagga Singh Sunga, J.N. Sharma, and Surain Singh Dhillon. Extracts from Messages, 3.

221. *Voice of India*, September 1946, 324.

222. Ibid.

223. *India To-Day*, July 1946.

224. *Voice of India*, ibid.

225. His speech *Cong. Record*, 79th Cong., 2nd sess., June 25, 1946, 7458.

226. Texts of these letters in *Cong. Record*, 79th Cong., 1st sess., 9524 October 10, 1945.

227. Lauchlin Currie may have had a hand in persuading President Roosevelt to support the bill. Jagjit's interview with Dr. Narayanan, 23; Venkataramani, *Quit India*, 261, 291.

228. President Truman to "Dear Dick" November 2, 1945, emphasis added.

229. *House Hearings March 1945*, 67.

BIBLIOGRAPHIES

Works listed below contain bibliographies on various aspects of the struggles and achievements of Indian immigrants to the United States.

Chandrasekhar, S., ed.. *From India to America: A Brief History of Immigration; Problems of Discrimination; Admission and Assimilation.* A Population Review Book. La Jolla, California, 1982, pp. 93-106.

Juergensmeyer, Mark, and Barrier, N. Gerald, eds. *Sikh Studies: Comparative Perspectives on a Changing Tradition.* Berkeley Religious Studies Series, Graduate Theological Union, Berkeley, California, 1979, pp. 215-219.

Melendy, H. Brett. *Asians in America : Filipinos, Koreans, and East Indians.* Boston : Twayne Publishers, 1977, pp. 299-325.

Singh, Ganda. "The Sikhs in Canada and California : A Bibliography." *The Panjab Past and Present*, IV, Part II, December 1970, pp. 380-400.

Manuscript and Archival Material

External Affairs and Commerce Department files in the National Archives of India, New Delhi.

India League of America Papers at the Indian Council of World Affairs, Sapru House, New Delhi.

In the Nehru Memorial Museum and Library. New Delhi.
Jagjit Singh papers
M. S. Hardikar papers.
Ramlal Bajpai papers.
Dr. Syud Hossain papers.
Oral History Transcripts of Jagjit Singh and Haridas T. Muzumdar.
Select Documents from the Roosevelt Library, Hyde Park, NY.
Select Documents from the Truman Library, Independence, MO.

The Reminiscences of Roger Nash Baldwin. Chapter VI, Indian Independence 1917-1947. New York: Columbia University.

U.S. Government Publications

House of Representatives, Committee on Immigrations and Naturalization. *Hearing on Restriction of Immigration.* December 6 and 11, 1913. 63rd Congress, sess. 2.

-----. *Hearings on Hindu Immigration*, February 13 and 19, 1914 ("The Sudhindra Hearings").

-----. *Hearings on Hindu Immigration*, April 16 and 30, 1914 ("The Bhutia Hearings").

United States Senate, Committee on Immigration. *Hearings on S.J. Res. 128 Providing for the Ratification and Confirmation of the Naturalization of Certain Persons of the Hindu Race*, December 9, 15, 1926.

-----. *Hearings on S. 868 Providing for the Deportation of Certain Alien Seamen, and for other purposes*. April 1934.

-----. *Hearings on S. 379 Providing for the Deportation of Certain Alien Seamen, and for other purposes*. April 1935.

House of Representatives, Committee on Immigration. *Hearings on HR 6795 to Autharize the Deportation of the Habitual Criminal.* April 1935.

-----. *Hearings on H.R. 7170 to Permit Certain Resident Oriental Veterans to Apply for Citizenship*. April 23, 1935.

-----. *Hearings on Petitions by Natives of India*, June 21, 1939.

United States Senate Committee on Immigrations *Hearings* on HR 6250 to Amend the Nationality Act of 1940 . February 1942.

House of Representatives, Committee on Immigration. *Hearings on HR 1882 and HR 2309 to Repeal the Chinese Exclusion Acts.* May and June 1943.

Senate Subcommittee on Immigration. *Hearings on S. 1595 to Permit Naturalization of Approximately Three Thousand Natives of India*. September 1944.

House of Representatives, Committee on Immigration. *Hearings on H.R. 173 (and others) to Grant a Quota to Eastern Hemisphere Indians and to Make Them Racially Eligible for Naturalization.* March 1945.

Senate Subcommittee on Immigration. *Hearings on S. 236 to Permit all People From India Residing in the United States to be Naturalized. April 1945.*

House of Representatives, Committee on Immigration. *Hearings on H. Res. 52 to Study Problems Relating to Immigration and Deportation.* August 1945.

-----. *Hearings on H.R. 3663 to Deny Admission to Certain Aliens and to Reduce Immigration Quotas*. February, March, May 1946.

Biographical Directory of the American Congress, 1774-1971 (1971).

United States Congress. *Congressional Record.* 62nd, 63rd, 64th, and 79th Congresses.

Interviews

Dr. R. Narayanan's interview with Jagjit Singh, 1972. Copy of transcript received courtesy of the interviewer.

Writer's interview with Mrs. Malti (J.J.) Singh in New Delhi, 1985.

Writer's interviews on the telephone with Haridas T. Muzumdar, 1984; Mrs. Vivian Thind, 1984, 1985, 1986; Marian Z. Kosa (Mrs. Saund), 1985; Mrs. Ruth Beck, formerly Office Secretary of the India League of America, 1985.

Recorded Naturalization Cases

Akhay Kumar Muzumdar v. United States, 299 Fed. 240.

Ex parte Shahid, 205 Fed. 812.

In re Akhay Kumar Muzumdar, 207 Fed. 115; United States v. Akhay Kumar Muzumdar, 296 Fed. 173.

In re Balsara, 171 Fed. 294, U.S. vs. Balsara, 180 Fed. 694.

In re Bhagat Singh Thind, 263 Fed. 683.

United States v. Bhagat Singh Thind, 261, U.S. 204.,

In re Feroz Din, 27 Fed., 2nd 568

In re Halladjian et al., 174 Fed. 834.

In re Mohan Singh, 257 Fed. 209.

In re Sadar Bhagwab Singh, 246 Fed. 496.

Kharaiti Ram Samras v. United States, 125 Fed., 2nd 879.

Kharaiti Ram Samras v. United States, 317 U.S. 634.

Takao Ozawa v. United States, 260 U.S. 178.

Shankar Laxman Gokhale v. United States, 278 U.S. 591.

Shankar Laxman Gokhale v. United States, 278 U.S. 662.

United States v. Gokhale, 26 Fed. 2nd 360.

United States v. Sakharam Ganesh Pandit, 15 Fed., 2nd 285.

United States v. Sakharam Ganesh Pandit, 273 U.S. 759.

United States v. Ali, 7 Fed. 2nd 728.

United States v. Ali, 20 Fed. 2nd 998.

Other Government Publications

Government of India. *Imperial Gazetteer of India.* Vol. 1. Punjab. Calcutta; Privincial Series, 1908.

U.S. Department of State. Papers Relating to the Foreign Relations of the United States, 1924, 1942, Washington.

U.S. Immigration Commission. *Reports of the Immigration Commission.* Washington, 1909-1911.

State Board of Control. *California and the Oriental*, June 19, 1920. New York: Arno Press, 1978

U.S. Department of Justice. *Laws Applicable to Immigration and Nationality*, 1953.

Newspapers and Journals

Indian

Akali Patrika Jallandhar.

Indian Review, Madras.

The Mahratta, Poona.

The Modern Review, Calcutta.

The Tribune, Lahore, Ambala.

American

Asia and the Americas.

Christian Century.

Harvard Law Review.

The Hindustanee Student (H.A.A.) spelled "Hindusthanee" from 1914 to 1918.

Independent Hindustan. San Francisco (Gadar Party).

India. New York (H.A.A.)

India and U.S.A. New York.

India News Service. New York (FFI).

India Today. New York (India League of America)

Indian Christian. New Haven, Connecticut.

Indian National Congress Association Newsletter, Los Angeles.

Missionary Review.

New India (India Welfare League).

New Orient (India Welfare League).

Open Court. New York.

Orient. New York.

Orient and USA. Washington.

The Oriential Magazine. New York

Outlook.

Outwest.

Overland Monthly.

Proceedings of the Asiatic Exclusion League. San Francisco.

United States of India. San Francisco (Gadar Party).

Theses and Dissertations

Deol, Dr. Gurdev Singh. "The Role of the Ghadar Party in the National Movement." Ph.D. diss., Punjab University, Delhi, 1969.

Khan, Salim. "A Brief History of Pakistanis in the Western United States." MA thesis, California State University, Sacramento, 1981.

La Brack, Bruce Wilfred. "The Sikhs of Northern California: A Socio-historical Study." Ph.D. diss., Syracuse University, 1981.

Mackett, Walter Charles. "Some Aspects of the Development of American Opinion on India 1918-1947. Ph.D. diss., University of Southern California, June 1957.

Misrow, Jagdish C. "East Indian Immigration on the Pacific Coast." MA thesis, Stanford University, 1915. (Reprinted by R&E Research Associates, San Francisco, California, 1971).

Puri, Harish K. "Ghadar Movement : Ideology, Organization and Strategy." Guru Nanakdev University Press, 1983.

Rathore, Naeen Gul. "Indian Nationalist Agitation in the United States: Lajpat Rai and the India Home Rule League of America 1914-1920." Ph.D. diss., Columbia University, 1965.

Schmidt, E.R. "American Relations with South Asia, 1900-1940." Ph. D. diss., University of Pennsylvania, 1955.

Schulz, Constance B. "Samuel Dickstein : Congressional Investigator, 1934-1939." MA thesis, University of Cincinnati, 1966.

Singh, Harnum. "American Press Opinion About Indian Government and Politics, 1919-1935." Ph.D. diss., Goeorgetown University, 1949.

Waldron, Gladys Henning. "Anti-Foreign Movements in California." Ph.D. thesis, University of California, Berkeley, 1956.

Reference Works

Benton's Abridgement of the Debates of Congress, Vol. 1. New York: 1857.

Collected Works of Mahatma Gandhi, Vol. XLIII. March-June 1930. The Publications Division Ministry of Information and Broadcasting , Government of India. New Delhi, India, 1971.

Sen, S.P. *Dictionary of National Biography*. Calcutta: Institute of Historical Studies, 1972.

Statesman's Year Book.

Thernstrom, Stephen, ed. *Harvard Encyclopedia of American Ethnic Groups*. Cambridge, Mass.: Harvard University Press, 1980.

Waiz, S.A., ed. *Indians Abroad Directory 1934.* The Imperial Indian Citizenship Association, Bombay, 1934.

White's *Conspectus of American Biography: Members of Congress up to 1937.*

Who's who in America.

Articles

Bose, Arun Coomar. "Indian Nationalist Agitators in the U.S.A. and Canada Till the Arrival of Har Dayal in 1911." *Journal of Indian History* 43 (1975): 227-39.

Bose, Sudhindra. "American Impression of a Hindu Student." *Forum* 53 (1915) : 251-57.

Chandrashekhar, S. "Indian Immigration in America". *Far Eastern Survey* 13 (1944): 138-41.

Dadabhoy, Yusuf. "Circuitous Assimilation Among Rural Hindustanis in California." *Social Forces* 33 (1954): 138-41.

Daniels, Roger. "Westerners From the East: Oriental Immigrants Reappraised. *Pacific Historical Review* (1966): 373-84.

De Motte, Marshall, "California - White or Yellow?" *Annals of American Academy of Political and Social Sciences* (January 1921): 18-23.

Dignan, Don K. "The Hindu Conspiracy in Anglo-American Relations During World War I." *Pacific Historial Review* 60 (1971) : 57-76.

Drury, C.M. "Hinduism in the United States." *Missionary Review*, April 1981: 281-83.

Garner, James W. "Denationalization of American Citizens." *American Journal of International Law* 21 January 1927: 106-107.

Hallberg, Gerald N. "Bellingham, Washington's Anti- Hindu Riot." *Journal of the West* 12 (1973) : 163-75.

Hay, Stephen N. "Rabindranath Tagore in America." *American Quarterly* Vol. 14, No. 3 (Fall 1962).

Hess, Gary R. "The 'Hindu' in America: Immigration and Naturalization Policies and India, 1917-1946." *Pacific Historical Review* 38 (1969): 59-79.

________. "The Forgotten Asian Americans : The East Indian Community in the United States," in Norris Hundley, Jr., Ed. *The Asian American* Santa Barbara, CA: Clio Press, 1976, pp. 157-77.

Jacoby, Harold S. "A Half-century Appraisal of the East Indians in the United States." *The Sixth Annual College of the Pacific Faculty Research Lecture*, May 23, 1956, Stockton.

Jayawardena, Chandra. "Migration and Social Change: A Survey of East Indian Communities Overseas." *Geographical Review* 58 (1968): 426-28.

Jensen, Joan M. "Apartheid: Pacific Coast Style." *Pacific Historical Review* 38 (3) (August 1969): 335-40

________. "The Hindu Conspiracy'" A Reevaluation." *Pacific Historical Review* 48 (1979): 65-83.

La Brack, Bruce. "Occupational Specialization Among Rural California Sikhs: The Interplay of Culture and Economics." *American Journal* (Fall-Winter 1982): 29-56.

La Brack, Bruce, and Leonard, Karen. "Conflict and Compatibility in Punjabi-Mexican Immigrant Families in Rural California, 1915-

1965." *Journal of Marriage and Family* 46 (August 1984): 527-37.

Leonard, Karen. "Marriage and Family Life Among Early Asian Indian Immigrants. *Population Review* (1981): 67-75.

________. "The Pahkar Singh Murders: A Punjabi Response to California's Alien Land Law." *Amerasia 11:1* (1984): 75-87.

_______. "Punjabi Farmers and California's Alien Land Law." *Agricultural History* IV (October 1985), 549-62.

McCrae, L. "Birds of Passage in California." *Missionary Review* (December 1918): 910.

McCrae, Lee. "Self-Exiled in America: Something About the Hindus in California." *Missionary Review* 39 (July 1916): 525-26.

Millis, H.A. "East India Immigration to British Columbia and the Pacific Coast States." *American Economic Review* 1 (1911): 72-76.

_______. "East Indian Immigration to the Pacific Coast." *Survey* 28 (June 1, 1912): 380-81.

_______. "The Hindu in America." *American Review of Reviews* 37 (May 1908): 604-5.

Narayanan, R. "Indian Immigration and the India League of America." *Indian Journal of American Studies* 2 (1) (1972) : 1-30

Olin, Spencer C., Jr. "European Immigrants and Oriental Alien: Acceptance and Rejection by the California Legislature of 1913." *Pacific Historical Review* 35 (August 1966): 303-15.

Raucher, Alan. "American Anti-Imperialists and the Pro-India Movement, 1900-1932." *Pacific Historical Review* 43 (1974): 83-110.

Scheffauer, Herman. "The Tide of Turbans." *Forum* 43 (June 1910): 616-18.

Shaplen, Robert. "Profiles: One-Man Lobby." *The New Yorker* (March 24, 1951): 35-55.

Singh, Amarjit. "The Ghadar Party Trial." *Panjab Past and Present*, Patiala (October 1970): 401-15.

Singh, Gurdial. "East Indians in the United States." *Sociology and Social Research* 30 (1946): 210- 11.

Spector, Ronald. "The Vermont Education of Taraknath Das: An Episode in British-American-Indian Relations." *Vermont History* 48 (1980): 89-95.

Spellman, John W. "The International Extensions of Political Conspiracy as Illustrated by the Ghadar Party." *Journal of Indian History* (April 1959): 23-45.

"The Hindu, the Newest Immigration Problem." *Survey* (October 1, 1910): 2-3.

Books

Abell, Tyler (Ed.). *Drew Pearson Diaries 1949-1959*. New York: Holt, Rinehart and Watson, 1974.

Abbott, Edith. *Immigration: Select Documents and Case Records.* Chicago : The University of Chicago Press, 1924.

Acheson, Dean. *Sketches From Life : Of Men I Have Known,* New York: Harper & Brothers, 1959.

Adams, Brooks. *The New Empire.* New York: The Macmillan Co., 1903.

The Autobiography of Robert Morss Lovett; All Our Years. New York: The Viking Press, 1948.

Bagchi, Moni. *Swami Abhedananda: A Spiritual Biography.* Calcutta: Ramkrishna Vedanta Math, 1968.

Banerjee, Kalyan Kumar. *Indian Freedom Movement : Revolutionaries in America.* Calcutta: Jijnasa, 1969.

Barnes, Mary Clark, and Barnes, Lemuel Call. *The New American: A Study in Immigration.* New York: Fleming H. Revell Co., 1913.

Bennett, Marion T. *American Immigration Policy: A History.* Washington, D.C.: Public Affairs Press, 1963.

Bogardu, Emory S. *Immigration and Race Attitudes.* Boston: D.C. Heath & Co., 1928.

Bose, Arun Coomer. *Indian Revolutionaries Abroad 1905- 1922: In the Background of International Developments.* Patna: Bharati Bhawan 1971.

Brinton, Crane. *The United States and Britain.* Cambridge, Massachusetts: Harvard University Press, 1945.

Brown, Emily C. *Har Dayal: Hindu Revolutionary and Rationalist.* Tucson: University of Arizona Press, 1975.

Buchignani, Norman, Indra, Doreen M., with Srivastava, Ram. *Continuous Journey: A Social History of South Asians in Canada.* Toronto, Canada: McClelland and Steward Ltd., 1985.

Buck, Pearl. *American Unity and Asia*. New York: John Day, 1942.

________. *My Several Worlds: A Personal Record.* New York: The John Day Company, 1954.

Burke, Marie Louise. *Swami Vivekananda in America: New Discoveries.* Calcutta: Advaita Ashram, 1958.

Celler, Emanuel. *You Never Leave Brooklyn: The Autobiography of Emanuel Celler.* New York: The John Day Company, 1953.

Chandrasekhar, S. *Indian Emigration to America.* Bombay: Oxford University Press, 1947.

Chase, Ray E., and Pandit, S.G. *An Examination of the Opinion of the Supreme Court of the United States Deciding Against the Eligibility of Hindus for Citizenship*. Los Angeles, 1926.

Cheng, Lucie, and Bonacich, Edoa (Eds.). *Labor Immigration Under Capitalisam: Asian Workers in the United States Before World War II*. Berkeley: University of California Press, 1984.

Complete Works of Swami Vivekanand. 8 vols. Calcutta: Advait Ashram, 1970-1979.

Daniels, Roger. Asian America: *Chinese and Japanese in the United States Since 1850*. University of Washington Press, 1988.

_______. *History of Indian Immigration to the United States*. New York: The Asia Society, 1989.

_______. *Politics of Prejudice: The Anti-Japanese Movement in California and the Struggle for Japanese Exclusion*. Berkeley: University of California Press, 1962.

Das, Frieda Hauswirth. *A Marriage to India*. New York: Vanguard Press, 1930.

Das, Rajani Kant. *Hindustani Workers on the Pacific Coast*. Berlin: 1923.

Dees, Joseph Lester. *Tagore in America*. USIS Calcutta, 1961.

Dharamavira. *Lala Har Dayal and Revolutionary Movement of His Times*. New Delhi: Indian Book Company, 1970.

Divine, Robert A. *American Immigration Policy 1924- 1952*. New Haven: Yale University Press, 1957.

Drury,, Allen. *A Senate Journal 1943-1945*. New York: McGraw Hill, 1963.

Fisher, Maxine P. *The Indians of New York City*. New Delhi: Heritage Publishers, 1980.

Flynn, Elizabeth Gurley. *The Rebel Girl: An Autobiography: My First Life (1906-1926)*. New York: International Publishers, 1955.

Franklin, Frank George. *Legislative History of Naturalization in the United States*. New York: Arno Press, 1969.

Garis, Roy L. *Immigration Restriction: A Study of the Opposition to and Regulation of Immigration into the United States*. New York: The Macmillan Co., 1927.

Gopal, Ram. *Lokmanya Tilak: A Biography*. London: Asia Publishing House, 1965.

Hardikar, N.S. *Lala Lajpat Rai in America*. New Delhi: Servants of the People Society, 1966.

Harris, Theodore F. *Pearl S. Buck: A Biography*. New York: The John Day Company, 1969.

Hess, Gary R. *America Encounters India 1941-1947*. Baltimore: Johns Hopkins University Press, 1971.

Hodges, Charles. *The Background of International Relations*. New York: John Wiley & Sons, Inc.,1931.

Hope, A. Guy. *America and Swaraj: The U.S. Role in Indian Independence*. Washington, D.C.: Public Affairs Press, 1968.

Hutchinson, E.P. *Legislative History of American Immigration Policy 1798-1965*. Philadelphia: University of Pennsylvania Press, 1981.

India and the War. Introduction by Lord Sydenham of Combe, Formerly Governor of Bombay. New York and London: Hodder and Stoughton, 1915.

Isherwood, Christopher. *Ramakrishna and His Disciples*. New York: Simon and Schuster, 1959.

Jackson, Carl T. *The Oriental Religions and American Thought: Nineteenth Century Explorations*. Westport, Connecticut: Greenwood Press, 1981.

Jenks, Jeremiah W., and Lauck, W. Jett. *The Immigration Problem: A Study of American Immigration Conditions and Needs*, 3rd ed. New York: Funk and Wagnalls, 1913.

Jensen, Joan M. *Passage from India: Asian Indian Immigrants in North America*. New Haven and London: Yale University Press, 1988.

Jha, Manoranjan. *Civil Disobedience and After: The American Reaction to Political Developments in India during 1930- 35*. Delhi: 1973.

Josh, Sohan Singh. *Baba Sohan Singh Bhakna: Life of the Founder of the Ghadar Party*. New Delhi: People's Publishing House. 1970.

Juergensmeyer, Mark and N. Gerald Barrier (Eds.). *Sikh Studies: Comparative Perspectives On a Changing Tradition*. Graduate Theological Union, Berkeley, 1979.

Kansas, Sidney, *U.S. Immigration, Exclusions and Deportations*. New York: M. Bender. 1941.

Ker, J.C. *Political Trouble in India 1907-17* Delhi: Orient Publishers, 1973.

Kitano, Harry H.L. and Englewood Clipps, N.S. *Asian American: Emerging Minorities*. The Prentice Hall, 1988.

Kondapi, C. *Indians Overseas, 1838-1949* New Delhi: 1951.

Konvitz, Milton R. *The Alien and the Asiatic in American Law*. Ithaca, New York: Cornell University Press, 1946.

Kopf, David. *The Brahmo Samaj and the Shaping of the Modern Indian Mind*. Princeton, New Jersey: Princeton University Press, 1979.

Lamson, Peggy. *Roger Baldwin: Founder of the American Civil Liberties Union: A Portrait*. Boston: Houghton Mifflin Co., 1976.

Landau, Captain Henry. *The Enemy Within: The Inside Story of German Sabotage in America*. New York: G.P. Putnam's Sons, 1937.

Lohia, Rammanohar. *Indians in Foreign Lands*. Allahabad, AICC, 1938.

Machell, Montague A. *"Muslim Valley Forge" : An Introduction to Mubarek Ali Khan*. Phoenix, Arizona: Privately published, 1949.

Mackenzie, De Witt. *India's Problem Can be Solved*. Garden City. New York: Doubleday, Doran and Co., Inc., 1943.

Majumdar, A.K. *Advent of Independence*. Chowpathy, Bombay: Bharatiya Vidya Bhavan, 1969.

Majumdar, R.C. (Ed.). *History and Culture of the Indian People: Struggle for Freedom*. Bombay : Bharatiya Vidya Bhavan, 1969.

Martin, Alfred W., A.M., S.T.B. (Harvard). *Seven Great Bibles*, New York : Frederick A. Stokes Company, 1930.

Mathur, L.P. *Indian Revolutionary Movement in the United States*. Delhi; S. Chand & Co., 1970.

Mears, Eliot Grinnel. *Resident Orientals on the American Pacific Coast : Their Legal and Economic Status*. Chicago : 1928.

Meier, August, and Rudweck, Elliott. *CORE : A Study in the Civil Rights Movement 1942-1968*. New York : Oxford University Press, 1973.

Mittal, S.C. *Freedom Movement in Punjab 1905-1929*. Delhi : Com-cept Publishing Company, 1977.

Moore, R.J. *Churchill, Cripps and India 1939-1945*. Oxford : The Clarendon Press, 1979.

Mukerji, Dhan Gopal. *A Son of Mother India Answers*. New York : E.P. Dutton & Co., 1928.

________. *Caste and Outcast. New York : E.P. Dutton & Co., 1923.*

Mukherjee, Sujit. *Passage to America : Reception of Tagore in U.S. 1912-1941*. Calcutta : 1964.

Murphy, Bruce Allen. *Brandeis-Frankfurter Connection : The Secret Political Activities of Two Supreme Court Justices*. New York : Oxford University Press, 1982.

Muzumdar, Dr. Haridas T. *America's Contributions to India's Freedom*. Allahabad : Central Book Depot, 1962.

Nehru, J.L. *A Bunch of Old Letters Written Mostly to Jawaharlal Nehru and Some Written by Him*. New York : Asia Publishing House, 1958.

Parmet, Robert D. *Labor and Immigration in Industrial America*. Boston : Twayne Publishers, 1981.

Pilat, Oliver. *Drew Pearson : An Unauthorized Biography*. New York : Harper's Magazine Press, 1973.

Rai, Lajpat. *The Arya Samaj*. London : Longmans Green, 1915.

________. *United States of America : A Hindu's Impressions and a Study*, 2nd ed. Calcutta : R. Chatterjee, 1919.

________. *Young India : An Interpretation and a History of the Nationalist Movement From Within*. New York : Howard Fertig, 1968.

Rice, Howard C. *Rudyard Kipling in New England*. Vermont : Stephen Daye Press, 1936.

Riggs, Fred W. *Pressures on Congress : A Study of the Repeal of Chinese Exclusion*. New York : Kings Crown Press, 1950.

Royce, Josiah. *Race Questions, Provincialism and Other American Problems*. New York : Macmillan Co., 1908.

Sarda, Harbilas. *Life of Dayanand Saraswati, World Teacher*, 2nd ed. Ajmer : Paropkarini Sabha, 1968.

Satprakashananda. *Swami Vivekananda's Contribution to the Present Age*. St. Louis : The Vedanta Society of St. Louis, 1978.

Saund, Dilip Singh. *Congressman From India*. New York : E.P. Dutton, 1960.

Shridharani, Krishnalal. *My India My America*. New York : Duell, Sloan and Pearce, 1941.

________. *Warning to the West*, New York : Duell, Sloan and Pearce, 1942.

Siegfried, Andre. *America Comes of Age : A French Analysis*. New York : Harcourt, Brace & Co., 1927.

Singh, Dewakar Prasad. *American Attitude Toward Indian Nationalist Movement*. New Delhi : Munshiram Manoharlal, 1974.

Singh, J.J. *India and America*.New York : India League of America, 1947.

Singh, Dr. Pardaman. *Ethnological Epitome of the Hindustanees of the Pacific Coast*. Stockton, California : The Pacific Coast Khalsa Diwan Society, 1922.

Sitaramayya, B. Pattabhi. *History of the Indian National Congress*, Vol. II (1935-1947). New Delhi : S. Chand & Co., 1969.

Swisher, Carl Brent. *American Constitutional Development*. New York : Houghton Mifflin Company, 1954.

Symes, Lilian, and Clement, Travers. *Rebel America : The Story of Social Revolt in the United States*. New York : Harper and Brothers Publishers, 1934.

Thomas, Wendell Marshall. *Hinduism Invades America*. New York City : Beacon Press, 1930.

Sareen, Tilak Raj; *Indian Revolutionary Movement Abroad (1905-1921)*. New Delhi : Sterling, 1979.

Tinker, Hugh, *The Banyan Tree : Overseas Immigrants from India, Pakistan and Bangladesh*. Oxford : Oxford Unviersity Press, 1977.

________. *Separate and Unequal : India and the Indians in the British Commonwealth 1920-1950*. Vancouver : University of British Columbia Press, 1976.

Venkataramani, Dr. S., and Shrivastava, B.K. *Quit India : The American Response to the 1942 Struggle*. New Delhi : Vikas Publishing House Pvt. Ltd., 1979.

Venkataramani, M.S. *Bengal Famine of 1943 : The American Response*. Delhi : Vikas Publishing House Pvt. Ltd., 1973.

Vivekananda Rock Memorial Committee. *India's Contribution to World Thought and Culture*. Triplicane, Madras : 1970.

Vyas, Pramod. *Dawning on the Capitol : U.S. Congress and India*. Calcutta : Mascot Publications, 1966.

The Works of Charles Sumner. Vol. XIII. Boston : Lee and Shepard, 1880.

Yash Dev, Dharam, *Our Countrymen Abroad*. Allahabad : AICC, 1940.

A Note on Transliteration

The word "gadar" (rhymes with "brother") is an Arabic word meaning mutiny or rebellion. Written غدر, its first letter (it is on your right, the one with a dot on it) is غ when standing alone. It is not the equivalent of "g" in English. Its sound resembles the one we produce when trying to dislodge a fishbone stuck near the throat. It definitely is not the "g" in Gandhi.

We are here dealing with three different sounds represented in the Urdu alphabet by two letters and one combination of two letters غ - گ - گھ respectively from left to right, "g" of Gadar, "g" of Gandhi, and "gh" as in ghost. One should be very reluctant to use one sound for the other.

The men of 1857 as well as the Punjabis and other Indians of San Francisco in 1913 clearly knew the differnce between those sounds and the letters that represented them. The poet Galib of the court of Bahadar Shah wrote a diary of the Mutiny. He spelled the event like his own name with غ - غالب غدر - not گالب گدر , much less. گھالب گھدر (Ghadar, Ghalib)

No Sikh in California would have pronounced the word gadar as if spelled with gh because he knew the differences between the sounds of the words غدر gadar, گورو guru, and گھر ghar (house).

Writing غدر in English as gadar or ghadar are techinally wrong transliterations. Placing a dot under or above 'g' simply begs the question. All Punjabis pronounce غدر with a relaxed concern for linguistic puritanism. They pronounce it with a 'g' sound as in guru without the sound made while dislodging a fishbone. However, no Punjabi, (Sikh, Hindu or Muslim) will ever pronounce 'guru' as if spelled with 'gh'.

In this work, the word is spelled the way it is pronounced by the people who now practically own it namely, the people of the Panjab. They pronounce the 'g' of Arabic word غدر exactly as the English 'g' in God, good, great, gracious not with "gh" because that would be a ghastly mispronunciation.

The Sikhs are experts in pronouncing the letter "g" because some of the most sacred words in their religious literature begin with this kind of "g", words such as Guru, Granth, Gobind Singh, gurbani, gurdwara, gurmukhi, gurmata, granthi, gutka, Goindwal and the "g" in langer.

By the way the vowel "i" in Sikh is short as in "wick," "slick," "prick."

A word of caution : a participant in a "mutiny" is a "mutineer", a participant in a rebellion, a "rebel", both honorable words if you are not on the British side. The person who joins "gadar" is "gaddaar". It has one and only one meaning, "traitor" a dishonorable word. The *Gadar* was betrayed by the *Gaddaars* (here and in Lahore) and the *Gadarites* suffered in consequence. Har Dayal, Taraknath Das, Sohan Singh Bhakhna were *Gadarites* not *Gaddaars*.

APPENDIX I

Extracts from a letter dated January 20, 1914 from Secretary of Labor W.B. Wilson to the Speaker of the House of Representatives. House Document No. 652, Sixty-third Congress, second session, Hearing on Hindu Immigration before the House Committee on Immigration, April 16, 1914, 141-144. Emphasis added.

> But owing to the time that will necessarily elapse, even if H.R. 102 should be favorably considered in the two Houses of Congress before it can become a law, the department desires to urge the passage as an *emergency measure* of either H.R. 9044 or H.R. 6440, for the reason that there now confronts the immigration Service of this department *the urgent and imperative problem* constituted of the Hindu—a problem which has been met for the past several years with such *expedients and makeshifts* as could be devised from time to time with a view to prevent a large and ever-increasing influx of laborers of that race, who to all intents and purposes are "coolies" in the same sense that Chinese were regarded when the necessity arose over a quarter of a century ago for affording statutory means of exclusion. The Immigration Service has been excluding as many of these laborers as possible under the provisions of existing law which relate to physically defective aliens and to aliens likely to become a public charge. Numbers of the Hindus, however, *are not physically defective* in the sense of the existing statute, *if at all*; and while there are facts and circumstances with regard to these people, such as clannishness, caste ideas, superstitions, and habits of life, as well as economic conditions in the sections of the country in which they are wont to locate, which have in a number of instances been regarded as sufficient to justify the holding that they are likely to become public charges if landed, their immigration is now becoming systematized and financed in such a way as to *reduce the efficacy of this holding*, which at best is accomplishing by indirection something which ought to be brought about by direct methods.

The Dominion of Canada has legislated on this subject in a manner even more drastic than that proposed by the pending bills, though in so doing it is dealing with subjects of the Empire of which it is a member. The people of Canada, like those of our country who have come into contact with the Hindus and gained experience and knowledge of them, are opposed to their coming. That Government, notwithstanding the adverse ruling of one of the higher Canadian courts, has had recourse to the emergency clause of its immigration laws, which provides prohibition of the entry of all laborers, so as to preclude those of India and allow the Government time to consider needed changes in its system; and only on the 17th instant additional protective measures were promulgated by an "order in council," thus meeting the necessities of the situation in the western Provinces, particularly British Columbia.

Australia, New Zealand, and other colonies of England have taken as radical steps to stop the *contemplated invasion* of these people.

Can we, who are not connected by governmental ties or obligations with the Hindus, afford to do less for our people and country than those who are bound by a common citizenship under the Imperial Government ?

If this movement of Hindus is not checked by legislation—for that, in my judgment is the "only effectual and certain way to meet the issue now presented—California and the West will not have a monopoly of this kind of labor, as climatic and industrial conditions in the southern States and other sections of the Union offer an extensive field for a people who can come in practically *unlimited numbers* if, by failure to do as Canada and other British colonies have done, they are tacitly invited.

. . . .

APPENDIX II

Prominent Participants in the Struggle

DR. SUDHINDRA BOSE : born, Keothkali near Dacca, Bangladesh, 1883; came to America, May 2, 1904; Ph.D., 1912; Appointed Lecturer State University of Iowa City, 1912; elected President Hindusthan Association of America, 1914; appeared at the House Hearings on Hindu immigration, February 1914; naturalized, 1917; contributed extensively to Indian periodicals on American and Indian subjects; visited India, 1928; member Executive Council, India League of America; died, May 25, 1946.

Modern Review, April 1912, 446-447; June 1914, 624- 628; May 1919, 521-526; June 1923, 691-695; June 1927, 760-761; May 1928, 736; July 1928, 92, 231; March 1933, 277-280; March 1940, 344-347; June 1946, 413; November 1948, 365-373. The *Hindusthanee Student*, January 1914, 2; November 1915, 18; December 1916, 12-25, 21; March-April 1917, 25; September-October 1925, 28; *Voice of India*, June 1946, 319; *Sudhindra Hearings*, 3-21, J.C. Ker, *Political Trouble in India*, 402.

DR. TARAKNATH DAS : born near Calcutta, May 15, 1884; came to the United States, July 12, 1906; naturalized U.S. citizen 1914; imprisoned for Gadar 1918; Ph.D., 1924, taught at several universities; lost citizenship as result of the *Thind* decision; citizenship restored 1928; visited India 1952 after almost 46 years; died in New York December 22, 1958.

For Taraknath Das : *Who's Who In America*, Chicago, 1932, Vol. 17, 654; S.P. Sen (Ed.), *Dictionary of National Biography*, Calcutta, 1972, Vol. IV; J.C. Ker, *Political Trouble*, several references, especially p. 410; Ronald Spector, "The Vermont Education of Taraknath Das," *Vermont History*. Vol. 48 (1980), 89-95; Chinese Repeal Hearings 1943, 33, 34, 38-42; *The Hindusthanee Student*, January 1914, 2, 21; Manoranjan Jha, "Britain and the Pro- India Activities in the U.S.A., 1917-1922," *Political Science Review* (India), 1973, 21-23, 102-103; Senate Hearings of December 1926, 2, 3, 5; Taraknath Das, *Open Letter to Srinivas Sastri*, N.S. Hardikar Papers, Subject File No. 1, Nehru Memorial Museum & Library; "Anti-Indian Propaganda in America," *The Mahratta*, February 12, 1922; Taraknath Das from Geneva, Switzerland to Lala Lajpat Rai, November 1, 1926, Nehru

Memorial Museum & Library. Acc. No. 512; Muzumdar, Oral History Transcript, 25, 26; Muzumdar, *America's Contributions*, 9, 10; The Watumull Foundation Newsletter No. 4 in India League of America Papers, File Miscellaneous No. 46; S. 1595 Hearings, 28; *Modern Review*, January 1911, 109; October 1934, 374-379; November 1934, 496-503; Gobind Bihari Lal, "Dr. Taraknath Das in Free India," July, 1952, 36-38; Praffula C. Mukerji, "Demise of a Great Patriot," January 1959, 47-48; *New York Times*, December 30, 1958, 35 : 2, January 24, 1959, 18 : 5.

GOBIND BIHARI LAL : born about 1888 in Bikaner State, educated at the same college, St. Stephen's, in Delhi as Har Dayal; came to America, 1911, convicted for Gadar, 1918; started as a journalist, 1924; appointed Science Editor of the Hearst Newspapers, 1930; won the Pulitzer Prize, 1936; Dr. Taraknath Das, "An Indian Journalist Receives Signal Honour in America," *Modern Review*, July 1937, 49-51; February 1941, 123; Deol. *The Role of the Ghadar Party*, 165; Diwakar Prasad Singh, *American Attitude Towards the Indian Nationalist Movement*, New Delhi, 1947, 187; *Voice of India*, Washington, D.C., April 1946, 282.

PROFULLA CHANDRA MUKHERJI : born, Dhubri, Assam, 1888; came to U.S.A. 1907; organized the Hindusthan Association of America, 1911; graduated as Metallurgist, 1914; joined Carnegie Steel Corporation, 1914; naturalized, 1920; retired from U.S. Steel 1956; died, New York, April 22, 1982.

Maxine P. Fisher, *The Indians of New York City*, New Delhi, 1980, 12-16; *The Hindusthanee Student*, January 1914, 11; September-October, 1925, 29; *Dr. Taraknath Das*, "Worthy and Successful Indians Abroad," *Modern Review*, October 1932, 431-433; *New York Times*, April 23, 1982.

VAMAN RAMCHANDRA KOKATNUR : born Athani, Bombay, December 16, 1886; came to the United States, 1912; Ph.D., 1916; naturalized, 1921; died, April 14, 1950.

Who's Who In America, 1951-1960, 487; Dr. Gurdev Singh Deol, *The Role of the Ghadar Party in the National Movement*, Delhi, 1969, 119, fn. 1; *The Hindusthanee Student*, September 1915, 13; March 1916, 7-9; October 1916, 19; *Modern Review*, December 1928, 745; November 1938, 590- 591; *New Republic*, September 20, 1943, Editorial; M.S. Venkataramani and B.K. Shrivastava, *Quit India : The American Response to the 1942 Struggle*, New Delhi, 1979, 55-56;

New York Times, April 15, 1950, 15 : 1. N.S. Hardikar, *Lala Lajpat rai in America*, 47-51.

The following appeared in *India To-Day*, November 14, 1940.

> "We congratulate the following Indians, whose contributions to the culture of America were recognized in a ceremony at the World Fair : Dr. Ananda Coomaraswami, Dr. V.R. Kokatnur, Dr. Taraknath Das and the late Dhan Gopal Mukerjee.
>
> We also congratulate Mr. Gobind Bihari Lal, Science Editor, on being elected President of the National Association of Science Writers of the United States."

Taraknath Das was never on the League Executive Committee and twice declined to be on its Advisory Board. He Occasionally gave donations to the League, kept up a steady correspondence with Jagjit Singh, reviewed books for *India To-Day*, was fittingly the chief speaker at the dinner held to celebrate the passage of the Luce-Celler Act in 1946.

Gobind Bihari Lal contributed articles to *India To- Day*, addressed several League functions and gave donations. He was one of Jagjit Singh's close friends.

Profulla Mukerji and Sudhindra Bose were on the League's Advisory Board.

APPENDIX III

Text of H.R. 3517 as enacted

To authorize the admission into the United States of persons of races indigenous to India, to make them racially eligible for naturalization, and for other purposes.

Be it enacted by the Senate and House of Representatives of the United States of America in Congress assembled, That section 303 of the Nationality Act of 1940, as amended (54 Stat. 1140; 57 Stat. 601; 8 U.S.C., Supp. 703), be amended to read as follows :

"Sec. 303. (a) The right to become a naturalized citizen under the provisions of this Act shall extend only to—

"(1) white persons, persons of African nativity or descent, and persons who are descendants of races indigenous to the continents of North or South America or adjacent islands ;

"(2) persons who possess, either singly or in combination, a preponderance of blood of one or more of the classes specified in clause (1) :

"(3) Chinese persons and persons of Chinese descent, and persons of races indigenous to India; and

"(4) persons who possess, either singly or in combination, a preponderance of blood of one or more of the classes specified in clause (3) or, either singly or in combination, as much as one-half blood of those classes and some additional blood of one of the classes specified in clause (1).

"(b) Nothing in the preceding subsection shall prevent the naturalization of native-born Filipinos having the honorable service in the United States Army, Navy, Marine Corps, or Coast Guard as specified in section 324, nor of former citizens of the United States who are otherwise eligible to naturalization under the provisions of section 317."

"Sec. 2. With the exception of those covered by subsections (b), (d), (e), and (f) of section 4, Immigration Act of 1924 (43 Stat. 155; 44 Stat. 812; 45 Stat. 1009; 46 Stat. 854; 47 Stat. 656; 8 U.S.C. 204), all persons of races indigenous to India entering the United States annually as immigrants shall be allocated to the quota for India computed under the provisions of section 11 of the said Act. A preference up to 75 per centum of the quota shall be given to Indians and other aliens racially eligible to naturalization, born and resident in India or its dependencies.

"Sec. 3. (a) For the purposes of section 2 of this Act, the term 'persons of races indigenous to India' shall mean any person who is as much as one-half of the blood of a race indigenous to India and who is eligible to naturalization under section 303 of the Nationality Act of 1940, as amended by section 1 of this Act.

"(b) For the purposes of section 2 of the Act of December 17, 1943 (57 Stat. 601; 8 U.S.C., Supp. 703), the term 'Chinese person' shall mean any person who is as much as one-half Chinese blood and who is eligible to naturalization under section 303 of the Nationality Act of 1940, as amended by section 1 of this Act.

"(c) Notwithstanding the two preceding subsections, any quota immigrant who is of one-half Chinese blood and one-half the blood of a race indigenous to India shall, if born in India, be chargeable to the quota for India; if born in China, to the quota for the Chinese, or if born in neither of those countries, to whichever of the said quotas has the least applications for visas against it at the time the application for visa is made."

APPENDIX IV

Jagjit Singh - George Russell Encounter

The story of Jagjit Singh's lobbying crusade against Senator Russell comes to us in two versions both from the same source and about twenty-two years apart. We may call one "the 1950 version" which was used by Robert Shaplen for the *New Yorker*[1] and the other "the 1972 version"[2] related by Jagjit Singh at an interview in India. This latter is now being examined and compared with the earlier version here for the first time.

The Singh-Russell encounter is one of Jagjit's numerous lobbying efforts that started in 1943 and solidified his reputation as a "one-man lobby" in 1946 after the Luce-Celler bill was enacted."[3] His talent in this field had been recognized by American journalists.[4] He mentions his lobbying visits to Washington in several of his letters, telegrams, and public statements.[5] This one he seems to have been particularly proud of and the only one he ever described in detail.

President Truman told Celler that he had failed to convince the Georgian of the need for the India bill.[6] Jagjit saw the letter,[7] ingested its meaning and challenge, and decided to loosen the Senator's grip on the bill by using "certain techniques" that he claimed to have learned.[8] He persuaded ecclesiastical circles in New York who favored the bill to write letters to "their representatives" in Senator Russell's constituency. Those representatives "began to propagate the bill" in Georgia, "the pressure started to show" in the Senator's office in Washington. Several times[9] Jagjit had knocked at his office door but had been denied a meeting. Now Russell let him in and they talked.[10]

Jagjit: Good Morning, Sir.

Russell: Morning, Mr. Singh. I am dead against your bill and I will be damned if I let the bill pass.

Jagjit: (to himself) That is the kind of man I like, he is a straightforward guy.

(to the Senator) Senator, you are the kind of guy I like. I like a man who shoots straight from the shoulder. You know, I too am a fighter.

Russell: Don't misunderstand me Mr. Singh. I am not against you Indians but by God if we remove one barrier, dirty, filthy people from all over the world will just be entering the United States of America.

Jagjit: Senator, we both are fighters. We agreed upon that. And I think as fighters we have to be fair. You will agree with me.

Russell: Yes, I am perfectly fair. I am not at all against your people.

Jagjit: How are you going to be fair with me when you don't even bring this bill before the Committee ? If you bring the bill before the Committee and the Committee opposes the bill and it is thrown out, that is fair enough. But you are not giving me a chance. I have tried to see you. You have tried to put me off. This is not fair. I want you to fight fairly with me.

(Jagjit believes this argument touched something in the Senator.)

Russell: God damn it, I will bring the bill before the Committee. I will give you a fair fight.

Jagjit: (After hearing these words. "I just got up shook hands and said") Thank you very much, Senator, I have your word that you will bring this matter before the Committee.

This is the story. Now let us try to understand why Jagjit published it to the world as an achievement.

The passage of H.R. 3517 through the Senate in the manner of a routine business without debate and without a division appears like the tame finish of a fight that initially promised to be hotly contested. This surprising but historically significant anticlimax is tied up very closely with the circumstances that forced Senator Russell to place the bill in the hands of the Committee after having defiantly blocked it for almost seven months.

The fact that the bill passed indicated in a general way the increasing strength of the forces that saw a new Asia coming. Particularly, of course, we have seen the President, his advisers, and the official representatives of the British Government seeking the bill's passage. And there were the nationalist Indians who spent years hoping and working for a better day.

On the other hand there were the forces represented by the Senator from Georgia. The liberating forces had worked upon his colleagues to the extent that, according to his own admission, he had lost a majority in the Committee.[11] The facile way in which the bill went through the Senate shows that the other 59 Senators present on June 14[12] were not eager to fight the absent George Russell's battle.

Yet Russell could have won the battle by just holding on to the bill for another few weeks thereby killing the bill.[13] Jagjit Singh claims he prevented this from happening. If his claim is found to be grounded on solid evidence his meeting with Russell and victory in argument over the Southerner could be the most crucial and the most decisive single act of the 2-1/2 year history of the India bills in Congress. He brought about what no one else—including President Truman—could, i.e., persuade Russell to submit the bill to his Committee.

The liberating forces had worked on Russell's colleagues not on Russell himself who stood stubbornly for his views even after the bill had been enacted.[14] For seven months he had served his cause by just keeping the bill bottled up in the Committee while his other conservative colleagues were abandoning him. He held the trump card. He was the Chairman. He could kill the bill no matter how many colleagues walk over to Jagjit's side.

But he gave up his advantage, came down from his strategic high ground to play according to Jagjit's rules. The League President maneuvered the Senator into a position which could not but lead to the passage of the bill. This is the significance of the Singh-Senator meeting if it took place.

It probably did take place. It was not in Jagjit's character to invent stories. Senator Russell was alive at the time when the 1950 version was published in the *New Yorker* identifying the Senator without naming him.[15] Even a serious difference of recollections would have drawn a rejoinder from him.[16] Thirdly the India League newsletter reported in May 1946 that Senator Russell "has *promised* to call a meeting of the Committee in the near future to take up the India Immigration and Naturalization Bill."[17] The report concluded with the latest news flash printed in italics that the meeting had been fixed for June 5. The word "promise" may indicate the Senator's promise made to Jagjit at their meeting and the early date seems to have been a pleasant surprise for the League's President.

We may concede that there indeed was a Jagjit-Russell face-to-face argument out of which Jagjit got what he wanted but there are internal contradictions in the available evidence that have to be resolved before he gets from history the credit he seems to claim.

Both the 1950 and 1972 versions contain statements which seriously harm his credibility. The earlier version for instance places the meeting after "The President had talked to him, but he wouldn't budge. This would date it after May 7, 1946. The last sentence of this version, however, says, "I didn't waste any time after that (promise), because I knew I had the Committee with me, three to two."

This "three to two" ties the meeting to the Fulbright Sub Committee of 5 members which held a hearing on H.R. 3517 on April 15, weeks before Russell defied the President or even Celler had occasion to complain to him about the Senator. There are serious mistakes in the second version. The Committee had 13 not 19 members. Russell served with the United States Naval Reserve in the First World War where he could not have "met . . . Sikh fighters."[18]

In this version Jagjit claims to have "already won 11 members out of 19." The contemporary documented figure is 6 out of 13. He did not have a majority on the night of June 3 when he left for Washington feeling "almost sure that I will secure another vote tomorrow."[19]

"Three to two" of the 1950 version may have been a current figure because Senators Fulbright, Ball and Ferguson favored the passage of the bill and the other two members of the sub-committee, Senators Eastland and Maybank could reasonably have been considered to be hostile. But even these two acquiesced in making a favorable report to the Committee. For reasons explained in the text Jagjit Singh and his friends may have been winning silent support of which they were not aware. We know for a fact that Senator Russell was left friendless both in his Committee and on the Senate floor over H.R. 3517. "Promise of support" may have come to Jagjit only from six members of the Committee by the evening of June 3. He was looking for the seventh vote when he entrained for Washington that night. But unknown to him all opposition except that of Russell himself had collapsed so that the bill blocked by him for seven months sailed through the rest of the Senate's legislative process in just nine days.

The Chairman's promise to place the bill before the Committee may have hastened and also widened the already growing consensus in favor of resigning to the inevitability of the repeal of Indian exclusion. Credit goes to the man who persuaded Senator Russell to make that promise. Let us give Jagjit that credit and forget the errors in his statements. There are two reasons why we should forget. For the 1950 version he may have been too excited to find himself the subject of a *New Yorker Profile* than go about checking each fact related by the author. In 1972 he was too sick and prematurely too old to keep his facts straight. Anyway his hold on the facts directly relevant to the conversation with the Senator is basically consistent. He was not just reading from the *New Yorker* at the interview in 1972. It is an independent account.

1. Robert Shaplen, "One-Man Lobby," *The New Yorker,* March 24, 1951, 45, 46.
2. Transcript of Narayanan's recorded interview with Jagjit Singh. The pages of the Transcript relevant to this incident, 19-21.
3. Fern Marja "India's One-Man Lobby," New York *Post,* 31 July 1946, Shaplen calls Jagjit "a lone-wolf lobbyist," *The Profile*, 43.
4. "It wasn't long before word of the new personality got around and people were asking other over cocktails, "Have you seen this Indian yet—J.J. Singh?" *The Profile*, 43. Shaplen is here talking about journalists.
5. Direct mention of his lobbying visits to Washington, D.C. are in Jagjit's telegram to Jagga Singh Sunga, the Secretary Sikh Temple Stockton, Sher M. Quraishi, Dr. J. N. Sharma, all dated October 5, 1945, Jagjit to Louis Johnson, January 31, 1946, Press Release, June 3, 1946.
6. President Truman to Rep. Emanuel Celler, May 7, 1946.
7. His claim to have seen the letter, transcript to Narayanan's interview, 19.
8. Ibid.
9. *The Profile*, the 1950 version quotes Jagjit saying that the Senator saw him "Along about the sixth time I called," 46; in the 1972 version he complains to the Senator, "I have tried to see you a dozen of times."
10. The dialogue is a merging of both versions in the interest of clarity.
11. Russell's speech, *Cong. Record*, 79th Cong., 2nd sess., June 25, 1946, 7458.
12. Of the total 65 Senators present, 6 were members of the Senate Immigration Committee, *Cong. Record*, 79th Cong., 2nd sess., June 14, 1946, Call of the Roll, 6884-6885.
13. The 79th Congress was due to recess from August 2, 1946.
14. *The Profile*, 46.
15. Senator Russell's speech, *Cong. Record*, 79th Cong., 2nd sess., June 25, 1946, 7458.
16. The Senator was identified as a Southerner and chairman of the Committee. *The Profile*, 46. The Senator died in 1971. The article would hardly have escaped the Senator's notice because he often picked up metropolitan newspapers published in America's larger cities. *Cong. Record*, 79th Cong., 1st sess., March 8, 1945, 1902.

17. *India To-Day*, May 1946. Emphasis added.
18. Biographical Directory of the Congress.
19. Press Release dated June 3, 1946, I.L.A. Papers.

INDEX